THE ATTACK OF THE BLOB

THE ATTACK OF THE BLOB

HANNAH ARENDT'S CONCEPT OF THE SOCIAL

HANNA FENICHEL PITKIN

THE UNIVERSITY OF CHICAGO PRESS

CHICAGO AND LONDON

HANNA FENICHEL PITKIN is professor emerita of political science at the University of California, Berkeley, and the author of *Fortune Is a Woman* (1984), *Wittgenstein and Justice* (1972), and *The Concept of Representation* (1967). She is a member of the American Academy of Arts and Sciences, and in 1997 she received the Lippincott Prize of the American Political Science Association, the same prize awarded in 1975 to Hannah Arendt.

The University of Chicago Press, Chicago 60637
The University of Chicago Press, Ltd., London
© 1998 by The University of Chicago
All rights reserved. Published 1998
07 06 05 04 03 02 01 00 99 98   1 2 3 4 5
ISBN: 0-226-66990-4

Library of Congress Cataloging-in-Publication Data

Pitkin, Hanna Fenichel.
  The attack of the blob : Hannah Arendt's concept of the social / Hanna Fenichel Pitkin.
    p. cm.
  Includes bibliographical references and index.
  ISBN 0-226-66990-4 (alk. paper)
  1. Arendt, Hannah—Political and social views. 2. Political science—Philosophy. I. Title.
JC251.A74P57 1998
320.5′092—dc21   98-13333
                                                                  CIP

Contents

	Acknowledgments	vii
ONE	The Problem of the Blob	1
TWO	Jewish Assimilation: The Pariah and the Parvenu	19
THREE	Biographical Interlude: Philosophy, Love, Exile	35
FOUR	The Refugee as Parvenu and the Conscious Pariah	52
FIVE	The Birth of the Blob	69
SIX	Writing *The Human Condition*	98
SEVEN	Absent Authorities: Tocqueville and Marx	115
EIGHT	Abstraction, Authority, and Gender	145
NINE	The Social in *The Human Condition*	177
TEN	Excising the Blob	203
ELEVEN	Why the Blob?	226
TWELVE	Rethinking "the Social"	251
	Notes	285
	Bibliography	329
	Index	339

Acknowledgments

Many people have helped me with this book. Hubert Dreyfus, Hans Sluga, and Elisabeth Young-Bruehl lent me their expertise to answer specific questions. Peter Euben listened attentively and, at just the right time, suggested, "You really ought to say *some*thing about Marx." Meta Mendel-Reyes illuminated Arendt's writings on the 1960s for me. Bonnie Honig edited and greatly improved the essay that eventually became this book. Sara M. Shumer shared with me in an endless conversation about the prospects for politics in our time—and carried the heavier pack. Michael Paul Rogin, George Shulman, Dee Dee Skinner, and John H. Schaar read the manuscript—most of them more than once—and gave me wise, productive, detailed advice and steady encouragement. Two referees who read it for the University of Chicago Press also made many helpful suggestions. Olga Euben was admirably efficient and patient in processing my words. And the many students who, over the years, read Arendt with me generously fed, criticized, and reshaped my thinking. I am deeply grateful to them all.

A few paragraphs in chapter 11 first appeared in "Rethinking Reification," published in 1987 in *Theory and Society* 16, pp. 263–93. Parts of chapters 1 to 4 and 8 first appeared in "Conformism, Housekeeping, and the Attack of the Blob," a paper presented at the annual meeting of the American Political Science Association in San Francisco in 1990.

ONE

The Problem of the Blob

This book traces the career of one problematic concept in the thought of one major political theorist of our time. The concept merits attention not because the theorist got it right and used it to teach an important truth, but quite the contrary, because the concept was confused and her way of deploying it radically at odds with her most central and valuable teaching. If studying it is nevertheless worthwhile, that is because its significance transcends the technicalities of textual interpretation and the critique of a particular thinker's work. If the concept was a mistake, that mistake was not just idiosyncratic or careless, and the problem that the concept was intended to address remains problematic.

The thinker is Hannah Arendt, arguably the greatest and most original political theorist of the mid–twentieth century; the concept is what she called "the social." Arendt wrote a dozen books, and her thought ranged widely, encompassing journalism, history, and philosophy, but "political theorist" is what she ultimately came to call herself, and her primary contribution surely centered on the constellation of three interrelated concepts that she treated as almost synonymous: "action," "politics," and "freedom." Though we all use these words, she thought, we do not really understand what they mean, because we lack the experiences from which they spring, the activities in which they belong. She regarded these experiences and activities as the most valuable available to human beings, called them our "lost treasure," and tried to restore our access to the full significance of these words so that we might also recover the corresponding forms of life.

By these three complex, interrelated terms Arendt meant, first of all, the human capacity for initiative, spontaneity, innovation, doing the unexpected, launching an unprecedented and worthy undertaking. Human beings, she stressed, have the capacity to interrupt the causal chain of events and processes, to intervene in history and begin something new that may then be taken up and carried forward by others. She called this the capacity for action, and thought that we mostly deny and hide from it, both because of the profound instability it seems to threaten and because of the enormous responsibility it implies. Recognizing the full extent of our powers, we might have to make major, uncomfortable changes in the way we live.

Second, because we tend to associate initiative and creativity with science, technology, and the material world, Arendt stressed doing rather than making, *praxis* rather than *poiesis*. She focused on innovation in nonmaterial culture, which she called the "web of relationships": the institutions, norms, customs, standards, practices, rituals, and ideas that make up a civilization. Our cultural arrangements do not just grow naturally, like a tree; they are founded, practiced, and enacted by people. But Arendt thought that we resist acknowledging the degree to which the patterns by which we live are our own doing—if not originally created by us, nevertheless sustained right now by nothing more than ourselves. Of course no one of us alone can do much to change these patterns, but since they consist in what we, together, are doing, together we can surely change them.

Therefore, lastly, by contrast with the modern tendency to privatize and personalize, to withdraw into psychology and introspection, Arendt stressed the large scale: our collective powers and responsibilities, politics and public life. Real freedom, she held, means jointly bringing the human capacity for action to bear on whatever is wrong in our present shared arrangements.

These were Arendt's most valuable themes, and they have rightly received the most attention from commentators. They are not the focus of this book. It concerns not what Arendt considered valuable and lost to us, but what she considered harmful and very much with us, what blocks recovery of the lost treasure. Each of the three elements in that treasure has its negative, evil counterpart for Arendt. Freedom contrasts with what she called "necessity," action with "behavior," and the negative counterpart to politics is society, or "the social." It is primarily the social that keeps us from our lost freedom, and that is the topic of this book.

Exploring these negative concepts may seem superfluous, since we have not lost them and thus should find them perfectly familiar. Focusing at such length on a single, isolated mistake by a great thinker, moreover, might seem downright petty and mean-spirited. Indeed, I had initially intended only a short conference paper on what then seemed to me a fairly technical problem of Arendt scholarship, but the topic gradually revealed deeper and more significant aspects. Sometimes what is most familiar can be as difficult to perceive accurately as what is wholly missing from our experience.

If our lost treasure had merely been inadvertently misplaced, if our failure to understand action and freedom were simply a matter of ignorance, then teaching about the treasure might suffice to restore it. That would fit one traditional image of political theory's task: to set forth a vision of the shining city on a hill toward which one should strive. But if what keeps us from that city, from the treasure, is something about ourselves—something we are doing—then merely extolling and explicating the goal, no matter how eloquently, may not suffice. We may need a better understanding of what is in the way: of how and why we block our own and each others' freedom. Those are not easy questions to formulate, let alone answer. Before approaching the technicalities of Arendt's words and texts, therefore, it may be wise to provide at least a rough sketch of the larger issues at stake, of where this book is going and why the journey may prove worthwhile.

The Social as Blob

What first engaged my curiosity about the social was that Arendt employs the concept in such an obviously counterproductive way, undermining her own central teachings. In her best known and most systematic work of political theory, *The Human Condition,* clearly we moderns are in a bad fix, about which we urgently need to do something.[1] Yet if one asks whose fault that is, what has put us in this alarming situation, the answer seems to be society, the social. Arendt depicts it as a living, autonomous agent determined to dominate human beings, absorb them, and render them helpless.

There is, first off, Arendt's puzzling hypostasization of the adjective "social" into a noun, almost as if she were readying the word to serve as this monster's proper name. She does nothing comparable with what she regards as the contrasting adjective, "political." And she hypostasizes "social" even though there is a perfectly good noun, "society," already available, which she continues to use alongside, and more or less synonymously with, her neologism. Even more telling is how often and how powerfully her imagery personifies and even demonizes this entity.

It is worth cataloguing the verbs that Arendt employs with these nouns, to make explicit the extent of the menacing activities of this "curiously independent Moloch," as Dagmar Barnouw has called it.[2] In *The*

Human Condition, society is variously said to "absorb," "embrace," and "devour" people or other entities; to "emerge, "rise," "grow," and "let loose" growth; to "enter," "intrude" on, and "conquer" realms or spheres; to "constitute" and "control," "transform" and "pervert"; to "impose" rules on people, "demand" certain conduct from them, "exclude" or "refuse to admit" other conduct or people; and to "try to cheat" people. The social, then, is very lively indeed.

This vision of the social contributes greatly to the most basic structural paradox of *The Human Condition*. Having traced at great length the inexorable advance of this monster engulfing us, the book concludes, in a manner one can only call blithe, that "needless to say" this does not mean we have lost any of our capacities. The last paragraph invokes the capacity for critical thought in particular, calling us back to Arendt's "very simple" proposal in the prologue that we "think what we are doing."[3] What *we* are doing? But we are doing less and less; our troubles are the work of the social, which is doing this *to* us. Why would a thinker whose intent is so clearly liberatory and empowering develop a concept so blatantly contrary to that intent? How did this happen to her?

It's like a science-fiction fantasy: Arendt writes about the social as if an evil monster from outer space, entirely external to and separate from us, had fallen upon us intent on debilitating, absorbing, and ultimately destroying us, gobbling up our distinct individuality and turning us into robots that mechanically serve its purposes. Such a science-fiction vision, coming from a thinker whose main effort was to teach human agency and freedom as part of a realistic understanding—that human institutions are humanly made, and that it is therefore up to us to change them—is truly astonishing.

Arendt's remarkable way of depicting the social is, of course, the source of my title, *The Attack of the Blob*. Initially I employed the phrase in my teaching without giving it much thought, to capture the clichéd, horror-fantasy quality of Arendt's images, but the expression in fact derives from one of the rash of kitsch science-fiction films popular in the 1950s, the period in which Arendt wrote *The Human Condition* (and in which I reached adulthood). The particular film, which, it turns out, was called simply *The Blob,* concerned a monstrous, jellylike substance from outer space, which has a predilection for coating and then consuming human beings and grows with each meal.[4]

Susan Sontag, Michael Rogin, and Naomi Goldenberg have suggested that the sudden appearance in the 1950s of numerous science-fiction motion pictures about large-scale disasters reflected a widespread popular mood, that these apocalyptic fantasies were displaced or projected versions of people's more realistic anxieties.[5] All three suggest that the real fear was psychological, reflecting people's sense of personal isolation, fragmentation, helplessness, and dehumanization. The fantasy of some monstrous "it" trying to take "us" over was really about how people were "disappearing to each other every day," as they increasingly related only to machines and to images on a screen.[6] Yet all three also recognize an objective public threat; they suggest that the monster films reflected a widespread sense of collective life out of control, headed in disastrous directions in the age of Cold War nuclear confrontation.[7]

These authors remark that typically such a movie opens by showing ordinary people doing ordinary things before the monster strikes, and depicts this daily life in ways so profoundly banal, conventional, and boring that one welcomes the horror when it comes.[8] Indeed, although in many of these films part of the horror is that people taken over by the monster or the aliens look just like everybody else, the opening scenes reveal that people were already all alike, "interchangeable parts, members of a mass society."[9] The monster appears, Goldenberg says, as the only interesting part of the stereotyped human characters, who are in a sense already dead before the catastrophe occurs.[10] At least the monster is alive; at least it makes people feel something; at least it makes manifest the hidden horror that had previously been experienced only as boring routine. We were already monstrous: dead, numb, paralyzed, identical robots, insects, slime, without individuality or boundaries, dissolving into a jellied mass.

All this is suggestive, and reminiscent of Arendt's presentation of the social as a Blob, and in due time we shall return to it, but its import for our investigation is far from clear. Arendt, who grew up in Europe, did not share the science fiction craze of 1950s America; on the contrary, she proposed that this genre be studied as symptomatic, "as a vehicle of mass sentiments and mass desires."[11] In any case it was I, not Arendt, who introduced explicit talk of the Blob and of monsters from outer space, finding them implicit in Arendt's metaphors and word choice. As a reminder that the Blob is my construct, I shall capitalize the word throughout.

Political Theory and the Paradox of Modernity

Though the atmosphere of the 1950s will prove relevant to our investigation, explaining Arendt's treatment of the social will not be any such simple matter. Just for starters, we shall see that Arendt herself warned against the sort of mystification in which she nevertheless engaged—ascribing the results of human action to some abstract, personified agency beyond human influence—and she criticized other thinkers for having done so. Nor was she the only modern political theorist who both warned against and nevertheless also engaged in such thinking. This surely suggests that more is going on here than any idiosyncratic foolishness on Arendt's part or any peculiarity of pop culture in 1950s America.

In this respect, too, one might speak of an "attack of the Blob," meaning now not some extraterrestrial monster gobbling up people but an insidious imagery that seems to overtake the minds of theorists despite their explicit awareness of its threat, making them depict human beings as helpless just when these theorists want to stress agency and freedom. Does the difficulty arise from the nature of abstract thought, as Arendt sometimes suggests? Or only from certain abstractions, perhaps those used for referring to human collectivities?[12] Or does it instead arise from the reflexivity of the particular problem Arendt sought to address: the paradoxical notion that people might be collectively getting in their own way? Perhaps there is even something about the enterprise of political theory as such at stake. That would certainly give the investigation of Arendt's concept of the social an importance extending well beyond the technicalities of Arendt scholarship.

Ultimately, however, this topic opens out into issues of even broader scope than the nature of political theory. Despite the Blob imagery in which Arendt couches her concept, despite all the difficulties in interpreting her meaning, she intended that concept to address a real problem she saw in the actual world of politics and history in which we all live, a problem she regarded as of the utmost urgency and importance. If she was right about that—and I am inclined to think she was—then the ultimate point of studying the social surely lies in thinking more clearly and realistically about that problem, hidden or distorted by Blob imagery, and doing something more effective about it.

The real-world problem that Arendt intended her concept of the social to address—if some oversimplifying is permissible as a way of getting started—concerns the gap between our enormous, still-increasing powers and our apparent helplessness to avert the various disasters—national, regional, and global—looming on our horizon. On the one hand, in so many respects, human beings in modern times have available more extensive powers than ever before in history. Our achievements are truly astonishing. We have accomplished things of which earlier centuries only dreamed, things they used to exemplify the humanly impossible (flying to the moon, say), things of which they did not even dream. We cure and prevent diseases and even hereditary defects. We are beginning to control genetic structure, to create new species and alter our own heredity. We harness the energy not merely of wind and water but of the atomic nucleus. We cultivate deserts, level mountains, create substances unknown in nature, design new materials at will. We transport people and materials and transmit messages with unbelievable, ever-increasing efficiency. We have created machines to aid our thinking that already surpass us in many tasks and that can be programmed to create others of their kind of even greater power. We have developed astonishing techniques of communication, persuasion, indoctrination, organization. We are more sophisticated than any previous era about human motivation and malleability. We can deploy people on an unprecedented scale, shape not just their conduct but their desires, get them to buy products, confess crimes, enlist in causes, believe anything.

Yet these extraordinary capacities somehow have not made people happy or free or even powerful. The power seems always to belong to someone else, who does not in fact employ it in ways that serve our lives or needs. Not only are the benefits of these extraordinary powers confined to a small and shrinking minority of human beings, but even those who benefit from them do not really control them. We do not direct these, our alleged powers; if anything, they direct us and determine the conditions of our lives, developing with a momentum of their own in ways we cannot foresee and that are often obviously harmful to human life and civilization. For every new cure discovered we seem to create another disease or debility. Every technological breakthrough seems to come at some new ecological price. The astonishing evaporation of the Cold War, removing the continual threat of nuclear annihilation that it involved, has already been followed by new nuclear proliferation and by local conflicts that make the use of these weapons more likely than ever. We are destroying species, exhausting resources, fouling the earth so that it may soon be unfit for habitation. Daily people's television sets bring into their living rooms the latest looming disaster, from acid rain to holes in the ozone layer, from cancer to AIDS, from collapsing banking systems and debt structures to famine among some accompanied by obscene waste among others, from torture to drug addiction, from ethnic and racial hatred to child abuse. We are ruining our world and seem unable to stop.

We watch in fascinated horror—both metaphorically and literally, in front of our television sets—as these various disasters rush toward us inexorably. But of course that is an illusion. They are not approaching us; we are approaching them, simply by doing as we do. These are not natural disasters that befall us accidentally, as storms or earthquakes used to do, nor are they mysterious divine punishments for someone's sins. They are the large-scale, long-run consequences—the by-products—of our own activities. More than ever before in human history, the conditions in which we live are humanly fashioned rather than just naturally given, so that more than ever before our troubles are of our own making. That is the paradox of modernity that has struck so many nineteenth- and particularly twentieth-century thinkers: more and more, as our power grows, the results of our own activities confront us like an alien and hostile force, beyond our influence.

It may, of course, be that the widespread apocalyptic feeling of public helplessness in the face of looming disaster is illusory and not to be trusted. Certainly some commentators so regard it, arguing that what characterizes modernity is an increase not in collective helplessness but, on the contrary, in the foolish assumption that humans might not be fundamentally helpless and dependent.[13] What is modern, they say, is the greedy, hubristic, Promethean, Faustian, or just defensively masculine expectation that humans *should* be able to control everything, to master the world, to produce heaven on earth.

This book cannot address the validity of the apocalyptic vision of crisis in our time, nor would I be competent to do so. The last chapter will undertake to deflate that vision somewhat, to sketch, briefly and inadequately, some ways of thinking about the problem without invoking a Blob, without apocalyptic mystification. But that there is an urgent problem to be thought about, which Arendt intended her concept of the social to address, this book will simply assume. It takes Arendt's sense of foreboding seriously, if only because ignoring it would—if she should prove to have been right—be so irremediably disastrous.

The larger underlying issues, then, are our power and our powerlessness, the possibilities and limitations of human agency, both theoretically, in general, and practically for ourselves, in particular. What is at stake, to put it another way, is our freedom and our conditions of unfreedom, particularly our freedom to change, to alter intentionally who we are and what we do. As Thomas Hobbes so strikingly observed, humans are both the "matter" and the "artificer" of "commonwealth," that is, of institutions, norms, conventions, culture.[14] Far more than any other species we humans are shaped by the particular situation into which we are born and in which we are raised, by our relationships to those who raise us, and by their institutional practices and cultural commitments, which we internalize. Yet those shaping practices and commitments are themselves humanly shaped, historically developed, not just humanly initiated in the past, but even now existing only as they are practiced.

What can freedom mean for such a dual being, both creature and creator? As shaped products and victims, we can never be free. As shapers we appear to be wholly free at every moment. Yet beyond these conflicting absolute positions lies the complex practical reality of what is and is not within our power, individually and collectively. Each individual's freedom to choose, create, or change intentionally is severely limited by the practices and commitments of the rest. Collectively, we could do a lot more, if only we could get together. If we are the problem, surely we can also be the solution. But then, why do we keep doing as we do?

Many lines of argument are possible: that most people are in fact content with their lives, and nothing much is wrong; that humans are in fact helpless and have always been so, at least on the large scale; that humans are now helpless as a result of some earlier free but bad decisions that have left us entrapped; or that the "we" is illusory, because *some* people (the rich, capitalists, Europeans and their descendants, "whites," men, heterosexuals) have power and privilege and are content with existing arrangements, while *others* are discontented and oppressed but helpless.[15] And yet, does power not rest on the complicity, obedience, or acquiescence of the powerless? If the victims were wholly powerless, how could they ever become free agents? Power and freedom are so difficult to think about partly because they are so entangled with responsibility, guilt, and blame—always contestable in relation to individuals and even more problematic in relation to human collectivities.

Such themes are familiar enough in the history of political theory and in the literature about modernity and contemporary public problems. Often, arrangements that human beings freely create ossify into constraining habits and empty rituals, hindering rather than expressing people's freedom and their power. Marxists, following Georg Lukács, have spoken of this phenomenon as "reification" and associated it particularly with modernity and capitalism.[16] Theodor Adorno and Max Horkheimer have seen it as symbolized in the myth of Ulysses and the Sirens: we acquire knowledge and the freedom that it seems to offer only at the price of self-imposed impotence. That is why the "mythic terror" that modern people experience is a fear that the world may "be set on fire by a totality which they themselves are and [yet] over which they have no control."[17]

Examining the concept of reification some years ago, I found this puzzling circularity epitomized in Franz Kafka's astonishing "Little Fable":

> "Alas," said the mouse, "the world is growing smaller every day. At the beginning it was so big that I was afraid, I kept running and running, and I was glad when at last I saw walls far away to the right and left, but these long walls have narrowed so quickly that I am in the last chamber already, and there in the corner stands the trap that I must run into."
>
> "You need only to change your direction," said the cat, and ate it up.[18]

The mystery is how we, with our enormous scientific sophistication and technical capacities, have come to be so helplessly trapped by our own activities. Or should one say, have come to *feel* so helplessly trapped, when in fact we are not? Or have come to *be* trapped *because* we feel trapped? Can it be that though the Blob is an illusion, believing in it we nevertheless make it real, becoming—as Arendt at one point formulated the view she opposes—"the helpless slaves of what we do"?[19] Can it be that though there is no Blob, we are the Blob? Does that even make sense? How could impotence be self-imposed, or people's own conduct constrain them?

What Is "the Social"?

These larger and most difficult issues will hover in the background throughout our investigation, but they must now be set aside as we turn to Arendt's concept of "the social" itself. What she means by this phrase is far from obvious, so the place to begin is in medias res, with *The Human Condition*, where the phrase appears explicitly and the concept is most fully developed. In that book, Arendt acknowledges that the idea of society is very old, our English words "society" and "social" deriving from the Latin *societas*, which she says meant "an alliance . . . for a specific purpose," such as "to rule others or to commit a crime" (23). Similarly, she acknowledges that the mistranslation of Aristotle's *zoon politikon* as meaning that man is a social animal (rather than a political one) is of ancient origin, occurring first in Seneca. Nevertheless, the social as Arendt understands it is modern: "The emergence of the social realm . . . is a relatively new phenomenon," no older than "the modern age."[20]

The focus, then, is society in this—the modern—sense, which Arendt variously calls "the social realm," "the social sphere," or most succinctly, "the social." One looks in vain for a definition of these expressions, for Arendt never defines her terms. The nearest thing to a definition occurs shortly before a chapter called "The Rise of the Social," in a passage equating "the rise of society" with "the rise of the 'household' (*oikia*) or of economic activities to the public realm."[21] Contending that the ancient Greeks located all activities concerned exclusively with survival, the needs of the body, and biological necessity in the household, and noting the derivation of our word "economics" from *oikia*, Arendt claims that for the Greeks economics was private. When, in modern times, it went public, it became the social. Society is "the form in which the fact of mutual dependence for the sake of life and nothing else assumes public significance."[22]

So the rise of the social seems to involve the development of a complex economy: trade, money, division of labor, a market system, and eventually the extensive, centralized, intricate network of production and exchange of our time, in which people are profoundly interdependent, yet no one is in charge, outcomes being determined, as we say, by "the market." The large-scale consequences of people's own conduct therefore confront them as inevitabilities, as if imposed by some alien, irresistible power.

This quality of irresistibility or inevitability fits well with Arendt's linking of economics to biology and natural necessity. It also suggests a plausible interpretation for her opposition between the social and politics: if the social is consequences out of control, political activity must be an effort to direct or take charge of those consequences. In the ancient household, Arendt suggests, biological process and natural necessity were kept under restraint because they were contained within the walls of privacy and subjected to human decisions by the paterfamilias. They are dangerous only when they emerge and become extensive, beyond the control of any household head; or, in economic terms, when production is no longer mainly for use, and money and trade begin to generate market forces. When what used to be housekeeping goes large-scale and collective, "an unnatural growth, so to speak, of the natural" is "let loose," with "the life process itself . . . [being] channeled into the public realm" (47, 45). Politics, then, would supply the collective body with a head to reassert human direction of its biological processes, of the socioeconomic forces generated by large numbers of interdependent people making their livings.

Such a reading might align Arendt with the Hegelian view of how civil society must be regulated by the state, if one reads Arendt's "political" as referring to the state. Or it might align Arendt with Marx's "On the Jewish Question," if one reads Arendt's "political" as equivalent to Marx's "human emancipation." But Arendt is neither a Marxist nor a Hegelian, and the social is considerably more complex and problematic than has emerged so far. Not only does her notion of politics differ from that of the state and from Marx's understanding, but the social is not (or not merely?) the locus of ruthless, competitive individualism and conflict for Arendt, to be unified by some central authority or communal harmony. Indeed, the social is not (or not merely?) economics or biological necessity.

The social includes not merely the shift from *oikia* to market economy without central direction but also central control of that economy; it includes not only "free market" laissez faire but also socialist or communist regulation, economies directed by a government on a technical, administrative basis, in a sort of "gigantic, nation-wide administration of housekeeping" (28). Replacing the paterfamilias by the state to contain the dangerous biological forces apparently is no solution, and the social encompasses not only an unregulated market economy but also a centrally regulated and administered one. But in what sense could the latter be construed as forces of biological necessity out of control? Is the point that a large-scale economy cannot be controlled? Or that modern governments are so different from the ancient paterfamilias that they cannot control their national households as he controlled his domestic one? Or is it that, on the contrary, national administrations are too much like the paterfamilias preoccupied with housekeeping? All three possibilities have some foundation in the text, and all three also encounter difficulties.

If the social is equated simply with *oikia* economics grown large, the first answer seems most plausible. Yet Arendt never advocates dismantling our economy, abolishing trade and money, and reverting to household production for use. The second answer is strongly suggested by her brief history of modern governmental forms, which begins with monarchy, analogous to the paterfamilias in his household, and ends with bureaucracy, "the most social form of government," where "government gives place . . . to pure administration" (40, 45). The expert administrators solve their specialized, technical puzzles about the most efficient means toward ends that they—and everyone else—leave unexamined, as simultaneously both uncontroversial and unavoidable—ends such as "growth" or "development." Thus while the bureaucracy runs the economy, no one is responsible for the larger questions, the overall direction, which determines the parameters within which the experts make their technical decisions. An overall direction nevertheless emerges, as if a resultant of some autonomous force, so that bureaucratic government resembles the market.

Why, then, does Arendt complain that modern government is too much like a household? One answer may be that the idea of the household has a second meaning unconnected with the Greek term and its English derivatives: the household is the locus of family life, and Arendt does say that when it became public, "*all* matters pertaining formerly to the private sphere" became " 'collective' concern[s]" (33, my emphasis). Of course, a nation-state is not literally one family, but Arendt claims that we understand it "in the image of a family," which makes it social, since "society always demands that its members act as though they were members of one enormous family" (28, 39). Indeed, Arendt here offers another quasi definition: "the collective of families economically organized into the facsimile of one superhuman family is what we call 'society' " (29).

But what does this mean, and how is it related to the first quasi definition, which invoked economics? Arendt offers at least three different lines of explication. First, a family is a biological unit. Its members are genetically related (except of course that the family is continually augmented by marriages, which then produce new genetic connections). The household, moreover, is where one is supposed to tend to one's personal biological needs, so social may equal familial because "society constitutes the public organization of the life process itself."[23]

A second line of explanation is that a family "has only one opinion and one interest," which, "before the modern disintegration of the family," were assumed to be represented by the paterfamilias (39). Similarly, in our collective life today we assume "one interest of society as a whole in economics . . . [and] one opinion of polite society in the salon" (40). The first assumption, about a single interest, Arendt says originated in the "communistic fiction," as nineteenth-century liberal political economists called it, that an "invisible hand" guides economic outcomes. Marx, she says, "proposed to establish [this fiction] in reality" through revolution, but we have in fact established it—in a sense different from what Marx intended—by creating the "reality of a national household" (44). We focus our collective life and attention on housekeeping questions and administer our collective affairs centrally through a corps of experts to whom we defer because we assume that there is—and that they know and serve—an objectively ascertainable "interest of society as a whole."[24]

The second assumption in our collective life—that society has only a single opinion, as in "polite society in the salon"—invokes yet another familiar sense of the word. While its connection with society as economics or biology remains obscure, the notion of "polite society" provides a third connection between social and familial matters. Society not only "demands" that people conduct themselves as if members of a single family but also regulates people's conduct in many other respects. As "action" corresponds to politics for Arendt, "behavior" corresponds to the social, and society seems to be bent on making us behave, as an irritated parent might impose rules of conduct on children in the family. This is no minor matter for Arendt; she says "it is decisive." Society by its very nature "excludes the possibility of action," and instead "expects from each of its members a certain kind of behavior, imposing innumerable and various rules, all of which tend to 'normalize' its members, to make them behave, to exclude spontaneous action or outstanding achievement."[25] Society, then, means a leveling of people into uniformity, the destruction of individuality. "The best 'social conditions,' " that is, the most "social" of social conditions, "are those under which it is possible to lose one's identity" (214).

But what is the connection between, on the one hand, suppressing individuality, imposing rules of behavior, the polite conformity of the salon, and, on the other hand, economics, necessity, and biology? Salon behavior and biological urges seem almost polar opposites. Arendt does suggest that behavioral regulation and normalization have something to do with group size, with people in large numbers, and one might argue that a large population presupposes a complex economy. But just how a large population and a complex economy are supposed to "account . . . for conformism, behaviorism, and automatism in human affairs" remains unclear, as do the connections among the various quasi definitions of the social (43).

Relating the social to family, moreover, seems to imply an unhealthy expansion of private into public life, so that some commentators have read Arendt as equating the social with an overgrown or triumphant private realm. But Arendt insists explicitly that the social threatens and ultimately destroys privacy, just as much as it threatens and ultimately destroys public life. Private and social are "at least as sharply opposed" as private and political.[26] Indeed, modern privacy "was discovered [by Rousseau] as the opposite . . . of the social" (38). Rousseau saw that society not only threatens individuality and privacy, Arendt claims, but also is an "unbearable perversion of the human heart," because it invades "an innermost region in man which until then had needed no special protection" (39). The social, then, is "neither private nor public" but some kind of "curiously hybrid realm" (28, 35). "Curiously," indeed, since the social is supposed to be an improper expansion of *oikia* and family but not of the private realm.

But the puzzle of definition is only the first and least interesting problem about the social. Considerably more important is the way Arendt envisages the concept as a Blob. The symbolic role it plays in her argument, the predicates she attaches to it, and the metaphors in which she embeds it run directly counter to her central teaching and replicate the fault she most criticizes in other thinkers. Arendt charges Marx, for example, but also Locke, with presenting what are in fact human choices and deeds as the inevitable result of natural forces. These thinkers unrealistically "wished to see the process of growing wealth as a natural process, automatically following its own laws and beyond willful decisions and purposes" (111). Yet Arendt later concedes that Marx's and Locke's view is in fact "correct." It is correct "only in a laboring society," to be sure, but a laboring society is precisely what Arendt claims we have, or are.[27] So she herself endorses as true what Marx and Locke unrealistically "wished to see."

Perhaps Arendt means to say only that what was untrue in Locke's and Marx's time has become true in ours, yet her awkward obscurity on this point is only one example of a pervasive tension in *The Human Condition:* she stresses human agency and condemns those who hide it by invoking superhuman entities and forces, yet she herself invokes the social in just this way. The social connects with biology and natural process; one of its "outstanding characteristics" is its "*irresistible* tendency to grow, to devour" (45, my emphasis). So the social is not merely "beyond willful human decisions and purposes" but is itself alive, eating and growing. Its growth, moreover, proceeds through identifiable "stages" (40, 45, 256). First was the stage of "expropriation," which "created both the original accumulation of wealth" and the mobile people, needing wages, who would transform "this wealth into capital through labor" (255–56). In this early stage, society already imposed "its rules of behavior," but only on certain sectors of the population and in certain aspects of their conduct (45). The corresponding governmental form was monarchical: "one-man rule in benevolent despotism and absolutism" (40). (How capital accumulation, a rule-governed elite, and despotic monarchy are related and form aspects of the social at this stage, Arendt does not explain.)

As the social continued to grow inexorably, it devoured more and more people, until now—in the form of "mass" society—it "embraces and includes all members of a given community" (41). Concurrently, monarchy was displaced by more inclusive governmental forms that culminate today not, as one might suppose, in democracy, but in bureaucracy, "a kind of no-man rule" or "the rule of nobody" (40, 45). But though (or rather, because) bureaucracy is rule by no human, it nevertheless involves a ruler, as we have already seen: it means rule by the social, which by now is not merely alive and growing but has a mind and (evil) intentions. In this stage, society has become a "subject"—admittedly an ambiguous term—"the 'collective subject' of the life process," as the family once was (256). Arendt insists repeatedly that this is no mere "fiction" or "fantasy," nor merely "a matter of theory or an ideology," nor "even merely a scientific hypothesis." It is a "factual historical development" in which, as we already noted, the national household "by no means remained an intangible entity" but became "reality" (33, 44, 46, 117, 256).

Mostly, in Arendt's various narrations of this story, the inevitable process of growth was set off by some ill-advised human actions in the past. Or is it some lack of action or failure to act? Occasionally even this initial human agency vanishes, and the social is mysteriously preexistent, arranging even its own appearance in the world; for example, society "first entered the public realm" in a deliberately deceptive form, having "assumed [a] disguise" (68).

The Task

Eventually this book will argue that by "the social" Arendt means a collectivity of people who—for whatever reason—conduct themselves in such a way that they cannot control or even intentionally influence the large-scale consequences of their activities. This is a surprising reading, not only because Arendt never puts things this way herself, but also because it seems so far removed from the ordinary meanings of "society" and "social" and from the meanings assigned to Arendt's concept by earlier commentators. The most common reading of the social in Arendt scholarship equates it with economics and reads it in Cold War terms as expressing her opposition to communism, socialism, and perhaps even the welfare state. This interpretation has considerable textual foundation, not only in what Arendt explicitly says about the social, but also in her hostility to Marx, her critique of the French Revolution, and her invocation of ancient Athens—a self-styled democracy, but from a modern perspective a highly elitist, slave-holding, inegalitarian polity.

More recently, as currents of academic interest have shifted, this dominant reading has been supplemented and increasingly displaced by one focused more on Arendt's earlier writings and attentive to issues of identity, diversity, and empowerment, rather than economics. On this newer reading, the social means disciplinary normalization, oppressive conformity to mainstream values, the obliteration of individuality. This interpretation, too, has considerable foundation in the texts. Yet neither the older nor the more recent way of interpreting the social even begins to get at the full range of theoretical difficulties in, or the significance of, Arendt's concept. The most astute commentators who have given explicit and somewhat extended attention to the social have seen that it is a complex composite, somehow involving both economics and normalization, but they have not found an overall, unifying meaning or importance in the complexity.

The questions of what Arendt means by "the social" and why she envisions it as she does were already posed, if briefly, by Margaret Canovan in her pioneering *The Political Thought of Hannah Arendt,* the earliest book-length study of this thinker, published in 1974.[28] Canovan argued that the concept of the social is internally incoherent, a conglomerate never brought to any satisfactory "synthesis" (108). In particular, the concept seemed to Canovan an unsuccessful effort to fuse "two separate strands of meaning" of the word "society" without acknowledging their distinctness, with the result that they remained "entangled" but their relationship was "not at all clear." In the first strand of meaning, society is the *oikia* enlarged; in the second strand it means "high society with its characteristic manners and vices: the fashionable world, originally composed of only a tiny segment of the population" (105, 108). This duality is revelatory, Canovan argued, not only methodologically, with respect to Arendt's "manner of thinking, which is unusually multidimensional"—confusing because she develops "a great many lines of thought simultaneously"—but revelatory in a substantive way, with respect to Arendt's basic purposes as a theorist (109). The concept of the social engages "another and deeper ambivalence" in her thought, the problem of "man's power in the modern age and his powerlessness," which Canovan also called "the general question of the capacity of modern men for action" (108).

Canovan was surely right in these observations, but she took them no further. Nor was she in a good position to do so, since Elisabeth

Young-Bruehl's rich biography of Arendt was not yet available, and Arendt's early essays had not yet been conveniently assembled in book form.[29] Only relatively recently have commentators begun to reinterpret *The Human Condition* in terms of the circumstances of Arendt's own life and the ideas of her earlier works.[30] Among these, Seyla Benhabib, in particular, has given attention to the concept of the social. Unlike Canovan, she distinguishes not two but three "dominant meanings of the term 'social' in Arendt's work." One is the economic, as in Canovan, but instead of Canovan's "high society," Benhabib contrasts to the economic both "mass society" and "sociability," meaning by the latter "the quality of life in civil society and civic associations."[31] How these three meanings are related, she does not discuss.

This book builds on the achievements of Canovan and subsequent commentators. It attempts to clarify the meaning of Arendt's concept of the social by tracing its gradual formation in the sequence of her works up to, and slightly beyond, *The Human Condition,* locating each work in the context of its writing—both the personal context of the author's life and the political, historical context that shaped the conditions of that life. Most of the book thus is devoted to a genealogy, tracing the provenance and vicissitudes of a concept—a vocabulary and a set of images—through a series of steps that arrive ultimately at a vision that is simultaneously plausible and yet also idiosyncratic and significantly counterproductive.

This way of proceeding may tax the reader's patience, for it requires painstaking attention to each of a series of texts and contexts. It also may easily be misunderstood. This book is not a psychohistory, let alone a causal explanation of Arendt's ideas. Its focus is not causes but reasons, meanings: what Arendt intended by what she said at each stage, how it might have made sense to her then and there. Nor is this book a general assessment of her thought; its focus is narrow, following only a single concept. It thus leaves uncriticized much that is blameworthy in Arendt's thinking and unpraised much that is meritorious. It does not examine in any general way the historical accuracy of Arendt's claims, their factual adequacy, or the political commitments or personal prejudices they may reveal. It pursues such matters only insofar as they illuminate the questions here adumbrated: what the social is (addressed primarily in chapter 9), why Arendt envisions it in such a counterproductive imagery (summarized in chapter 11), and how one might think about the real-world problem that Arendt meant to address, without succumbing as she did to (images of) the Blob (attempted in chapter 12).

TWO

Jewish Assimilation: The Pariah and the Parvenu

Long before society was a Blob for Arendt or was connected with economics, housekeeping, or biology, it figured in a very different sense in the first work she undertook after completing her university studies—a historical biography called *Rahel Varnhagen*.[1] In that work, society was "high," "respectable," "fashionable," or "good society," in which socialites once attended social functions, which debutantes used to enter at coming-out parties, and whose doings were reported in the social pages of newspapers. Although such matters clearly presuppose some wealth, they have little to do with economics as such or with the needs of the body, and the issues that then concerned Arendt were those of status and deference, snobbery and social climbing, assimilation and identity. Nevertheless, this is the right place to begin investigating Arendt's concept, because the book already contains, in embryonic form, what will become the basic distinction of *The Human Condition*, that between the social and free political action. Thus it reveals something of what was at stake for Arendt, and it will repay our detailed attention.

Arendt wrote most of *Rahel Varnhagen* in Berlin between 1929 and 1933, finished it in exile in Paris in 1938, but did not publish it until nearly twenty years later in the United States. Subtitled *The Life of a Jewish Woman*, it concerns an eighteenth-century woman famous for the salon she kept for a time in Berlin. As Arendt narrates her story, Rahel Varnhagen, born Rahel Levin, tried very hard almost her whole life long to assimilate and to win acceptance into high society. She tried to do so by marrying a gentile aristocrat, but his family opposed the match, and he acceded to their wishes. She tried to do so by conducting a salon frequented by aristocrats and important personages. For a time she tried to flee the issue by means of a romantic withdrawal into an inner life, but found this equally unsatisfactory. She then tried again to assimilate by converting to Christianity and changing her name. Finally she succeeded by marrying a gentile, who even obligingly discovered some aristocratic ancestors. And then, having succeeded in her lifelong project, she changed her mind. She decided that the project had been a terrible mistake, and on her deathbed Varnhagen reportedly said: "The thing which all my life seemed to me the greatest shame, which was the misery and misfortune of my life—having been born a Jewess—this I should on no account now wish to have missed."[2]

Arendt opens the biography with these words, remarking that it took Varnhagen "sixty-three years to come to terms with a problem which had its beginnings seventeen hundred years before her birth" and which "was slated to come to an end . . . one hundred years after her death."[3] Varnhagen died on March 7, 1833; the problem she faced was the Jewish Question, and specifically the question of assimilation. It came to an end with the rise of the Nazis, when assimilation was no longer an option.

Arendt herself was having personal experience of this problem when she wrote *Rahel Varnhagen,* as we shall see and as is perhaps indicated by a grammatical shift immediately after the book's opening, from the narrative third person to the first person plural: "It may well be difficult for us to understand our own history when we are born in 1771 in Berlin and that history has already begun seventeen hundred years earlier in Jerusalem."[4]

Though the "we" cannot be meant literally, it is by no means merely editorial. If we fail to understand our history, Arendt continues, it "will take its revenge, will exert its superiority and become our personal destiny" (3). But what does that mean? Can understanding one's history help one escape one's destiny? Should one want to escape it? This seems to be one of Arendt's earliest attempts to formulate what later becomes the distinction between social and political modes of conduct: the difference between being a product or victim of historical forces and helping to shape one's own destiny as a free and autonomous agent, the latter a capacity exclusively of human beings. "What is man without his history?" Arendt quotes from a letter of Varnhagen's, "product of nature—not personality" (4). Coming upon the letter, Arendt, who had read Kant while still of high-school age, may well have thought of his distinction between natural causation and human freedom.

Understanding one's history includes the awareness that history is humanly made, that we and our present situation are conditioned by people's past actions, and that we, being people, are capable of action too. Lacking that understanding, we will remain unaware of our powers, and what befalls us will seem like the predestined "unfolding and realization of what we already were." If one is fortunate in one's birth, this can result in a happy life. Insofar as we are (like) natural products, we are "dependent upon luck as seed is on good weather." But if the weather turns bad, our destiny may then loom as an agonizing and untimely death. At such inclement times, "the person who has no recourse but nature is destroyed by his own inexperience, by his inability to comprehend more than himself" (4).

The penultimate chapter of the biography, "Between Pariah and Parvenu," introduces distinctions that Arendt will later elaborate and then abandon but that prefigure the categories of *The Human Condition*.[5] Following Bernard Lazare, Arendt holds that the Jews are a pariah people, and Varnhagen was, like any Jew living in an anti-Semitic gentile society, a pariah—that is, an outcast, ascriptively defined as biologically inferior and excluded. (The term was originally brought back by the British from India, where it designated the largest of the low castes, those at the bottom of the caste hierarchy.) Pariah status, being ascriptive, is something that befalls one by, and like, one's birth. Some pariahs, raised in the subculture of a coherent and fairly isolated pariah group, may feel entirely at home in it. Others, feeling no pariah cultural ties, may be shocked to find themselves so classified.

Pariah status is often associated with various markers—stereotypes—some of which may be unchangeable, but others of which can be altered or disguised by effort, such as one's name, dialect, or social manners. Status lines may also be more or less rigidly drawn, and the consequences attaching to pariah status more or less severe.

Thus most pariahs do have options within the limits of what befalls them. A significant option for German Jews in this period was assimilation, which Arendt calls becoming a "parvenu," someone who tries to "climb by fraud into a society, a rank, a class, not [his] by birthright."[6] The word is from the French, where it literally means someone who has arrived, but it was particularly employed by the French aristocracy to designate those of the nouveau riche middle class who sought, or even achieved, aristocratic status. Thus it connotes the *only recently* arrived, with their crass, pushy manners, their ostentatious display of wealth, their lack of noblesse oblige.

In *Rahel Varnhagen* Arendt applies this originally class-oriented term to Jewish assimilation into gentile society. As a result, it shifts slightly in meaning, for Arendt is concerned not with all who have recently risen, but only with those who have risen from pariah status, and indeed not with those who have risen so much as with those aspiring to do so. She is interested neither in the acceptance actually achieved by the parvenu nor in the continuing denial of acceptance implied by the pejorative connotations of the word, but in the *striving* for acceptance that is one of the options open to pariahs. As Richard Bernstein says, she is "primarily concerned with types of *response*" available to the pariah and the consequences each entails.[7] In explicating her concept, then, we shall speak of the parvenu in Arendt's sense: as the social outsider desperate for admission.

What makes the parvenu strategy attractive to pariahs is, quite simply, that it sometimes works. In certain times and places, an individual pariah facing a class rather than a caste system, with lines not very strictly drawn, may be able to "pass" into the forbidden ranks. In Varnhagen's milieu, "a personal solution of the Jewish problem, an individual escape into society," social acceptance for a wealthy Jewish woman of assimilated manners and speech, while difficult, was "not flatly impossible."[8]

Paying the Price

Even a successful parvenu rarely manages to achieve full acceptance, however, entirely to shed his former status. The established elite never loses track of who really belongs. Even when Varnhagen was thirty-eight years old and a social success, her friend Wilhelm von Humboldt referred to her as "the little Levin girl," and even after she had married into society, he wrote: "Now at last she can become an Excellency and Ambassador's wife. There is nothing the Jews cannot achieve."[9]

Whatever degree of external success the pariah achieves as parvenu, moreover, comes only at a price, and in Arendt's view, "the price demanded of the pariah if he wishes to become a parvenu is always too high."[10] That is because, for a pariah, becoming a parvenu requires not some isolated instance of deception but a long-term and total commitment affecting every aspect of life and self. The price of success as a parvenu is becoming a parvenu-ish sort of person. However well he may fool "society," the parvenu must live with the one observer whom he cannot fully fool—himself.

Succeeding as a parvenu requires internalizing the standards of those to whom one would assimilate. While in theory it may seem that one could be a consummate deceiver toward others and yet retain perfect integrity toward oneself, in practice this is just about impossible. The successful parvenu must have an intense, even an uncontrollable impulse "to honor [him]self in [his] superiors, and to track down their good qualities in order to love them." Mere "obedience" or "simple and undisguised servility" may suffice for a career serving one's betters, but "for social success and for positions in society," more is required: "a strenuous effort to love." The effort to love helps to control the "inevitable but intolerable resentment" involved, resentment that must be controlled if one is to succeed. Thus, "those who are resolutely determined to rise, to 'arrive,' must early accustom themselves to anticipating the stage they hope to attain by simulating voluntary appreciation; must early set their sights higher than . . . blind obedience . . . ; must always act as if they were performing freely, and as their own masters, the things that are in any case expected of hirelings and subordinates" (199).

What is most costly to the pariah turned parvenu is not internalizing standards as such, however, no matter how zealously, but internalizing standards by which the likes of himself are worthless. He must train himself zealously to despise who he is, or at least who he has hitherto been. "In a society on the whole hostile to the Jews . . . it is possible to assimilate only by assimilating to anti-Semitism also" (224). This means that the parvenu must both endorse existing stereotypes about the characteristics of his pariah group and strive to eradicate those characteristics in himself.

The parvenu strives to get by as an exception, "to penetrate society solely as [an] individual" (85). Success therefore depends on maintaining both his exceptionality and the appropriateness of pariah status for the others. Jews who sought assimilation in Varnhagen's time endorsed the Enlightenment's view of traditional Judaism as superstition, of the Jews as "an oppressed, uncultured, backward people who must be brought into the fold of humanity." They confessed "fervently" that the Jews were a "deservedly despised nation" (8, 220).

Both Jewish tradition and the gentile legal system tried to reinforce the distinctness and unity of Jews. The Prussian state, for example, made the entire Jewish community responsible for the tax debt of each individual member, forcing the rich and prominent Jews to acknowledge their connection to their poor and backward co-religionists. All the more did the assimilationist parvenus seek to deny the connection, cherishing the secret hope that "there would be no civil reform, no emancipation," for only as long as the others deserved their exclusion could they themselves merge with anti-Semitic society as exceptions.[11] Every assimilated, parvenu Jew "felt like a Grand Sultan in contrast to his poor, backward co-religionists. From their degradation, from the great gap that separated him from them, he drew his consciousness of being an exception, his pride in having come so gloriously far" (216). In short, the parvenu must not merely separate himself from his pariah group but also join and support those who condemn it. For successful assimilation, therefore, Jews must become "unable to distinguish between friend and enemy, between compliment and insult; and [must] feel flattered when an antisemite assures them that he does not mean them, that they are exceptions."[12] Seeking acceptance from those who despise (the likes of) him, the parvenu must learn to identify with his oppressors. He "begs from those whom he ought to fight" and appraises his pariahhood "by the standards of those who have caused it." Thus "he becomes automatically one of the props which hold up a social order from which he is himself excluded"; he becomes, in short, "a scoundrel."[13]

But severing connections with the people of one's birth, parentage, and ancestry is no easy task, nor is it accomplished in a single, decisive moment. Every assimilated, sophisticated, parvenu Berlin Jew remained "connected to the Jewish people and the old manners and customs he had discarded," both through his memories and through his "inescapable provincial Jewish relations."[14] Separating himself from them required denying a part of himself.

Here we arrive at a second aspect of the high price of becoming a parvenu. One must not only become a scoundrel and turn against one's fellow pariahs but also establish a permanent division within oneself, declare war on oneself, become a " 'battlefield' " (79). To succeed in his goal, the parvenu must commit himself to an inner change that can never be accomplished.

Varnhagen's self-assessment is captured in the title of the first chapter of Arendt's biography, "Jewess and Schlemihl." The latter is a Yiddish word meaning a hapless unfortunate who, through no fault of his own, lacks grace, talent, and skill, for whom things never turn out right. Varnhagen specifies her own schlemihl limitations: "not rich, not beautiful, and Jewish."[15] Of these defects, the last is "the greatest shame," the one that Varnhagen most wants to "escape" or deny (3, 7): "The Jew must be extirpated from us, that is the sacred truth, and it must be done even if life were uprooted in the process" (120). Jewishness is like a genetic physical defect, "as inescapable as a hump on the back or a club foot," yet the parvenu must struggle precisely to escape it, to convert it into "a character trait, a personal defect in character," which by effort and discipline might be overcome.[16]

This peculiar kind of discipline, however, itself becomes a character trait, an obsession, and the inner struggle is interminable, for precisely in order to overcome this "defect," one must be eternally on one's guard, must in fact keep it alive. In order to "become another person outwardly," Varnhagen could not afford to forget the "shame" of her Jewishness even "for a *single* second. I drink it in water, I drink it in wine, I drink it with the air, in every breath" (120, emphasis in original). The inner struggle being endless, even where a parvenu meets with outward success, he fails. Construed "as a personal problem the Jewish question was insoluble" (221).

One becomes a parvenu, then, at the price of any stable or integrated sense of self: one cannot afford to know, yet cannot afford to forget. Varnhagen was highly introspective and enormously preoccupied with herself. Yet during most of her life that introspection and preoccupation amounted at most to a romantic escape from reality; they did not result in self-knowledge: "For she did not possess herself; the purpose of her introspection was merely to know what could happen to her, in order to be armed against it; in introspection she must never let herself know who she was, for that might possibly be [was bound to be] a 'schlemihl or a Jew'" (23). Even as Varnhagen so assessed herself, she added, "I shall never really grasp it" (9).

Similarly, the parvenu can achieve no stable, realistic sense of his own powers. Defining himself and his goal in terms of acceptance by certain "superior" others, he fluctuates between delusions of grandeur (they, being so superior, can make me into anything, give me everything, as soon as I fool them into accepting me) and equally exaggerated visions of his own hopeless inadequacy (by comparison with them, I can do nothing; besides, I'll never fool them). Thus, "the parvenu's overestimation of himself, which often seems quite mad," is the counterpart of "the tremendous effort, and the straining of all his forces and talents," required for him "to climb only a few steps up the social ladder." His mood, therefore, is totally volatile, fluctuating wildly with the latest "sign" from society: "The smallest success so hard-won, necessarily dazzles him with an illusory: everything is possible; the smallest failure instantly sends him hurtling back into the depths of his social nullity" (201–2).

In addition, the parvenu must constantly be on guard against any personal or spontaneous impulses, perceptions, judgments, or feelings that might betray him. Every personal wish and reaction must be subordinated to the central goal of social acceptance, and that goal requires craving and enjoying what "they"—not oneself—define as valuable. Thus the parvenu is "gnawed" inwardly by an insatiable craving for "a multitude of things which he [does] not even really want, but which he [cannot] bear to be refused." He must "adapt his tastes, his life, his desires to these things," and thus must learn "to sacrifice every natural impulse, to conceal all truth, to misuse all love, not only to suppress all passion, but worse still, to convert it into a means for social climbing" (205, 208). Thus he no longer dares to be himself in anything, even for a moment. The parvenu condemns himself "to lead a sham existence" and is able to "seize possession of all the objects of a world not arranged for him only with the pseudoreality of a masquerade."[17]

Here we arrive at yet a third part of the high cost of the parvenu strategy: the loss of reality. No more than he can afford a stable sense of his own self can the parvenu independently assess what is real in the world. For most of Varnhagen's life, "her consciousness of reality was dependent on confirmation by others."[18] The others defined what there was, what it was like, and what it was worth. "The world and reality" had, for Varnhagen, "always been represented by society. 'Real' meant for her the world of those who were 'socially acknowledged.' "[19] Not only was her own reality dependent on social recognition, but she had to suppress her own perceptions and responses lest they compete with the social definition of the world. Varnhagen had to pay for her social acceptance "in the coin of 'true realities' "—the simple, personal pleasures and perceptions unrelated to status that she could not afford: "green things, children, love, weather," or (at another point), "a bridge, a tree, a ride, a smell, a smile" (210, 213).

Along with reality, truth had to be sacrificed: truth became whatever society says is true. The parvenu must focus on impression management. Varnhagen had to master the "art of representing her own life: the point was not to tell the truth, but to display herself; not always to say the same thing to everyone, but to each what was appropriate for him." So "an honest parvenu . . . is a kind of paradox," because one enters society "only at the price of lying, of a far more generalized lie than simple hypocrisy."[20] What was successfully presented and socially accepted became true. It was a power of sorts, if one was a gifted deceiver, but also a constraint: "One is not free when one has to represent something in respectable society."[21] The constant need to manipulate, to present a persuasive version of things, combines with the parvenu's self-imposed constraints on perception and on thought. To fit in with society's view of reality, it is best to have none of one's own. To succeed as an exception, it is best not to generalize. The parvenu becomes "ultimately incapable of grasping generalities, recognizing relationships or taking an interest in anything but his own person" (214). To focus on the task, one may have to wear blinkers.

The parvenu, then, "must not act, not love, not become involved with the world" (8–9). Incapable—of autonomous judgment or action, of perceiving others accurately or relating to them nonmanipulatively, hence of intimacy or love, of mutuality or solidarity, of taking pleasure in the real world—the parvenu is bound to remain isolated, a victim, and unhappy.

At times Varnhagen withdrew from parvenu striving into romantic introspection, but this left her equally out of touch with reality and truth. In the isolation achieved by introspection, there are no others, there is no objectivity, and "without reality shared by other human beings, truth loses all meaning." In "the inner self," Arendt says, "everything is eternally present and converted back into potentiality"; that makes introspection comforting, but "at the price of truth" (11). For romantic Varnhagen, the importance of her own feelings and emotions was entirely independent of any real action or consequences in the world. For example, as she herself said, when she loved a man, her own feelings were "more important than [their] object" to her (92). "Facts mean nothing at all to me," she wrote, and signed the letter "Confessions de J. J. Rahel," invoking that other romantic, Rousseau, whom Arendt calls "the greatest example of the mania for introspection," whose own life "acquire[d] reality [for him] only in the course of confessing it" (11, 20).

In introspection, "thinking becomes limitless because it is no longer molested by anything exterior," neither by action and its consequences nor by the testimony of others (10). Accordingly, "introspection accomplishes two feats: it annihilates the actual existing situation by dissolving it in mood, and at the same time it lends everything subjective an aura of objectivity, publicity, extreme interest. In mood the boundaries between what is intimate and what is public become blurred." So personal matters are imagined as having public importance, and public issues "can be experienced . . . only in the realm of the intimate—ultimately, in gossip," as in salon conversation (21). Thus introspection here does what Arendt will later charge against the social: it blurs the line between private and public. And romantic withdrawal inward, although an alternative to parvenu striving, is equally "social" in the self-centered isolation, the lack of realism, and the irresponsibility with respect to worldly consequences that it entails.

Varnhagen's Change of Mind

In the end Varnhagen abandoned her parvenu strivings, finding their costs too high, and instead accepted and even cherished her pariah status. The change was not a sudden conversion but a gradual process, a struggle. It began when Varnhagen, having tried and failed to win social acceptance through love and marriage, at the age of thirty went to live in Paris, where she knew almost no one and thus could not present a fraudulent, social self. This freed her for a time from her self-preoccupation and gave her her first opportunity to enjoy nature and people simply for what they were, undistorted by manipulative purpose or self-referential anxiety. In Paris she "slowly and happily learned the joy of 'denying one's own existence,' the receptivity to enjoy new things without always and obstinately referring them to herself, the freedom to love a person as he was, to have a male friend without making demands upon him" (72). One need only open one's eyes to the beautiful world, she learned, and take pleasure in it; one need not, does not even want to possess it but only "to see it blooming. . . . [W]e can never possess anything but the capacity to enjoy" (77).

But this was an interlude abroad, an experiment. Returning to Berlin, Varnhagen returned also to her former ways and character. The enjoyment of nature and love soon became romanticized into another sentimental, introspective withdrawal from reality. She began yet another narcissistic and obsessive relationship with a man and, when it failed, returned even more seriously to the project of parvenu assimilation. She did so, however, precisely at a time of resurgent anti-Semitism in Prussia and of financial difficulties for her brothers, on whom, as a single woman, she was financially dependent.

Unable for both these reasons to resume a successful salon, she changed her name in 1810, had herself baptized in 1814, and then chose the one form of assimilation that in her time and place really "could succeed," at which "all her women friends who had come from the same background and who wanted to escape from Judaism had succeeded": she married the gentile August Varnhagen, who—partly under her ambitious prodding—made high-level connections and eventually discovered some aristocratic ancestors in his own family tree (177, 176). Still, despite this success, or perhaps because of it, she continued to move away from her assimilationist striving.

Arendt suggests two explanations for this continuing change, in addition to Rahel Varnhagen's limited discovery of self and reality in Paris.

First, the resurgence of anti-Semitism and of hard times forced her to recognize the extent to which her former success had been dependent on historical, humanly made circumstances. "Only now, in a time of breakdown, did Rahel realize that her life also was subject to general political conditions," or as she put it, that she had lived and prospered only "under the auspices, in the strictest sense under the wings, of Frederick the Second." This fact, Varnhagen said, had been "shattered over [her] head," employing a phrase that Arendt would later apply to her own rude awakening to political reality (121). We learn through suffering.

Arendt's second explanation for Varnhagen's continuing turn away from the parvenu strategy is that her success, in the form of marriage, proved disappointing. On the one hand, her husband—partly in response to her ambition—proved to be a parvenu, and Varnhagen in effect saw in him a caricature of what she herself had been trying to become, and could not bear what she saw. At the same time, on the other hand, Varnhagen discovered that the route to social acceptance she had chosen carried its own kind of renewed pariah status for her. A woman could assimilate through an appropriate marriage, but only because a wife did not exist as a person; she became part of her husband. Now she was expected to behave "as if I were nothing more than *my husband;* in the past I was *nothing,* and that is a great deal" (210, emphasis in original). She was not socially welcome without him, for instance, when he was abroad, and the marriage brought with it new social pressures, the need "to represent something in respectable society, a married woman, an officer's wife, etc." (213).

Even as she changed her name, was baptized, married, Varnhagen began what Arendt calls a "passionate protest, [a] furious attempt to undo everything again, to repudiate all she had achieved as something never desired" (212). She resumed using Hebrew in letters to her brothers, and she resumed contact with a woman who had been the most socially disreputable friend of her youth, wholly outside the pale of respectable society. To this friend she wrote that the two of them had "been created to live the truth in this world" and were "excluded from society. You because you offended it . . . I because I cannot sin and lie along with it" (205). She was, in short, starting to take pride in her outsider status and to see social acceptance as founded on deceit and hypocrisy.

In the end Varnhagen proved too honest to succeed as a parvenu, lacking the requisite "virtuoso capacity for self-deception" (211). She also had too much compassion, "'too much consideration for a human face'"; she could not bear the condescension toward other pariahs that was involved in separating "herself from the dark mass of the people" (214, 219). And she preferred, ultimately, to pretend nothing, and to be herself.

Except in a very few passages, *Rahel Varnhagen* never explores what alternatives to becoming a parvenu might be open to pariahs. Twice Arendt makes reference to an alternative she calls "political": once at the book's opening and once in the conclusion. In introducing her subject, she remarks that "a political struggle for equal rights might have taken the place" of Varnhagen's personal struggle "for recognition in society" (7, 6). This alternative Varnhagen never in fact pursued. The opening chapter suggests that this was no failure on her part, since the political alternative "was wholly unknown to" her entire generation of Jews (7). Arendt also remarks later that Varnhagen "never saw the other possibility, of joining those who had not arrived, of throwing in her lot with [them]." But this passage concerns a time before Varnhagen's change of mind, indeed, before her marriage, and although the phrase "the other possibility" clearly implies a dichotomous choice, the passage then continues with a dual interpretation of that second alternative: "she had never ventured into criticism of the society, or even to solidarity with [other pariahs]" (177).

In the concluding chapter, Arendt does seem to blame Varnhagen for not taking this last alternative, charging that she "had resolutely refused to share the general fate of the Jews, to place her hopes in political measures which would benefit all."[22] All this is somewhat confusing, since Arendt's telling of the story shows that Varnhagen did, in the end, become willing to share the general fate of the Jews and did specifically criticize society for its hypocrisy. Indeed, she came to call herself "a rebel after all," with a "*great* love for free existence," and Arendt remarks that Varnhagen had always wanted "to be esteemed as a peer," an expression that might suggest Arendt's later notion of citizenship.[23] Nevertheless, Varnhagen did not become political or enter into any political action on the basis of her criticism and private rebellion.

Instead of a political understanding of her situation and correlated political action, what Varnhagen achieved in the end was a biblical understanding of her fate as divinely destined and therefore meaningful, to be affirmed by acceptance rather than resisted through either parvenu or political striving: "Thus in the end she understood her '*whole* fate [as] an historical, inexorable, Old Testamentarian fate, indeed [as] the *curse* which the children of its adherents vainly try to flee in all quarters of the globe.'"[24] This understanding gave meaning to her suffering and enabled her to "see life as a whole," to generalize in a way that parvenus cannot permit themselves: "If, though unable to revolt as an individual against the whole of society, he disdains the alternative of becoming a parvenu, [the pariah] is recompensed for his 'wretched situations' by a 'view of the whole.' That is his sole dignified hope: 'that everything is related; and in truth, everything is good enough' " (215).

Not only did Varnhagen's life gain meaning, but where previously she had purchased social acceptance "by sacrificing nature," now as she gave up social acceptance she regained nature, the simple pleasures, her natural self. But she did not gain politics or use her capacity for action. Thus, although Arendt opened the book by saying that "if we do not understand [our own history, it] . . . will take its revenge . . . and become our personal destiny," Varnhagen's ultimate understanding of her own life as part of a meaningful history was precisely what enabled her to accept and welcome it as her destiny (3). Even at the end of her life, she still could only "let everything pour down upon me like rain without an umbrella."[25] But now, she welcomed the rain.

Society in *Rahel Varnhagen*

In *Rahel Varnhagen*, "society" and "social" almost always refer to high society as the parvenu understands it: an elite "they, up there" who hold a monopoly on power and privilege, control access to everything worthwhile, and indeed define what is worthwhile. They are members by birth, but so great is their power that occasionally they can admit an outsider to their ranks as a reward for exceptional adherence to their rules, or because they have been fooled by the outsider's exceptional capacity for fraudulent cleverness, or (somehow) both. For the most part, then, society is high society, and it is omnipotent.

But the message of the book as a whole, based on Varnhagen's retrospective judgment of her own life, is that this view is illusory. Having always felt that doors were closed against her by society, Varnhagen concluded in the end that she did not really want what lay behind those doors and that the things she really wanted, the "true realities" of natural pleasure—"green things, children, love, weather . . . a bridge, a tree, a ride, a smell, a smile"—could be neither withheld from her nor given to her by any elite. At that point the doors on which she had been hammering were no longer closed against her, not because they had opened, but because she no longer wanted to go through them. And other doors, of which she had not even been aware, turned out to have been open all along. At that point, one might say, the terrible power of society over her vanished, and society was revealed as a paper tiger. One might say that, but neither Arendt nor Varnhagen ever does say it in this book. Nor can it be said unproblematically, for Varnhagen remained a pariah even after she stopped being a parvenu, and whoever or whatever agency makes certain people into pariahs surely is wielding real power.

Indeed, in a number of passages in *Rahel Varnhagen* "society" and (particularly) "social" and "socially" do not mean the elite of high society, but refer to the entire system of status hierarchy of which high society is only the top layer. Parvenus seek "a higher social position" by climbing "up the social ladder" (119, 202). A salon where members of all classes may mingle is "socially neutral" in welcoming "visitors from all social circles" (38, 55). In this sense, everyone, not just the elite, is part of what is social; society is a hierarchy of "circles" into which people are born. In becoming a parvenu, someone born into a pariah circle seeks to escape his own "natural social ground," the "stage-set . . . given him at birth" (220, 217).

So the word "society" and particularly the corresponding adjective and adverb are sometimes used in this book in a way that reaches beyond high society to other familiar meanings, including both what one might call the sociologist's sense—where society is (almost) all the people who live in a certain region and share the local culture—and the sense epitomized in "sociability" and meaning something like one's "associates," the company one keeps.[26] Even when the words appear in these latter senses, however, their meaning is still pervaded by the parvenu's outlook. Even when they refer to one's social circle or the collectivity of all such circles, those circles are always *understood as* ranked and ordered in a status hierarchy, even if members of lower circles can also strive to climb into higher ones. Thus, when Arendt remarks that the nobility "set the tone in society," the latter noun clearly includes not just the nobility themselves but also "the bourgeois[ie] as well as the Jews who became parvenus" (203). Similarly, to reject the parvenu outlook would be "to revolt as an individual against the whole of society"—not just against the elite, but against all who regard them as the elite and honor the tone they set, who are prepared to "submit to" that tone, to conform to the "social rigors and conventions" (215, 208, 57). In other words, in this book, even when society is the company one keeps or the ensemble of all social circles, it is characterized by what holds those circles together, the "social" outlook they share, which is the parvenu's outlook: a concern with rank and status, a striving to conform to the rules and standards set by "higher" ranks, a suspension of autonomous judgment and truth in favor of submission, deference, and hypocrisy.

There is one passage, however, that points problematically beyond the uses of "society" and "social" in this book, a mere inadvertent hint at issues not yet salient for Arendt. Varnhagen, at the end of her life, "could not help thinking that Jews like herself had been lured into society by fraud and deception, . . . by a secret, spiteful alliance between state and society which combined to withhold from the Jews first civil rights and then social equality." Here the deception is practiced not by the parvenu seeking to enter society but by the "spiteful alliance," and specifically by society itself, whose "hypocrisy" is "pretend[ing] to treat assimilated Jews as if they were not Jews." Furthermore, though it may at first seem that the hypocrisy consists simply in falsely promising the Jews something they already want, Arendt's account of Varnhagen's thought is more complex. The spiteful alliance, she says, "inoculated" the Jews "with the poison of ambition" and "led them desperately to want to attain everything" by denying them even "the simplest rights."[27]

So the location of pariah and society in relation to each other is problematic in this passage, as is the question of blame. Clearly society is high society, and the Jews are outside it wanting in, rather than members of one social circle seeking admission to another. Yet society has also gotten inside of the Jews, shaping their character by its hypocrisy; it constrains them not only outwardly, by making them into pariahs, but also inwardly, by making them into parvenus. It is not clear whether the society that does the inoculating is high society, one's immediate social circle, or the sociological (almost) everybody, but it is surely no paper tiger. Its power seems close to omnipotence. Insofar as Arendt speaks of society this way, in effect blaming it even for what she mostly treats as the pariah's free choice of whether to become a parvenu, she herself adopts the parvenu's perspective. Envisioning society's "alliance" with the "state," moreover, she casts doubt on her own distinction between social, parvenu conduct and its "political" alternative.

There are problems in the background, then, unexamined in *Rahel Varnhagen*, about the ontological status of this entity called society, about the extent of its power, and thus about the power and freedom of individual pariahs. Neither these background perplexities nor the alternatives to parvenu striving are explored further in this book. Their complexly problematic implications are visible only in hindsight, in light of the later development of Arendt's ideas. In *Rahel Varnhagen* the concept of society is not examined critically at all; the word mainly reflects the parvenu's point of view, which the book as a whole rejects. Yet we shall see that in important respects this is what society continues to mean for Arendt throughout her work, so that her idea of the social as Blob cannot be understood without reference to the parvenu perspective, the way of the parvenu in the world, and the costs it entails.

THREE

Biographical Interlude: Philosophy, Love, Exile

Arendt claimed to have written Rahel Varnhagen's story as Varnhagen herself might have told it, using her letters and "reflections upon herself," and making no criticism of her that did not "correspond to [her] self-criticism."[1] No doubt she was able to proceed in this way because Varnhagen's fundamental retrospective self-criticism contained the lesson Arendt wanted to teach and which probably drew Arendt to her story in the first place.[2] Moreover, the issues raised and the categories introduced in *Rahel Varnhagen* importantly structured all of Arendt's subsequent thought, and specifically her concept of the social. Why did the lesson that Varnhagen taught matter—and matter so much—to the young Arendt? What, indeed, did it mean to her, in terms of her own life and world? Commentators are quick to point out a certain identification of the biographer with her subject, but obviously Arendt's Germany was not much like Varnhagen's, and the two women were not at all alike. Both were assimilated Jews encountering anti-Semitism, certainly, and were shy, highly intelligent, and gifted women. But Arendt was no social climber anxious for acceptance by respectable society, nor did she experience her Jewishness as a misfortune to be extirpated.

To understand Arendt's interest in Varnhagen's life, particularly in Varnhagen's ultimate rejection of her own parvenu striving, one needs, I believe, to look beyond such actual parallels to psychological ones, and specifically to Arendt's relationship with her teacher, Martin Heidegger. But that sort of rude, if posthumous, intrusion into Arendt's personal life requires some advance justification, particularly because she herself so vehemently rejected our modern tendency to personalize, introspect, and reduce the public and political to the intimate and psychological.

Arendt doubted the "legitimacy" of our contemporary "eagerness to see recorded, displayed and discussed in public what were once strictly private affairs and nobody's business."[3] Writing Varnhagen's biography, she sought strenuously to avoid "that modern form of indiscretion in which the writer attempts to penetrate his subject's tricks and aspires to know more than the subject knew about himself or was willing to reveal; what I would call the pseudoscientific apparatuses of depth-psychology, psycho-analysis, graphology, etc." For just this reason she excluded from consideration an obviously relevant topic, "the Woman Problem, that is, the discrepancy between what men expected of women 'in general' and what women could give or wanted in their turn."[4]

It is true that a psychobiographical approach to political theory can easily become reductionist, dismissing political doctrines as "really" merely about the theorist's psychic conflicts or fantasies. But in Arendt's case, almost the reverse is true. Only when the highly abstract, seemingly remote, Grecophile concepts of *The Human Condition* are traced back to their roots in Arendt's life do their true political significance and contemporary relevance emerge. To understand Arendt's concept of the social, one must not merely, as Michael Rogin once put it, "look through the Greeks to the Jews," but also look through the problems of Rahel Varnhagen's life and times to those of Arendt's own. But the proof of that pudding will have to wait until it has been dished up, a task that this chapter begins by examining Arendt's life up to the time when she fled Germany, including her complex relationship—both intellectual and personal—with her most significant teacher.

Arendt's Early Life

Like so many middle-class, urban German Jews, Arendt grew up assimilated, though aware of her Jewishness. Her parents were not religious, but they had social contact with rabbis, and she was sometimes taken to synagogue by her paternal grandfather. Arendt said that "the word 'Jew' was never mentioned at home" during her early childhood, that she first encountered it in the anti-Semitic remarks of other children, whereupon she "was, so to speak, 'enlightened'" (the German word also suggests sexual enlightenment and might best be translated here as learning "the facts of life"). As an older child, she was aware that she "looked Jewish," but, she said, "not as a form of inferiority, just as a fact." One source claims, however, that as a child, Arendt had wished she was blond and blue-eyed.[5]

The anti-Semitism that she encountered did not "poison" her soul (or psyche, *Seele*), she said, because her mother always "protected" the child's "dignity" by insisting that "One may not knuckle under [*Man darf sich nicht ducken*]! One must defend oneself!" This sounds almost more like a duty than like a protection, however, and the story Arendt proceeds to tell is not exactly or merely about self-defense, but reflects the complex relations between assimilated German Jews and the embarrassingly uncultivated Jewish immigrants from the East, relations which also figured in Varnhagen's life:

> If my teachers made anti-Semitic remarks—mostly not about me but about Jewish girls, for example, eastern Jewish pupils—I was instructed to get up immediately, to leave the class, come home, . . . [where] my mother would write one of her many registered letters. . . . But if remarks came from other children, I was not allowed to tell about it at home. That didn't count. Against what comes from other children, you have to defend yourself.[6]

There is, then, a duty—not a right or privilege—of self-defense and of solidarity, together. The child's duty is relatively limited with respect to insults from adults, more extensive with respect to insults from peers.

Of her mother, Arendt said that, although "completely areligious," she was "of course Jewish. She would never have had me baptized! I assume she would have boxed my ears if she had ever discovered that I had denied being a Jew. Simply out of the question, so to speak."[7]

Arendt was a highly intelligent, precocious child. By the age of five she could both read and write; at fourteen she was reading Kant's *Critique of Pure Reason*, then Jaspers's *Psychologie der Weltanschauungen*, as well as Kierkegaard. At that point she decided that if she could not study philosophy, "I'd drown myself, so to speak."[8] In school Arendt was ambitious and very successful. Nevertheless, when she was fifteen she responded to an offensive remark made by one of her teachers—we are not told its content or whether it was anti-Semitic—by organizing a student boycott. For this she was expelled from school, but with her mother's help she was able to enroll for classes at the university in Berlin and finished high school by examination.[9] Clearly, by this time Arendt spurned parental protection when her honor was at stake.

On the whole, Arendt insisted that Jewishness was a matter of low salience in her childhood. So, it seems, was gender. Arendt's parents' friends were professionals, teachers, and musicians. Her mother had studied music in Paris; she read Proust in French with Hannah. Arendt's father was an engineer. He suffered from syphilis, contracted and supposedly cured in his youth but reappearing in its tertiary stage when she was two. She was four when he became bedridden, five when he was institutionalized, just turning seven when he died. Elzbieta Ettinger says, without attribution, that to please her mother the child pretended "that her feelings for her father were unaffected by his looks, which were disfigured by syphilis," but aside from that, we know very little about what this experience meant to her, what she was told or what she thought about this socially embarrassing illness.[10] She became very close to her paternal grandfather—the one who took her to synagogue, who was also a great storyteller—in this period. But he too died, shortly before her father's death. The next year, so did an uncle with whom she had just vacationed.

The year after that, World War I broke out, and Arendt's mother took her to Berlin, where their life was financially strained, at least until her mother remarried in 1920. Apparently Arendt was never close to her stepfather, who already had two teenaged daughters of his own.

In a short, crucial period, then, Arendt lost her father and two surrogate fathers, along with the familiar, provincial, relatively well-to-do world of her childhood. Her mother recorded that the child showed no reaction to her father's death but turned inward and became "opaque."[11] Ettinger adds, again without attribution, that after the father's death, "her adored mother travelled frequently to take the waters or visit relatives, and each absence left the child upset, fearing that her mother would not return."[12]

Arendt's mother was much influenced by ideas of progressive education, including those that encouraged "girls to go the educational routes long reserved for boys."[13] Later Arendt said that she owed to her mother "above all an education without any prejudices and with all opportunities."[14] Yet her mother seems also to have had quite conventional and traditional ideas about femininity and sexual conduct. Arendt later said that she herself had never been very interested in "the Woman Question" and that on this question she had been "old-fashioned," having always held that "certain occupations are not suitable for women, do not become them, if I may put it that way. It doesn't look good when a woman issues orders. She should try not to get into such positions, if she is concerned to retain feminine qualities." At the same time Arendt added, however, that she herself had always "simply done what I wanted to do." To another interviewer she averred that she was "not disturbed at all about being a woman professor because I am quite used to being a woman."[15]

Politics, too, Arendt claimed, was of little concern to her in her youth. Her parents were socialists and progressives, active in the Social Democratic movement, though affiliated with its gradualist rather than its radical, Spartacist wing. Nevertheless, Arendt's mother, the politically more engaged of the two, was "an ardent admirer" of the Spartacist Rosa Luxemburg, and when the Spartacist uprising began in 1919, excitedly told her daughter to "pay attention, this is a historical moment!"[16] Ettinger was told by Arendt's cousin that in this same period the young girl had been "fascinated by family tales about a beautiful vanished aunt who, involved in subversive political activities, led a secretive life, surreptitiously crossing frontiers, carrying messages, and being adored by her co-conspirators, who knew her stunning face only from behind a thick veil."[17]

Later in her life Arendt rejected the suggestion by Gershom Scholem that she was among the "intellectuals who came from the German left." She responded, "I was interested neither in history nor in politics when I was young. If I can be said to 'have come from anywhere,' it is from the tradition of German philosophy."[18] This is a puzzling remark from the daughter of an engineer, the stepdaughter and granddaughter of businessmen. But Arendt clearly was referring not to family influences but to her own preoccupations. Her academic brilliance and ambition had led her early not only to German philosophy but also to the ancient Greeks, particularly their poetry, which she loved.[19] These interests brought her to her university studies with Heidegger, Husserl, and Jaspers.

Arendt and Heidegger

When the eighteen-year-old Arendt came to the university in Marburg in 1924, it was primarily to study with Martin Heidegger, to whom, as she explained much later, students flocked from all over Germany, drawn by rumors that in his classes "thinking has come to life again; the cultural treasures of the past, believed to be dead, are being made to speak. . . . There exists a teacher; one can perhaps learn to think."[20] As for what Heidegger saw when he looked at Arendt, a friend and fellow student testifies that she was "shy and turned inward, with striking, beautiful facial features and lonely eyes, [and] she immediately stood out as 'unusual' and 'singular.'"[21]

Since the appearance of Young-Bruehl's biography of Arendt, recently supplemented by Ettinger's interpretation of the Arendt-Heidegger correspondence, everyone knows what happened when the brilliant young professor, reserved and awkward, aged thirty-five, unhappily married and the father of two boys, met the brilliant student half his age who had read Kant in high school and memorized Greek poetry in the original language for fun: they had an affair, a romance. According to Ettinger, it was Heidegger who "initiated the affair... with forethought."²² Two months after Arendt appeared as a student in one of his classes, he wrote her a formal note inviting her to a conference in his office. A brief note dated less than three weeks later "indicates... the beginning of physical intimacy" (16). Heidegger wrote poetry to Arendt, and letters that Ettinger calls "sentimental and romantic," as well as "suffused with sensuous love," and he "promised to love her forever" (14, 25, 3). He set the detailed terms for their secret meetings (17–19).

After a year Arendt left Marburg, first to study briefly with Husserl, then to write a dissertation with Jaspers. Ettinger says both that it was Arendt who first "started to think about moving to another university" and that Heidegger "pressured her to leave" (18, 21). What is clear is that Heidegger, who later averred that Arendt had been "*nun einmal* the passion of his life," did not leave his wife.²³ Nor, Ettinger says, is there any "evidence to suggest that [Arendt] ever thought or wished" that he might.²⁴ Though Arendt left, the affair resumed, apparently at his initiative, and continued for two more years, until Heidegger ended it after being appointed to Husserl's chair at Freiburg. Arendt responded with a letter that Ettinger says displayed romantic "high drama" but was also genuinely "desperate," closing with lines from Elizabeth Barrett Browning's forty-third Sonnet from the Portuguese:

> ... and, if God choose,
> I shall but love thee better after death.²⁵

As a young adult, Arendt once told a friend that her father's dream for her had been that she become a famous scholar. Her father having been institutionalized when she was five, one does not know what to make of this; perhaps it was a story her mother told her, or perhaps she meant her stepfather, though that seems unlikely.²⁶ Much less ambiguous is her remark while praising Jaspers (not Heidegger) as her teacher: "I grew up fatherless."²⁷ Jaspers in fact conducted himself in a fatherly fashion toward her, guiding her studies and becoming—along with his wife—her good friend. Young-Bruehl reports that Arendt referred to her encounter with Heidegger as her "first amour" and adds, "Philosophy was her first love; but it was the philosophy incarnate in the person of Martin Heidegger."²⁸ Arendt encountered him, as she herself later put it, as "the hidden king [who] reigned in the realm of thinking" (44).

All else aside, one imagines it must have been thrilling to be singled out by this master teacher with his coterie of adoring students, this king of the realm of philosophy to which she most desired access, this paternal figure who preferred her to his wife. Later Arendt came to see the affair in a rather different light. While mostly remaining publicly loyal to and protective of Heidegger, Arendt spoke of him privately with a kind of indulgent contempt, finding in his letters, for example, "the same mix of vanity and deceitfulness—or better, cowardice—as before" and noting that he "lies notoriously always and everywhere, and whenever he can."[29] She called this dishonesty "intricate-childish" and found it "unbearable," but ascribed it to a certain "lack of character—but in the sense that he literally has none, certainly not a particularly bad one."[30]

Arendt also came to see her own past conduct with Heidegger as deceitful, as a kind of inauthentic, romantic self-abnegation. After he publicly attacked *The Human Condition,* she wrote to Jaspers:

> I know that it is intolerable for him that my name appears in public, that I write books, etc. All my life I have pulled the wool over his eyes, as it were, always acted as . . . if I, so to speak, could not count to three, except when it came to giving an interpretation of his own works, where it was always very welcome to him when it turned out that I could count to three and sometimes even to four.[31]

In Jaspers Arendt encountered a different conception of philosophy from Heidegger's. For Heidegger, as she would put it later, philosophy was an inherently solitary enterprise in which the individual turns away from all conventions and relationships to become an authentic self and achieve self-certainty. "The most essential characteristic of this Self is its absolute egoism, its radical separation from its fellows." Jaspers, by contrast, understood philosophy as dialogue, on the Socratic model, intended to illuminate rather than to reject the world of human conventions and relationships. "Fellow humans are not (as in Heidegger) an element of existence that, while structurally necessary, inevitably interferes with one's self-being." Rather, one only becomes human through contact with one's fellows.[32]

Under the supervision of Jaspers, who knew nothing of Arendt's affair with Heidegger until decades later, she found a dissertation topic that enabled her both to develop her scholarship and to work through her feelings about Heidegger: Saint Augustine's concept of love. In particular, the dissertation focused on love of one's neighbor, which is neither the sinful, exploitive *cupiditas* of lust nor the selfless, adoring absorption of *caritas,* as the Christian's love for God, but a mysterious third alternative.[33]

On the one hand, loving God means turning away from the world and from oneself. From the perspective of eternity, this world matters not at all, and "no individual means anything in comparison" to God. How can a Christian even have a "neighbor"?[34] Yet, on the other hand, humans were put on this earth by God, concretely embodied as particular persons with particular neighbors, endowed with free will and commanded to choose the good. While the Christian is alive on earth, he must live in the world among other people, struggling against evil, just as he must live in his own body in "a constant struggle against sin that will not end until death" (107). Consequently, love for one's neighbor is concrete, yet not uncritical; on the contrary, the Christian owes his neighbor admonition in his struggle against sin (96, 100, 106, 108–9). The Christian is not to love the sin in his neighbor any more than in himself, but only that which is of God in the neighbor, what "is eternal in him." And yet this loving of God and the eternal "in" the neighbor must somehow be love of this particular individual "in isolation," concretely embodied like oneself (95–96, 111).

The words "society" and "social" play an undistinguished role in the dissertation, referring simply to interpersonal, human collectivity (which is why we began our investigation with *Rahel Varnhagen* rather than here). Yet Arendt does explain neighborly love in terms of the Christian's membership in human society, calling it "social *caritas*" (95). Since the Christian must live in the world, and the world is "constituted by" human beings, humans are responsible for its maintenance.[35] For Augustine, Arendt says, membership in human society is thus twofold: given and chosen. People "belong to Adam (that is, to the human race) by generation," created by God and connected to each other by common descent. In that sense each of us is born into a preexisting "situation," into a world that is humanly established but not by us, into the "interdependence" that "essentially defines social life" (100–103). Yet we are capable of replacing that given interdependence, which is "inevitable and a matter of course," with a "freely chosen" connection in mutual love, in "imitation" of Christ, and in the egalitarian recognition of shared sinfulness and a shared hope for grace (102, 100, 103, 106, 108–9). What makes possible such a freely chosen community of neighborly love is the combination of our shared given membership in Adam with the unique individuality of each human being. "By virtue of" this individuality we are "lifted out of the self-evident dependence in which all people live with each other" and enabled "to detach ourselves from human history and from its irrevocable enchainment by generation" to move from necessity to freedom (112).

Anticipating the terminology of *Rahel Varnhagen,* one might say that all humans are pariahs, sojourners on earth, but the Christian acknowledges that status in solidarity with other pariahs, while the parvenu lives in sin—a bad Christian for Augustine as he is a bad Jew for Arendt. But of course these were not yet Arendt's terms. A less anachronistic and more revealing way to understand her dissertation is as identifying the essence of human love neither with possessive exploitation of the beloved as object, nor with a romantic fusion of self into a vastly superior being, but with a mutuality between "neighbors," who perceive each other realistically, in their generic human limitations and concrete particularity, each loving the other for what he truly is, without romance. Ironically, Arendt came to express this idea through a line from Augustine that Heidegger quoted to her: *Volo ut sis,* "I want you to be"; I will your being, just as you are, recognizing your weaknesses and your capacities, realistically affirming your unique individuality.[36]

Having finished her dissertation, and explaining that she "wanted to be free," Arendt declined to pursue an academic career.[37] She moved to Berlin in 1929, revised her dissertation for publication, and began work on a study of German romanticism focused specifically on Rahel Varnhagen.[38] After a brief affair with a former fellow Heidegger student, Arendt reencountered another former Heidegger student in Berlin, began living with him, and soon married him.[39] Günther Stern was, like Arendt, from a middle-class, assimilated Jewish background; he was the son of two psychologists, joint authors of a famous book on child development based on meticulous observation of their own three children. A member of the Communist Party, he was politically radical but seems to have been by character a dutiful son. After her affair with Heidegger, as Arendt put it later, "I was absolutely determined never to love a man again, and then I married, just someone, without loving him."[40] Asked what had attracted her to Stern, she replied that he was kind and gentle, that her mother got on well with him, and that she herself liked and admired his mother for her "generous nature."[41] The marriage lasted about four years in substance, twice that long before the formal divorce.

Permitting ourselves to speculate once more, we might say that Arendt was trying hard to give up the entrapments of romantic self-abnegation and to pursue realistic possibilities. Giving up fantasies of an academic career, she moved to the big city and commenced independent intellectual work. Giving up Heidegger, the king of the philosophical realm, she chose her ordinary fellow subjects in that realm. Giving up dreams of romantic merger and self-abnegation, she turned to disenchanted neighborliness with a vengeance, determined to do without love.

"Nightmare and Flight"

The simultaneously philosophical and personal discoveries Arendt made in her dissertation work were soon enriched and displaced by increasingly urgent external concerns: the rise of anti-Semitism and Naziism. As we have seen, Arendt had been aware of her own Jewishness and of the anti-Semitism around her, yet for her intellectual and scholarly interests, in which she was passionately involved, her Jewishness had seemed wholly irrelevant.[42] Or rather, when she first fell in love with philosophy as a teenager and found it inextricably intertwined with theology—notably in Kierkegaard—she was for a time deeply troubled, worried "how one goes about it, then, if one is a Jewish woman." But she soon found that those "severe worries" could "be dispelled without further ado."[43] One obvious measure of the apparent personal irrelevance of her Jewishness is surely her choice of dissertation topic: of all possible thinkers, she chose to specialize in a Christian saint.[44] What's a nice Jewish girl doing with a topic like that?

By 1931, under the influence of Stern and his friends, Arendt was seriously reading Marx, Lenin, and Trotsky and attending to public affairs. She held political opinions, read the newspapers "intently," and as early as 1931 became "firmly convinced" that the Nazis would eventually come to power.[45] In Berlin, Arendt had also reencountered Kurt Blumenfeld, a Zionist known to her family in Königsberg, now the chief spokesman for the Zionist Organization of Germany. Blumenfeld became her friend and her "mentor in politics," and Arendt spent increasing amounts of time in the circle of his Zionist associates and friends as her marriage began to come apart. Later she wrote that on "the so-called Jewish Question" she had been "simply naive" and had found it "boring" until Blumenfeld "opened my eyes."[46]

What opened her eyes more forcefully, however, was the rapid rise of the Nazis. In early 1933, after Hitler became chancellor and after the Reichstag fire, there began a wave of illegal "arrests," beatings, torture, and disappearances of radicals, Jews, and people who happened to look Jewish. Arendt wrote later that she "had been primarily occupied with academic pursuits. Given that perspective, the year 1933 made a lasting impression" on her. Not that she had been blind to the Nazis before: "That the Nazis were our enemies—God knows we did not need Hitler's seizing of power to demonstrate that! That had been clear to everyone who was not feebleminded for at least four years prior to 1933." At that point, however, the "generally political became a personal fate."[47] Already "around 1930" she had argued with Jaspers, who maintained that she was "of course" ethnically German, Arendt responding, "No, I'm not. After all, anyone can *see* that!"[48]

Of even greater impact than her personal risk, however, was what was happening to other people. What befell those seized by the Nazis at the time "was an immediate shock to me, and from that moment on I felt responsible. That is, I was no longer of the opinion that one could be simply an observer." At this point, Arendt said, "Finally it hit me over the head like a hammer, and called me to my own attention."[49] She was forced to ask herself what she had been doing, what the institutions and people with whom she had been connected, and from whom she had sought approval, had been doing. Today we might call it a "consciousness raising" experience.

Heidegger, in particular, became a Nazi. It is not clear at precisely what point that became evident to Arendt; she was certainly aware early that his wife was anti-Semitic.[50] Nor do we know whether Arendt's being Jewish played any role in her affair with Heidegger. But she surely meant both Heidegger and others of her intellectual "friends" when she later said that what had been hard to come to terms with was not Naziism, but collaboration with it: "The problem, the personal problem was not what our enemies did, but what our friends did." People about whom she would earlier have said "we" were cooperating with the Nazis when there were not yet any penalties for withholding such cooperation, when it was still "relatively voluntary."[51] That was what was hard to get one's head around, what left one feeling isolated, as if a yawning "empty space was opening up around" one. And intellectuals were the worst of all; among them, Arendt found, collaboration was "so to speak, the rule," as it was not among other people. The "terrible thing" was that the intellectuals collaborated with Naziism not to protect their jobs or their families but because "they actually believed in it," even if only for a short time.[52]

Arendt's way of understanding this collaboration was generally in terms of social conformity, the parvenu mentality. But more specifically with regard to intellectuals, academics, philosophers, she reached a conclusion that in effect allowed her to forgive Heidegger even while condemning what he did. Academic intellectuals, and particularly philosophers like Heidegger, are liable to a sort of *"déformation professionelle."*[53] The isolation and abstraction demanded by their professional thinking blinds them to the simple, ordinary realities of political history and human relationship, the realities that are obvious to everyone else ("everyone who was not feebleminded") and that shape political life. Heidegger was "a philosopher's philosopher," and in proportion as he was philosophically brilliant, he "lacked political judgment and discernment about people."[54]

Academics and abstracted romantic philosophers, it now seemed to Arendt, were seduced by Naziism because they were in love with their own, abstract ideas. Karl Kraus, the celebrated Viennese humorist, was once asked why he did not produce some satire on Hitler and the Nazis. His sad response, widely circulated in leftist and Jewish circles at the time, was *"Mir fällt zu Hitler nichts ein* [In connection with Hitler, nothing (humorous) comes to mind]."[55] Clearly making reference to this comment, Arendt later said about the abstracted academics and philosophers, *"Zu Hitler fiel ihnen was ein."* In connection with the name Hitler, "ideas came to them, some of them enormously interesting! Quite fantastic and interesting and complicated ideas, that hovered far above the level of the ordinary. . . . They fell into the trap of their own ideas." As in Varnhagen's romantic introspection, thinking becomes "limitless" when it is not "molested by . . . any demand for action," whose consequences might provide a reality check. Arendt found it "grotesque" and drew her own conclusions. She herself now gave up introspection and philosophy as, in Young-Bruehl's phrase, a "youthful error."[56]

Her husband, involved in radical politics, left Germany a few days after the Reichstag fire. Though she also intended to leave eventually, Arendt at first stayed on, making their apartment available to leftists and others hiding from the Nazis and undertaking some illegal research for Blumenfeld's Zionist organization. For this work she was herself arrested, but released after eight days. Crossing the border illegally, she too went abroad, beginning her own personal "nightmare and flight" into exile. (This phrase is the title of an essay Arendt wrote in 1945.) She left Germany, she later said, "dominated by the idea—always exaggerating a little, naturally—Never again! I will never again touch any intellectual undertaking. I want nothing to do with that bunch. . . . I was of the opinion that it was a matter of this profession, of intellectuality."[57]

Arendt went to Paris, where she found employment with Zionist welfare agencies, taking care of Jewish refugee children on their way to Palestine. She wanted nothing more to do with the life of the mind. Nevertheless, she took the Varnhagen manuscript along and eventually finished it there. Rereading it after the war, she felt distanced from its tone and manner of reflection, but not from its foundation in "the Jewish experience that I acquired for myself with much effort and difficulty." That experience had taught her, as she then formulated the lesson, that "When one is attacked as a Jew, one must defend oneself *as a Jew*." She began to learn Hebrew and Yiddish.[58]

As Arendt fled to Paris and, she thought, gave up not just a university career but intellectual life as such in favor of work that was nurturant, close to traditionally feminine roles, and Jewish, she also saw—as she later put it—that "the Jewish problems I was discussing in [*Rahel Varnhagen*] were not my personal problems," because the Jews in Varnhagen's time "were pariahs only in the social sense." Now, however, "being Jewish had become my own problem." And her own problem, Arendt stressed (maybe protesting too much), "was political, purely political! I wanted to do practical work—and exclusively and only Jewish work."[59] One can see here the beginnings of the contrast between social and political; but the connection of the latter with the final sentence in this passage is striking. Apparently "political" here means practical, Jewish, and— though Arendt notably does not say so—nurturant (indeed, what *we* might identify as "social work"). To Arendt at this point "social" seems to imply not only parvenu and assimilationist but also abstracted and romantic, unrealistic, impractical; and it connects with intellectual work and with ambitions toward a profession considered problematic for a woman.

By the time Günther Stern and Arendt fled Germany, their marriage was essentially over. After a while in Paris Arendt met another man, Heinrich Blücher, who became her lover and, in 1940, her husband. Although also from the German left, Blücher seems to have been an altogether different sort of man from Stern: a lover of adventure and conspiracy, greatly averse to sentimentality, a gentile of working-class rather than middle-class origins. His father having died in an industrial accident before Heinrich was born, he was raised by his mother, who was a laundress. He was a street fighter who returned from World War I to take part in that Spartacist rebellion in Germany which had excited Arendt's mother—from a distance—into admonishing her daughter to "pay attention!" Unlike Stern, Blücher did not get on well with Arendt's mother, treating her with the same toughness he had developed early toward his own demanding and dependent mother. But he did get on well with Arendt herself, and she with him.⁶⁰

The marriage was happy. In it, one might say, Arendt discovered real "neighborly love," real love but without romantic self-abnegation. In her affair with Heidegger, Arendt had felt invisible when he did not see her, reduced to utter passivity and dependence. When he was not with her, she felt "alone and utterly helpless"; there seemed "nothing I could do but let it happen, and wait, wait, wait."⁶¹ Stern did not have this romantic power over her, but she did not love him. With Blücher, however, she not only experienced what Ettinger calls "erotic pleasure" for the first time but also, as Arendt herself said, finally "wasn't afraid any more." With him she realized the "unbelievable" possibility "that I can have both, the 'great love,' and retain my own identity." He confirmed it: "You will be who you are, and so will I [be who I am]" (26, 41–42).

Arendt as Parvenu and *das Man*

During the period in which she was writing the bulk of *Rahel Varnhagen*, then, Arendt was making a series of interdependent discoveries, all of them linked to something like the costs of being a parvenu, taking that term in a broad sense. She made discoveries about love: about the thrills and the costs of romantic devotion with its unrealistic fantasies of merger, its inauthentic self-abnegation and hidden, desperately self-centered craving; but also about the possibilities of a different sort of loving, more like neighborliness. She made discoveries about ambition and the intellect, and particularly what they might mean for a woman and a Jew fantasizing an academic career for herself in a German university—and most particularly in a field like philosophy, subject to its *déformation professionelle,* which is liable to make one humanly and politically blind, as well as a scoundrel. And of course she made discoveries about Jewishness and assimilation, about how self-interest relates to duty in the face of persecution, but also about the capacity for autonomous action and for solidarity in action with others. These lessons were profoundly interrelated, and all of them together—political and personal, intellectual and emotional—shaped Arendt's understanding of the parvenu and consequently of society. Omitting Heidegger from the story would make these links incomprehensible.

It seems likely that Arendt was interested in Rahel Varnhagen's parvenu social climbing and its costs partly because of the ways in which it paralleled her own personal romantic interlude with her teacher. Both involved a kind of inauthentic self-disparagement and self-denial, supposedly serving but in fact damaging self-interest, and based on a romantic overvaluation of some superior person or group who supposedly can ratify one as real and valuable, if only one conforms or submits. Both Varnhagen's parvenu striving and Arendt's romance, furthermore, proved not just to be damaging to the self and inauthentic but also to contain a hidden political danger: both proved complicit with anti-Semitism.

But the matter is still more complicated, because the lessons that Varnhagen learned from her life and Arendt from her romance also parallel a philosophical doctrine of Heidegger's developed in *Being and Time*, the book on which he was working during his affair with Arendt and which they often discussed: the doctrine of "*das Man*."[62]

Das Man is not easy to translate, since normally *man* is a pronoun in German and takes no article. The phrase is usually translated as "the they," although the pronoun *man* can be variously translated as "people," "others," "they," "public opinion," "one," and even "we" ("What will people think?" "They say that...." "One doesn't expect...." "We don't do that!"). *Das Man* means other people in the abstract, generic sense—not as a set of individuals, nor as an organization or body, but generically as the postulated carriers of cultural mores, expectations, or norms. Heidegger says it means "the Others," but "not *definite* Others." It "is not this one, not that one, not oneself, not some people, and not the sum of them all."[63] *Das Man* thus is a sort of horizontal version of the parvenu's "they, up there": a "they, out there" or "they, all around me."

Heidegger maintains that in our ordinary, day-to-day living we conduct ourselves with reference to this projected, generic "they," deferring to it, ascribing to it responsibility for what we do, and seeking fulfillment through it. This way of living Heidegger calls our "they-self." It is not, however, our real or authentic self. The latter can emerge only after the individual isolates himself from the others and questions conventions and habitual assumptions by philosophical inquiry.

This Heideggerian notion is surely one source of Arendt's concept of the social, but that is emphatically not to say that her concept is merely derivative from Heidegger's. For one thing, we do not know the details of who influenced whom in their conversations about his work. For another, Arendt had herself read Kierkegaard and others on whom Heidegger drew. And, most important, Arendt became a *critic* of Heidegger's doctrine after the end of their affair and his emergence as a Nazi. Out of her rejection of Heidegger's doctrine of *das Man* came a further important aspect of what she meant by the social.

Both Heidegger and Arendt opposed conformism, and both suggested that the supposed coercive and ratifying power of the generic "they" is not real, but a myth of the conformist's own making. Yet Arendt found Heidegger's ways of challenging convention and public opinion unsatisfactory. At the personal level, his own disdain for convention evidently reached to an illicit affair with a student, but not to a divorce. Politically, his philosophical questioning of conventions did not protect him against naive illusions about Naziism. And philosophically, his approach was vulnerable to philosophy's characteristic *déformation professionelle:* too abstracted, too individualistic or egoistic, too romantic. "This whole mode of behavior has exact parallels in German Romanticism," Arendt wrote about Heidegger immediately after the war. "Heidegger is, in fact, the last (we hope) romantic."[64] In effect, Heidegger himself was like Varnhagen: unrealistic and irresponsible.

So while Arendt and Heidegger both addressed the problem of conformism, she thought that his proposed solution merely continued the problem and was every bit as inauthentic and ineffectual as the "they-self." As early as 1930, Arendt was already publicly questioning Heidegger's attribution to *das Man* of a timeless universality: "There may not always have been and may not always be something like the 'they.'"[65] Later, while praising Heidegger for rejecting the philosopher's traditional claim to be a "wise man" with special access to "eternal standards," Arendt added that specifically in the concept of *das Man,* however, one still finds "the old hostility of the philosopher toward the *polis.*" Consequently, even Heidegger's philosophical innovation "never reaches but always misses the center of politics—man as an acting being" (432–33). For Arendt, in short, *das Man* abstracted into timeless inevitability an outlook or mode of conduct that was in fact historically created and maintained at a particular time by human beings, who consequently bore responsibility for it because they could have changed it, not—as in Heidegger—by individual philosophical insight, in the mind, but by joint political action, in the world.

Seen in this way, society is neither, as the parvenu supposes, an omnipotent "they" nor, as the parvenu's critic and Heidegger's argument imply, a paper tiger merely projected by parvenus. It is instead something closer to the sociologist's "(almost) everybody": the actual culture and conduct of particular collectivities of people at particular historical times, making pariahs of one group (say, Jews) at one time and place, of another group (say, people with dark skin) at another; attaching certain penalties to pariahdom here, and different ones there; relatively permeable to parvenus here, and virtually closed against social climbing there. In this sense, society is objective and wields real power; it is no paper tiger. Yet it is neither omnipotent nor inevitable; humanly produced, it is humanly changeable, its power real but limited. *Das Man* as a generic, ontological condition may be all very well for philosophy, but what matters in the living of a human life is precisely such historical differences.

And yet, the sociological "(almost) everybody" is transhistorical, like Heidegger's *das Man;* only its form and content vary with time. Arendt, however, precisely in order to oppose Heidegger's irresponsible abstraction, wanted to insist that society is an exclusively modern phenomenon—a parvenu concept—that only in our historical era do people characteristically conduct themselves in terms of an inauthentic "they-self." So even as she moved beyond the parvenu's omnipotent society and the critic's merely projected "society," Arendt also wanted to retain the connection between society and parvenu ways. Society seen as pariah-maker was real and perhaps universal, though one might hope and work for more tolerant arrangements, but society as *das Man* or as the parvenu response to pariahdom was exclusively modern.

But these ideas were not yet clear enough in Arendt's thought even for their inconsistencies to be fully apparent. They began to become more explicit, and the ontological status of society and its power therefore more problematic, only when Arendt's attention shifted from Jewish assimilation in the eighteenth century to Jewish refugees in the twentieth.

FOUR

The Refugee as Parvenu and the Conscious Pariah

From France, the exiled Hannah Arendt moved in 1941, together with her second husband and her mother, to New York, where she soon began writing articles for refugee, Jewish, and left-wing publications. These New York essays, the most important of which were later collected by Ron H. Feldman in *The Jew as Pariah*, address the refugee's situation against the background of the developing war, which the United States entered before the end of the year. In these essays, the concepts of "pariah," "parvenu," and "society" reappear and are further developed, but as they are applied to this new topic, they also change. Thus the scope and importance of Arendt's ideas increase, but so do their difficulties.

As her attention shifts from the eighteenth-century salon to the twentieth-century internment camp, the problems adumbrated in *Rahel Varnhagen*, concerning the ontological status of society and the reality of its power, are not resolved but rather intensified. Clearly the Jews under Nazi persecution face a pariahdom far more extreme, with consequences far more severe, than anything threatening Varnhagen. No one would want to call the Nazis a paper tiger or suggest that their power is illusory, a mere projection of parvenu anxieties and ambitions. While not of course omnipotent, the Nazis wield real power that must be taken with the utmost seriousness, power that will not vanish with philosophic insight and will not allow Jews to withdraw into any happy pariah privacy among trees and children. Whereas previously society could be recognized as "a nobody in a dress-suit," now it has become "a masquerade with a death's head grinning behind every mask."[1] Society has not only shifted from empty foolishness to lethal fanaticism, but also enlisted the resources of the state. So the parvenu's vision of social omnipotence has become considerably more realistic in the twentieth century than it was in Varnhagen's day.

At the same time, however, the apparently opposite view has also become more plausible, for the parvenu strategy of conformity and deference has now become hopeless. Under the Nuremberg race laws, assimilation is no longer a viable option for Jews. Now their pariah status is legally defined, and enforced with increasing severity, not merely by social sanctions but by legal ones as well. "So long as the Jews of Western Europe were pariahs only in a social sense," Arendt writes in a New York essay, "they could find salvation, to a large extent, by becoming *parvenus*." To secure this "outward freedom," unfortunately, they had to sacrifice inner freedom, but whoever found that price too high had the option of remaining a "mere" pariah in "social isolation." Such a life would lack "political significance" but would be "by no means senseless." For Jews in Nazi times, by contrast, "social isolation is no longer possible.... The old escape mechanisms have broken down," and "only flight around the globe could offer salvation" from the Jews' "political outlawry" (89–90, 121). So even though the parvenu illusion of society's overwhelming power has become truth, the parvenu strategy for dealing with that power has become totally unrealistic, pathologically dissociated.

Yet something very like parvenu conduct and outlook was precisely what Arendt now found widespread—even epidemic—among the victims of Nazi persecution, as she observed them during her own refugee experience: in secret resistance, in jail, in flight, in internment, in exile, and in her work with refugee social service agencies in Paris. The refugee is of course the pariah par excellence, cast out by his own society and a (mostly unwelcome) stranger in his new land: awkward in speech and manner; lacking political rights and often even legal status; bereft of home, friends, work, resources; in many cases disoriented by recent brutalizations; and dependent on the charity of strangers, who become increasingly less charitable as the flood of refugees mounts. The prisoner in the clutches of the lawless state, the exile trying to get by in a new land *must* adapt and conform; the refugee without resources *must* supplicate from those with power and wealth; where visas or jobs or seats in the lifeboat are limited, one person's salvation *has* to mean another's disaster. Arendt had seen and had herself experienced how desperate is the plight of this twentieth-century pariah and how its necessities constantly impel him toward the dangerous line where prudent resourcefulness turns into parvenu collaboration with the persecutors.

The Refugee as Parvenu

To begin with, the refugee finds himself starkly alone, thrown back on his own resources and isolated from everything and everyone familiar, a debilitating experience for almost any human being: "Man is a social animal and life is not easy for him when social ties are cut off.... [M]ost of us depend entirely upon social standards; we lose confidence in ourselves if society does not approve us; we are—and always were—ready to pay any price in order to be accepted by society" (62, 65). There may be something of the parvenu in us all, but historical circumstances really matter here. To the generic human dependence on sociability one must add the refugees' desperate practical situation and the psychological needs it generates. To sustain the enormous continual effort imposed by their situation, refugees need to keep alive some hope for the future, some belief in the eventual resumption of normal life. And that need can all too easily turn into a pathological denial of the realities they face.

Arendt opens the essay called "We Refugees" with the observation, "In the first place, we don't like to be called 'refugees'" (55). Those fleeing the Nazis would much rather be seen as ordinary immigrants, she says, who won't constitute any special drain on their host's resources or threat to their host's security, who are ready to forget all they have been through and settle into a happy new life, already patriots of their new homeland. "After four weeks in France or six weeks in America, we pretend to be Frenchmen or Americans" (56). This cheerful adaptability rings all the more hollow as it is repeatedly revised each time the refugee is forced to flee to yet another country. Indeed, the refugees adapt so cheerfully and change identity so often "that nobody can find out who we actually are"—least of all they themselves (62).

Among the refugees, then, Arendt encounters a kind of surplus adaptability: "We adjust in principle to everything and everybody" (63). Many of them, indeed, display a "perfect mania for refusing to keep their identity," a mania whose roots Arendt thinks antedate the Nazi era and lie in a parvenu character structure. Accustomed all their lives to define themselves in terms of how others see them, they become "failures in their own eyes" as soon as the deference and the emblems of status they have always demanded and received are withdrawn or—worse yet—are inverted in Nazi brutalities and refugee humiliations (64, 60). Lacking autonomous inner resources, the refugees respond to external blows in the only way they know, by trying ever harder to conform to the rules and to mollify their persecutors, redirecting their natural anger inward against themselves or against their fellow victims.

Like other parvenus, therefore, these refugees oscillate between an "insane optimism" about their fate and self-destructive depression, between megalomania and hopelessness. Even as they declare themselves infinitely adaptable and cheerful, "there is something wrong with our optimism. There are those odd optimists among us who, having made a lot of optimistic speeches, go home and turn on the gas or make use of a skyscraper in quite an unexpected way" (59, 57). No doubt Arendt had in mind not only the specific tragedy of her friend Walter Benjamin's needless suicide at the Spanish border but also more broadly the competitive and self-destructive conduct she observed among the inmates of a French internment camp where, as she later put it, she "had the opportunity of spending some time."[2]

Arendt was in Paris when Germany invaded France in 1940 and France decided to intern all "enemy aliens"—persons of German nationality in France—even though the greatest number of these were refugees and passionate enemies of the Nazis. She was duly sent to a camp at Gurs, in the south of France. There, with the aid of a spokeswoman, because she herself was too shy to speak in public, Arendt helped organize the inmates.[3]

At one point, in a discussion of possible means of resistance, someone suggested a collective suicide pact, "apparently a kind of protest in order to vex the French." When "some of us" pointed out that the inmates had in any case been shipped there by the French precisely *pour crever*—to croak, or kick the bucket—the mood instantly changed, as people were brought back to a more realistic sense of who was friend and who enemy. No longer blaming their misfortunes on "some mysterious shortcomings in themselves" or in each other, they promptly recovered the capacity for solidarity and a "violent courage of life." Yet these "same people, as soon as they returned to their own individual lives, being faced with seemingly individual problems," reverted to the parvenu's "insane optimism which is next door to despair."[4]

A few weeks later, when France surrendered to Germany, there came a brief period of administrative chaos when "all communication broke down," and it was possible to obtain fraudulent "liberation papers" with which one could walk out of the camp. The opportunity was brief, however, and to take advantage of it, "one had to leave with nothing but a toothbrush, since there existed no means of transportation." Those who still trusted the authorities and deferred to the rules, those who could not walk off into the unknown with nothing but a toothbrush, stayed in the camp. The opportunity passed. Those who remained were later turned over to the Germans, and most of them died in Nazi extermination camps. Arendt was one of about two hundred women, out of some seven thousand in the camp, who left.[5] Later she would tell the story of

Gurs, Young-Bruehl reports, whenever she wanted to illustrate concretely the price paid for indecisiveness and misplaced deference (160).

A characterological strategy that in Varnhagen's time had held fair promise of paying off for the individual pariah—though even then at a price that Arendt judged too high—becomes for twentieth-century refugees simply lethal. Under Naziism the parvenu fares badly because he mistakes powerful enemies for friends and brutal persecutors for legitimate authorities to be placated, collaborating with them and suppressing his rage to the point of apathy or even suicide, striving to get by as an exception and thus incapable of solidarity with his fellow refugees, but even in isolation lacking the self-confidence for autonomous judgment and decisive action, such as walking out despite the rules and without possessions. The parvenu strategy has come to mean "inevitable destruction," and those who follow it finally "die of a kind of selfishness."[6] The personal price of being a parvenu has gone way up.

So has the cost to other pariahs of the parvenu's scoundrel conduct. The parvenu was always "automatically one of the props which hold up a social order from which he [was] himself excluded" (78). But in the eighteenth century the objective impact of Jewish parvenu conduct on others was relatively minor, not only because the Jews were few and social anti-Semitism could flourish nicely without their support, but also because fellow pariahs still had a number of alternative options. In the twentieth century, however, the consequences for other pariahs of the parvenu's conduct have escalated into such horror that "scoundrel" hardly seems the appropriate word. This is particularly true because, though the Jews are still few and the anti-Semites many, something very like parvenu conduct is becoming visible to Arendt outside Jewish ranks as well.

Nonpariah Parvenus

For Jews, Arendt found, the parvenu pattern had preassimilation roots in Jewish community life, with a division between the wealthy few, who held a high "position in [Jewish] society," and their impoverished dependents, who felt constrained to "beg . . . from those whom [they] ought to fight." Once assimilation to gentile society became an option, the majority of Jews thus faced a "double slavery": dependence on both gentile and Jewish high society, which were "somehow in league."[7] Jewish tradition required charity from the wealthy toward their less fortunate brethren, but once the rich Jews themselves became parvenus seeking admission to gentile society, the poor and less "refined" Jews were not just a burden but a threat to them. Already in the eighteenth century wealthy, assimilated German Jews sought to disown their less assimilated and less "civilized" fellows from the East. Now the genteel society of established, respectable Jews in the various countries of refuge looked down on and felt threatened by the immigrants who made claims on their resources, endangered their social position, and brought political complications. Besides, the refugees' stories of horror could easily be doubted as exaggerations.

Of this phenomenon, too, Arendt had personal experience. Working with refugees in Paris, she saw how the wealthy, philanthropic French Jews scorned and feared the exiles and turned a deaf ear to their appeals, increasingly as those appeals continued to mount. For a time she worked for the Baroness Germaine de Rothschild, who was *not* like that, but the job gave Arendt the opportunity to observe other members of the Rothschild family who were. In May 1934, for example, Robert de Rothschild warned the General Assembly of the Consistoire of Paris—the major religious association of native, mostly wealthy, French Jews—that the influx of German Jews presented two grave dangers. In Young-Bruehl's words, "The first was that the immigrants, with their old-country dress, habits, and manners, would aggravate the anti-Semitism and the xenophobia of the French. The second danger was that the immigrants would continue their unfortunate political habits, involving themselves in French politics, particularly in leftist politics."[8] Arendt also remembered "a director of a great charity concern in Paris" who, whenever he received the calling card of a German Jewish intellectual seeking help—the card inevitably bearing all the German honorifics, "*Herr Doktor*" or "*Herr Professor*" or even "*Herr Doktor Professor*"—would shout "at the top of his voice," using the Yiddish word for beggar, "*Herr Doktor, Herr Doktor, Herr Schnorrer, Herr Schnorrer!*"[9]

Even before the Nazis, Jews all over Europe habitually stereotyped and felt contempt for Jews from other countries, each group developing its own set of derogatory terms for the others (62). Now established, assimilated Jews everywhere tried to disown the refugees: "The defeat of the Jewish people started with the catastrophe of the German Jews, in whom European Jews were not interested because they suddenly discovered that German Jews constituted an exception. The collapse of German Jewry began with its splitting up into innumerable factions, each of which believed that special privileges could protect human rights" (109).

The pattern of parvenu conduct fed anti-Semitism, but that pattern was not confined to pariahs or to Jews. Rich, established Jews and all sorts of gentiles were also often afflicted by the same disease, thinking for example that the Nazis were a threat only to Jews, or only to German Jews, and seeking at all costs to disassociate themselves from the victims. So parvenu conduct and failures in solidarity with the pariahs can originate in all kinds of conformism and short-sighted selfishness, not just in Jewish assimilationism, and can widen into appeasement: "the outlawing of the Jewish people in Europe has been followed closely by the outlawing of most European nations. Refugees driven from country to country represent the vanguard of their peoples" (66). It seemed that, thanks to the Nazis, history had become a morality play that taught a "moral": failures in solidarity with the victims will soon be punished by one's own victimization (106, 108). Nonpariah people who conduct themselves like parvenus will soon be made pariahs in their turn. "The comity of European peoples went to pieces when, and because, it allowed its weakest member to be excluded and persecuted" (66).

Apparently, then, one did not have to be a pariah to become a parvenu in character and conduct. All sorts of people were doing it. Indeed, instead of pariahs becoming parvenus one now found nonpariah parvenus destined soon to become pariahs. Looking at the world of Nazis and their victims, one might even want to say that everyone always faces the choice between accommodating deferentially to existing arrangements, in order to succeed as an individual, and thinking critically about those arrangements and rebelling against them in solidarity with those they victimize. This would greatly enlarge the scope, and in that sense the importance, of Arendt's doctrine, since its application would no longer be confined to Jews or even to pariahs. At the same time, however, this broadened precept would also play havoc with the meaning of her categories. Just when the practical choices people face in the real world look increasingly stark and urgent—either you oppose the Nazis or you aid them—the theoretical analysis of such choices seems to become blurred and problematic.

Someone who is not a pariah, after all, *cannot* become a parvenu in Arendt's sense of that term—striving for acceptance as an individual exception at the expense of fellow pariahs—because he does not *lack* acceptance and he *has* no fellow pariahs. And what is now the alternative: rebellion against what, and in solidarity with whom? Against the Nazis, no doubt, and in solidarity with the Jews. Or is it with one's "own people," whoever they be? Or with all whom the Nazis victimize or threaten?

Even worse, what of the Nazis themselves? If everyone faces the same dichotomous choice between becoming a parvenu and resisting, that must be true of the Nazis too. By 1945, opposing the notion of universal, collective German war guilt, Arendt argued that for the vast majority of Germans, "the real motives which caused people to act as cogs in the mass-murder machine" were parvenu anxieties (though she did not use that phrase) about "security," an "earnest concern" to make a living for one's family, "respectability," and "normality" (231–32). This passage concerned only the majority, suggesting that there were also some true or committed Nazis to whom these parvenus deferred. But if even these fanatical Nazis faced the same choice, then either they too were parvenus—so that there were nothing but parvenus on the side of evil, all trying to accommodate but without anyone to whom they might conform—or else the committed Nazi is one of the rebels, thinking for himself and acting in solidarity—but with whom? The former alternative points toward the social, as we shall see; the latter points to the urgent need for Arendt to clarify the "political" alternative to becoming a parvenu. Apparently it is not enough simply to mobilize parvenus to autonomy and activity; they could become active Nazis.

In short, "pariah" and "parvenu" are increasingly problematic categories when applied to the world of refugees and Nazis. Not only does the parvenu option become somehow both more realistic (because the oppressive power is all too real and growing) and more delusional (because appeasing that power or "passing" cannot succeed), not only do the pariahs persist in parvenu conduct even when it is manifestly senseless, but nonpariahs engage in it as well, feeding the oppressive power that will soon turn them too into pariahs, a power that now must either consist only of parvenus or else centrally include some who have refused the parvenu option.

Society in the New York Essays

Not surprisingly, given how closely Arendt linked the concepts of parvenu and pariah to that of society, the latter concept is also in trouble in the New York essays. Clearly, "society" and "social" no longer refer to high society, for the difficulties that refugees face are not those of respectability and the salon, and parvenus need not even be pariahs, but can appear in the highest social ranks. Yet the words still seem to connote ranking, deference, and conformity to norms in these essays, as society is said to establish "social distinction[s]," "standards," and "unwritten social laws" enforced by its "weapon" of "public opinion." Society seems, moreover, to have formed a connection with the state and to use written laws as well, reaching beyond the pariahs' "social" to their "legal status," making "legal or political outlaws" out of what used to be "pariahs only in the social sense" and discovering the lethal potential in "passports or birth certificates, and sometimes even income tax receipts" (62, 65, 89). Whether this new connection results from society's taking over the state or from the state's—the Nazis'—exploiting "social," parvenu submissiveness, or from some mysterious merger of the pariahs' old enemy, society, with their new one, the Nazis, is not clear.

If everyone always faces the parvenu option, either Arendt's concepts need to be redefined, or else everyone must be in some sense a pariah. This seems a strange idea: if everyone is outside, excluded, then there is no inside, no society, and thus no one to exclude them, unless they exclude themselves. And yet, if they face a choice between accommodating to or resisting established arrangements, that does perhaps imply a kind of "standing outside" those arrangements. Are pariahs self-excluded from the arrangements to which parvenus uncritically accommodate, with society a mere projection, its power imaginary, as Varnhagen found at the end of her life?

The established arrangements and norms do exist. If it is the parvenus who uphold and enforce them, perhaps society is real but consists simply of the parvenus. Though they imagine themselves excluded and some "they" as included, in fact the parvenus are society. Either way, society begins to sound distressingly like Heidegger's *das Man:* the eternal human proclivity to accommodate unthinkingly to existing institutions, norms, and assumptions, to be escaped only by individual philosophical withdrawal, rather than the specifically modern condition Arendt had in mind, remediable only by political action in solidarity with others.

If being a parvenu is now to mean conforming uncritically to established arrangements in order to get by or get ahead as an individual, while the alternative means criticizing and sometimes rejecting those arrangements, the latter option can come to seem very mysterious. For each of us is raised in some particular culture, whose norms and arrangements we internalize as we grow up. How can an individual thus formed judge critically the very norms and practices that formed him? At most, it seems, we criticize some of those arrangements by the standard of other such arrangements, making them more coherent. We are all bearers of the norms and practices; we are all society, all of us insiders, even those who rebel. Now society seems to approach the sociological sense of the word, as meaning (almost) everybody, everybody who shares in a particular culture, or "all members of a given community," as Arendt will later put it.¹⁰ But then the distinction between conformism and resistance, crucial to Arendt, gets lost.

The New York essays, shifting the context of inquiry from assimilation to refugees, only intensify the puzzles and confusions about society, what it is and whether it has real power, that were adumbrated in *Rahel Varnhagen* and in Arendt's encounter with *das Man*. These puzzles are nicely epitomized in a short story by Kafka, "Description of a Fight," discussed in one of those essays, the first time that Arendt explicitly addresses the ontological questions about society. Kafka's tale, she says, is "concerned, in a general way, with the problem of social interrelations." Quoting from the story, she interprets it as claiming that society "is composed of 'nobodies'—'I did wrong to nobody, nobody did wrong to me; but nobody will help me, nothing but nobodies'—and has therefore no real existence." Society being unreal, all its members are nobodies. In a footnote Arendt seems to praise Kafka as "the first to have started from [this] basic truth." Yet she immediately continues in a way that implies the opposite, saying that, "nevertheless, even the pariah, who is excluded from [society], cannot account himself lucky, since society keeps up the pretense that it is somebody and he is nobody, that it is 'real' and he 'unreal.'" The reality of society, then, is a mere pretense. Yet society is also the one that does the pretending, and that (presumably) excludes pariahs. Arendt further proceeds to envision the "conflict" between this real pariah and the unreal society, in which "the point at issue is simply whether it or he has real existence." Finally, she says that "the greatest injury" society inflicts on the pariah "is to make him doubt the reality and validity of his own existence, to reduce him in his own eyes to the status of nonentity," in short, to make him imagine himself a nobody and thus like the members of the society from which he is excluded.¹¹

But surely an unreal entity cannot truly injure a real one? Accordingly, Arendt is unclear and inconsistent about society in the New York essays, claiming sometimes that it has "no real existence," sometimes that its weapons can be lethal; sometimes that no "isolation" from it is possible, that it gets inside the pariah's mind, at other times that he must "face" society and "struggle against" it (82, 65, 90, 83).

Kafka's characteristic paradoxical conundrums are an excellent vehicle for expressing Arendt's logical difficulties but do nothing to resolve them. Imagining enormous Nazi power, many people behave as parvenus, falsely conceiving themselves as both able thereby to secure their personal survival and helpless to resist. As a result, that power grows unopposed, and a falsely imagined power becomes real. Parvenu illusions have real, dreadful consequences for real people. One might be tempted to say that there is real power at work here, dominating real pariahs, but power that nobody has or wields, neither the "nobodies" who are its victims and collaborators nor the imaginary "they" that the parvenus project. Such people, one might say, *are* power but do not *have* it. But then, who or what does have it? This way of talking threatens to enter into the very outlook it is meant to criticize; the Blob is in the offing.[12]

The "Political" Alternative

As a corollary, the alternative to becoming a parvenu—choosing to become a "rebel"—also increasingly needs clarification. Arendt continues in the New York essays to urge pariah refugees to "fight" rather than accommodate, to "come out openly as the representative of the pariah," to enter "the arena of politics," and to translate their problems "into political terms".[13] The equation of becoming a parvenu with social concerns—and of its alternative with political activity—suggests the contrast, originating in Hegelian and Marxist thought but long since familiar in general usage, between "civil society" and the state. That distinction, we saw, was invoked once in *Rahel Varnhagen*.[14] But now that society and the Nazis are allied with the state and are imposing pariahdom in "political" ways, engaging politically can no longer be the criterion distinguishing parvenu conduct from its alternative.

In *Rahel Varnhagen* only a single alternative was envisaged; it was "political," made one a "rebel," guaranteed one's "reality," and helped one understand "history" (7, 222, 209, 224, 177, 3). Beyond that, it was left unexamined. Yet we noted that the narrative of the book already belied this simple dichotomy, since even at the end of her life Varnhagen did not in fact engage actively in political struggle but only became reconciled to her fate.

In the 1944 essay "The Jew as Pariah: A Hidden Tradition" Arendt begins to catalogue alternatives to the role of parvenu, only one of them political, and she explicitly acknowledges that the sort of fatalism at which Varnhagen ultimately arrived means a life "shorn of political significance."[15] Each of the essay's four sections is devoted to one alternative to the parvenu role: the role of the poet, or "lord of dreams"; the role of "the suspect," exemplified by Charlie Chaplin's movie persona (Arendt acknowledging in a footnote that Chaplin was not Jewish); the role of the "man of goodwill," exemplified in Kafka's *The Castle;* and the role of the "conscious pariah" explored by Bernard Lazare.[16] The essay also mentions additional possibilities, such as a cheerful acceptance of ghetto life or bohemianism ("a society of pariahs . . . in utter detachment from reality") and Varnhagen's ultimate biblical fatalism (82, 90). Yet by the end of the essay Arendt has once more constricted the multiple options and reimposed dichotomy, arguing that under conditions of twentieth-century Naziism the role of conscious pariah, the political alternative, is the only *viable* one.

For our purposes, it will suffice to examine two of the essay's options: the lord of dreams and the conscious pariah. The phrase "lord of dreams" comes from Heinrich Heine, the German Jewish writer, who applied it to his own role as poet. The lord of dreams, he said, is descended from the *Schlemihl*, whose hallmark is innocence (70). *Schlemihl* is of course what Rahel Varnhagen called herself in self-disparagement, meaning thereby not so much innocence but haplessness, ineptitude. But in this essay Arendt celebrates the lord of dreams as a worthy alternative to parvenu assimilation. To Heine it meant enjoying both his German and his Jewish heritage with detached humor, for instance, by composing German poetry in praise of traditional Jewish food (74). His innocence was a "gay, insouciant impudence" in solidarity with "the common people," the lower classes, who were also excluded from respectable society. He shared the "simple *joie de vivre* which one finds everywhere in children and in the common people" and saw through empty social conventions and distinctions to the essential natural equality of all human beings "in the presence of such universal things as the sun, music, trees, and children—things which Rahel Varnhagen called 'the true realities' " (71). The category of "lord of dreams" thus seems to merge Varnhagen's romantic withdrawal to an unreal inner world of beauty ("dreams") with the simple, real, natural pleasures she regained after abandoning parvenu striving.[17]

Nevertheless, while celebrating Heine's achievement and acknowledging real value in these options, Arendt rejects them for her own time, where they have become childishly irresponsible. The lord of dreams draws freely on his multiple cultural inheritances but does nothing to protect the communities—the people—from whom these cultures sprang and in whom they are perpetuated. The lord of dreams allies himself with Jews and the common people spiritually, but he does not make common cause with them in action. He celebrates his pariah alienation not just from the empty conventions of respectable society but from "all the works of man," as if these could take care of themselves (72). His natural universalism remains an abstraction, incapable either of practical, political enactment or even of sustaining a culture on which a poet might draw (75). He is thus, despite his creativity, still what Rahel Varnhagen called a "product of nature," at the mercy of events, like a plant dependent on the weather.[18] And the twentieth century has brought the sort of politically inclement weather that rules out his cheerful, creative, irresponsible naturalism.

The only alternative that Arendt sees as now open to pariahs is what, following Bernard Lazare, she calls the role of "conscious pariah." Lazare recognized "where the solution lay" to the problem of pariahdom: "In contrast to his unemancipated brethren who accept their pariah status automatically and unconsciously, the emancipated Jew must awake to an awareness of his position and, conscious of it, become a rebel against it."[19]

The alternative to becoming a parvenu has now acquired a name, but what that name means and whether it is appropriate, especially when applied to refugees rather than to assimilators, is problematic. The passage from Lazare is not entirely clear: the conscious pariah has woken to awareness of what, exactly? "His position," Lazare says, but this cannot mean simply that he is a pariah, for even isolated ghetto Jews must have been aware of their pariah status, if only as a result of periodic pogroms, and even the assimilationist Varnhagen was highly conscious of being a pariah ("I drink it in water. I drink it in wine. . . .").[20] What Varnhagen lacked consciousness of in her parvenu life, one might even argue, was not her pariahdom but precisely the opposite. She failed to see that she was *not* (really, intrinsically) a pariah, did *not* deserve to be considered and treated as one, did *not* need social approval in order to be real and valuable. Even at the end of her life, she did not in fact rebel against her pariahdom but welcomed it as divinely decreed.

The conscious pariah, Lazare says, will no longer "*accept* his pariah status automatically and unconsciously." So it's not that the pariah was previously unaware of that status; it's that he was unaware of accepting it, inwardly ratifying it and disparaging himself. Becoming a conscious pariah, he sheds, as Arendt put it half a year later, "the old mentality of enslaved peoples, the belief that it does not pay to fight back, that one must dodge and escape in order to survive."[21]

What Arendt, following Lazare, means by becoming a conscious pariah is rejecting pariah status on principle, consciously and openly, as unjust, and opposing it actively in solidarity with others. Unlike the refugee who lacks "the courage to fight for a change of [his] social and legal status," the conscious pariah "enters the arena of politics" and thereby becomes "perforce a rebel," not merely in Varnhagen's abstract sense of no longer feeling deferential and worthless but in actual shared engagement against pariahdom (62, 77).

This category too, however, becomes problematic in the context of Naziism, where even nonpariahs can behave like parvenus (or refuse to do so). If one is not in fact a pariah, *can* one become conscious of being one or of having hitherto ratified one's status as one? Perhaps, but surely only as a delusion, and is that really to be recommended? We noted earlier that, at minimum, Arendt will need a new vocabulary for the new context, but a lot more than vocabulary is at stake.

Identity and Solidarity

For a pariah, the choice between becoming a parvenu and becoming a conscious pariah is intimately tied to identity, and the duty to fight thus coincides with self-knowledge and true self-interest. For the nonpariah, this connection is at least more problematic and may not exist. A duty of solidarity with one's "own" people seems different from a general duty to fight injustice. The former involves acknowledging the pariah group as one's own; the latter does not. With respect to both who one is and whom one owes solidarity, moreover, there is the question of who is to say: who has authority to define you, your people, your interest, your duties?

Arendt presents becoming a conscious pariah as a kind of adult acceptance of responsibility, by contrast with the childish naturalism of the lord of dreams. Lazare, she says, demanded "that the pariah relinquish once and for all the prerogatives of the *schlemihl,* cut loose from the world of fancy and illusion, renounce the comfortable protection of nature, and come to grips with the world of men and women" (77). This passage is intriguing, among other things because, most unusually for her, Arendt here speaks of "men *and women.*" One suspects that this might be because of the underlying contrast with childishness, the role of adults in providing nurturance and security perhaps reminding Arendt of her mother's protective militancy and of her own unfortunate lack of a protective father. In any case, even when withdrawal into the ghetto, into nature, or into dreams was a viable alternative, it meant a shirking of adult responsibility for maintaining the world and the institutions humans have fashioned to protect themselves against historically inclement weather.

Arendt also equates accepting this with accepting responsibility for oneself, even though one did not create that self. The passage continues, "*In other words,*" Lazare required the pariah "to feel that he was himself responsible for what society had done to him. . . . However much the Jewish pariah might be, from the historical viewpoint, the product of an unjust dispensation . . . , politically speaking, every pariah who refused to be a rebel was partly responsible for his own position" (77). Though we are in fact, historically speaking, products, what has been produced is a creature capable of choice, action, and responsibility, thus not really a mere product.

On the whole, although Arendt calls on her readers to become conscious pariahs, in this essay she presents that option as a duty and a sacrifice, made necessary by Naziism. One must "relinquish" and "renounce" the "comfortable protection" one might otherwise prefer. The simple, natural pleasures of "green things" that were still the "true realities" in *Rahel Varnhagen* have become in Nazi times as unrealistic and irresponsible a choice as parvenu striving and the fantasy world of the lord of dreams. The essay thus conveys an implicit undercurrent contrary to its explicit intent: would that one could remain a child!

Is parvenu conduct selfish and self-interested, and becoming a conscious pariah dutiful and self-sacrificing? Arendt sometimes seems to say so, and of course the context of refugees and Nazi collaborators strongly suggests it. But matters are actually considerably more complicated. For one thing, if the parvenu is selfish, it is a short-sighted selfishness indeed. Even for Varnhagen the price of becoming a parvenu was too high not merely because it meant becoming a scoundrel but also because it required abdicating one's powers and losing oneself, reality, the world, and the simple, natural pleasures. These pleasures are no longer an option in Nazi times, but a more negative reinforcement of duty by self-interest has appeared instead: pariah parvenus "die of a kind of selfishness" (60). As for nonpariah parvenus, "history" intervenes to align their duty with their self-interest, because their selfishness empowers the Nazis, who will soon turn them into pariahs too. Of course, much depends on what one means by "self" and "interest," matters which we cannot and fortunately need not pursue further here.[22]

As to the morality and dutifulness of the conscious pariah, the central questions are to whom that duty is owed and with whom one is to pursue it. Initially, when Arendt focused only on Jews and assimilation, the answer seemed clear: the duty was to fellow Jews, to fight alongside them for the "admission of Jews *as Jews* to the ranks of humanity." As

Arendt fled Germany, her precept was "when one is attacked as a Jew, one must fight back *as a Jew*," and though she was no Zionist, it was with Zionist organizations that she worked. Later she came to see this precept as "letting the enemy define you" and called instead for solidarity with all pariah groups.[23] Following Lazare, she tended, however, to meld these alternatives into one: being "the champion of *an* oppressed people" (one's own?), becoming the "representative of *the* pariah" (all pariahs?), and fighting "for freedom" along with "all the down-trodden of Europe" are more or less the same, all reflecting, as Lazare said, "the duty of every human being to resist [one's own? one's people's? anyone's?] oppression."[24]

Yet there are important differences here, not only with respect to how this duty connects with self-interest, but also with respect to policy and consequences. A pariah who chooses conscious pariahdom recovers himself because he stops identifying inwardly with his oppressor. This may still be true, though a little less obvious, if he fights in solidarity with all pariahs rather than just his "own" people. But for the nonpariah who chooses to fight alongside and on behalf of pariahs it does not seem true at all. And who defines which are "my people," and thus which solidarity entails realistic self-recognition for me? If the Nazis decree that anyone with even a single Jewish great-grandparent is a Jew, is that decisive? If Judaism has rules about Jewish descent, are they decisive? Or does it all depend on how I feel, so that a parvenu who does not feel Jewish is not?[25]

Such difficult issues of identity and membership will be discussed further in chapter 8. They can have important political consequences, especially if some pariah group's struggle proves successful and they come to power or acquire a state of their own. If duty is equated with loyalty to one's own people and conscious pariahdom with "a mobilization of the people against its foes," then success in their struggle may mean imposing new pariahdoms on others.[26] With respect to Jews, Arendt foresaw this danger already during the war, supporting the establishment of a Jewish homeland and refuge in Palestine but opposing a specifically "Jewish" state.[27] By 1948, after the partition of Palestine and establishment of Israel, she warned of "the dangerous tendencies of formerly oppressed peoples to shut themselves off from the rest of the world and develop nationalist superiority complexes of their own."[28] The definition of Israel as a Jewish state was "plain racist chauvinism" no different from other "master race theories" and "hopelessly out of touch with the realities of this world," which here included the prior "presence of Arabs in Palestine" (183–84, 185).

But by 1948 Arendt was already hard at work on what would become *The Origins of Totalitarianism*. Her New York essays, astute and insightful as they may be, are not primarily works of theory, and they open up theoretical difficulties without resolving them. Even the distinction between pariah and conscious pariah is not yet stable in Arendt's thinking.[29] The essay form does not push an author into systematic theorizing; Arendt's intended audience of refugee Jews perhaps kept her from realizing how far she had moved from the assimilationist issue; so did the wartime outlook, which suggested a simple, unambiguous distinction between Good Guys and Bad Guys. Complexities and problems, it seemed to many at the time, could and must be postponed until after the war.

This chapter, accordingly, has posed far more questions than it has answered. Arendt's way of thinking about society is here in transition, compounded still of the parvenu's "social" outlook, the realist's critique of that outlook, the sociological (almost) everybody (in relation to which neither pariah nor parvenu makes much sense), "civil society" somehow allied with the state yet contrasted to "political" engagement, and probably other elements as well. Their contradictions and complexities will not be resolved in Arendt's later works. Instead, their fertility, even further enriched in *The Origins of Totalitarianism*, will generate the threatening Blob, which will hide them from view. The elusive political alternative, the role of conscious pariah, meanwhile, will receive no more attention until *The Human Condition*, where it will reappear transformed into the concepts of action, politics, and freedom.

FIVE

The Birth of the Blob

As Arendt's focus shifted from assimilation to refugees, the tensions in her thinking about society increased, though hidden by the simplifying urgencies of war. After the war ended, she reengaged those tensions in her magisterial study, *The Origins of Totalitarianism*. It presented Nazi Germany and Stalinist Russia as two instances of an unprecedented new form of government, but it had begun as a study of Naziism alone, and even its final structure remained oriented to one central question: the mystery of the holocaust. How could it have happened that a policy of genocide—of systematically exterminating a whole category of people, defined biologically and thus having committed no crime—was pursued with a fanaticism exceeding any rational motive, indeed, even contrary to rational self-interest? Totalitarianism was Arendt's answer, linking Naziism with Communism, but the comparisons on which that answer rested remained poorly integrated into the book and hastily drawn.[1] The holocaust remained the book's core, as is evident from its tripartite topical division, which progresses from question to answer: anti-Semitism, imperialism, totalitarianism.

What befalls Arendt's schema of ideas about society and the parvenu in *The Origins of Totalitarianism* is simply astonishing. After a brief appearance in its familiar form, it first undergoes a remarkable reversal and then largely disappears from view. Only a few key passages link it explicitly to the words "social" and "society," which appear only rarely in parts 2 and 3, and in part 3 never in Arendt's special sense. Yet, with the benefit of hindsight one can see the schema of ideas she had connected with those words cropping up everywhere, transformed, extended, like variations on a musical theme. The schema of ideas earlier linked to society and parvenu characterizes each of the three main structuring topics of *The Origins*, as well as the two subtopics of imperialism: racism and bureaucracy. It characterizes—in one or another transformation—each of the specific categories of people whom Arendt identifies as contributing to the rise of totalitarianism: anti-Semites, colonial administrators, adventurers, secret agents, the Boers, "the mob," and "the mass." It characterizes the epitome of totalitarianism, the concentration camp. And, by the end of the book, it emerges as the Blob.

Not that Arendt intentionally kept reapplying an explanatory device that had previously succeeded. Rather, looking back from *The Human Condition,* it is as if in *The Origins* Arendt's special explanatory schema had gone underground, where it had begun to proliferate and diversify, sending up new shoots everywhere in a rich but utterly unsystematic plethora of applications. Of this plethora, three transformations stand out. First, particularly in part 1 of *The Origins,* on anti-Semitism, although Arendt's familiar schema of ideas first appears unchanged, it is soon joined by its mirror image, though Arendt never acknowledges the shift. In a truly remarkable reversal, what had begun as a tool for understanding Jewish assimilation under conditions of anti-Semitism becomes the key to understanding anti-Semitism itself, Naziism, the holocaust.

Second, particularly in part 2, on imperialism, the other half of what will eventually become Arendt's concept of the social is introduced. To the original notions of high society and social climbing she here adds ideas about economics and biology, the body, its needs, and the activities by which people satisfy those needs, natural processes, and biological necessity. Only rarely are these matters called social, but the familiar schema of ideas is clearly visible. Now, in effect, when parvenus abdicate their autonomous powers it is not to some "they, up there" or "out there" but to a *process,* not a static entity but a moving force that grows, spreads, and thus is far more menacing. Having abdicated her autonomy to "they, up there," Rahel Varnhagen remained free to change her mind at the end of her life. Such second thoughts become far more problematic if one abdicates to a process of inexorable expansion, what Arendt will later call "necessity *in motion.*"[2]

Finally, in part 3, the Blob appears as this inexorable process acquires a will and purpose of its own. That purpose is, of course, evil, and its essence—the nature of totalitarianism—consists in actively depriving people of their autonomy, of precisely those capacities for initiative and judgment that, in the early writings, had been voluntarily abdicated by the parvenu.

Before turning to these developments in greater detail, a word of warning. It seems particularly important in relation to *The Origins* to underline the limited scope of the critique here undertaken. Arendt's writings are enormously rich and often highly controversial; there is much in them to question and to criticize. The interest of the study in which we are engaged, however, is narrow. Only those topics and problems relevant to that interest are addressed here.

Anti-Semitism: Extrapolating the Way of the Parvenu

To begin, then, at the beginning, the explicit concepts related to society, and even the particular examples from Arendt's early writings, reappear virtually unchanged in the first section of *The Origins*. Rahel Varnhagen is there with her salon. The parvenu appears, as does the pariah, and they are expressly tied to society and things social. The "conscious pariah" is not mentioned as such, although politics—with which he was explicitly linked in the early writings—is very much in evidence. The deployment of these ideas continues to be relatively unself-conscious, as if their meanings were transparent and obvious.

The topic of this book, however, is radically different from that of Arendt's earlier writings. Not the options open to Jews under conditions of anti-Semitism, but the sources of the holocaust—and therefore of anti-Semitism itself—are now the focus. As a result, the Jew's personal choice whether "to remain a pariah and stay out of society altogether, or become a parvenu" disappears from the text almost as soon as it is introduced, but its substance—without the terms "pariah" and "parvenu"—remains in two significant forms.[3] In the later sections of the book, we shall see, something like pariah origins or parvenu conduct or both characterizes each of the specific categories of people Arendt identifies as contributing to the rise of totalitarianism. And in part 1, addressing the sources of that particular kind of central and western European anti-Semitism Arendt regards as making genocide possible, she calls those sources "social," repeatedly contrasting social to political matters in a way that replicates her earlier contrast of parvenu and conscious pariah.

Arendt begins by tracing the history of Jews in early modern central and western Europe. Initially, the European states then being officially Christian, Jews were excluded from all civil and political rights, but a few wealthy Jews were welcomed at court as exceptions, because they were financially useful. With the rise of the bourgeoisie, a few gifted Jews were similarly welcomed in salon society, not for their financial services but for the esoteric titillation their presence provided. Still later, after emancipation, the Jews no longer being legally different and exotic, their social welcome ended. Anti-Semitism, Arendt argues, originated both in bourgeois hostility to the royal court, symbolized by the financial "exception Jews," and in a lingering sense of the Jews as a distinct enclave, not really part of "the nation."[4] Certain political candidates and parties exploited this popular anti-Semitism for their own purposes, thereby also increasing it.

Thus, Arendt remarks, the Jews "always had to pay with political misery for social glory and with social insult for political success," and "political antisemitism developed because the Jews were a separate body, while social discrimination arose because of the growing equality of Jews with all other groups" (56, 54). Here "political" seems to mean no more than state-related, but "social" could mean either civil society, in the conventional contrast to the state, or respectable society, the object of parvenu striving. As Arendt continues, however, the latter notion prevails.

All who advocated Jewish political emancipation, she says, associated it with Jewish "assimilation, that is adjustment to and reception by society," either as a prerequisite or as an immediate consequence. "In other words, whenever those who actually tried to improve Jewish conditions attempted to think of the Jewish question from the point of view of the Jews themselves, they immediately approached it merely in its social aspects." So "social aspects" is synonymous ("in other words") with "assimilation," parvenu striving. Then comes the contrast: "It has been one of the most unfortunate facts in the history of the Jewish people that only its enemies, and almost never its friends, understood that the Jewish question was a political one" (56). The Nazis made the Jewish question political in the sense of official, the subject of racist laws; earlier candidates and parties had made anti-Semitism political by exploiting it in order to mobilize voters. These no doubt were the enemies of the Jewish people. But why is it "unfortunate" that "friends" have not also seen the question as political? Surely Arendt is not arguing for either anti-Semitic laws or ones that particularly favor Jews. Instead, one suspects, the Jewish question is political rather than social in the sense that it cannot be dealt with successfully in parvenu ways, but only in the way of the conscious pariah, through principled resistance in solidarity with others.

But there is also a second, related theme involved. The Jewish question is political rather than social also because the very category, "Jew," is a human convention masquerading as a biological fact, and anti-Semitism cannot be successfully dealt with until this masquerade is revealed as such, the role in it of human choice and responsibility rediscovered. Already in the 1940s Arendt had written that anti-Semitism must be recognized as "a political and not a natural phenomenon."[5] Now she adds that the tendency to regard Jewishness as a natural rather than a conventional, humanly established category is "social"—characteristic of society.

The contrast between social and political ways of regarding such matters appears repeatedly in part 1 of *The Origins,* the issue always being a realistic recognition of human agency and responsibility. The contrast appears, for example, in some seemingly parenthetical observations on the concept of equality, where Arendt again distinguishes in terms of human agency, calling the "modern" understanding of equality its "perversion . . . from a political into a social concept." The ancient Greeks rightly saw that people are not by nature equal but must be made so by human arrangements if they are to become fellow citizens in a free polis. In ancient Greece, equality was "recognized simply as a working principle of a political organization in which otherwise unequal people have equal rights." The modern understanding of a universal natural human equality first emerged in Christian thought, rooted in God-given rights, but as this understanding was secularized it was also naturalized and made biological. The modern outlook thus relegates equality to "the dark background of mere givenness," confusing it with likeness or normality, so that the exceptional human being seems defective. Instead of fostering initiative, autonomy, and political action, the concept promotes parvenu striving to fit in and be accepted as normal. The modern, social view thus not only hides human responsibility for enacting an equality that is not naturally guaranteed but also undermines the very capacity for action by teaching conformism. That is why it "constitutes a permanent threat to the public sphere," to politics. The actual modern equality of social conditions, while "certainly a basic requirement for justice" and accordingly "among the greatest . . . ventures of modern mankind," is therefore also among the "most uncertain" and "all the more dangerous."[6]

Another version of the same theme appears in a section called "Between Vice and Crime," in which Arendt discusses Marcel Proust as a kind of nineteenth-century Rahel Varnhagen, welcomed in the salons of the Faubourg Saint-Germaine because of the titillating dual fascination of his being both a homosexual and a Jew (actually a half-Jew, but "in emergencies ready to identify himself as a Jew"). Presumably with respect to his sexual orientation, Arendt says that society, in its "morbid lust for the exotic, abnormal, and different as such," transformed what had hitherto been considered a crime to be punished into a vice to be entertained. It changed "an act of will into an inherent, psychological quality which man cannot choose or reject but which is imposed upon him" biologically. Arendt calls the shift "the victory of bourgeois values over the citizen's sense of responsibility." Without explaining at this point what bourgeois values have to do with it or indeed what they are, she adds that in Proust's time, "society had emancipated itself completely from public concerns," so that "politics itself" became subsumed in "social life," political issues decomposed "into their dazzling fascinating reflections" in salon gossip, without policy consequences. This society may still be high society, a particular class of actual people who might have, but chose not to, become political leaders. But one can begin to discern in Arendt's locution here hints of a superhuman agency at work, society as a personified abstraction. By its very nature, "society denies all responsibility and establishes a world of fatalities in which men find themselves entangled."[7]

Yet, though society entangles people in false fatalities they feel helpless to alter, it does not exactly render them passive or apathetic. Instead, they become frantically, obsessively active in a special way, the way of the parvenu, diametrically opposed to responsibility and politics. Even as society shifts crime into vice, choice into biological fatality, the parvenu is motivated to an endless personal striving to shed or disguise (what he nevertheless agrees with society in regarding as) his biological, irremediable flaw. Precisely as emancipation changed the social understanding of what being a Jew meant from a willful, quasi-criminal refusal to convert to Christianity into an interesting biological debility, it transformed the Jews' experience of Judaism into the "psychological quality" of "Jewishness."[8]

This meant, first, that Judaism became a private concern, "an involved personal problem for every Jew," as each had to choose whether to become a parvenu; second, if he became one, it meant entering upon an interminable, paradoxical activity: "The more the fact of Jewish birth lost its religious, national, and socio-economic significance, the more obsessive Jewishness became; Jews were obsessed by it as one may be by a physical defect or advantage, and addicted to it as one may be to a vice." Because striving to overcome by effort what is (seen as) biologically unchangeable cannot succeed, the goal of the parvenu can never be achieved. "The social destinies of average Jews were determined by their eternal lack of decision." This endless ambiguity was intensified by society's conflicting demands: Jews, being socially welcome for their distinctive "vice," had to be different (bad) in order to be acceptable (good) (66, 84, 67).

The rise of the Nazis, one might suppose, by making parvenu assimilation impossible, should have freed these Jews from this obsessive temptation. Yet we have seen that it did not end parvenu conduct. Even in theoretical terms, it did not simply change being a Jew back from a vice into a crime. Though the Nazis "punished" Jewishness like a crime, they defined it biologically, without ascribing any criminal action or offering any alternative choice. They thus simultaneously *revealed* the Jewish question to be in fact political (a matter of policy, of human choice), *made* it political (enacting it into law and enforcing it by state machinery), and *made* it *social* (basing their policy and their law on what they falsely presented as a biological category imposed inescapably by nature).

Arendt cuts through this theoretical tangle by saying that the Nazis imported into politics a social conception of Jewishness, meaning that they enacted laws and employed the power of the state in the service of a category that they presented and perhaps regarded as natural, for which they claimed to bear no responsibility, and which those labeled as "Jewish" could not avoid, no matter how hard they tried. That is why society's transformation of the crime of Judaism—the refusal to convert to Christianity—into the interesting vice of Jewishness, welcomed in the salons, had been "dangerous in the extreme." From Judaism, Jews could escape by converting; "from Jewishness there was no escape. A crime, moreover, is met with punishment; a vice can only be exterminated." Thus modern, Nazi anti-Semitism "cannot be understood . . . as a mere political movement" but must be seen in terms of "social factors," which fundamentally "changed the course that mere political antisemitism would have taken if left to itself" (87).

Specifically, it was social discrimination and not political anti-Semitism that created "the phantom of '*the* Jew' " as a general, abstract category independent of any individual's religion or conduct.[9] Without that spuriously biological category, there might have been "anti-Jewish legislation and even mass expulsion but hardly wholesale extermination" (87). This is what happens, Arendt warns, "whenever the legal and political machine is not separated from society so that social standards can penetrate into it and become political and legal rules."[10] Society and social ways will be Arendt's solution to the mystery of the holocaust.

The argument of this opening section of *The Origins* is extremely dense and hard to survey, partly because Arendt is entangled in her own rapidly diversifying notions without analyzing them explicitly. Somehow, in the course of this difficult section, alongside the familiar story of Jewish pariahs who become parvenus, the same narrative structure becomes an explanation of anti-Semitism. To be sure, Arendt's Jewish parvenu was always a scoundrel, contributing to anti-Semitism. But one could hardly construe all anti-Semites as parvenus, pariahs seeking assimilation. Some important shifts in emphasis within the basic narrative make possible the transition by which Arendt's account of Jewish assimilation becomes an explanation for anti-Semitism and genocide.

Not only must the contrast between parvenu and conscious pariah be replaced by that between social and political, but, as a corollary, agency shifts from individuals to society as such. In particular, the parvenu's abdication of his human powers and responsibilities, of agency and of judgment, is replaced by society's imposition of its categories as natural, its discovery of "the Jew in general" as a biological creature, its transformation of crime into vice. Society now not only defines some people as pariahs and then seduces them into becoming parvenus, but it also disguises this activity as a natural, inevitable process beyond human power.

Society and Natural Process

These confusing shifts in emphasis are accompanied by a changed perspective on nature and natural things. In *Rahel Varnhagen,* we saw, nature was ambiguous, signifying both the inescapable, biologically given, like a hump or a club foot, and the gratifying "green things," the simple pleasures directly enjoyed.[11] In both respects, however, nature contrasted with society, with social artifice, convention, and parvenu pretenses. Being social meant turning away from nature, giving up the simple pleasures, and striving to overcome or conceal the club foot. In the New York essays this began to change, as the simple pleasures of "green things" seemed, in the face of Nazi horrors, not merely inaccessible but downright escapist, an irresponsible pretense entirely akin to—instead of opposed to—parvenu social striving.

Now, in *The Origins,* as the emphasis shifts from the parvenu to society as agent, nature and society are classed together. That which is given biologically and cannot be changed, and that which is falsely presented as biological, are paradoxically confounded in their shared contrast to a realistic perception and responsible exercise of human agency. This becomes a central theme in all of Arendt's subsequent writings, probably enhanced by the influence on her thinking of Kant, the first philosopher she read (at the age of fourteen), whose sharp distinction between causally determined nature and the human realm of moral responsibility is well known.[12]

But, Arendt's confusing treatment of nature also reflects the complexities in that word's ordinary uses. We do, indeed, contrast nature now to the cultivated or civilized, now to the perverse or artificial, so that it fluctuates between being a deprived condition in which human powers remain undeveloped and being an Eden of health and ease. In addition, we often call "natural" whatever has not been affected by human intervention, so that nothing humans do or produce can be natural. Yet we also and rightly regard human beings as one among many natural species on earth, which might imply that everything humans do is part of nature. It is thus not surprising if Arendt's use of the term also fluctuates. By failing to recognize and to examine these fluctuations, however, she made trouble for her own thought in two ways.[13] First, merging nature and society meant losing the crucial distinction between what is truly biological and inevitable and what is falsely, socially, regarded as such, a loss whose consequences will be traced in chapter 9. Second, as nature merges with society, gratification and motivation become problematic. If one must give up the simple pleasures of "green things" in order to be political and responsible, agency looks more like self-sacrifice than fulfillment. Either some other, "higher" kind of pleasure will have to be invoked, or politics is likely to seem either empty vanity or mere duty, reluctantly performed, charges that critics have often brought against *The Human Condition*.

These difficulties, however, become manifest only later. In the argument of *The Origins*, the assimilation of society to nature becomes a central theme of part 2, on imperialism, in the form of the idea of "process." Through the idea of process, part 2 introduces what will eventually become the other half of Arendt's concept of the social: its connections with economics, biology, the body, and necessity. Social process, like natural process, defies human agency.

The "central political idea of imperialism," Arendt postulates, is expansion, endless expansion pursued for its own sake as the "permanent and supreme aim of politics," not as a means to wealth or any other goal but as "a supposedly permanent process which has no end or aim but itself."[14] The idea derives, Arendt says, from economics, "the realm of business speculation," where expansion was "an adequate concept" because in the nineteenth century "industrial growth was a working reality." But as a political aim or policy goal, endless growth proved disastrous because it "is not really a political idea at all" and can never serve successfully as "a principle of politics."[15] More concretely, the idea was introduced into politics by "the bourgeoisie," whose characteristic "privateness and primary concern with money-making had developed . . . from the experience of a society of competitors" (138).

Arendt calls the first chapter of the imperialism section of *The Origins* "The Political Emancipation of the Bourgeoisie," because before imperialism the bourgeoisie had achieved "economic preeminence without aspiring to political rule"; it turned to politics "when the nation-state proved unfit to be the framework for the further growth of capitalist economy" (123). This was the bourgeoisie's "political emancipation" in the sense that now "businessmen became politicians and were acclaimed as statesmen, while statesmen were taken seriously only if they talked the language of successful businessmen" and applied "bourgeois convictions" in their political activity. Thus imperialism was not, as Lenin claimed, the "last stage of capitalism," but rather "the first stage in political rule of the bourgeoisie" (138). Significantly, Arendt explicitly equates the bourgeoisie here with society. As the bourgeoisie began to struggle openly for control of public policy, she says, "the latent fight between state and society [became] openly a struggle for power" (123). There are echoes here of the familiar contrast between the state and civil society, and one also suspects the influence of Arendt's native language, since the German for "civil society," *bürgerliche Gesellschaft,* can also be translated more literally as "bourgeois society." In any case, the seizure of state power by the bourgeoisie that launched imperialism was clearly, to Arendt, also a victory for society over either the state or politics, or both.

Within imperialism Arendt distinguishes "two new devices" that facilitated ruling foreign peoples without their consent: racism, to rationalize the apparent inconsistency between the ideal of self-government at home and imposed domination abroad, and bureaucracy as a mode of administering that imposed domination (185). Like anti-Semitism, racism deceptively naturalizes humanly created arrangements and categories into biological inevitabilities. Racism originated, Arendt thinks, in the Europeans' encounters in Africa and Asia with peoples whose appearance and culture differed so fundamentally from the European that these peoples seemed to lack any culture at all, to be merely part of a nature that the Europeans overseas then experienced as "particularly hostile." These alien beings seemed part of this threatening inhuman environment in "that they behaved like a part of nature, that they treated nature as their undisputed master, that they had not created a human world, a human reality."[16] With respect to anti-Semitism, Arendt explicitly calls such spurious naturalizing "social"; with respect to racism, she does not, but the parallels are evident.

The same is true about bureaucracy, the other component of imperialism. Although she does not yet call it, as she later will, "the most social form of government," she does present bureaucracy here as an abdication of human initiative and judgment reminiscent of the parvenu.[17] "Always a government of experts, of an 'experienced minority,'" bureaucracy is inherently hierarchical, each rank focused on its specialized task and deferential to those above.[18] It is inherently—if benevolently—contemptuous of those it rules, who seem only to hamper its efficient performance. Trying to insulate itself against the governed, bureaucracy therefore favors secrecy over publicity, relying on ad hoc decrees rather than settled, publicly accessible law. Thus, while racism is "an escape into ... irresponsibility," denying the humanity of native peoples and therefore any responsibilities toward them, bureaucracy is the assumption of too much responsibility, "of a responsibility that no man can bear for his fellow man and no people for another people" (207). If the racist is like the anti-Semite, then, the bureaucrat is like the parvenu, unquestioningly deferential to those "above," unhesitatingly contemptuous of those "below," abdicating his human capacities in both respects.

Who Is to Blame?

These parallels to the early writings emerge even more clearly in Arendt's treatment of the various categories of people she identifies as contributing to the historical rise of imperialism and later of totalitarianism. The anti-Semites and the bourgeoisie play the earliest role. In the nineteenth century they are joined by the colonial bureaucrats, secret agents, adventurers, the Boers in South Africa, and a category Arendt designates merely as "the mob." In the twentieth century, the latter is joined, in totalitarianism, by "the mass." None of these categories precisely fits the image of the parvenu from Arendt's early writings, and Arendt never calls them parvenus; nor are they all alike. But there is something like a family resemblance; each category involves at least some parvenu features. All are in some sense pariahs to begin with, even if not literally so. All consist in some way of isolated individuals, incapable of solidarity or mutuality, who abdicate their human capacities and responsibilities to a projected "they" or "it," with disastrous consequences, both for other people and eventually for themselves.

Begin with the colonial administrator and the secret agent, the "two key figures" in the development of nineteenth-century overseas imperialism. They were not literally pariahs; on the contrary, they were often "of illustrious origin," the younger sons of aristocratic families.[19] Yet Arendt says they chose their roles overseas out of an intense revulsion at the stifling conventionality and hypocrisy of established society, "the world of dull respectability whose continuity had become simply meaningless."[20] Once Arendt even calls them "born adventurers ... who by their very nature dwelt outside society" (218).

Although they craved honor and heroic adventure, however, the imperial bureaucrats and secret agents did not seek public glory. On the contrary, like a parvenu abjectly striving for acceptance, they wanted to serve anonymously, to merge themselves into some great and meaningful cause. Imperialism offered them such a cause, since bureaucracy requires expertise and shuns publicity, and a secret agent's work is clandestine by definition. Imperialism "required a highly trained, highly reliable staff whose loyalty and patriotism were not connected with personal ambition or vanity and who would even be required to renounce the human aspiration of having their names connected with their achievements. Their greatest passion would have to be for secrecy ..., for a role behind the scenes" (213). The agents of imperialism, then, were not selfish; but precisely their "sense of sacrifice" for the backwards peoples they ruled, and their "sense of duty" toward their homeland, readily turned into a mindless devotion reminiscent of parvenu conformism. Though their rebellion against social respectability was virtually the opposite of conformism, they nevertheless shared the parvenu's readiness for "degrading themselves voluntarily into mere instruments or mere functions." Only, instead of subordinating themselves to a hypothetical projected respectable society, they became "secret and anonymous agents of the force of expansion" itself (211, 215).

A variation of the same story concerns the Boers in South Africa, Arendt's paradigm of racism. While again not exactly pariahs, the Boers were certainly self-exiled from European society, "completely isolated from the current of European history," and may well have felt abandoned in the wilds of Africa. Even more, like the colonial administrators, they rejected European society and civilization, repeatedly fleeing inland before the advance of British law and propriety. They were "the first European group to become completely alienated from the pride which Western man felt in living in a world created and fabricated by himself," and they abandoned responsibility for its upkeep (191, 194).

For Arendt, the Boers epitomize virulent racism, not just classifying people in biological categories but unable to see the natives as people at all. They perceived Africans simply as natural "raw material," to be used in the same manner "as one might live on the fruits of wild trees." Denying outright "the Christian doctrine of the common origin of men," the Boers felt entitled to massacre or enslave those they encountered, to live "parasitically from their labor," and to exploit them "in absolute lawlessness" (193–95).

The combination of this racist exploitation with their rejection of European tradition and civilization meant, first, that the Boers refused to work, feeling "contempt for labor and productivity in any form," settling for what they could extract from the labor of their slaves (193). Because that production was too meager to sustain a high civilization, second, they accepted "living in an environment which they had no power to transform into a civilized world" (197). Their refusal to work and their repeated flight from civilization meant, third, that they remained trekkers, lacking the traditional European "feeling for a territory, a *patria* of [one's] own," a land inherited from ancestors and for whose care one bears responsibility, a feeling that Arendt associates with self-government in European nation-states.[21] Finally, this also meant that the Boers no longer saw or treated even each other as fellow members. They lost "their civilized feeling for human fellowship. 'Each man fled the tyranny of his neighbor's smoke' was the rule of the country," so that the Boers were bound into "no body politic, no communal organization."[22]

By their racist invocation of biological categories and by their rejection of any sort of solidarity, the Boers let loose forces that subsequently took them over: "they embarked upon a process which could only end with their own degeneration."[23] Rather than striving to assimilate to respectable society like the parvenu, they rejected and fled it. Rather than merging themselves into an impersonal "higher cause" like colonial bureaucrats and agents, they abandoned all commitments. As a result, however, they regressed into nature, like permanent babies unwilling to take responsibility for the upkeep of the human world and fleeing the authority of those who might have kept it up for them. Reverting to nature, by this time, means to Arendt being at the mercy of process.

In this respect the Boers resemble and anticipate "the mob," which also pays the price of regression. Unlike the other categories of people in *The Origins*, Arendt's mob is a genuine pariah group, expelled from society; it consists of the dregs, "the residue," or "the *déclassés* of all classes," those who "had not stepped out of society but been spat out by it."[24] A "by-product" of capitalism, the mob comprises the accumulated "human debris that every [economic] crisis, following invariably upon each period of industrial growth, eliminated permanently from producing society."[25] The mob is thus the *Lumpenproletariat,* but it is also the "underworld": petty criminals, punks, grifters, pimps, and prostitutes (155, 332, 337). Proverbially "fickle" in its "essential irresponsibility," the mob has always been drawn to "evil and crime" (108, 155, 307).

Although the mob consists of pariahs, these pariahs respond to their status neither with a parvenu's assimilationist striving nor with the conscious pariah's political resistance, but rather, like Arendt's Boers, with a resentful withdrawal from responsibility. The mob "hates society from which it is excluded, as well as Parliament, where [—being outside the class system—] it is not represented" (107). Whereas the parvenu is automatically compliant toward whatever society decrees, the mob rejects those decrees with equally automatic scorn, in a "rebellious nihilism" that is "satisfied with blind partisanship in anything that respectable society [has] banned" (317, 331).

Here Arendt makes explicit what with respect to the Boers she had only suggested: that the mob's conduct is a kind of inverted parvenu dependence. Seeking at all costs *épater le bourgeois,* the mob orients itself by society's standards just as thoroughly as the parvenu does, only in the opposite direction, "in perverted form" (314). Like the stereotypical adolescent rebel, it knows what it is against but has no positive vision of its own. The mob accepts as truth "whatever respectable society [has] hypocritically passed over, or covered up with corruption"—or rather, whatever sounds like the sort of thing respectable society would want to pass over or cover up.[26] The mob is thus cynical but at the same time also profoundly susceptible to conspiracy theories and quasi-paranoid suspicions. Trusting its own direct perceptions and common sense no more than the parvenu trusts his, the mob is always "inclined to seek the real forces of political life in those movements and influences which are hidden from view and work behind the scenes" (108). This cynicism, the apparent opposite of parvenu deference, thus proves just as isolating, just as incompatible with solidarity, and just as crippling.

In the development of imperialism, the "superfluous men" of the mob, the "scum of the big cities," became adventurers and prospectors abroad. "Fed up with being counted among the pariahs and want[ing] to belong to a master race," they discovered in the colonies that through racism and violence overseas a pariah group could "create a class lower than itself."²⁷ After World War I, when "they could no longer escape into exotic lands" from the hypocritical respectability of society, they turned to violence at home and to anti-Semitism, which served not only as a substitute for overseas racism and a way of shocking the bourgeoisie but also as fodder for their quasi-conspiratorial cynicism. The Jews became their symbol for society and everything they hated in it, "for the hypocrisy and dishonesty of the whole system."²⁸

Initially active and rebellious, though in an utterly selfish and exploitive way, the mob now submitted itself to a cause as selflessly as any parvenu. As colonial bureaucrats had seized on imperialism to escape from social conventionality, so the mob turned to a "self-willed immersion in the suprahuman forces of destruction," to violence and anti-Semitism, both as their only "salvation" from the established roles society offered them and as a way of disrupting its automatic functioning. Both halves of this "seemingly contradictory" combination were essential: the violent activity and the utter submission to an "overwhelming force of sheer necessity." Preferring "terrorism" to any conventional social or creatively political way of expressing their "frustration, resentment, and blind hatred," and of "forcing the recognition of [their] existence on the normal strata of society," the mob sought "access to history even at the price of destruction," perhaps especially at the price of destruction (331–32).

But respectable society, as it turned out, was as titillated by the mob's transgressions as it had earlier been by selected exotic Jews and homosexuals. On this point Arendt herself sees the parallel with her earlier ideas: "The mob of the twentieth century followed faithfully the pattern of earlier parvenus," not in the sense of imitating them or of conforming deferentially but in discovering "that bourgeois society would rather open its doors to the fascinating 'abnormal,' the genius, the homosexual or the Jew, than to simple merit." In its attraction to the mob, bourgeois society was further supported by "the elite," who were "pleased when the underworld frightened respectable society into accepting it on an equal footing" and watched with "genuine delight" the resulting destruction of society's banal respectability (332–33). (This is one of the rare passages where Arendt distinguished between respectable bourgeois society and "the elite," a point to which we shall return shortly.)

It was the mob, according to Arendt, that initially supplied the leadership for totalitarian movements and regimes.²⁹ The membership, however, was recruited from a different category of people, whom she calls "the mass." Mass man is characterized primarily by "his isolation and lack of normal social relationships."[30] In the nineteenth century the mob was already outside the class system, but in the twentieth century "the class system broke down" altogether, so that, in effect, everyone was outside it; there remained nothing but "unorganized masses" (314–15). Having "lost their home in the world," both socially and spiritually, having lost all traditional "communal relationships," people were left "atomized" and outside, but without any society excluding them (350, 352, 318).

The masses, like the mob, "stand outside all social ramifications and normal political representation" (314). Thus they are not bound together by any shared interest; neither do they pursue diverse private interests. All that they share is a resentful cynicism like that of the mob, a "vague apprehension . . . that all the powers that be [are] . . . equally stupid and fraudulent." They are, however, apathetic, and—unlike the mob—take no initiative to act on their resentful cynicism. It remains a mere feeling, an introverted, "self-centered bitterness" (315). Though each of them has this feeling, it does not constitute a common bond among them, let alone an interest, common or private, on which they might act. Indeed, like the parvenu's striving and the romantic's withdrawal inward, the mass man's self-centeredness goes "hand in hand with a decisive weakening of the instinct for self-preservation, . . . [a] radical loss of self-interest . . . and [a] general contempt for even the most obvious rules of common sense" (315–16).

Like the pariah in his lack of social location, mass man is without confidence in the judgment of his peers but equally without confidence in his own autonomous judgment or capacity to perceive reality, hence also like the parvenu: "modern masses . . . do not believe in anything visible, in the reality of their own experience; they do not trust their eyes and ears but only their imaginations" (351). This leaves them vulnerable to, even eager for, "the fantastically fictitious consistency of an ideology," and thus to the same sort of conspiracy theories as attract the mob (352).

All of these characteristics prepare the mass to be deployed by the mob for its own resentful, criminal, and violent purposes, and ultimately to be the cannon fodder of totalitarianism. Totalitarian movements recruit their followers from "this mass of apparently indifferent people whom all other parties had given up as too apathetic or too stupid for their attention."[31] Mass man, like the bureaucrat and the secret agent before him, yearns "for anonymity, for being just a number and functioning only as a cog" in some great, significant machine (329). Although, historically speaking, the mob arose earlier than the mass, played a role in imperialism, and supplied the leadership for totalitarianism, eventually the mob disappears from the scene, leaving nothing but leaderless, apathetic, atomized individuals congealed into a single unarticulated, "structureless mass."[32]

At that point everyone is as isolated as the parvenu, but without any high or respectable society by which he has been excluded or to which he can aspire. Everyone has become a would-be parvenu, desperately seeking a substitute for that society, something to which he might aspire and conform, an authority to which he might defer, as if such self-annihilating merger into an undifferentiated whole had become the only possible mode of human relationship. In effect, for Arendt, it is only with the disappearance of society (in the sense of a class system of rank and status) that the social (in the sense of parvenu assimilationism) can be perfected and become universal.

Where, then, does Arendt locate the origins of totalitarianism? Before there was a mass, there were the mob, the colonial bureaucrat and the secret agent, the racist Boer, the early anti-Semite. But behind them all looms the bourgeoisie. Although Arendt never says so explicitly, the genealogy of totalitarianism seems to lead back to two basic features of bourgeois life: the capitalist profit motive in economics and the fake respectability of the salon. As entrepreneurs seeking profit, the bourgeoisie launched imperialism abroad, bringing their competitive "privateness and primary concern with money-making" into political life, and they promoted a process of economic growth that first created the mob as a "by-product" and then destroyed the class system altogether, producing the mass.[33]

It was also the bourgeoisie who introduced social climbing and the salon, into which they invited the nobility as well as the exceptional Jew, the homosexual, and the petty criminal. Although Arendt never says so, the word "parvenu," which she adopted for Jewish assimilationism, previously had a class reference, designating members of the bourgeoisie who aspired to aristocratic rank. Long before Jews sought admission to bourgeois salons, members of the bourgeoisie were themselves imitating noble ways and seeking to win acceptance from the aristocracy, enforcing standards of "respectability" on their children and on each other and scornfully attributing to those below themselves in rank the very same "qualities which the nobility despised as typically bourgeois."[34]

Accordingly, although again Arendt does not quite say so, the Jewish parvenu was really only taking the bourgeois as a role model, imitating the imitator. So, in their respective ways, were the mob and the mass. As Arendt does say, the petty criminals and cynics of the mob were not only reacting resentfully against bourgeois hypocrisy but also imitating that class's ruthless selfishness. The utter isolation of mass man is only an exaggerated version, the culmination, of bourgeois competitive individualism. The "last . . . product of the bourgeoisie's belief in the primacy of private interest" is "the philistine's retirement into private life, . . . the atomized individual . . . the mass man." Acquisitive, competitive self-interest thus somehow turns into self-abnegation, for, in the end, "nothing proved easier to destroy than the privacy and private morality of people who thought of nothing but safeguarding their private lives."[35]

The two features of bourgeois life on which Arendt seems to focus here—capitalist profit-seeking and the striving for social respectability—clearly anticipate what will become the puzzling dual features of the social: economics and conformism. It was the *inconsistency* between these two features of bourgeois life, moreover, that specifically constituted the profound hypocrisy, the "smugness of spurious respectability," which so repelled the colonial bureaucrats and secret agents and which so enraged the mob, the mass, and perhaps the Boers (327). The bourgeoisie "confounded all moral issues by parading publicly virtues which it not only did not possess in private and business life, but actually held in contempt" (334). Arendt herself recognizes "how justified disgust can be in a society wholly permeated with the ideological outlook and moral standards of the bourgeoisie" (328). So if the justified rage of the elite, the mob, and the mass also brought totalitarianism, the bourgeoisie was ultimately to blame. The elite—the former nobility—of course also despised the bourgeoisie for its hypocritical smugness. Indeed, the elite's fateful temporary alliance with the mob, which played an important historical role in the rise of totalitarianism, "rested largely on the genuine delight with which" the elite watched the mob destroy and mock bourgeois respectability.[36] (It cannot be wholly irrelevant that, writing to her husband from Europe in 1952, Arendt refers to the influence that Heidegger's jealous, anti-Semitic wife exercised over him as basically "a tie between mob and elite, in this case most intimately bound.")[37]

What began in Arendt's thought as the parvenu's characteristic hypocrisy and became society's deceptiveness reflects bourgeois hypocrisy and the inherent emptiness of the conventions that the parvenu strives to internalize. Furthermore, if one accepts the identification suggested earlier of the bourgeoisie with civil society (*bürgerliche Gesellschaft*) and thence with society as such, it becomes likely that for Arendt hypocrisy is the essence of society, that the *tension* between the two halves of Arendt's concept—between underlying acquisitive greed and surface conformity to polite conventions—will itself be crucial to the social.

All of the categories of people that Arendt depicts as contributing historically to the rise of totalitarianism display one or another mix of the bourgeoisie's original combination of ruthless, competitive exploitation with inauthentic, self-disparaging conformism. Sometimes the selfishness is more evident, as in the mob; at other times the self-abnegation is more prevalent, as in assimilationist Jews, bureaucrats, and secret agents. But these two kinds of groups also form a chronological sequence for Arendt. Historically speaking, the more openly selfish groups appear earlier, letting loose the forces of totalitarianism and leading the others toward it. Conformist apathy, on the whole, comes later and characterizes the followers; ultimately the followers wholly constitute totalitarianism as the earlier, selfish groups disappear. In the end, when all are mass, the very capacity for selfishness is gone. At that point the mass, no longer led by any humans, is deployed by totalitarianism itself.

Totalitarianism as Blob

This happens in the third part of *The Origins,* where totalitarianism appears, "a novel form of government" previously unknown in the annals of political thought and differing "essentially from other forms of political oppression known to us such as despotism, tyranny, and dictatorship."[38] Being unprecedented, totalitarianism cannot be understood, like earlier forms of domination, as the ruthless exploitation of some people by others, whether the motive be selfish calculation, irrational passion, or devotion to some cause. Understanding totalitarianism's essential nature requires solving the central mystery of the holocaust—the objectively useless and indeed dysfunctional, fanatical pursuit of a purely ideological policy, a pointless process to which the people enacting it have fallen captive.

It became evident that the Nazis' fanaticism had reached the level of "open anti-utility when in the midst of the war, despite the shortage of building material and rolling stock, they set up enormous, costly extermination factories and transported millions of people back and forth."[39] This had nothing to do with expediency, no matter how exploitive or perverse. Seen in "strictly utilitarian" terms, "the whole enterprise [had] an air of mad unreality" beyond anything that had ever been intended: even "totalitarian dictators do not consciously embark on the road to insanity" (445, 411). This mad unreality of Nazi genocide, writ large and extended into a form of organization and a way of life, is totalitarianism.

In a totalitarian system, everyone is engaged in constant self-sacrifice in order to serve and merge with the system, which itself serves no one's interest, nor that of any group, nor of the polity as a whole. Its "most conspicuous external characteristic" is that it requires of each individual member "total, unrestricted, unconditional, and unalterable loyalty," so that it amounts to "the permanent domination of each single individual in each and every sphere of life" (323, 326). There are forces involved here "that cannot be trusted to follow the rules of common sense and self-interest—forces that look like sheer insanity, if judged by the standards of other centuries" (vii). Numerous European scholars, Arendt says, had foreseen the rise of mass society and the possibility of popularly based tyranny, but no one knows what to make of this new phenomenon: "the radical loss of self-interest, the cynical or bored indifference in the face of death or other personal catastrophes, the passionate inclination toward the most abstract notions as guides for life, and the general contempt for even the most obvious rules of common sense" (316).

How are people brought to conduct themselves in such an unprecedented, irrational manner? Arendt answers that it can be done only by destroying individuality, utterly suppressing the distinctive human capacities for initiative or spontaneity and for autonomous judgment, which make us capable of action, responsibility, freedom, and politics. Totalitarianism turns people into "a kind of human species resembling other animal species whose only 'freedom' would consist in 'preserving the species.'" It reduces human beings to mere "bundles of reactions" so that each person "can be exchanged at random for any other," because only people who have been so reduced can be organized without any regard for individual variation, "as if all humanity were just one individual" (438). The demand that individuals sacrifice themselves for their collectivity is of course perfectly familiar and may often be justified, particularly in times of crisis, but totalitarianism, unlike earlier forms of collectivity, possesses its members entirely, "to the point of complete loss of individual claims and ambition, . . . extinguishing individual identity permanently and not just for the moment of collective heroic action" (314).

One way in which totalitarianism does this is by isolating people from each other, "interrupting all channels of communication" among its subjects, making mutual support and joint action impossible (495). It does so not only by forbidding illicit groups and subversive ideas but also more subtly and effectively by destroying interpersonal trust, cultivating spies and informers everywhere, until "the most elementary caution demands that one avoid all intimate contacts" (323). The resulting "isolation of atomized individuals" extends even into the ranks of the leaders, who "are not bound together by equal status in the political hierarchy or the relationship between superiors and inferiors, or even the uncertain loyalties of gangsters" (407).

A second way in which totalitarianism destroys individuality is that it deprives people of any fixed reality by which they might orient themselves. Everything is kept in flux, in process, subject to constant change, "creating a state of permanent instability" (391). Like imperialism, according to Arendt, totalitarianism adopts process as such as its only goal; it has a mania for perpetual motion. Totalitarian movements can retain "power only so long as they keep moving and set everything around them in motion" (306). This means, paradoxically, that for such a movement success in seizing state power is problematic, threatening to generate a new stability, which "would surely liquidate the movement itself" (391). Like imperialism, therefore, totalitarianism in power cannot operate by fixed, generally accessible laws. "The never-resting, dynamic 'will of the Fuehrer'—and not his orders, a phrase that might imply a fixed and circumscribed authority—becomes the 'supreme law' in a totalitarian state" (365). Instead of law, totalitarianism uses ad hoc decrees, and even these are often "intentionally vague," the recipient being required to guess what is intended. Many valid and operative regulations are never made public at all (399, 394).

For the same reason, Arendt says, totalitarianism develops its own distinctive governmental form—a kind of bureaucracy, but not, as one might imagine, a supremely disciplined hierarchical administrative machine, for "every hierarchy . . . tends to stabilize," and stability is what must be avoided (364–65). Moreover, "there is no hierarchy without authority," and authority reduces unpredictable motion.[40] Nor is this governmental form a series of nested hierarchies, a "multiplicity of principalities" in which "each little leader is free to do as he pleases [within his jurisdiction] and to imitate the big leader at the top" (405).

Instead of a hierarchical pyramid, totalitarian government is structured in a series of concentric circles or spheres, with the leader at the center. Each layer shields the next layer inside it from external reality like "a protective wall" and guards the movement's secrets from the next outward layer, which is less fully initiated than itself.[41] Indeed, secrecy is to this form what clear, stable lines of authority are to a pyramidal bureaucracy. Here, each layer "knows" that the inner layers must be privy to secrets it does not share, secrets that presumably explain and justify everything that is going on; each looks down on the outer layers that have to be kept in the dark because they are not trustworthy. There is thus a "graduation of cynicism expressed in a hierarchy of contempt" (384).

This organizational schema begins while totalitarianism is still a mere movement, with distinctions between party leaders and followers, party members and members of front organizations, sympathizers, and the general public. Once totalitarianism is in power, however, the scheme displays its greatest advantage: it "keeps the organization in a state of fluidity," so that the essential instability is preserved by "constant additions of new layers and shifts in authority" (368–69). The Nazis, Arendt explains, "made sure that every function of the state's administration would be duplicated by some party organ"; they continually created new offices and shifted duties without ever abolishing any of the old agencies, producing no mere duplication but a "multiplication of offices."[42] As with intentionally vague orders, people "had to develop a kind of sixth sense to know at any given moment whom to obey and whom to disregard" (399). In such a system, all one can know for sure is that one cannot know, since "the more visible government agencies are, the less power they carry. . . . Real power begins where secrecy begins" (403).

Arendt's metaphor for this pattern of "planned shapelessness" is the onion. As she explains in a later essay, "each layer forms the facade in one direction and the center in the other, that is, plays the role of normal outside world for one layer and the role of radical extremism for another. . . . The onion structure makes the system organizationally shockproof against the factuality of the real world."[43]

Through this instability, uncertainty, and severance from the real world, totalitarianism undermines the very notion of agency—people's responsibility for deeds and the consequences of those deeds. It has many devices for creating complicity—both actual and symbolic—with the regime's policies, and it metes out "punishment" at random, to guilty and innocent alike, so that a "grotesque haphazardness" is the only rule.[44] Ultimately it thereby "destroys all sense of responsibility and competence" (409). Everyone is merged into the regime and thus shares in its successes, while failures are no one's fault. Naturally no failure is the fault of the leader at the mysterious center, and even his close "entourage . . . in case of disagreement with him, will never be very sure of their own opinions" (388). But agency vanishes even in the outer layers, as "nobody ever experiences a situation in which he has to be responsible for his own actions or can explain the reasons for them" (375). One may be "punished," but punishment is no longer related to any misdeed. Not even personal failures need to "be recorded, admitted, and remembered" (388).

Without any stable external reality, without any reliable sense of agency—their own or that of others—people become incapable of judging or choosing for themselves: "A world which is complete with all sensual data of reality but lacks [any] structure of consequence and responsibility . . . remains for us a mass of incomprehensible data" (445). It is not that totalitarianism exploits some basic human credulity or somehow creates a new gullibility. Quite the contrary: Arendt argues that through "the eternally shifting party line" it produces a debilitating kind of cynicism; no one believes the propaganda and all regard it as intended for "others," yet all continue to conduct themselves as if they believed it and to enforce it against each other (451). Precisely this instability and the resulting cynical disbelief create a desperate need for security that manifests itself as fanatical loyalty. Thus, paradoxically, devoted obedience increases in proportion to the cynical lack of belief, since people's only source of security is the regime. Finally people reach a point at which they "can be reached by neither experience nor argument; identification with the movement and total conformism seem to have destroyed the very capacity for experience" (308).

As a cement to hold these isolated, desperate people together and as a way of motivating them, since interests will not work, totalitarianism offers them the shelter of ideology: an alternate, "entirely fictitious world" (362). The form of what ideology offers—infallibility—thus becomes "more important than the content" of its propaganda.[45] People not only feel incapable of testing the ideology's claims against any independently perceived reality, but they fear and actively resist any such testing, since it threatens their only security. We encountered earlier the anti-Semite's originally "social" notion of " 'The Jew' in general," an abstraction unrelated to concrete experience, which followed only "the peculiar logic of an ideology."[46] In totalitarianism this "social" mode of knowing becomes pervasive as ideological abstraction everywhere replaces fact and experience. People "escape from reality into fiction, from coincidence into consistency," into a systematic explanation of things in which the homeless mind "can feel at home" (352–53).

The ultimate organizational device by which totalitarianism finally destroys individuality altogether, and which thus is the perfect epitome of totalitarianism itself, is the concentration camp, "the most totalitarian society ever realized."[47] Concentration camps are "the true central institution of totalitarian organizational power," which therefore "stands or falls with [their] existence."[48] For the ultimate aim of totalitarianism is changing not the world or society but "human nature itself," and the camps "are the laboratories where changes in human nature are tested."[49] There the totalitarian system carries out its "experiment of eliminating, under scientifically controlled conditions, spontaneity itself," the capacity for initiative that has hitherto distinguished human beings from the rest of creation; there it "transform[s] the human personality into a mere thing."[50]

The destruction of inmates' individuality and humanity in the concentration camp proceeds in three stages, Arendt says. First comes destruction of the juridical person, as people are stripped of their rights, their citizenship, all legal status. The camps are outside the normal judicial system, the innocent are condemned along with the guilty, and all records are secret, so that people simply disappear from the world into the camps without a trace. The physical death of an inmate in such "organized oblivion" merely sets "a seal on the fact that he had never really existed."[51]

Second comes destruction of the moral person, of conscience. "This is done in the main by making martyrdom, for the first time in history, impossible" (451). Not only has the inmate become anonymous, but the combination of enforced complicity and arbitrary "punishment" in the camps undermines all morality, "making the decisions of conscience absolutely questionable and equivocal" (452). Finally comes destruction of individuality itself, of the "differentiation of the individual [from others], his unique identity . . . shaped in equal parts by nature, will, and destiny" (453–54). The individual becomes a robot, incapable of any initiative or self-defense, indifferent to everything.

The role of individuality in all of this is very confusing, and Arendt does nothing to sort it out. Individual separateness seems to cause totalitarianism, to be caused by it, and yet also to be the best defense against it. The processes that lead to totalitarianism are launched by the competitive individualism of the bourgeoisie and the anxious self-concern of the parvenu trying to get by as an exception. They are augmented by the isolated self-abnegation of colonial bureaucrats and secret agents and by the Boers' regressive flight from all human company into isolation. They end up in the utterly atomized mass man, ultimately both produced by totalitarianism and constituting it. Yet, though there is no discussion of alternatives or remedies in *The Origins* (or at least none prior to the 1958 epilogue), references in Arendt's earlier writings to politics, resistance, and conscious pariahs also imply individuality in the sense of individual initiative and judgment, though certainly expressed through solidarity. The ties of solidarity, moreover, are utterly different from the way in which isolated atoms congeal into a headless mass in totalitarianism, and the distinguishing criterion is surely that individuality in some sense is retained in political membership. That is the individuality totalitarianism seeks to destroy. It is all distressingly unclear.

In actual concentration camps, real human beings were in fact often reduced to a robotlike apathy by the brutalities inflicted on them by other real human beings. But the concentration camp also functions for Arendt as a symbol, revealing the essence of totalitarianism, the direction in which that process moves. Totalitarianism by its very nature aims at reducing all people to the condition of camp inmates. The guards eventually come to resemble the prisoners, and the subjects of totalitarian power not yet in camps also undergo very similar processes. Eventually guards are no longer needed, camps are no longer needed, leaders are no longer needed, nor are any available. The system rests on everyone's apathetic obedience and goes its own way.

Beyond Totalitarianism

This sort of extrapolation of apparent trends can easily become, as it does for Arendt, a story of the self-development of an autonomous power that intends things and deliberately imposes them. Thus, when Arendt calls the camps experiments in transforming human nature, she does not mean to suggest that actual Nazi or Soviet leaders literally said to each other, "Let's set up some centers where we can scientifically test the possibility of turning humans into robots." Rather, she is discerning an emerging pattern of events, giving it a name, and then thinking of that name as an intentional, active force, composed of humans who have lost their human agency—in short, a Blob.

But of course the story requires a "before," when there still were human agents, and—since the Blob did *not* come from outer space—something those agents did must have produced the Blob. We have by now encountered numerous versions of this tale, some entirely contained within *The Origins*, others reaching back into *Rahel Varnhagen* and the New York essays.

For example: at first the parvenu, striving to get by as an exception, is a scoundrel contributing to anti-Semitism. Then the refugee who collaborates with the Nazis, the established Jews elsewhere who refuse to help, the gentiles who won't stand up to Hitler are all appeasers, whose acquiescence makes the Nazis a serious threat. They are destined to become the Nazis' next victims. The trend is evident: soon all will be self-made victims, no humans left to be their oppressors; yet the oppression will be entirely real.

Or again, it begins with bourgeois capitalists who, seeking to expand their profits, launch imperialism with its attendant racism and bureaucracy, create an economy at home that produces first mob and then mass, and teach hypocrisy and false deference. The mob, enraged at bourgeois hypocrisy and seeking to profit from (or survive by) petty crime as the bourgeoisie does from investment, manipulates the mass; but as its success grows, there is more and more mass and less and less mob. The trend is evident: soon all will be mass parvenus, desperate for something to which to submit themselves, but no human agents will be left for the role of leader; the submission will be very real, and irreversible.

Similarly, anti-Semitism, first developed as a social phenomenon, is imported into politics by leaders and parties that seek to exploit its appeal for their political self-interest. But soon their invocation of biological, natural inevitability becomes an ideological necessity that they can no longer afford to abandon, and then it takes them over as well, as nature took over the Boers. So the Nazi system continues to pursue genocidal policies long after these have become obviously dysfunctional. Now the ideology is in charge, not the leaders.

Finally, although totalitarian organization, ideology, and new devices of enforcement at first give unprecedented power to the ruling elite and particularly to the *Führer*, as the domination increases it becomes more and more efficient, allowing fewer guards and fewer leaders to control more and more roboticized people, for "totalitarianism had discovered a means of dominating and terrifying human beings from within." The trend is evident: soon even the all-powerful leader at the center will be superfluous, a mere hypothetical "function" postulated by the system but perceptible to no one, and thus wholly expendable. Hitler already was no Alexander or Tamerlane, no mighty conqueror founding a great empire to bear his name, but himself a mere resentful parvenu, incapable of "the master's privilege" of founding anything much. "The totalitarian leader is nothing more nor less than the functionary of the masses he leads; he is not a power-hungry individual imposing a tyrannical and arbitrary will upon his subjects" (325). An onion *has* no center.

Although initially let loose by bad human decisions and deeds, totalitarianism triumphant is a superhuman force, and Arendt's narrative becomes a Sorcerer's Apprentice tale. Of course, Arendt is not intentionally personifying or demonizing totalitarianism in *The Origins,* any more than she will intentionally personify and demonize the social in *The Human Condition.* Indeed, she often writes quite realistically about things that totalitarian leaders tend to do or about features characteristic of totalitarian movements; she uses the adjective. But particularly in part 3 of *The Origins,* the noun "totalitarianism" also appears repeatedly as the subject of some remarkable verbs: "using," "striving," "establishing." Each such passage is doubtless intended only as metaphor, yet their combined effect is more than metaphorical, and it reflects something more than metaphor in Arendt's thinking as well. As the title of the book's last chapter (of the original edition) reveals, in the end it is "Totalitarianism" itself that comes to be "in Power." And what totalitarianism in power does, as Arendt sums it up, is that it

> uses the state administration for its long-range goal of world conquest and for the direction of the branches of the movement; it establishes the secret police as the executors and guardians of its domestic experiment of constantly transforming reality into fiction; and it finally erects concentration camps as special laboratories to carry through its experiment in total domination. (392)

Thus totalitarianism is an autonomous power that merely "uses the state as its outward facade" but that ultimately strives not toward despotic rule over people but toward a system without people.[52] In short, as Jewish assimilationism reversed into anti-Semitism in part 1 of *The Origins,* at the end of the story, in part 3, totalitarianism imposes on its members the helplessness and depersonalization that parvenus once chose and by which they helped produce totalitarianism.

A clear indication of the extent to which Arendt has demonized this ultimately leaderless juggernaut by the end of her book is that she identifies it explicitly with what Kant called "radical evil," a diabolical danger which she claims even Kant did not take seriously enough.[53] Totalitarianism, like the concentration camp that epitomizes it, "is the appearance of some radical evil, previously unknown to us," an evil involving the intrusion into modern politics of something "that actually should never be involved in politics as we used to understand it."[54] Totalitarianism is an "unforgivable absolute evil which [can] no longer be understood and explained by the evil motives of self-interest, greed, covetousness, resentment, lust for power, and cowardice" (459). *The Origins of Totalitarianism* rests its claim to fame on offering the first correct interpretation of the true nature of this unprecedented radical evil, which had remained opaque to all traditional explanations and classifications. The mystery of the holocaust, which the book set out to address, has a genealogy, but no rational solution. The solution is itself mystical: radical evil.

In the last part of *The Origins,* in other words, the Blob is born. To be sure, its name is "totalitarianism" rather than "society." And though in parts 2 and 3 the words "society" and "social" appear only rarely, and in part 3 are never used in the Arendtian sense related to the parvenu, nevertheless the Blob of this book is profoundly connected to the ideas Arendt associated with society.

Furthermore, although the Blob here is called totalitarianism, by the end of the book Arendt has begun hinting that it may not yet have reached its real or ultimate form—that an even worse monster is yet to come. By the time the book was written Hitler had been defeated, and by the time of its last edition the Stalin myth had been dismantled, yet Arendt by no means concludes that the threat whose origins she has been tracing is over. "Totalitarian solutions may well survive the fall of totalitarian regimes," she warns somewhat cryptically at the close of the original concluding chapter (459). Earlier in the book, noting the gradual disappearance of the mob, which initially supplied totalitarian leadership, Arendt remarks uneasily, "What will happen once the authentic mass man takes over [completely], we do not know yet" (327).

By her 1953 essay, "Ideology and Terror," appended to the second edition of the book, this foreboding has grown: "It may even be that the true predicaments of our time will assume their authentic form—though not necessarily the cruelest—only when totalitarianism has become a thing of the past" (460). And in an article explaining the new, enlarged edition of her book, she remarks that totalitarianism "certainly corresponds better to the inherent tendencies of a mass society than anything we previously knew."[55]

Thus the final stage is not yet, there is still time to turn around, but the danger is also closer to home than we had supposed. It looks more like what we now have (or are) than like the defeated totalitarian regimes. The "authentic form" of our "true predicaments" may be some extreme, onionlike version of bureaucracy in which even the ostensible leaders efface themselves to serve the process, so that no one—no human—is in charge of the juggernaut that is our joint activity. That form may not be as "cruel" as totalitarianism, because it will require no guards, no punishments, no prisons or camps. The enforcement, torture, and terror still imposed under Hitler and Stalin will no longer be needed once all are roboticized, and the ultimate stage of the Blob may look more like an apathetic, administered consumer society than like a ruthless dictatorship.[56] These hints, however, are not further developed in *The Origins of Totalitarianism*.

SIX

Writing *The Human Condition*

Like any major theoretical work, *The Origins of Totalitarianism* left a number of unfinished tasks, the one most evident to Arendt herself being the book's inadequate treatment of the Soviet case. Introduced relatively late in the book's writing, as we noted, the Soviet case received only sketchy treatment, even though the very concept of totalitarianism required that the Soviet Union in fact be comparable to Nazi Germany. Accordingly, Arendt proposed as her next project a more thorough study of Soviet totalitarianism, its distinctive features, and the role of Marxism in it.[1]

Instead of a study of Russia and Marxism, however, she ultimately produced *The Human Condition,* in which the Soviet Union scarcely appears and Marx plays only a muted role. That book did, however, address a number of other theoretical tasks, which—at least to us, in retrospect—look like loose threads left dangling from the theoretical fabric of *The Origins,* even if Arendt did not think of them as such.

First and most central for our concerns were the mounting tensions in her concept of society. Was society real, possessed of enormous power, perhaps even omnipotent, or was it a mere abstraction, a projection, a paper tiger? Was society a timeless feature of human life, a historically changing product of human action, a phenomenon that ended in the nineteenth century, or a specifically modern process culminating in totalitarianism? Was it the cause of parvenu conduct or its result? Already troublesome in *Rahel Varnhagen,* as we saw, these questions only intensified in the New York essays, and in *The Origins* they went underground, cropping up everywhere in diverse forms. In *The Human Condition* this fecund but confusing complexity becomes the concept of the social.

Second, there remained Arendt's ill-defined alternative to parvenu conduct and social ways, present in shadowy form from the outset, repeatedly linked with "politics," but never elaborated. At first, we saw, it seemed to be singular, *the* alternative, but by the time it was named, as the "conscious pariah," it was only one among several options. Though Arendt thought it the only alternative viable in her time, she did not make clear its distinguishing features; nor did *The Origins* do so, since that book had a different project. In *The Human Condition* the political alternative becomes the central counterplayer to the social.

Precisely because this book thus explicitly addressed what people must now do, third, it had to engage the emergent historical conditions of its time, a world in which Nazi totalitarianism had been defeated and Stalinist totalitarianism was showing signs of strain. What now required elaboration were the vague forebodings Arendt had expressed at the end of *The Origins* about another, even greater danger that might follow totalitarianism. In *The Human Condition* the social emerges as this new, less cruel but even more terrible threat.

Finally, implicit in these questions about the nature of society and of politics in our time was the methodological but also personal issue of Arendt's own work: What was she doing? Was she a historian, a social scientist, or a journalist addressing current events? Was she continuing her practical, political engagement on behalf of pariahs? Or was she examining ideas, theorizing, perhaps even philosophizing? The materials treated in *The Origins* and the early writings now fairly cried out for theoretical systematization, yet in what terms could Arendt justify to herself returning to the abstract intellectual pursuits she had sworn, in leaving Germany, "never again [to] touch"? Writing *The Human Condition* threatened to draw Arendt back into Heidegger's kingdom.

The worldly background against which Arendt addressed these tasks was the mid-1950s, the era of the Cold War. The initial euphoria of Allied victory had long since worn off, the urgent tasks of rescue and repair in Europe were being addressed, and the simplifying polarization of wartime had vanished. One could no longer postpone all the hard questions, blame problems on the war or the enemy, suppress the complexities of distinguishing degrees of friendship and enmity, alliance and opposition. Broadly speaking, it was an era of disenchantment and disappointment. With the defeat of the Axis powers, the wartime alliance among the victors had resolved itself into a new configuration of two superpowers, each with attendant satellite and client states, confronting each other with nuclear weapons poised. All the effort and sacrifice of the recent war obviously had not succeeded in achieving either stable democracy or secure peace in the world.

The Cold War as such, although certainly disappointing, still fit within the conceptual framework of *The Origins of Totalitarianism*.

Since Arendt saw the Soviet Union as totalitarian, the new alignment of states was a sort of continuation of World War II for her, with the United States still leading an alliance of free, democratic nations. Indeed, *The Origins* itself came to function as a significant Cold War document, whether or not Arendt so intended it.[2] With the death of Stalin in 1953 and Krushchev's revelations about the "crimes of the Stalin era" at the Twentieth Party Congress in early 1956, followed by uprisings in Poland and Hungary, there was even some reason for optimism that the last bastion of totalitarianism might be about to fall.

Regarding America

But even as the Cold War fit into the conceptual framework of *The Origins* and gave some basis for hope, its domestic manifestations in the United States challenged that framework in ways that reminded Arendt painfully of the last days of the Weimar Republic. Clearly America was not another Nazi Germany, but Arendt did fear that it might be turning into some version of that post-totalitarian danger she had vaguely anticipated in *The Origins*. That worry may have been rendered more plausible as various social scientists of the time articulated "convergence theories" about an increasing resemblance between the two Cold War powers, both turning into bureaucratically administered, conformist, repressive welfare states.[3] *The Human Condition* was Arendt's first book about America. Even though its thesis was universal, the book took conditions in the United States as foreshadowing the likely future of the world, perhaps as characterizing modernity as such.

What had struck Arendt most forcefully about America on her arrival in 1941 was its surprising combination of stifling social conventionality with a genuine, lively tradition of political freedom. Soon after landing in New York, Arendt secured through a refugee agency a two-month placement in a private home in New England, to help her improve her English and master American ways. Her husband and mother remained in New York, so her impressions are recorded in their correspondence, reported by Young-Bruehl. Arendt's New England hostess, a third-generation American, was apparently puritanical, high-minded, and somewhat self-righteous. Arendt was repelled by her small-town, petit-bourgeois ways, her racist prejudices, her rigid vegetarianism and hostility to smoking (Arendt was permitted to smoke in her room, but the husband of the family was required to do his smoking outdoors), and her strict pacifism, impervious to the refugee's tales of Nazi horrors. One suspects that Arendt was also put off by her hostess's quasi-maternal, somewhat condescending efforts to supervise and improve the ignorant foreigner, who had, after all, been placed there for just that purpose.[4]

At the same time, however, Arendt got a strongly favorable impression of this American woman's principled political activism. When the wartime order interning Americans of Japanese descent was announced, Arendt's hostess and many of the hostess's friends immediately and spontaneously wrote letters of protest to their Congressmen, "insisted on the constitutional rights of all Americans regardless of national background, and declared that if something like this could happen, they no longer felt safe themselves." Such readiness with letters of political protest, one suspects, might also have reminded Arendt of her mother's protesting against incidents of anti-Semitism; but this American woman was neither Jewish nor Japanese by ancestry, was in no way a pariah. Arendt wrote to Jaspers early in 1946, "people feel that they share in responsibility for public life here to a degree unknown to me in any European country." This responsible readiness to act, she wrote, this "great political-practical understanding and passion to *straighten things out*," flourishes in the United States despite the "social conformism that rules everywhere," despite the land's "fundamental *Ungeistigkeit* [mindlessness, lack of spirituality, anti-intellectualism]," and despite the racism by which American society "organizes and orients itself."[5]

Two years before this, in 1944, Arendt had already remarked in an essay that America is "not a national state in the European sense of that word."[6] Now she explained to Jaspers that not only is it a land of immigrants from many nations, but the uniformity of "the melting-pot" is "not even its social ideal, let alone a reality." Instead, each of the national groupings shows a "monstrous need for cliquishness." Jews are not welcome in gentile society, but neither do they seek admission to it. Yet this does not mean, as it would in Europe, that gentiles would sit idly by if the political rights of Jews were threatened. On the contrary, the very pluralism of Americans' social cliquishness "creates a free, or at least a non-fanatical atmosphere," so that "there really is such a thing as freedom here, and a strong feeling among many people that one cannot live without freedom."[7]

America thus confounded some of the ideas Arendt had earlier formulated about Europe. In America she found neither the extraordinary German deference to established authority nor a social elite to which parvenus could aspire. Widespread parvenu conformism and social pressure here enforced an egalitarian subservience to peers rather than a snobbish or hierarchical deference to superiors. America's was a horizontal rather than a vertical conformism, yet it did not eventuate—as Arendt's previous theory about Europe would have suggested—in totalitarianism but co-existed with political freedom.

America thus at first offered Arendt a great reassurance: it might be bland, monotonous, puritanical, and *ungeistig*, but politically it was truly the land of the free. This must have seemed all the more striking given New Deal social policies and the engagement of American troops for freedom and democracy against the Axis powers. In the 1946 letter to Jaspers, Arendt observed that "the fundamental contradiction of this land is the coexistence of political freedom with social servitude."[8] In the late 1940s, when European intellectuals, particularly of the left, began to see America in a more critical light, as an arrogant nuclear bully siding with its European allies against emerging independence movements in their colonies, Arendt defended her new homeland. Europeans, she thought, misled by the country's social conventionality, failed to see the power of its political freedom. They did not understand its "fundamental contradiction."

The mid-1950s, however, were bound to call into question such a sunny view of America. It was increasingly apparent that the gigantic, centralized administrative machinery created for pursuing the war mostly would not be dismantled but instead was crystallizing into what President Eisenhower was soon to call the "military-industrial complex." The Cold War abroad was accompanied at home by witch-hunts against those labeled un-American, disloyal, red, or radical. By 1949 these manifestations of hysteria were reminding Arendt of conditions she had seen before, in Germany. In June of that year she wrote to Jaspers that although "American foreign policy is really excellent," the general domestic political atmosphere was alarming: "the red scare is in full swing."[9]

After passage of the McCarran-Walters Act of 1952, Arendt and her husband worried that he might be deported at any time if the government learned of his former connection with the Communist Party.[10] After Senator Joseph McCarthy of Wisconsin was reelected by a wide margin and began making widely publicized charges of disloyalty in the State Department and other federal agencies, Arendt reported to Jaspers "how far the disintegration has gone and with what breathtaking speed it is advancing." All opposition to the anticommunist hysteria, she said, was melting away "like butter in the sun." Explaining how congressional committees manipulated the Fifth Amendment privilege against self-incrimination to trap subpoenaed witnesses, Arendt said that invoking the privilege now carried a "social . . . presumption of guilt." Thus wherever the congressional committees "do not stick their dirty noses themselves, an extraordinarily effective self-censorship takes place," in which editors, employers, or faculty quietly "purge" their own organizations of any suspected radicals. "In this way the informer system is carried into society" through a spreading witch-hunt. Ultimately "everyone really censors himself. It all happens without any force, without any terror."[11] Arendt warned Jaspers that "it is no longer possible, as it still was only a few years ago, to stand up for America without any reservations, as we both did. Naturally that does not mean that one may join in the European chorus of anti-Americanism. But the dangers are clear, *clear and present.*"[12] Arendt's concern about the threat to political freedom resulting from the domestic Cold War, in other words, was beginning to complicate her vision of America.

By the following summer, however, Arendt began to see some encouraging signs of resistance to McCarthy, and the worst danger seemed to be over. Having lectured in 1953 at Princeton on America and Europe, Arendt published a series of three articles on this topic in September 1954, once more defending America against European skeptics.[13] Europeans, she wrote, worry too much about America's conformist witch-hunting and its nuclear technology. Although it is true that these two issues— "the political organization of mass societies and the political integration of technical power"—are now "the world's central problems," nevertheless European fears are based on a misperception. "America has, of course, a much longer experience with conformism than Europe," having been a mass rather than a class society from early on, and Europeans have worried, at least since "Tocqueville's insight" into the power of public opinion, that "under conditions of majority rule, society itself would be the oppressor, with no room left for individual freedom." Yet this supposed danger has never materialized, thanks to "the specifically American safeguards": the Constitution with its Bill of Rights and the country's functioning political institutions.[14]

Throughout these letters and essays Arendt still construes the danger as totalitarianism, speaks of "fascism," and repeatedly stresses to Jaspers—obviously because it is counterintuitive for both of them—that these developments in America do not involve anti-Semitism. On the contrary, Jews are playing an "outstanding" role among the witch-hunters.[15] Yet Arendt also sees that the danger takes another form here than it did in Europe. By the fall of 1954, she explains retrospectively that what she had really feared in McCarthyism was not an exact replication of Naziism but something unprecedented: "totalitarian developments out of the lap of society, of mass society itself, without any 'movement' and without any set ideology."[16] A year earlier she had already remarked to Jaspers about developments in America: "One might say that society is doing in the republic."[17] Insofar as *that* was the danger, it did not end with the fall of Senator McCarthy.

Arendt discusses the McCarthy phenomenon one last time in a letter to Jaspers months after the senator's fall from power, breathing a great, joyous sigh of relief: "The political tradition of this land has prevailed once again, and we—God be thanked and praised—were wrong." She also calls the sudden collapse of McCarthy's power "one of the most interesting and also most uncanny phenomena known to me under the heading 'public opinion,'" adding, "only Tocqueville had the slightest inkling of this story."[18] What exactly Arendt intends by the phrase "this story," whether merely McCarthy's astonishing rise to power or also (or exclusively) his decline thanks to "the political tradition of this land," is not entirely clear. Context suggests that she means the latter, in which case her image of Tocqueville may have shifted between her 1954 articles and this 1955 letter. Whereas before he was one of those Europeans who mistakenly worry about American social conformism, he is now the only thinker who even suspected the capacity of America's "political freedom" for overcoming that threat. Tocqueville was, of course, both these things, and in the period when she was writing *The Human Condition,* Arendt seems to have looked at this country increasingly through Tocquevillian lenses, a matter to be investigated in the next chapter.

The Jewish State

But America was not Arendt's only concern in this period, nor was Tocqueville the only intellectual influence on her ideas. She continued also to be preoccupied with the fate of the Jews, her own people, who in this period had acquired a homeland in Palestine, which in May 1948 became the state of Israel. Here, too, initial hopes for great possibilities gave way in the 1950s, for Arendt, to disappointment and increasing concern.

In her New York essays Arendt favored a separate Jewish contingent in the Allied armies and a Jewish homeland in Palestine, hoping that they might bring about a new Jewish identity and, as Young-Bruehl says, "the beginning of a political life for the Jewish people."[19] Having an army of their own and a state for which they were responsible as citizens might rid the Jews of their proclivity to parvenu subservience, might make them self-reliant, might end their childish hope for "some big brother [to] come along" and save them, and might allow them to choose and constitute their unity instead of being "a group of people held together by a common enemy."[20]

Accordingly, Arendt resolutely opposed identifying the new state exclusively with any national or ethnic group; it must be a polity in which all related as equal citizens, whatever their biological, religious, or ethnic memberships. America could serve as a model.[21] We saw that Arendt warned during the war that a formerly pariah people obtaining territory and power might inflict new pariahdoms on others. Now she insisted that peace in the Middle East could not be "imposed from the outside" but could be the result only of direct "negotiations, of mutual compromise and eventual agreement between Jews and Arabs."[22] Only direct personal contact and joint engagement on concrete issues could overcome the abstract mutual stereotyping that aligned Jews against Arabs in two hostile camps. Without such cooperation, "the whole Jewish venture in Palestine is doomed," she wrote, and consequently the "only realistic political measures" for the new state to take would be ones instituting "local self-government and mixed Jewish-Arab municipal and rural councils, on a small scale and as numerous as possible" (186, 192). Such active, face-to-face local interaction might then undergird some form of federation at the national or regional level, the only alternative to a hopeless "Balkanization" of the area (161, 191, 217, 221–22). In 1948 Arendt also still hoped that the kibbutz, the Jewish collective farm, might model for the world "a new form of ownership, a new type of farmer, a new way of family life and child education, and new approaches to troublesome conflicts between city and country, between rural and industrial labor" (185). In the prospect of Arab-Jewish cooperation she even saw the potential for a "new concept of man" that might demonstrate decent human relations for a "constantly shrinking world which we are bound to share with peoples whose histories and traditions" differ radically from our own.[23]

What Arendt envisioned did not come to pass. She watched in dismay as tensions between Jews and Arabs increased, while "terrorism and the growth of totalitarian methods [were] silently tolerated and secretly applauded."[24] Seeing the underlying structural sources of these tensions, Arendt nevertheless insisted that wrong political choices had permitted the structural developments. Jews and Arabs in Israel failed to recognize and treat each other as fellow human beings, she wrote in 1950, primarily because the two groups lived structurally separate lives, functioning in almost completely distinct economic and social systems. The Arab economy remained backward and poor, while the Jewish economy prospered. This was not deliberate policy, but it was economic fact; not political, therefore, but rather "the social aspect of Jewish-Arab relationships." Yet this seemingly inevitable "social" fact was itself the result of policy, or rather of a failure to enact policy. It was, after all, "no accident that Zionist officials had allowed this economic trend to take its course," rather than making Arab-Jewish cooperation and interaction "the chief objective of major policy," as Judah L. Magnes, for one, had recommended (203). As a result, "the solution of the Jewish question merely produced a new category of refugees, the Arabs."[25]

Not only were the former pariahs creating a new internal pariahdom, but in the Cold War international context of nuclear confrontation, the very survival of human life on earth seemed to be at stake in their policies. In late 1956, when the Israeli Sinai campaign precipitated French and British bombing of the Suez Canal, Arendt worried whether "we Americans" might get involved, and feared that "the Third World War" might really be "at the door."[26]

Thus, while America suggested both new dangers in parvenu conformism and a new importance for political action in forestalling those dangers, events in the Middle East were demonstrating the inadequacy of simple, unspecified activism. Merely mobilizing inert, deferential parvenus into action—any action, at any price—clearly would not suffice, not only because their success in seizing power was no guarantee of better policies, but also because in the age of nuclear weapons the wrong forms of activism might endanger inherited civilization and even the earth itself. The need to clarify just *what sort* of activism was called for must have seemed increasingly urgent to Arendt. In June 1949 she wrote in a note to David Riesman, "If we can blow up the world, it means that God has created us as guardians of it" (255). As her book began to take shape, she initially intended to call it *Amor Mundi,* love of the world (324). The phrase was clearly meant to contrast with the philosopher's traditional rejection of earthly concerns, *contemptus mundi,* and it may also contain an echo of Nietzsche's *amor fati;* but, as Arendt wrote to Jaspers in 1955, she also chose this title "out of gratitude," because she herself had "begun truly to love the world so late, actually only in recent years."[27] What exactly she meant by this remark is not clear, but the letter is the same one in which she breathed her final sigh of relief about McCarthy's fall from power. It seems likely that concern about the new, post-totalitarian danger in a context of potential nuclear war sharpened Arendt's awareness of how precious and how fragile are human civilization and life on earth. The modern world, she wrote in *The Human Condition*, "was born with the first atomic explosions."[28]

The Resistance in Retrospect

Similar concerns and similar disappointments in the postwar world were also being articulated in these years in the third theater of Arendt's personal involvement: Europe. French intellectuals of the left, in particular, were trying to come to terms with the disappointing Fourth Republic, product of the wartime resistance struggles and the liberation yet so distressingly similar to the despised Third Republic, which had collapsed in the face of the Nazi invasion. Despite all the wartime sacrifice, postwar France remained a deeply divided society, the many French sympathizers with Nazi policies having by no means vanished with the German defeat. Once more the country had a vacuous, factional parliament and an elitist, bureaucratic civil service. Nothing had changed; nothing positive had been accomplished.

France remained of special concern to Arendt as the land where she had spent the first eight years of her exile, been interned, escaped, and lived illegally. It was the only country for which she sometimes felt homesick in America.[29] What the intellectual ferment on the French left meant to Arendt in the period in which she was working on *The Human Condition* can best be captured—at the risk of some anachronistic distortion—by reaching ahead two or three years to the preface of *Between Past and Future*, a collection of essays she wrote between 1954 and 1961.[30]

That preface addresses in retrospect "what four years of the *résistance* had come to mean to a whole generation of European writers and men of letters," but also, I suggest, to Arendt, who identified with them.[31] Looking back on their wartime resistance activities from the mundane and disappointing postwar scene, these French intellectuals felt not only that an opportunity had been missed but also that something valuable had existed and then been lost, that in some obscure way things had been *better* in those terrible years of Nazi occupation. In the resistance experience there had been a special clarity and commitment, a special companionship and dignity, a kind of freedom.[32] Yet one could hardly wish for a return of the occupation and the war, with all their ghastly costs.

Arendt herself felt some of this same, paradoxical and unacceptable nostalgia for the wartime years. Looking back on them later she said that things had been "occasionally a little difficult, we were very poor, we were persecuted, one had to flee, and one had to swindle one's way through and whatever—that's just the way things were. But we were young. For me it was even a little fun at times. I couldn't put it any other way." But she immediately added that of course she did not mean the genocide, the death camps; *those* were another matter, "completely different. Personally, one could deal with everything else," but not with that. That was something to which "none of us will ever be able to reconcile ourselves," which "should never have been allowed to happen."[33] As in 1933, when the facts of life hit Arendt over the head and called her to her own attention, what was unendurable was the suffering of others. Thus nostalgia for the challenging adventures, for the "fun" of the wartime years must not be allowed even for a moment to become a wish for their actual return. On the contrary, the terrible costs paid by others had yet to be justified by transformations in the world for which one had hoped in those years but which had not been realized.

In the preface to *Between Past and Future* Arendt writes that to previously apolitical French intellectuals, the "totally unexpected" collapse of France before the German invasion "had emptied, from one day to the next, the political scene of their country, leaving it to the puppet-like antics of knaves and fools." These intellectuals now found themselves joining the Resistance, "sucked into politics as though with the force of a vacuum." In that way, these hitherto apolitical people, "without premonition and probably against their conscious inclinations, . . . had come to constitute willy-nilly a public realm where—without the paraphernalia of officialdom and hidden from the eyes of friend and foe—all relevant business in the affairs of the country was transacted in deed and word."[34] That Arendt might construe this mobilization of previously private intellectuals into organized action as analogous to the transformation of parvenus and abstracted romantics into conscious pariahs is not surprising. What is, however, startling and therefore illuminating in this passage is that she should construe the Resistance as a "public realm." What could be less public than a clandestine resistance organization, "hidden from the eyes of friend and foe"? Even the members may not know each other as such, lest they betray others if captured and tortured. Clearly, what prompts Arendt to call the Resistance a public realm must be the goals or principles that motivated the members, their serious commitment to the cause of France, of justice, of freedom, of self-government, thus to the real "affairs of the country," so ignominiously abandoned by the official politicians.

At the time, the members thought of the need to resist as an unfortunate "burden" that they had to take up. But the enterprise "did not last long," and only after it had ended did they realize that it had briefly given them something of inestimable value, something they could not even identify. Arendt quotes from a prescient essay by the poet and Resistance member René Char that speaks of a "lost treasure." With the return to normalcy after the war, Char says, former members of the Resistance were "thrown back into what they now knew to be the weightless irrelevance of their personal affairs, once more separated from 'the world of reality' by an *épaisseur triste,* the 'sad opaqueness' of a private life centered about nothing but itself." At the same time, Arendt adds, they saw the country's public life, for which they had temporarily made themselves responsible, revert "to the old empty strife of conflicting ideologies which after the defeat of the common enemy once more occupied the political arena to split the former comrades-in-arms into innumerable cliques which were not even factions and to engage them in the endless polemics and intrigues of a paper war" (4).

The members of the Resistance were "neither the first nor the last" to have experienced this retrospective sense of loss after a period of difficult, dangerous engagement in public life. Indeed, "the history of revolutions[,] . . . which politically spells out the innermost story of the modern age, could be told in parable form as the tale of an age-old treasure which, under the most varied circumstances, appears abruptly, unexpectedly, and disappears again, under different mysterious conditions, as though it were a fata morgana" (4–5).

This lost treasure of the Resistance has "as it were, . . . two interconnected parts." First, someone who shed his private preoccupations or apathy to join the Resistance discovered—again quoting Char—"that he who 'joined the Resistance, *found* himself,' . . . that he could afford 'to go naked' . . . stripped of all masks—of those which society assigns to its members as well as those which the individual fabricates for himself in his psychological reactions against society" (4). Again this metaphor of stripping off masks may seem surprising in connection with this most clandestine of organizations, but it should not be. Like Rahel Varnhagen at the end of her life or even in her brief, happy interlude in Paris, like the refugee who stops pretending that all is well, parvenus who accept their pariah status gain new awareness of who they really are, not because some public now recognizes a different, truer image of them but precisely because they stop depending on other people's perceptions of them and instead regain contact with their own capacity to experience and to judge.

Joining the Resistance meant taking on a new and far more serious secretiveness than any the members had previously known—and new pretenses—but taking them on knowingly, without self-deception. In the process, those who joined discovered, like Rahel Varnhagen, that a thousand things they had previously considered vital no longer mattered to them, could now be seen never really to have mattered. A thousand earlier constraints and anxieties vanished. Precisely as they took on a new double life, they escaped the psychic ambiguities of a parvenu's inner striving and discovered their true selves in action. They knew that discovery to be of the true self both because, being clandestine, that self could not have been assumed for mere show, and because, its role being lethally dangerous, it could not be hypocritically self-serving. Even if initially adopted in a hypocritical pretense of heroism, the new role would soon be cashed out in action.[35] The courage and integrity revealed in resistance action, moreover, were quite independent of whether the action proved "successful," for against a military occupation very few resistance actions will in fact succeed. They do have practical purpose, of course, but the deed itself must suffice; it reveals (if only to oneself) a true self that is better and braver than one had ever supposed. That self-realization—both the making real and the becoming aware of one's true self—is the first "part" of the treasure possessed in the Resistance and lost in postwar normality.

Its second part, "interconnected" with the first, is that in their shared secret enterprise the members of the Resistance were "visited for the first time in their lives by an apparition of freedom." This was not just because they joined the fight against Nazi tyranny, since every soldier in the Allied armies was engaged in that fight without encountering any such apparition. Nor was it just the shedding of anxieties and pretenses that had previously constrained. Rather, it was because, in joining the Resistance, people began to *act* on their true beliefs, *created* their own organization for this purpose and consciously sustained it, willed and enacted their ties to each other. It was, Arendt says, "because they had become 'challengers,' had taken the initiative upon themselves and therefore, without knowing or even noticing it, had begun to create that public space between themselves where freedom could appear."[36]

Again, Arendt uses the surprising adjective "public," this time suggesting not merely the principled commitment to France and the liberties of fellow citizens but also the capacity to form and change one's institutional ties, taking charge of one's commitments to others. In organizing, the resisters actively created a new web of relationships, thereby realizing in a practical way their freedom to initiate and to change institutions. Of course they were not free. Under military occupation, engaged in clandestine activities punishable by death and worse, they were about as unfree as people can get. And yet they had discovered their own capacities for action, for founding organizational ties, for looking after the affairs of a public that they were assuming, projecting, creating by their commitment. Those are the elements, the prerequisites of freedom. Arendt quotes Char: "At every meal that we eat together, freedom is invited to sit down. The chair remains vacant, but the place is set."[37] In a 1960 essay, she even says that their self-organizing initiative on behalf of a projected self-governing public *itself was* freedom—the "freedom of Brutus: 'that *this shall be* or we will fall for it.' "[38]

In one sense, then, the members of the Resistance had experienced freedom and now missed it. In another sense, the whole Resistance enterprise had been only a means toward the goal of freedom. The terrible sacrifices—especially the burden of guilt entailed in the sacrifices made by *others* to whom one was committed—could be justified only in retrospect, by actually achieving in the postwar world the goals that the Resistance had projected. At the close of the war, left-wing and populist members of the Resistance formed groups such as *Mouvement de Libération Nationale* and *Libérer et Fédérer*, striving to reorganize France on the basis of local, participatory councils loosely linked in federation. Arendt, in New York, moved among intellectuals who followed these developments with intense interest, as Gregory D. Sumner has recently documented.[39] But by the time she began work toward *The Human Condition*, most such former members of the Resistance felt not hope but a sense of profound failure and loss: the intense awareness of personal freedom had vanished with the return to normalcy, and the goal of a freer and more just France—let alone a freer, more peaceful, and more just world—had not been achieved.[40] Having lost their treasure, the former fighters against Nazi oppression now had to face, as Arendt wrote in 1954, the "ominous silence that still answers us whenever we dare to ask, not 'What are we fighting *against*?' but 'What are we fighting *for*?' "[41]

Why had the treasure of freedom—whether actually realized or only prepared in the Resistance—been lost in the postwar normalization of life, as it had been lost after each revolution of "the modern age"?

Was it, as there are "many good reasons to believe," because the treasure had never been real, but only "a mirage"? Arendt claims otherwise: it was lost because of "a failure of memory," not just on the part of those who came later, but even on the part of the participants themselves, "the actors, the witnesses, those who for a fleeting moment had held the treasure in the palms of their hands." The treasure "fell into oblivion" because—at least for us moderns—it lacks "a name."[42]

The Project of *The Human Condition*

Here was a task, then, for thought and writing, a task that became increasingly clear to Arendt as she reflected on postwar disappointments and dangers in America, in Israel, in Europe: How might one effectively "name" that lost treasure, capture it in words that could convey its reality to others who had forgotten or never experienced it? And how might one do this without the unthinkable expedient of creating once again—or even wishing back into existence—the horrible conditions of the Nazi occupation, without conjuring up another war that might destroy the earth? This, I suggest, became the project of *The Human Condition*: to articulate a general theory of free citizenship that would recapture the principled but tough-minded realism of the wartime Resistance without the dreadful, unacceptable costs that those years had entailed and without the external constraints on freedom that the occupation had imposed. What Arendt needed to write was not a better account of Soviet or Marxist totalitarianism but a sustained and serious exploration of the positive, "political" alternative to parvenu conformism and social process, an alternative to which she had been alluding since her earliest writings but which she had never yet articulated.

That task was difficult, for what had been so valuable in those troubled times seemed very much context-bound. Members of the Resistance, after all, had been a small group of self-selected volunteers, while a general theory of free citizenship would have to include everyone.[43] The central concern of the Resistance, second, had been *resisting*, opposing an enemy in power. A general theory of free citizenship would lack the unifying force exerted by such an enemy, and it must not conjure up a new one. Developments in Israel demonstrated the danger of creating new categories of pariahs, and the international Cold War together with nuclear weapons demonstrated the danger in postulating an external enemy. Arendt's new book, as its initially intended title suggests, would have to theorize a free citizenship that ruled out pariahdom and protected the world, caring for inherited human civilization and for the earth itself, "the Mother of all living creatures" and the "quintessence of the human condition."[44] Citizenship would have to mean taking responsibility for this care as the Resistance had taken responsibility for France, so ignominiously abandoned by the "knaves and fools" officially in charge, except that a general theory of free citizenship would have to apply to all, including knaves and fools as well as pariahs.

The Resistance, third, had arisen in response to an emergency that created nearly intolerable conditions, in which life could not continue as usual in any case. A general theory of political freedom would have to engage the mundane, everyday concerns of ordinary people. How could it possibly recreate the sense of high purpose and meaning, the intensity of commitment, the heroic companionship in danger of the Resistance? Or, lacking these, how could it nevertheless offer citizens the self-discovery that the Resistance had provided, even while they remain immersed in precisely such mundane, everyday concerns?

Fourth, not only the special intensity but also the special simplicity created by enemy occupation would be lacking to a general theory of free citizenship. It would no longer be easy to separate the Good Guys from the Bad Guys, nor to overcome the ambiguities involved in ruthlessness toward the latter. The single, overriding goal of getting rid of the occupying enemy would be lacking. A general theory of free citizenship would have to address a context of multiple, conflicting goals and allow for a variety of conflicting perspectives and interests. It would have to engage precisely the divisive question—"What [were] we fighting *for*?"—that had previously been hidden behind the desperate agreement on what one was fighting against. None of this is meant to suggest that either during the war or afterwards, contemplating the Resistance experience, Arendt's thinking was binary or Manichaean, denying the humanity of collaborators, appeasers, or the Nazis themselves.[45] But during the war and in writing *The Origins* Arendt had not felt required to articulate a vision of free politics that might contain Nazis and Jews as fellow citizens. Now, gradually, she did.

Young-Bruehl is brilliantly right, therefore, to choose as the epigraph for the chapter on this period in Arendt's life a stanza from a poem by Bertold Brecht that itself dates from this postwar era of disillusionment:

Die Mühen der Gebirge liegen hinter uns
Vor uns liegen die Mühen der Ebenen.

[The hardships of the mountains lie behind us
Before us lie the hardships of the plains.][46]

As the *maquis* of the Resistance took to the mountains between forays, so the entire period of the Nazi occupation could be seen as a time of heroic, "high-profile" politics, costly in the extreme but drawing people out of their apathy and their superficial daily concerns. A general theory of ongoing free citizenship would have to suit people's everyday concerns, their ordinary, low-profile interests and conflicts, without succumbing to triviality, apathy, or privatization. What was needed was a vision of "normal," ongoing, ordinary politics that was not really normal or ordinary: not in accord with the now conventional understanding of politics, nor like the now ordinary practice of politics—petty, banal, and quotidian. The commitment and power of resistance had to be transferred into normal politics so that the amalgam became more than resistance and more than normal.[47]

Paradoxical as that requirement might seem, it was not beyond possibility, since there was a grave new post-totalitarian danger to be resisted, and politics rightly understood was the only effective way to resist it. The very flatness of the quotidian "plains" constituted the new danger to freedom, but an invisible, insidious danger, which no one recognized as such. Flattened into invisibility, this new danger would have to be revealed in high relief by a theory of free citizenship if such a theory hoped to succeed. And so, articulating a vision of free politics would also require an account of what stood in its way—the social.

In order to articulate such a vision and provide such an account, finally, out of the chaotic complexities of *The Origins* and in relation to the world's current situation, Arendt would have to risk a level of generality and abstraction that she perceived as dangerous, not just to herself personally but also to precisely the enterprise of recovering the lost treasure. She would have to find a mode of political theorizing sufficiently abstract or philosophical to provide a coherent overview and the perspective of distance, escaping the characteristic blindnesses of the time, yet sufficiently concrete and in touch with ordinary human reality that it did not also abstract away human agency, the capacity for freedom.

SEVEN

Absent Authorities: Tocqueville and Marx

In addition to what was going on politically while Arendt began work on what would become *The Human Condition*, two important intellectual influences seem to have been shaping her thought. "Seem to," because these influences—authorities of a sort for Arendt—were never acknowledged as such publicly by her. Though she often referred to and quoted great thinkers of the past, Arendt rarely acknowledged any major sources of her own ideas. Being neither an academic critic commenting on the great texts nor a historian of ideas in the usual sense, she mostly spoke in her own voice about the substantive issues. Yet there were authorities hidden behind that voice; it was not unproblematically her own, for her relationship to those authorities was deeply ambivalent. That this was so in relation to Heidegger we have already seen, and the issue has received detailed attention in recent scholarship.[1] Two other great thinkers from the tradition of political theory, however, seem to have decisively shaped her ideas in this period, though in different ways: Alexis de Tocqueville and Karl Marx.

Tocqueville's influence can only be surmised as extremely likely in light of the striking parallels between *The Human Condition* and his *Democracy in America,* but it cannot be established with certainty, since Arendt never publicly acknowledged his importance to her. Marx, by contrast, plays a prominent role in *The Human Condition,* which is not surprising, since the book was initially to be a study of his contribution to totalitarianism. Marx appears in the book almost exclusively as the object of Arendt's severe criticism, but there is something odd about that criticism. Although its overall thrust may well be valid and is surely defensible, its detailed formulations are almost always mistaken, sometimes blatantly so. Arendt's account of Marx, moreover, leaves out about half of that admittedly inconsistent thinker, and what is missing from her Marx remarkably resembles Arendt's own ideas in *The Human Condition,* particularly those about the social. Indeed, what makes Arendt's hidden intellectual debts important for this study at all is the extent to which they occur in the very terrain occupied by the social as Blob.

Begin with Tocqueville. Arendt's debt to Tocqueville will strike a careful reader as very extensive, and in a 1959 letter she mentions his "great influence" on her work.[2] Yet she never publicly acknowledged that debt nor discussed Tocqueville's ideas systematically, citing him only rarely. Nor do we know when Arendt first read *Democracy in America*. Others of Tocqueville's works are occasionally cited in *The Origins of Totalitarianism*, but the first mention of *Democracy* is in Arendt's 1953 lectures on America.[3] Did she read the book as part of her European formal education, or perhaps in the last idle weeks in France while waiting for an American visa, so that Tocqueville from the outset shaped her expectations about this land? Or did she encounter his impressions of America only after forming her own, and find them strikingly parallel?

All we know is that twice in the 1950s Arendt mentioned Tocqueville's view of the danger to political freedom in America that social conformism might become. The first time, she classed him as one of the Europeans overly worried about that danger; the second time, she hailed him as the only European thinker who had had any inkling of the resilience of American political freedom.

Tocqueville on Democracy

Tocqueville was, of course, both those things. As Arendt began to systematize her ideas about society and the parvenu, on the one hand, and politics and the conscious pariah, on the other, Tocqueville's simultaneous fears and hopes for America may have helped to crystallize her thinking into a dichotomous form. In the process, *Democracy in America* may also have pushed her to elaborate her image of totalitarianism as Blob and transfer it to the social, since Tocqueville himself envisaged the dangerous alternative precisely in such ways.

In America, Tocqueville said, he saw "more than America." He sought "lessons" from which Europeans "might profit," because America was pioneering the path that Europe must also take, a path toward increasing "democracy," by which Tocqueville meant not so much a form of government as a "social state," a "great social revolution" that involved both an increasing "equality of conditions" and a consuming passion for such equality.[4] About this coming equality there was no choice; it had to be accepted as "irresistible," "fated," "imposed by Providence."[5] But there was a choice about what political institutions would accompany this democratic social condition, and that was the choice Tocqueville hoped to guide by the lesson learned from America.⁶ His standard for the right choice, his passion, and his cause was *liberté*—freedom, or liberty—which he saw as both threatened and promoted by the advancing social equality. His aim therefore was to warn against the former tendency and stimulate the latter.⁷ The two futures he imagined awaiting respectively the nations that chose badly or well strikingly resemble Arendt's vision of the new, post-totalitarian social danger and its still only vaguely defined political alternative.

On the one hand, Tocqueville thought, social equality makes people confident, independent, active, and self-reliant, even rebellious and intractable. On the other hand, that independence can all too easily become a debilitating isolation and privatization that leaves people weak, helpless, indifferent to others and to long-range concerns, and therefore apathetic. The first tendency "leads men directly to independence," the other, by a more "roundabout and secret but also more certain" route, to "servitude."⁸ Both tendencies were powerfully at work in America. For Tocqueville's reader, the inherently difficult task of distinguishing them is made harder both by the rich, diverse detail of his book and by its formulation in two installments, the first volume appearing five years before the second. Those years were eventful in Tocqueville's life, and they altered his views in ways of which he himself does not seem to have been fully aware.⁹

Tocqueville found Americans a very independent and a very political people, full of energy and initiative, and irreverently skeptical of traditional authority. The American "trusts fearlessly in his own powers."¹⁰ Frontier conditions have accustomed him not only to autonomous action but also to cooperation, and particularly to initiative in forming new cooperative relationships wherever they are needed, what Tocqueville calls "the art of being free" or "the art of association."¹¹ Americans are a nation of joiners, "forever forming associations"; they readily get together to take care of whatever needs doing, rather than waiting for some authority to provide.¹² Accordingly, they are also a highly political people, an active rather than a merely obedient or deferential citizenry. The political activity prevailing in the United States is so extensive and enthusiastic that a European must see it to believe it. In a passage likely to astonish the contemporary American reader, Tocqueville says that taking a hand in politics and discussing public affairs are the American's "most important business and, so to say, the only pleasure he knows"; if an American were "reduced" to occupying himself exclusively with his private affairs, that would mean "half his existence [had been] snatched from him; he would feel it as a vast void in his life and would become incredibly unhappy" (243).

At the same time Tocqueville also sees in American society an intense pressure toward conformity, which not only keeps men of distinction from gaining power but nearly prevents men of distinction from developing at all (197–99, 57). In the first volume of *Democracy*, this leveling social pressure takes two forms. Tocqueville finds it in the "immense," almost irresistible power of the majority of citizens acting through the democratic political institutions against minorities, exercising the "tyranny of the majority" (248, 257). He also finds it in the majority's informal, extralegal power of public opinion, which is "almost as great," because enforced by "all kinds of unpleasantness and everyday persecution." The latter power in America is stronger than any despot in Europe, for it is internalized: "it leaves the body alone and goes straight for the soul." As a result, despite America's constitutional guarantees, Tocqueville knows of no country where "there is less independence of mind and true freedom of discussion than in America" (248, 254–55).

In volume 1, on the whole, the danger Tocqueville foresees is that this "omnipotence of the majority," exercised primarily through government but also by controlling thought, may crush the *liberté* of minorities and individuals (246, 248, 253). Accordingly, the remedies he invokes, and to which he attributes America's continuing *liberté*, are devices that check, restrain, divide, and reduce majority power, damp down political passion, and distract people from politics. They include institutional checks and balances, federalism, autonomous local institutions that can resist central power "like so many hidden reefs retarding or dividing the flood of the popular will," indirect elections, the extensive territory and the absence of large cities, deferential respect for courts and lawyers as well as for the authority of religion, and finally, the Americans' zealous pursuit of wealth, which both draws them away from intense political engagement and makes them value stability, as they see "order and property linked together and marching in step."[13]

In volume 2, however, Tocqueville says that the intervening five years "have not lessened [his] fears but have changed their object."[14] The danger he now fears has no name as yet, being a "type of oppression ... different from anything there has ever been in the world before." It is oppression without an oppressor, despotism without a despot, tyranny without a tyrant, so that the available terms do not fit it. For lack of a better name, Tocqueville calls it "democratic despotism" or "administrative despotism."[15]

He envisions democratic despotism as "more widespread and milder" than past oppressions, tending to "degrade men rather than torment them."[16] It involves "an innumerable multitude of men, alike and equal," but without relationships and incapable of forming any (691–92). "Each one of them, withdrawn into himself, is almost unaware of the fate of the rest," so that "each citizen drawing separately aside, the fabric of society must fall into dust" (692, 667). Being thus "isolated and weak," people ultimately become totally apathetic.[17] Tocqueville imagines this condition as imposed on them by a stifling, benevolent, administrative government, "an immense tutelary power which is . . . absolute, thoughtful of detail, orderly, provident, and gentle." This power is "not at all tyrannical" but merely "hinders, restrains, enervates, stifles, and stultifies," and it "covers the whole of social life with a network of petty, complicated rules that are both minute and uniform."[18] After a time, the habits formed by continual subjection to such paltry rules lead people "to give up using their free will"; thus the tutelary power "robs each citizen of the proper use of his own faculties," until all cease being human and become "a flock of timid and hardworking animals with the government as its shepherd" (694–95, 692).

Although Tocqueville imagines this condition imposed on people by a "government," which takes "each citizen in turn in its powerful grasp and shape[s] him to its will," he also foresees an ultimate condition in which force is no longer used and no one is in command, because entropy has overcome all (692). Each obediently lets himself be collared because "he sees that it is not a person, or a class of persons, but society itself which holds the end of the chain."[19] Such an "orderly, gentle, peaceful slavery . . . could be combined, more easily than is generally supposed, with some of the external forms of *liberté*," including regular elections and "the shadow of the sovereignty of the people." At that point, in a sense, there are no people left; the remaining beings will still be active, like sheep or insects, in "trivial, lonely, futile" ways, but despite all the "constant agitation," Tocqueville fears, "humanity will make no advance."[20]

This is a very different nightmare from the "tyranny of the majority," for that phrase suggests opposing views on some public issue, a struggle, energy, a clash of wills. The new danger is one of entropy and drift. Fear of majority opinion and informal social pressure appears in both volumes, but in volume 1 Tocqueville still construes that danger as a majority threat to minorities or individuals. Anxiety about a more diffuse "public opinion" is found only in volume 2, and democratic despotism is associated not with any majority but with "the mass," and in the end the "immense protective power" that grasps and shapes each individual is no actual government, leader, party, or group but "society itself."[21] Tocqueville also speaks of this smothering power as resembling a monstrous parent that keeps its children permanently infantilized: "It would resemble parental authority if, father-like, it tried to prepare its charges for a man's life, but on the contrary, it only tries to keep them in perpetual childhood" (692). He does not consider whether, failing to be fatherlike, this monstrous power might in some sense be motherlike, might express some nightmare fantasy of maternal engulfment, though he does speak of public opinion that reflects "the mass" as "becom[ing] *mistress* of the world," a topic to be considered further in the next chapter (435, my emphasis).

By the time he composes volume 2 of *Democracy*, Tocqueville's "chief aim in writing" is to combat this new danger (671). How greatly it differs from the dangers he feared in volume 1 is best seen from the stunning shifts—often reversals—in the remedies he proposes. The new danger being entropy, Tocqueville holds that "there is only one effective remedy" against it, "and that is political *liberté*."[22] Accordingly, instead of checks and balances, barriers against power, and elections kept as indirect as possible, Tocqueville now favors popular empowerment and active, direct political participation. He still praises localism, but now because it draws people into active public life and mobilizes them politically, rather than because it is a "reef" against "the flood of the popular will."[23] He still regards religion as essential to *liberté*, but now because it promotes energetic action and calls men to engage with "the greatest problems of human destiny," rather than because it makes them obedient and orderly (444). As to the privatizing passion for money-making, which in volume 1 usefully distracted people from politics, replacing "ambition for power" with the "more vulgar but less dangerous passion" for "well-being," in volume 2 the latter has become "a breathless cupidity" that leads not so much to "forbidden delights" as to a "decent materialism . . . [tending to] soften and imperceptibly [to] loosen the springs of action." Accordingly, Tocqueville now warns legislators not to encourage this "fatal tendency" in hopes of "divert[ing] the citizens' attention from political passions," lest the tendency destroy both democracy and *liberté*.[24]

As a further corollary, Tocqueville now distinguishes among types of associations in a new way: Americans may be a nation of joiners, but some memberships distract from politics and enervate, while others promote citizenship and *liberté*. Actually, Tocqueville's interest in the power of association and the contrasting helplessness of individuals (no matter how numerous) who are isolated antedates even volume 1, appearing in his joint study, with Gustave de Beaumont, of the American penal system. In the penitentiaries of New York the two Frenchmen found prisoners locked in separate cells at night but required to work together in the daytime, "subjected to the law of rigorous silence," so that "their union in the workshops" had "nothing dangerous" about it.[25] This was particularly evident at Sing Sing, where "nine hundred criminals, watched by thirty keepers, work free in the midst of an open field," without chains. The guards easily control the prisoners who vastly outnumber them because the guards "communicate freely with each other, act in concert, and have all the power of association; while the convicts separated from each other by silence, have, in spite of their numerical force, all the weakness of isolation."[26] The administrative despotism that Tocqueville fears in volume 2, one might say, is a society composed entirely of such prisoners, no longer requiring any guards because they have internalized the prohibition against associative communication.

Association is power, but what matters for *liberté* is a certain kind of association. First, whereas European associations are internally hierarchical and confront each other like opposed armies, American associations are internally democratic, preserving "a place for individual independence" and requiring no "sacrifice" of each member's autonomous "will and reason."[27] That much is already in volume 1, where Tocqueville also remarks that participation in political affairs, particularly at the local level, gives the ordinary "man of the people" in America "a certain self-esteem," great "energy," and a "general taste for enterprise," which is then applied in economic entrepreneurship as well. But the participatory political role is still bestowed from above: the ordinary fellow is "*asked* to share in the task of governing" (244, my emphasis).

Volume 2 introduces further distinctions, as the issue is increasingly neither mere sociability nor mere energy but the capacity for joint self-government. Accordingly, the important kind of associations are those initiated from below, by the members, for only there do people realize their capacity for organizing new institutions and thus their responsibility for existing ones. Even in traditional aristocracies people are associated, and their relationships constitute power, but those relationships are given, not made: each aristocrat "is in practice head of a permanent and enforced association." In a democracy, people would "find themselves helpless if they did not learn to help each other voluntarily," and for this purpose, how to join together to form "associations of plain citizens" (514, 697). In a democracy, therefore, "knowledge of how to combine is the mother of all other forms of knowledge," and the "art of association" becomes central to *liberté* (516–17).

In addition Tocqueville now distinguished between "civil" and "political associations," in accord with his new doubts about the value of economic enterprise for *liberté*. In political associations people "combine for great ends . . . [concerning] important matters," whereas civil associations pursue "lesser affairs" (521). Thus political associations are like "great free schools to which all citizens come" not merely to learn how to combine but also to "acquire a general taste for association" and to become engaged in those "great and powerful public emotions" without which Tocqueville fears they will drift in "trivial, lonely, futile" private activity.[28] Political engagement may still promote economic enterprise as well, but Tocqueville no longer thinks this a good thing. Competitive acquisitiveness, even if pursued through associations, not only cannot teach or develop the taste for responsible, principled, public agency but actively draws people away from it.

This new stress on political associations as pursuing "great ends," however, also raises a new problem. Tocqueville has insisted all along that the art of being free can be practiced only in small, local, face-to-face settings of peer equality, but he now says that in order to accomplish "great ends" and thus provide participants the experience of principled personal efficacy, associations must be large. Only large associations can "make . . . plain" the "general value" of the art of being free, and thus overcome people's sense of isolation and impotence in a democratic society (521).

By the time he completed his second volume, then, Tocqueville was posing an increasingly sharp choice: there would come either something rather like Arendt's social—an innumerable multitude of isolated, apathetic animals who have been stripped "of the chief attributes of humanity" by "society itself"—or else political *liberté*, meaning widespread, active, vigorous, and engaged citizen participation in self-government, the "only . . . effective remedy" (693, 513). Indeed, America could serve as a model for Europe precisely because "the Americans have used *liberté* to combat the individualism born of equality, and they have won" (511).

Arendt and Tocqueville

This was Arendt's conclusion, too, as the immediate danger of McCarthyism receded. She shared both Tocqueville's enthusiasm for American political freedom and his nevertheless mounting fears about conformism and isolation in mass society. In the former respect, Tocqueville's influence may have encouraged and helped her to elaborate the healthy political alternative to parvenu conduct, now the only effective remedy for the danger of social power. Tocqueville's understanding of American *liberté* as conjoined with but overcoming social conformity, as rooted in New England Puritanism (like that whose remnants Arendt encountered in her early placement in an American household), as centered in active political participation, was wonderfully well suited to Arendt's need to elaborate the notion of the conscious pariah. Tocqueville's *Democracy* would have engaged Arendt's still largely implicit distinction between desirable individual autonomy and undesirable individual isolation; it involved the principled pursuit of "great ends," solidarity, public engagement, rather than the quest for competitive individual advantage as an exception; it stressed initiative and self-organization from below, which Arendt would have connected with the resistance experience; and it envisioned institutions that were local, small, and face-to-face, yet somehow combined through federalism into a large, diverse, and powerful nation, as Arendt had proposed for the Middle East.

Insofar as *The Human Condition* generalizes, develops, and improves on the notion of the conscious pariah, then, its debt to Tocqueville's *Democracy* seems enormous. To be sure, one could argue that Arendt did not borrow, or learn, enough from Tocqueville, that his insights are richer, his observations more detailed and circumstantial, his recommendations more nuanced and thoughtful than what she derived from them. But that is not to the point here. More important for our purposes is that Arendt seems to have acquired, along with Tocqueville's understanding of politics and *liberté*, some of the difficulties and dilemmas that plague his argument.

Most striking are the similarities between Tocqueville's nightmare vision of the tutelary power that is "society itself," problematic in a theorist of Tocqueville's activist, political persuasion in exactly the same way as Arendt's "the social" is in *The Human Condition*. Even before she wrote that book, of course, Arendt had not only contrasted active political engagement to the parvenu's "social" ways but herself envisaged totalitarianism as a Blob and anticipated an even more dangerous posttotalitarian threat. Since we do not know when she read Tocqueville's *Democracy*, the extent to which it merely confirmed tendencies in her own thinking or shaped and directed them cannot be determined.

The specific puzzle of Blob imagery in an otherwise demystifying and liberatory theory is, for both Arendt and Tocqueville, linked to a broader tension about the value and dangers of abstraction. Both sought ways of generalizing, of theorizing, that would do justice to human individuality, initiative, and politics. Both feared the tendency toward empty abstractions that hide the very possibility of political action, so that both of them sometimes seem to be their own best critics, warning against exactly what they themselves go on to do. The issue is difficult, and its extended discussion must be postponed to chapters 8 and 11. For now, note only that abstraction is another problem which Arendt shared with Tocqueville and which may either have drawn her to *Democracy in America* or heightened preexisting tensions in her own thought, or both.

More specifically, the tensions between large-scale historical or theoretical explanation, on the one hand, and individuality, action, and freedom, on the other, relate, for Tocqueville, to the problem of American exceptionalism and thus to the basic project of his book.[29] The more he succeeds in explaining what is special about America—what has enabled it to combine democracy with *liberté*—so that France may learn from its example, the less accessible that example seems for France, which is differently situated. Explanation, intended to serve intelligent action, is somehow at war with the very idea of action. Though Arendt's project is different from his, both are troubled about whether free politics has causal preconditions or is a perennial, unconditioned existential possibility. Most specifically, both face the difficult task of teaching *liberté*, or freedom, to people who have no experience of it and misunderstand the very idea. Praising its effects simply confounds the problem, since *liberté* cannot be understood as a means, but only as an end in itself: "whoever asks of *liberté* anything other than itself is born to be a slave."[30] In a later work, Arendt would quote this line from Tocqueville.[31]

There are still other tensions and problematic formulations that Arendt shares with Tocqueville's *Democracy* as well. If her elaboration of the conscious pariah into the theory of free citizenship in *The Human Condition* is indeed indebted to *Democracy*, then the debt is surely to the activist, participatory view of volume 2. But that view lives in an uneasy relationship of both interdependence and conflict with the more conservative and disciplinarian strictures of volume 1. In this respect, too, one can discern parallel difficulties in the two thinkers, for example, about the relationship between free politics and market economics or about the difference between liberty and license—the need for limits on the scope and substance of free political action.

The former topic is best reserved until we turn to Marx later in this chapter, but the problem of cautionary limits on freedom deserves some further attention here. Even in the activist volume 2, and certainly if one reads both volumes together and assumes their mutual coherence, Tocqueville surrounds his call for vigorous, widespread, assertive political contestation with a number of explicit restrictions and implicit limitations, as Mark Reinhardt has recently argued.[32]

Certain categories of people and certain kinds of issues had to be excluded if democracy was to be successfully combined with *liberté*. For Tocqueville, this was linked to the problematic issue of American exceptionalism, but the general notion that under certain circumstances free democratic politics cannot succeed, that certain issues are too divisive for it to handle, that it presupposes an underlying consensus on fundamentals, is familiar enough. Some of the specific limitations and exclusions by which Tocqueville makes safe his democratic activism are particularly interesting, however, if one imagines Arendt reading and reacting to *Democracy*.

Reinhardt argues that Tocqueville not only "greatly exaggerates the degree of material equality and cultural consensus in Jacksonian America" but makes democratic *liberté* dependent on such consensus specifically in religion, in gender relations, and in matters of "race," effectively placing all three beyond political contestation (60).

"Religious consensus does the most important work of containment" for Tocqueville, Reinhardt says, for *liberté* "cannot do without faith," specifically Christian faith (73–74). Tocqueville himself doubts whether people "can support complete religious independence and entire political *liberté* at the same time."[33] Not only does he trace American *liberté* back to New England Puritanism, but he insists that it still rests on an underlying moral consensus, indeed, on a consensual "great severity of mores" that limits Americans' boldness and initiative: "there are things which religion prevents them from imagining and forbids them to dare."[34] That religion is Christian. Although there are many diverse sects in America, "Christianity itself is an established and irreversible fact," beyond challenge.[35] The Christian consensus "imposes a salutary control" that allows Americans "to make good use of *liberté*" despite the "tumultuous agitation" of their politics (444, 434, 398).

Religion, in turn, is dependent on gender, for "it is the women who shape mores," not only by forming future citizens but also, crucially, in their role as wives. Tocqueville does not merely accept the exclusion of women from official public life that prevails in America and Europe but sees women's domestic submission as essential to American *liberté*. In Europe, he says, "almost all the disorders of society are born around the domestic hearth and not far from the nuptial bed. It is there that men . . . develop a taste for disorder, restlessness of spirit, and instability of desires." The American man, by contrast, comes home "from the turmoil of politics to the bosom of his family" to find there "a perfect picture of order and peace."[36] That order and peace, in turn, rest on the voluntary total submission of wives to their husbands. American girls, Tocqueville says, are educated like boys, so that the American woman "thinks for herself, speaks freely, and acts on her own" (590). She even takes an interest in politics and goes to public meetings (243). But on consenting to marry, she gives all that up and "loses her independence forever," leaving "her father's house," which has been "a home of *liberté* and pleasure," to enter that of her husband, which will be for her "almost a cloister" (592). Having been educated to think, moreover, she makes the choice with full awareness. Far from resenting men's "conjugal authority," American wives "seem to take pride in the free relinquishment of their will[s]," and they "boast" of having "freely accepted the yoke."[37]

Finally, the free and tumultuous politics Tocqueville saw in America also excluded issues of "race." Consigning the topic to a single, long chapter set apart from the rest of his argument, Tocqueville explained that race relations were mere "tangents to my subject," since the problem was "American, but not democratic," certainly not something for France to imitate (316). Though he greatly admired and respected "North American Indians" and reported having seen them suffering "afflictions beyond my powers to portray," Tocqueville suggested no remedy for those afflictions and regarded the destruction of the Indians as "inevitable" (324, 30). Similarly, though he was profoundly critical of American slavery, saw the "unprecedented atrocity" of slave laws in the South as contrary to "the order of nature," and thought the institution of slavery to be "in retreat," he regarded "race prejudice" as a "much more intangible and tenacious" problem, in fact, "immovable," since he himself took "race" to be a "physical and permanent fact."[38]

Thus, Reinhardt argues, Tocqueville effectively removed both slavery and "race relations" from the reach of practical, political confrontation, presenting these topics in a manner "oddly free of agents and struggles, as if there were no *politics* involved."³⁹ No doubt this results partly from the tension between explanation and action; Tocqueville's predictions about both minority "races" surely were prescient. Indeed, his presentation of certain issues as *unpolitical* and "fated" in America may have been part of his effort at *political* education of his own fellow citizens in France, for example, toward more egalitarian and liberal policies regarding women and marriage or toward more tolerant and less violent treatment of religion. For our purposes, however, what matters is this: if one imagines Arendt's encounter with Tocqueville's *Democracy*, whether in the 1950s or earlier, one cannot help but wonder what she, as a Jewish woman refugee from Nazi "race" policy, might have thought of the way the book tied free citizenship to a universally shared Christian faith and a Christian consensus on severe mores, of its excluding certain people and issues from political contestation on apparently biological grounds, and of its making *liberté* for men dependent on women's voluntary submission to a domestic "cloister" and exclusion from suffrage.

Someone who had read only Arendt's early works (and perhaps *The Origins*) might expect her to challenge Tocqueville on at least some of these themes in a book drawing on his ideas. That expectation would be foolish: she was not writing a book on Tocqueville, was not even acknowledging any positive debt to him; why should or how could she challenge him? The point, however, is that she herself was ambiguous and ambivalent on many if not all of these topics. On some, her ambivalences antedate *The Human Condition;* on others, they are evident for the first time in that book; on still others, earlier ambiguities have been developed and intensified. If Tocqueville's *Democracy* did indeed shape Arendt's transformation of her vague notion of conscious pariahdom into the conceptual constellation of action, politics, and freedom in *The Human Condition*, to what extent did she acquire along with this unacknowledged legacy certain theoretical difficulties that plagued her argument, notably our central concern: the social as Blob?

Marx: Authority by Ambivalence

Whereas Tocqueville's name appears just once in *The Human Condition*, Marx gets considerable explicit attention, almost all of it critical.⁴⁰ This is hardly surprising, since the book originally was to be a critique of his role in totalitarianism. As Arendt's project changed, Marx became less central, yet some of his ideas continued to play a crucial structuring role in ways that Arendt did not acknowledge and of which she may not even have been aware. While her detailed criticisms of Marx are often inaccurate, the overall thrust of her critique has considerable merit, except for the fact that it is directed against only one half of Marx's highly ambiguous teaching. The other side of Marx, which Arendt wholly suppresses or overlooks, remarkably resembles her own argument about the social in *The Human Condition*.

Arendt had seen early on that the role of Marx in (Soviet) totalitarianism was anomalous. Except for Marxist doctrine, every other factor involved in the rise of totalitarianism constituted an important break with the past, contributing to totalitarianism's unprecedented novelty and our resulting difficulty in understanding it. All of the other factors "emerged only when and where the traditional framework of Europe broke down," and none of them had any "connection with the great political and philosophical traditions of the West." Marxism, which obviously did have such connections, was the exception. Thus, Arendt explained, her omission of Marx from the argument of *The Origins* had been "deliberate," intended to preserve that book's internal coherence.[41] Now, however, she saw that totalitarianism could be—had in fact been—reached by two distinct routes: a "low road" taken by ordinary people and charted in *The Origins* and a "high road" taken by intellectuals under the spell of certain doctrines, such as Marxism in the Soviet case, which she now intended to trace.[42]

The task of assessing Marx's role on this high road was difficult not only objectively, because of the complex nature of Marx's writings, but also subjectively, because of their personal significance for Arendt. Objectively, Marx is an extraordinarily ambiguous and complex theorist, his teachings deeply riven by apparently incompatible commitments, somehow held in tension. The history of Marx interpretation surely demonstrates that there are at least two (if not many) Marxes. There is the scientist who discerns what must inevitably happen and who thus need not care what this or that person thinks or even what a class—the proletariat—"*pictures* at present as its goal," but only "*what the proletariat is in actuality*" and what it therefore "will historically be compelled to do."[43] But there is also Marx the political activist who hectors, exhorts, and organizes and who cares very much what people think because he is trying to move them to action, and not just to any action but to the one, right course of action, dangerously misperceived by rival organizers. While logically hard to reconcile, the two Marxes are also almost impossible to disentangle, and the objective task of sorting them out was, by Arendt's time, made more difficult by the several intellectual generations of Marx interpreters—both scholarly and activist—who had considerably muddied the terrain.

For Arendt personally, the task of assessing Marx's responsibility in Soviet totalitarianism was problematic also because so complexly interwoven with her past and present loyalties to various people, whose own relationships to Marxism were conflicted. She was, after all, the daughter of "socialist" parents, raised by a highly principled and demanding mother who was socially conventional yet admired the rebel Spartacist Rosa Luxemburg.[44] Because of the vagaries of "world history," Arendt's mother lived with her and Heinrich Blücher in America until 1948, when she decided to return to Europe, but died shortly after arriving.[45] *The Human Condition* was the first book Arendt undertook after her mother's death.

Arendt was also the former wife of a Communist Party member, under whose influence she had first read Marx and Trotsky in Berlin (95). Now she was the wife of another former party member, a Spartacist street fighter, a Trotskyist who had gradually become "an incisive critic of doctrinaire Marxism" (124). In America, Blücher had at first adopted an enthusiastic, uncritical Americanism, but had experienced difficulties adjusting to life here and finding work. Shortly after the departure and death of Arendt's mother, however, he experienced a "brainstorm" and a "surprise attack of productivity" that renewed his political thinking: he would abandon his "narrow" focus on "the American dream," along with Marxist and all other kinds of metaphysics. Dismissing Marx as a "despot," he would henceforth think in practical, political terms and identify himself only as "a citizen" (237–38). Their circle of friends in New York included many leftists and former leftists of all kinds, virtually all of them also trying to clarify their own particular positions in relation to Soviet policy and Marxist ideas. Finally, Arendt's former teacher and revered intellectual father-figure, Jaspers, although he had never been of the left, also had strong views on Marx, and he pressed them on Arendt in letters.

With respect to Soviet totalitarianism, for Jaspers, Marx was unequivocally to blame. "For my part," he wrote to Arendt when he heard of her project, "I harbor the hope that you will in the end after all find in Marx the intellectually responsible origin of what could lead to totalitarianism. . . . Demons don't exist, but there is something analogous in people like that."[46] At first Arendt resisted and argued with Jaspers, trying "to rescue Marx's honor in your sight," to defend Marx as a revolutionary in spite of himself, "whom a passion for justice had seized by the scruff of the neck." That passion, she said, connects Marx, in some "not entirely visible but very powerful way," to Kant.⁴⁷ Jaspers was outraged: "Marx's passion seems to me impure at its root, itself unjust from the outset.... I don't see a trace of Kantian spirit there.... I can't see anything else in him but an 'evil' person." Jaspers "would hope for support" in this view, he wrote, from Arendt's husband.⁴⁸ She soon reported that Blücher did agree with Jaspers "completely," but she continued the sentence in a way revealing that this was not quite true: Blücher held that Marx indeed "had no sense of justice, but did have one of freedom."⁴⁹

Defending Marx against Jaspers's charge that he and Hegel had "created" the modern illusion of history as caused by abstract forces, Arendt invokes Marx's early journalistic attack against Prussian laws forbidding wood gathering on private land. Such laws, which put property rights ahead of human need, she says, were what Marx had in mind when he warned against "the abstraction of society, and a rebellion against these things seems to me to be still alive in the later Marx as well." She wants to defend Marx not as a scholar, "and surely not as a philosopher, but as a rebel and a revolutionary."⁵⁰ Jaspers then responds even more strongly, but to Blücher, confessing that he himself has never been able to confront Marx "with anything but hatred." It was "Marx's thinking and his personality, with its sense of outrage, its violence, and its dictatorial character filled with hate" that bore "responsibility for what has happened" in Soviet Russia. Marx followed his own personal hatred "in the name of justice, into an abominable vision." Arendt, by contrast, Jaspers informs her husband, seems "in recent years" to be becoming "very just," and "her tremendous rage is almost extinguished."⁵¹

The published letters do not record whether Blücher agreed, but by May 1953, less than a year later, Arendt had obligingly changed her mind. The more she read Marx, she wrote to Jaspers, "the more I see that you were right. He's not interested in either freedom or justice."⁵² And in the fall of 1953 Arendt delivered a series of lectures at Princeton University subsequently published as an essay opening with the claim that "our tradition of thought," which began with Plato, was brought to a "definite end in the theories of Karl Marx," who located truth not in some transcendent realm but within "the sphere of human affairs" and sought to " 'realize' " it in " 'society,' " that is, in "the sphere of living together."⁵³ The opening paragraph thus sounds as if Marx had come to occupy for Arendt the diabolical, continuity-destroying role that in *The Origins* she had assigned to totalitarianism. But the essay is considerably more complex and ambivalent than that.

In the first place, it is still totalitarianism and not any thinker that accomplished the "break" with tradition (26–27). Second, Marx is also recognized as attempting "to 'realize' [philosophy] in *politics*," and the young Marx is acknowledged to have defined the human being as "*ein tätiges Naturwesen,*" which Arendt translates as "a natural being endowed with the faculty of action" (18, my emphasis, 39). Third, Marx is not alone; he is grouped in this essay with Kierkegaard and Nietzsche as standing "at the end of the tradition just before the break" (28). All three "tried desperately to think against the tradition while using its conceptual tools" (25). They were "the first who dared to think without the guidance of any authority whatsoever," but because they were "still held by the categorical framework of the great tradition," their effort resulted in "self-defeat" (28, 31). Less than a year later, moreover, Arendt was characterizing the task of "an authentic political philosophy"—the task in which she was then engaged—as focusing the traditional philosophical sense of wonder on "the realm of human affairs," understood not as "society" but as "the political realm."[54] In other words, she was undertaking the same task as Kierkegaard, Nietzsche, *and Marx,* but hoping to avoid their self-defeat.

In the same letter in which Arendt conceded to Jaspers that he was right about Marx, she anxiously recorded the advance of anticommunist hysteria in America, so that even as she turned fully against Marx, Arendt was profoundly concerned not to join those despicable former leftists who had become self-righteous Cold Warriors, now that (as she had put it in a slightly earlier letter) "every little idiot thinks he has a right and a duty to look down on Marx."[55]

Nothing remains visible in the text of *The Human Condition* of the personal struggle that Arendt underwent, except for the curiously oblique and awkward apologia with which she opens the chapter in which "Karl Marx will be criticized." Expressing her discomfort only indirectly, through the words used by Benjamin Constant as he set out to criticize Rousseau, Arendt says that, like Constant, she must "console" herself for appearing to join the petty detractors of this great thinker by striving to "disavow and keep these false friends away from me as much as I can."[56] In short, just as Arendt sought a solution different from both Soviet totalitarianism and American Cold War liberalism, she needed a way of understanding Marx that violated neither her ties to Jaspers and others whom she loved nor her own commitments "as a rebel and a revolutionary" to the pariahs of the world and against the unjust "abstraction of society."

Less than a year after beginning her intended study of Marx, Arendt came upon what struck her as a highly important distinction that seemed to promise a solution to these dilemmas. It was the distinction between two kinds of human production: labor and work, or in Locke's famous phrase, "the labor of our bodies and the work of our hands."⁵⁷ The former word, she saw, connected with laboriousness, with heavy, painful bodily effort, and specifically with women's travail in giving birth. The latter word, lacking these connotations, instead focused on the result, the product (as in "work of art," "all his works"), a lasting object formed by human artifice. The former thus sorted with the body, biological necessity, and natural processes independent of our will, while the latter sorted with know-how, technical skill, efficiency, and the enduring world of humanly fashioned objects. The importance of the distinction was underlined for Arendt by its ubiquity: "Every European language, ancient and modern, contains two etymologically unrelated words for what we have come to think of as the same activity." She mentions Greek, Latin, French, and the German distinction between *Arbeit* and *Werk*. In all these languages, she says, "only the equivalents for 'labor' have an unequivocal connotation of pain and trouble."⁵⁸

Not long after coming upon this distinction, Arendt connected it further with Aristotle's contrast between making, or production (*poiesis*), and doing, or action (*praxis*).⁵⁹ These overlapping contrasts she combined into the three "fundamental activities" of the *vita activa* that would ultimately organize *The Human Condition*. More immediately, their discovery seems to have been an intellectual breakthrough for Arendt, enabling her to begin the actual writing of her book. The triad seemed to suggest the third alternative she needed to both Soviet Russia and Cold War America, but also and perhaps more immediately, to offer a way of reading Marx that escaped her painful personal dilemma.

Marx, she now saw, had focused entirely on *Arbeit*, thereby becoming "the greatest of modern labor theorists" with his "seemingly blasphemous notion . . . that labor (and not God) created man or that labor (and not reason) distinguished man from the other animals." For Marx, labor alone, and not work, was "the source of all productivity," and labor rather than action expressed "the very humanity of man."⁶⁰

From this narrowness derived most of Marx's other theoretical faults. The focus on labor accounted for his "consistent naturalism"—he saw humans as a kind of animal, rather than distinguishing sharply as Kant had done between causally determined nature and human freedom. Marx "discovered 'labor power' as the specifically human mode of the life force," thus of "natural" or "biological process."⁶¹ He saw humans from a "purely social viewpoint," which is to say, one that takes "nothing into account but the life process of mankind" or "of society."⁶²

This meant that Marx neglected the lasting world of objects fashioned by work and of relationships created and sustained in action. "The question of a separate existence of worldly things, whose durability will survive and withstand the devouring process of life, does not occur to him at all."⁶³ Without an enduring world there can be neither meaning in human life nor secure individuality. Marx did not see the meaningless "futility" of a life defined only by endless process, and he had an entirely mistaken notion of human collectivity in which individuality disappears into a single, monolithic mass of "society" or "the species."⁶⁴ Neglecting work, he did not care enough about the world; neglecting action, he did not see our responsibility for protecting the world. Thus he missed our true lack, which is *amor mundi*: "not self-alienation, as Marx thought," but rather "world alienation" is our problem, "the hallmark of the modern age" (254).

Having missed action and individuality, finally, Marx utterly neglected politics and misunderstood freedom. Because of his "materialism," he took the web of human relationships and the action that sustains it to be a mere "facade . . . an essentially superfluous superstructure" on the determining base of bodily labor.⁶⁵ Thus, although Marx did want to promote freedom, his viewpoint left him unable even to understand it. In relation to freedom, consequently, Arendt locates "the fundamental contradiction which runs like a red thread through the whole of Marx's thought." Having defined humans in terms of labor, he nevertheless intends an ideal, postrevolutionary society in which people are freed precisely from labor. For Marx, Arendt says, "only when labor is abolished can the 'realm of freedom' supplant the 'realm of necessity.' "⁶⁶

All of Arendt's specific charges against Marx have some foundation in the texts, yet almost all of them involve misreadings and distortions, sometimes blatant ones. Begin with the central idea of Marx's alleged obsession with labor, his neglect of work. Marx of course wrote in German, and although *Arbeit* does translate the English "labor," it is by no means, as Arendt misleadingly claims, the German "equivalent for 'labor,' " for the two languages do not encode quite the same distinction. The range of words in the *werk-* family in modern German is extremely restricted. The verb, as Arendt notes, has become "rather obsolete," leaving only *arbeiten* for translating both "to labor" and "to work." And the noun, as Arendt fails to note, refers *only* to the product or result, so that only *Arbeit* is available for the process of production, be it labor or work.⁶⁷

Marx's frequent use of words from the *arbeit-* family, therefore, cannot indicate a preoccupation with labor to the detriment of work.⁶⁸ On the contrary, except where context indicates otherwise, when Marx says *Arbeit* or *arbeiten* he is just as likely to mean work as labor, or both together. Arendt is thus wrong to read Marx as if he had a choice between work and labor and opted for the latter; and she is doubly wrong, in passages where the context clearly shows that Marx meant work, to conclude that he must be caught in "contradictions," or reluctantly forced "to admit" something, or "misrepresenting" labor as work.⁶⁹

Marx's Other Half

Such errors about language would be silly and trivial were it not for the way they reflect Arendt's more general, systematic blindness to, or suppression of, one side of Marx. To show that and assess its significance, however, requires a brief account of the Marx that Arendt omits. The place to start is with Arendt's claim, cited above, that Marx wrongly diagnosed self-alienation rather than world alienation as our basic problem. Now, Marx never says that self-alienation is the basic form of alienation; he merely lists it along with several other forms in the *1844 Manuscripts,* without designating any one as fundamental.⁷⁰ If one nevertheless insists on asking, with Arendt, which form of alienation is "central" for Marx, or even what unifies all the forms into a single concept, the most persuasive answer is none of the listed forms but a different phenomenon, discussed both in the *Manuscripts* and in many later writings and sometimes designated as "alienation"(*Entäusserung* or *Entfremdung*), though some later Marxists, notable Georg Lukács, call it "reification."⁷¹

This phenomenon links all the various kinds of alienation for Marx, both conceptually and causally, and it lies at the center of one major facet of his theory about human beings and history, a facet that remains fundamentally unchanged from Marx's early writings right through *Capital,* though of course details vary and emphases shift. According to this theory and this notion of alienation, human beings are indeed a species of animal, but a unique one. What characterizes any species is its "life-activity," and the characteristic life-activity of our species is that we work or labor (*arbeiten*) on the natural world to produce what our bodies require for life. Production is our "species-life." But other animals also do this: gather food, build nests or hives, spin webs or cocoons. What distinguishes humans is "free, conscious" productive activity. While other animals are "immediately identical with" their life-activity, "Man [*der Mensch*] makes his life-activity itself the object of his will and of his consciousness." Other animals are conscious too, but they do not think in general concepts, do not abstract from their immediate experience to formulate generalizations, make plans, invent imaginary situations, or articulate principles and rules. Animals of other species produce only what they immediately need, driven by that need, but "man [*der Mensch*] produces even when he is free from physical need and only truly produces in freedom therefrom." Humans are creatures that naturally engage in *Arbeit* even when they do not immediately need its products. We putter and play, invent, improve, rearrange, organize, compose, because that is what fulfills us, our "life-activity, [our] *essential* being."[72]

Even with other animals, some of what they produce may continue in use for a considerable time, like a beaver dam or an anthill. But this is far more true of human beings, precisely because of our leisure-time productivity, whose products are not immediately consumed. These humanly produced, lasting objects gradually accumulate around us and form an increasing portion of our world. They all decay eventually, but some of what each generation produces becomes part of the quasi-natural "given" for the next generation, part of the objective world in which it must produce its livelihood. Increasingly with the passage of time, the material environment in which we produce what we need is itself humanly shaped, so that "man contemplates himself in a world that he has created."[73]

This contemplating involves our capacity for abstraction and generalization, which gives us foresight and imagination, so that some of our leisure production goes toward providing for future needs or toward improving future production. We are the toolmakers. This same capacity also allows us a versatility not available to other animals, whose activities are governed by instinct. Birds' nests and beavers' dams are always built in the same, species-specific way, but "man knows how to produce in accordance with the standard of every species" and thus also "in accordance with the laws of beauty." Third, our capacity for abstraction allows us to generalize about ourselves, to recognize other human beings as members of the same freely creative species, to imagine ourselves in their situation, and thus to become moral and political beings.[74]

For Marx, human *Arbeit* on the natural world produces not just physical substances and objects but also at the same time all of the intangible features of nonmaterial culture. While engaged in material productive activity we also produce relationships, habits, skills, institutions, language, mores, character. Here too, although much is transient, some of the transforming effects always continue, so that with the passage of time the human species cultivates and civilizes itself, developing specifically human, cultural achievements and pleasures. We are the species that produces itself, not just reproducing biologically like all natural species, but also creating and sustaining our specifically human cultures and character. Ultimately, "the *entire so-called history of the world* is nothing but the begetting of man through human *Arbeit.*"[75]

All this is explicated in the early writings, but Marx is still saying the same things in *Capital* at the end of his life. In the process of *Arbeit,* while changing the external world, the human being "changes his own nature. He develops his slumbering powers," both as an individual and as a species. As this happens, the form of our activity gradually changes from "its first instinctive stage" to ones that increasingly mark it "as exclusively human," as subject to our free, conscious control rather than instinctually driven. "A spider conducts operations that resemble those of a weaver, and a bee puts to shame many an architect. . . . But what distinguishes the worst architect from the best of bees is this, that the architect raises his structure in imagination before he erects it in reality" (344). The capacity for imagination characterizes the human species from the outset. Architecture, however, is an activity in which we can engage only because countless earlier generations gradually developed the necessary skills, tools, ideas, and character, including the disciplined self-control required for keeping one's will "steadily in consonance with his purpose" (345).

In theory, therefore, we modern human beings ought to feel—and be—enriched and fulfilled by this wealth of cumulative human accomplishment. We ought to feel—and be—at home in a world and in activities that are by now almost entirely humanized. They should wholly suit our needs. But in fact all of the species' powers and accumulated achievements have not made humans either powerful or free. Indeed, in Marx's time as in ours, the opposite seems to be the case. Marx sees in this a dual paradox: first, that those who do the actual *Arbeit,* the physical production of the material wealth underlying our nonmaterial culture, are increasingly impoverished thereby; and, second, that everyone, worker and capitalist alike, finds himself helpless in the face of socioeconomic forces, the "laws of the market." The workers live like animals, on the edge of starvation and physically debilitated by dreadful working conditions, the amenities of civilization unavailable to them because they have no money. But the capitalists, although safe from starvation, are not really much better off. They have money and what money can buy, though the bulk of profits must be constantly reinvested. But even the capitalists lack access to the actual riches of civilization, since they cannot relate to those riches in ways that bring real fulfillment. They relate to art, for example, only in terms of ownership and money, to knowledge only in terms of technology and profit, and to their fellow human beings only through the competitive selfishness that is forced on all alike by a market economy.

Like Arendt and following Hegel, Marx calls this pattern of competitive exploitation "society," but for him it is only one special kind: society "*as it appears* to the [bourgeois] political economist" (101, my emphasis). This is "*civil society,* in which every individual is a totality of needs and exists for the other person, as the other exists for him, insofar as each becomes a means for the other."[76] By society in general Marx means simply "the co-operation of several individuals, no matter under what conditions, in what manner, and to what end."[77]

Market capitalism is a highly intricate social system, a system of profound interdependence but one whose shared social arrangements require mutual exploitation and competitive isolation. These shared requirements make it impossible for people to cooperate in solidarity, as they would have to do in order to direct or control the overall consequences of what they are all separately doing. Instead, therefore, those consequences confront them like an external, coercive force by which they are all constrained—workers in order literally to survive, owners in order to survive *as* owners, to stay in business. "Modern bourgeois society," in the famous words of the *Manifesto,* is thus "like the sorcerer, who is no longer able to control the powers of the nether world whom he has called up by his spells."[78] It is a vicious cycle: precisely because "each tries to establish over the other an *alien* power, so as thereby to find satisfaction of his own selfish need," they jointly but unintentionally produce the market's coercive power over them all, a further "extension of the alien powers to which man is subjected," which forces him into continued competitive exploitation. Marx says this in the *1844 Manuscripts,* in *The German Ideology,* and in the *Grundrisse* and is still saying it in *Capital.*[79]

The increasing enrichment, productivity, civilization, and power of the human species, then, is paradoxically accompanied by an increasing immiseration for most (and specifically for those who do the actual

Arbeit) and an increasing (or at least an increasingly paradoxical) helplessness for all.⁸⁰ This is true of human history as such and of capitalism in particular, and it constitutes the central, basic form of alienation for Marx. The alienation of the worker (*Arbeiter*) means that his *Arbeit* "becomes an object, [acquires] an *external* existence" as a commodity in the market, which wields "a power of its own confronting him . . . as something hostile and alien." Similarly, in history and in capitalism generally, people "become more and more enslaved under a power alien to them" but which they in fact constitute, until finally "all is under the sway of an *inhuman* power," which people enact but do not have, cannot wield.⁸¹

Arendt thus is not just wrong about which form of alienation is central for Marx, but altogether misses or suppresses this whole line of argument, which greatly resembles some of her own ideas about the social.

In the course of explicating this line of argument in Marx, we have also touched on a number of details that Arendt gets wrong about Marx, besides the translation of *Arbeit* and the basic form of alienation. Thus it is clearly not true that Marx misses the importance of a lasting world of humanly fashioned objects, since the cumulative development of tools and technology is a central tenet of his theory. Nor is it true that Marx aims only at life and abundance for their own sake. Indeed, this is a charge that Marx himself brings against capitalist thinkers.⁸² Although Marx does aim at abundance, it is never abundance for its own sake, but always for the freedom and humanization to which he thinks abundance is prerequisite. Thus it is flatly false that freedom only begins for Marx where labor has come to an end, and in order to make this out as a "fundamental and flagrant contradiction" central to his thought, Arendt has to misread two passages and reshape a third by ellision.⁸³

For Marx, *Arbeit* can never disappear, both because we are embodied creatures and because it is our species characteristic; but *Arbeit* is not merely Arendt's labor. With respect to our natural needs and productive activity to fulfill them, freedom is not the disappearance of *Arbeit*, but instead "can only consist in socialized man, the associated producers, rationally regulating their interchange with Nature, bringing it under their common control, instead of being ruled by it as by the blind forces of Nature." Beyond the fulfillment of needs and this sort of freedom, however, lies "that development of human energy which is an end in itself, the true realm of freedom." For Marx, however, the first sort of freedom is prerequisite to the second, because only the first ends the basic kind of alienation and thus makes possible the subjection of those forces that have hitherto driven and determined human beings "to the power of the united individuals."[84] Having first said it in *The German Ideology,* Marx is still saying it in *Capital* (327, 413, 441). Abundance is a goal, but only because it is the means to freedom.

It is also the means to real individuality. Far from wanting to dissolve individuality in some monolithic mass called "society" or "the species," Marx aims to enhance it by having people take charge of the monolithic mass they *already are,* a collectivity presently out of control, driving and constraining them as individuals. The value of capitalism, of "modern industry," and of the abundance they create is that these eventually make possible the "humane development" of individual human beings, allowing each to give "free scope to his own natural and acquired powers" (413–15). Individual development presupposes relationships with others, material abundance, and advanced civilization. "Only in community [with others has each] individual the means of cultivating his gifts in all directions; only in the community, therefore, is personal freedom possible." In all the "previous substitutes for community, in the State, etc.," there was personal freedom for at most a few, and even that freedom was severely limited because their community, being only partial and "illusory, . . . always took on an independent existence in relation to them" and became their "fetter."[85] That is why, in his early critique of Hegel, Marx says that democracy is "*the essence of all state constitutions*" and "the solved *riddle* of all constitutions," revealing what a constitution really is by bringing the abstract, formal idea "back to its actual basis, the *actual human being[s],* the *actual people,* and establish[ing it] as the people's *own* work." Only in democracy does the constitution appear as what it really is, "a free product of man," because only democracy is—or continually re-creates—"the true unity of the general and the particular."[86]

In true community, "individuals obtain their freedom in and through their association," because a human being is by nature "in the most literal sense a *zoon politikon,* not merely a gregarious animal, but an animal which can individuate itself only in the midst of society."[87] Marx says this in the early writings; he says it most famously in the *Manifesto,* and he is still saying it in 1875.[88]

Arendt and Marx

Indeed, Arendt acknowledges that this was Marx's goal, that his "guiding model," like hers, was "the Athens of Pericles," which, Marx thought, "in the future, with the help of the vastly increased productivity of human labor, would need no slaves to sustain itself but would become a reality for all."[89] Nor is the model of Athenian politics all that they share. On repeated occasions in *The Human Condition,* we have seen, Arendt affirms some proposition she has earlier attacked Marx for affirming. She herself asserts that at a certain stage in the "process" of world alienation, "society became the subject of the new life process"; and she explicitly affirms that this is no mere metaphor. This "society as a whole, the 'collective subject' of the life process, [was] by no means ... an intangible entity," a fiction, but real.[90] Similarly, "Marx's contention that economic laws are like natural laws," which Arendt first dismisses as the illusory way Marx "wished to see" things, she later affirms as "correct." It is correct "only in a laboring society," but of course a laboring society is exactly what Arendt repeatedly claims we have, or are.[91] At one point Arendt even seems to acknowledge that what she calls world alienation, which she says Marx ignored in his fascination with self-alienation, in fact *is* what Marx "denounced" as self-alienation.[92]

Now, Arendt's notion of world alienation is not in fact identical either to what Marx means by alienation from self or to his basic notion of alienation, examined above, but it bears some striking resemblances to the latter.[93] So Arendt doesn't just get Marx wrong in detail but also fails to see, or refuses to acknowledge, the extent to which her own doctrine parallels a major aspect of his. Only a fool would claim that Arendt and Marx agree in general or think alike. I am arguing merely that there is an important area of overlap between their theories, that Arendt is blind to Marx's views within that area, and that the area corresponds roughly to her concept of the social. Of course they wholly disagree about much else, including economics and property; history, class conflict, and process; their different prescriptions and predictions; the absence of anything like Arendt's concept of the world from Marx's thought; and Marx's relative neglect of what politics might look like in a classless world. Arendt's overall critique of Marx, as distinct from her detailed claims and her selective blindness to the area of overlap, has much merit. Marx often is historicist, pseudo-scientific, determinist, reductionist, disparaging of politics and of ideals as mere "superstructure," the more so if one ignores the other side of his deeply ambivalent thinking. Nevertheless, given the fierceness of her criticism of Marx, the extent of this tacit parallelism is astonishing.

As we shall see in more detail in chapter 9, Arendt agrees with (at least part of) Marx as to what human beings are like, what distinguishes them from other animals. Though she attacks his "naturalism," the truth is that both she and Marx are—rightly—on both sides of the question of our relationship to nature. They both see humans as simultaneously a part of nature and different from all other species, precisely with respect to the natural human propensity to create culture, both material and relational. The ambiguity lies in the concept of nature itself. As Arendt said in *The Origins,* "Man's 'nature' is only 'human' insofar as it opens up to man the possibility of becoming something highly unnatural, that is, a man."[94]

Consequently Marx and Arendt largely agree also about what human fulfillment and freedom might look like, specifically that freedom would have to combine individuality with solidarity. They agree that in our present condition we are far from free because almost completely subjected to an enormous, seemingly alien power that debilitates and constrains us yet that is even now of our own making. And they agree that our hope for achieving freedom lies in the paradoxicality of this subjection—that the resultants of our own activity now dominate us only because that activity keeps us isolated from each other, incapable of solidarity. So we are not free, yet somehow are free-to-become-free. For Arendt, we have seen, this paradoxicality centers on the social as Blob. It gives rise to the puzzling questions we have encountered more than once already about the ontological status of society and its power: whether it is a mere *mentalité* or an objective reality that genuinely coerces.

Not surprisingly, entirely parallel questions are thoroughly familiar in Marx scholarship, though most do not focus on the concept of society. Marx himself did warn in his early writings that "what is to be avoided above all is the re-establishing of 'Society' as an abstraction *vis-à-vis* the individual."[95] A critic of Hegelian idealism, with its active, personified abstractions, Marx was determined instead to "set out from real, active men" and their objective doings in the world (154). Yet when he observed these doings, he saw that people in his time were in fact objectively driven and constrained by market forces, which were no illusion or empty abstraction.

The ambiguity can be seen clearly in Marx's apparently inconsistent treatment of the bourgeois political economists, whom he calls "fetishists" because they falsely present the market as omnipotent and its requirements as inevitable, yet whose assumptions in this regard he himself endorses as he proceeds to set forth the necessary laws of capitalist development.[96] The ambiguity is even more strikingly and persistently displayed in Marx's troubled relation to Feuerbach, to whose views on religion Marx often both compares and contrasts his own theories. Feuerbach saw religion as an illusion in which people ascribe the best powers, qualities, and aspirations of the human species to imaginary beings and then feel depleted, diminished, and depraved by comparison, helpless before the gods' power.[97] It is the same in history, in capitalism, in political economy, Marx says over and over again: people's own power, alienated, looms over them like a god.[98] But it is in fact their own power; that is why the bourgeois political economists are fetishists.[99]

Yet Marx also insists, over and over again, that his narrative differs fundamentally from Feuerbach's, because gods are merely imaginary, their power illusory, but the market is real and its power actually constrains. Consequently, whereas religion can be ended by insight, by a change in people's thinking, the power of the market can be ended "only by the practical overthrow of the actual social relations" that constitute it.[100] " 'Liberation [*Befreiung*]' is a historical and not a mental act" (169).

Marx himself, one might say, had something of a Blob problem. That is, he saw people in the grip of the market, a large-scale force they could not control or direct even though it consisted only in their collective activities, and he himself sometimes pictured that force as a superhuman monster with a will of its own—as does almost every newscaster reporting on Wall Street, relating what the market thinks likes, believes, intends, and so on. But Marx also thought that people were in his time—although previously they had not been—in a position to change this, that they could jointly take charge of the large-scale resultants of their various activities. So they were unfree but free-to-become-free, in the grip of a monster but only because they still believed in its autonomy and had not yet taken charge. Marx tended to handle this logically problematic teaching by a chronological division of before and after: hitherto determined (first by nature, later by humanly made arrangements out of control), henceforth free because at last in a position to take charge. That, however, leaves the transition, the present, highly problematic: the coming or making of the revolution, its difference from all previous revolutions, the nature and permanence of the changes it is to introduce.[101] These are familiar issues in Marx scholarship and Marxist movements.

One might have expected Arendt to attack Marx on this ground, to reject this chronological sequencing of necessity and freedom in favor of her own, more sensible view that freedom is a constant human possibility in history, rarely achieved and easily lost but always in principle available. One might have expected her to insist, against Marx, that freedom, even after the revolution, must surely depend on just *how* the collectivity will go about "regulat[ing] the general production": how that will be institutionalized and enforced, who will play what sort of role in it, what its politics will look like (160). She might, in short, have insisted on the need to teach people explicitly about action, politics, the lost treasure, might even have counterposed Tocqueville to Marx for this purpose and attempted a synthesis of their ideas.[102]

One could argue that this is in fact what *The Human Condition* does, implicitly and indirectly. But it patently is not what that book does explicitly and directly. Instead it acknowledges no debt to either Tocqueville or Marx, and it misrepresents the latter's theory. As a corollary, Arendt's account remains troubled precisely where it is tangent to Marx's. As in relation to Tocqueville, so in relation to Marx: she seems to acquire the theorist's difficulties along with her unacknowledged positive debt to him, because avoiding acknowledgment of the debt gets in the way of her seeing those difficulties and criticizing them. Thus, despite her criticisms of Marx, Arendt herself cannot regard freedom simply and flatly as a constant possibility, without preconditions; otherwise she could hardly maintain that things are getting worse in this respect. She herself, furthermore, needs some explanation of *why* things have been getting worse, why people persist in behaving in ways that leave them unfree, constrained, and endangered. And the very logic of such explanation, whether historical, psychological, or sociological, seems to conflict with the idea of action and political freedom that Arendt most wants to teach.

Putting the same point in a slightly different and more speculative way, one can imagine that, as Arendt worked on this book, the powerful parallels between her own thinking and (half of) Marx's must have driven her frantic. If Jaspers was right and Marx was diabolical, part of the "high road" to totalitarianism, then extirpating the dangerous parts of his thinking from her own had to be her most important task. Coming to her work on Marx from *The Origins of Totalitarianism*, with all the dangers of parvenu-like surrender to process still fresh in her mind, Arendt saw the diabolical element in Marx as his materialism, naturalism, determinism, all of which she identified with his focus on *Arbeit*. Those were the elements she must purge from her own thinking, against which she must protect freedom and the world. As a result, however, Arendt developed a dichotomy every bit as rigid and as problematic as Marx's chronological before and after, determined past and free future: the Arendtian contrast between the determined necessity of the social and free political action.

The point of tracing the possible influence of Tocqueville and Marx on *The Human Condition,* then, is multiple. First, and most simply, it raises the question of why these authorities remain hidden, if indeed they were authorities for Arendt. But that question only matters for our purposes insofar as, second, Arendt may have been encouraged to transform and modify her vision of totalitarianism as Blob into the social as Blob by certain related formulations and images in Tocqueville and Marx. There is also, however, a third, larger point involved. Instead of regarding the Blob as a personal failure of Arendt as theorist, we might note that here are three major political theorists who all encounter difficulties in this same area of their thinking. All three clearly write with liberating intent. All three want to enhance individuality in a good sense but warn against individual isolation in a bad sense. All three criticize other thinkers' deployment of empty abstractions as interfering with the understanding of freedom, and all three accordingly worry about how to theorize without invoking such dangerous abstractions. Surely it is remarkable that all three nevertheless end up, in their respective ways, envisioning some kind of Blob. Eventually we shall have to ask whether there are ways of treating these issues without a Blob, but we are not yet ready for that.

EIGHT

Abstraction, Authority, and Gender

The project that gradually replaced Marx as the focus of Arendt's new book, chapter 6 argued, was a general theory of free citizenship extrapolated from the experience of wartime resistance to the Nazis. Like coming to terms with Marx, this new project presented both objective difficulties, troubling for anyone, and subjective ones, personal to Arendt. Objectively and substantively, the task required a motivation for public engagement as powerful as Nazi occupation of one's country but without the risks of genocide and war. Objectively and methodologically, it required a way of theorizing—a mode of abstraction—that was not hostile or blind to politics. Subjectively, the new project entailed multiple psychic tensions for Arendt, reopening personal issues that had seemed settled long before: issues concerning vocation and ambition, aggression and guilt, authority, identity, and gender.

The conceptual triad of labor, work, and action that helped Arendt begin settling accounts with Marx also seemed promising for the newly emerging project, where it played the same moderating, synthesizing, tie-breaking role that the idea of neighborly love had once played in her dissertation. Henceforth, with regard to citizenship, abstraction, and Arendt's personal dilemmas, she would theorize not one but two distinct ways of getting things wrong in juxtaposition to the right way, which thus would become a third option, a way out. So the place to begin is with a more detailed look at the conceptual triad itself.

The first wrong alternative juxtaposed to action is labor, the *animal laborans*—human beings as one species of animal, a part of nature with its causally determined processes, driven by bodily needs and tending to them painfully. Laboring, for Arendt, is endlessly laborious: repetitive, cyclical, meaningless yet necessary, like the natural "processes of growth and decay" but also like the continual human struggle against those processes to feed and shelter the body and "to keep the world clean and prevent its decay," protecting the human artifice "against nature."[1]

The second wrong alternative is work, *homo faber*—human beings as workers, capable of initiative and creativity, unlike other animals, but exercising that capacity in relation to the material world: objects and substances. *Homo faber* produces not life-sustaining, necessary consumption goods but the more enduring use-objects that together comprise the " 'artificial' world of things," which we have "in common" and "inhabit . . . together" and which stabilizes our lives over time, even over generations (7, 52). *Homo faber*'s orientation is practical, aimed at the efficient achievement of some intended result. Himself creative, but only in relation to things, *homo faber* in effect recognizes no peers, no fellow creators. Other people are like objects to him: means or obstacles.

Neither the helpless, driven repetitiveness of labor nor the narrowly technical focus of work is suited to relationships among fellow creators, to founding, sustaining, or altering the institutions, norms, and practices that make up nonmaterial culture. Neither is capable of making life meaningful. Labor, although necessary, is inherently pointless because endless; work, although creatively expressive in its piecemeal projects, "gets caught in an unending chain of means and ends" on the larger scale.[2] Unable to recognize fellow creators, moreover, *homo faber* is both liable to treat people "as one treats other 'material' " and blind to the problems of joint goal-setting among multiple autonomous agents (188). He cannot see the large-scale limitations of the cost-benefit outlook itself.

The third alternative, contrasted to both labor and work, is action, which employs the creativity found also in *homo faber* but in a manner suited to relations among free equals. Action culminates in no tangible product, generating neither consumption goods nor use-objects. If it can be said to produce anything, its "specific productivity" lies in its "capacity for establishing relationships" and "stories" (191, 184). Its resultant is the "web" or "fabric of human relationships and affairs," which is "no less real than" material objects, though—despite the metaphor—it has no material existence (95, 183, 233). This web or fabric is not merely created by action at some initial moment, but even now consists only in ongoing human conduct. It is the medium in which action takes place and takes effect, so that in a sense action is always interaction, and the reality of the fabric it weaves "is entirely dependent upon the constant presence of others," each of whom is a unique individual capable of creative initiative.[3]

Central to this Arendtian way of conceiving action is not freedom of choice, which we tend to see as the essence of human freedom, but creativity in human relationships, what Arendt would later call "founding" and what Tocqueville called "the art of association."⁴ Freedom as choice is too circumscribed for Arendt's purposes, since it suggests selecting among a set of preexisting alternatives, whereas her point is that the alternatives are themselves humanly created. It is not just that existing arrangements always allow some choice between supporting and resisting them, but that we always have the capacity to initiate unprecedented new ones. Elaborating this idea near the end of her life, Arendt cites Henri Bergson's observation that even philosophers who believe in free will "have reduced it to a simple 'choice,' between two or several options, as though these options were 'possibilities' . . . and the Will was restricted to 'realizing' one of them." None seems "to have had the slightest notion" of our capacity for initiating something "entirely new," which Bergson says is, "after all[,] free action."⁵

With respect to the lost treasure, then, action contrasts both to the laborlike indifference to public affairs that, for so many people in Europe, preceded the coming of the Nazis, and to the worklike, narrowly self-interested ruthlessness of collaborators and exploiters. It thus addresses the substantive difficulties in Arendt's project by suggesting the enormous power potential of human freedom, yet always within bounds set by mutuality among fellow creators.

Methodologically, action suggests a way of abstracting, thus of gaining a large-scale perspective on reality and a critical perspective on existing conventions, without losing sight of the individual, both as the source of initiative and as the locus of moral value and dignity. Action, in other words, suggests a mode of thinking that is neither mired in the concrete present, like someone in intense physical pain, nor inhumanly abstracted, like Heideggerian philosophy. It was while writing *The Human Condition* that Arendt found a name for this mode of thought. She called it "political theory," applying that phrase first to the book's content and soon thereafter to her own vocation.⁶

Abstraction, Ambition, and Femininity

The remainder of this chapter, however, concerns neither free citizenship nor political theory but the personal dilemmas that Arendt's new project presented for her, and how the concept of action seemed to promise a way out that avoided both selfishness and self-sacrifice. Once more, therefore, we shall take up the psychological and gender-related concerns that Arendt sought so strenuously to banish from her work but which nevertheless continued to haunt it.

Given the multiple problems for which Arendt's conceptual triad seemed to promise solutions, it is not surprising that this triad became central to the structure of *The Human Condition*. Introduced at the outset of the first chapter, it informs chapters 3, 4, and 5, each of which is devoted to one of the three concepts. In between, however, stands chapter 2, which introduces the ancient Greeks as well as the social. Titled "The Public and the Private Realm," this chapter juggles two dyads: public versus private and (ancient Greek) politics versus the (modern) social. Although politics has already been linked to action in the opening chapter, chapter 2 elaborates that link and lends it authority by way of the ancient Greeks, in effect transferring to politics and free citizenship some of the liberating, generative conceptual role played by the idea of action in its triad.

At the same time, however, the ancient Greeks also import into Arendt's argument some problematic features she surely did not (consciously) intend to adopt: an agonistic, narcissistic, and misogynist striving for heroic glory, profoundly different from the heroism of anti-Nazi resistance, and a corresponding set of rigid, pejorative contrasts ranking Greek above barbarian, freeman above slave, public above private, and male above female. Arendt herself, of course, would not knowingly have endorsed any of these rankings. Specifically, she saw both public and private life as essential, and the two as mutually dependent; she wanted to invoke the Greeks' clear distinction between them but not their ranking. The (modern) social appears in chapter 2 as an evil third term to the dyad of public and private, blurring their distinction and ultimately destroying both, a threat as much to private individuality as to public political freedom.

As a result, structurally speaking, *The Human Condition* is built around two triads: labor, work, and action, where the third term is the desirable alternative; and public, private, and social, where the third term constitutes the evil threat. The two third terms—action and the social—therefore confront each other dichotomously. One might even argue that the social functions symbolically in the book to restore dyadicity, forcing a stark and simple choice where the original conceptual triad had opened possibilities for a more nuanced, richer, but also more ambiguous complexity. Such claims, however, are bound to seem hopelessly schematic and uninformative, arbitrarily postulating that triads are somehow inherently better than dichotomies. To put some flesh on the bones of this schematic arbitrariness, one must relate it in some detail to the issues of abstraction, authority, and gender confronting Arendt in the project of this book.

These personal issues, we have noted, stemmed from Arendt's undertaking of a general theory and thus reencountering the dangers of abstraction. As she says at the outset, *The Human Condition* proposes merely that we "think what we are doing," but thinking was itself profoundly problematic.[7] The preface to *Between Past and Future*, which introduces the idea of the lost treasure, stresses that recovering the treasure has become a task for *thought*; it makes an appeal to thought "no less urgent and no less passionate" than the appeal to action that had drawn apolitical people into the Resistance. The preface speaks of this double reversal in the intellectual history of the twentieth century: first apolitical people were driven from thought to action in resisting Naziism; now former activists are "forced . . . back into thought" to seek their lost treasure.[8]

As it happens, these are terms in which one might equally tell the story of Arendt's own life, seen retrospectively from the 1950s. The young Arendt, leaving Heidegger, the university, and Germany behind, turned from thought to action, from academic philosophy to practical, politically engaged, femininely nurturing work. Her second reversal—returning to thought—might be seen as a gradual process that began when she took the Varnhagen manuscript with her into exile; but it might also, perhaps better, be seen as centered in an acute crisis around writing *The Human Condition*, which forced Arendt back toward that dangerous abstraction she had sworn never to touch again.

Reviewing what we know of Arendt's biography in these terms, and permitting ourselves a certain speculative leeway, we might tell her story this way: in love with philosophy, the young Arendt was personally ambitious to enter the world of abstract thought. Early worries about "how one goes about it, then, if one is a Jewish woman" soon dissipated, yet abstract thinking was from the outset tied to questions of vocation, identity, and gender, to her relations with her parents and, in due time, with Heidegger. Having grown up "fatherless" (from the age of seven if not from the age of two), Arendt was left chronically hungry for an (idealized) father but also intensely focused on her one remaining parent, who seems herself to have been deeply ambivalent about the proper role for a woman. (It is difficult to be sure, given the discreet brevity of both Young-Bruehl's and Arendt's own remarks on the subject.)

Martha Arendt was a strong and cultivated woman and politically engaged, in a cautious, respectable way. Though she encouraged her daughter's education and raised her "without prejudices," she also had a fairly conventional bourgeois and, Young-Bruehl says, "warm and sentimental" notion of femininity, which her daughter experienced as "confining, particularly after she began her university studies."[9] This surely suggests that Martha Arendt would not have approved of her daughter's affair with a married professor and very likely was never told about it. Encountering Heidegger, Arendt in effect had to choose between two forms of ambition, both conventionally forbidden to a good woman: whether to *be* a philosopher, a professor, a man, or to *have* one, as an immoral woman sexually triumphant over his wife. The latter option seemed to require that she deny the former ambition by pretending that intellectually she, "so to speak, could not count to three"; it also seemed to violate her mother's demands, both those about conventional feminine propriety and those about solidarity among victims, in this case, women. In either option, Arendt could succeed only as an exception, a parvenu, at the price of becoming a scoundrel and—in the one case—of disappearing as an autonomous person and thinker or—in the other—of ceasing to be a woman (and a Jew).

Abandoning both of her ambitions in turn, Arendt then tried to settle for something more modest: an unromantic "neighborliness" in the form of a life without an academic or even an intellectual vocation and marriage without love or sexual fulfillment to a fellow subject in Heidegger's realm, a man of whom her mother approved. Ambition did too much damage in the world; her place must be with the victims, nurturing Jewish refugee children and perhaps also fighting on their behalf, in solidarity with fellow pariahs.

But these decisions did not hold either. The marriage dissolved, and Arendt continued to write. Her second marriage was to a man of whom her mother did not approve, whose working-class manners clashed with Martha Arendt's genteel sense of propriety, and who confronted his mother-in-law with the same toughness and "great fear of sentimentality" that he had developed long before in relation to his own demanding and needful mother (135, 236). In different circumstances, marriage to Blücher might well have drawn Arendt out of her mother's orbit; instead, "world history" intervened, as Arendt and Blücher liked to put it, creating circumstances such that the three of them continued to live in the closest proximity for a decade.

After the Nazi pogroms of 1938, Martha Arendt fled to Paris, where her daughter was already living with Blücher. Martha Arendt shared their apartment, joined them in the south of France after their internments, and emigrated to America very shortly after they did. In America she lived for seven years in the same rooming house as they, though on a different floor, and kept house for them.[10] In Paris, Martha Arendt had done well, being fluent in French and having numerous friends in the city where she had studied in her youth. Even there, however, and probably from much earlier, she already "concentrated her attention on her daughter," who felt "overmothered," as Young-Bruehl puts it. This became even more true in America, where Martha Arendt lacked a satisfying social life and "grew melancholy" in her isolation. The tensions between her and Blücher intensified; she found him crude and uncultured, resented his failure to find steady work, and felt that he had made her daughter "assertive and tough."[11]

Arendt herself, however, seems to have found in her second marriage and in her gradually developing career as a journalist, essayist, and historian a personal balance that worked for her, combining passion with realism, intellectual activity of scope and ambition with practical political concreteness, a successful career with family life, care for her husband with care for her mother, and genuine gratification with duty. In the period immediately preceding *The Human Condition*, however, two personal events unsettled this balance: Arendt's mother died, and she herself resumed contact with Heidegger.

In 1948, as Arendt was finishing *The Origins of Totalitarianism*, her mother decided to move to England, to live with her surviving stepdaughter, a woman from whom Hannah Arendt had long been estranged ("I have nothing to do with her," Arendt wrote to Jaspers in 1947).[12] On the ship to Europe, however, Martha Arendt suffered a heart attack, and soon after arriving she died. Arendt, on vacation alone when she received the news, wrote to Blücher about her complex feelings, referring cryptically to "the demand" her mother had chronically made on her, which she "could not simply refuse," yet "naturally . . . could also never completely fulfill," because that would have required "a radical destruction of myself and all my instincts." Indeed, she now saw that "for my whole childhood and half my youth" she had constantly striven "to conform to all expectations." Blücher tried to reassure his wife: "You did your best, and she would never have had enough, because when one has the passive love of a sponge, one always feels too dry. . . . Actually it makes me furious, her constant blood-sucking of you and her total lack of respect for your unbelievable work." He added that Arendt's mother had been "the one who, more than any other timid blockhead in our circle, simply and thoughtlessly took you for a man." Although the meaning of this remark is somewhat obscure, Martha Arendt's dependence on and investment in her daughter seems evident, as does her resentment of her daughter's involvement with Blücher and with her work. Arendt wrote Blücher that her mother's death left her "simultaneously sad and relieved."[13]

A year and a half later, visiting Europe under the auspices of the Commission on Jewish Cultural Reconstruction, Arendt looked up, first, Karl and Gertrud Jaspers, with whom she had been corresponding since 1945, and then Heidegger, with whom she had had no contact for twenty-two years. The latter encounter also involved Heidegger's wife, to whom he had confessed the affair. After that visit, Arendt and Heidegger resumed a correspondence, though never their affair; when she returned to Europe in 1952 to begin research toward *The Human Condition,* she saw him again.[14]

Resuming contact with Heidegger reawakened echoes in Arendt of her earlier, romantic self-abnegation toward him, as is clear from the detailed, if unreliably speculative, account of their correspondence offered by Elzbieta Ettinger. Though her love for and marriage to Blücher were never threatened, Arendt was both drawn to the now personally pitiful but philosophically still idealized Heidegger and frightened by the masochistic yearnings he still aroused in her, even though she now saw him clearly as a habitual liar. Each return to him was suffused for her with a feeling of temptation. In 1955, on yet another visit to Europe, during which Heidegger proved reluctant to see her, Arendt wrote to her husband that "the unspoken *conditio sine qua non*" of her whole relationship with Heidegger had been and remained her behaving "as though I have never written a word and will never write one."[15] And yet, while recognizing this as well as his deceitfulness, she nevertheless found that, as before, "the long and short of it" was: "I am at the brink of doing the same thing I did 30 years ago, and somehow I cannot change it. Caption: following the law that started 'it' off" (102). Although this remark is somewhat cryptic, it clearly does not mean that she was on the brink of resuming the affair. The real temptation concerned her relationship with herself: her yearning for self-denial in a romantic merger with an idealized, paternal, philosophical "other."

Arendt had long ago learned her lesson. The problem now was just how to construe its content: That abstraction leads to complicity in genocide? That ambition for a masculine profession, for abstraction, is unsuitable for a woman? That affairs with older, married men are forbidden?

That mother knows best and you must obey her even if it means your own "radical destruction"? That if you disobey her in quest of either ambition or erotic gratification, you will become "assertive and tough" to the point of causing her death? Is there no nurturant, responsible way for a woman to affirm herself and find both emotional and intellectual fulfillment, in both love and work, in both personal and public life, no way of combining gratification with care and commitment?

Psychoanalytic theory holds that the death or loss of a central person in one's life is likely to provoke intense unconscious feelings, in addition to whatever conscious mourning, relief, or anxiety it may arouse. Unconsciously, the bereaved are likely to feel abandoned and helpless, and therefore angry, and thus guilty, as if they had killed the deceased. The bereaved are also likely to identify more intensely with the lost person, whether this be construed as creating an idealized inner image to replace the lost person or as no longer having the real person available against whom to test inner images. All this is the more intense in proportion as the death or loss occurs early in childhood, when the psyche is not yet well developed and reality not yet reliably distinguished from fantasy.

One need not accept such psychoanalytic theory, however, to recognize that Arendt's early loss of her father might have left her hungry for fathering and vulnerable to idealized father figures, that her encounter with Heidegger might have left her wary of such figures and of her own yearnings, and that the (much later) death of her beloved but demanding mother might have reactivated psychic conflicts that had seemed settled. Her actual mother was no longer around, so an insistent pressure in her personal balance had suddenly been removed; yet, at the same time, being bereaved in a context of anger and strain as her mother went off to live with Arendt's estranged step-sister, Arendt surely must have felt new inner reproaches, a renewed concern to protect and obey parental—and particularly maternal—figures, perhaps including the world, which she had begun "only in recent years really to love" (*amor mundi*), and more specifically the "Earth, who was the Mother of all living creatures."[16]

Arendt on Women

There can be little doubt that issues of gender and relations between the sexes troubled Arendt. She was profoundly aware of what, in setting it aside at the beginning of *Rahel Varnhagen,* she called "the Woman Problem," meaning "the discrepancy between what men expected of women 'in general' and what women could give or wanted in their turn."[17] Yet she steadfastly refused to address the issue publicly, to focus her intellectual attention on it, or to support political organizing on its basis. Arendt was no feminist.

Personally, she was strong, resourceful, assertive, rebellious, ambitious, and of course fiercely intellectual. As a teacher she was authoritative, sometimes even authoritarian in manner. Yet she was also shy about speaking in public, avoided face-to-face conflict, and felt that she lacked "quite a number of qualities" required for political leadership. Indeed, she was "skeptical about whether women should be political leaders" and told an interviewer that she regarded "certain occupations . . . [as] not becoming to women," because it just "doesn't look good for a woman to issue orders."[18] When Arendt gave personal advice to younger women, Young-Bruehl reports, it "was as bourgeois and conventional in its details as it was, in important matters, open-minded and unsentimental."[19]

Like many academic women prior to the 1970s, moreover, Arendt was utterly unself-conscious about the masculine identifications implicit in the English language, not only in generic pronouns and terms such as "mankind" but also in more revealing individually crafted locutions. In 1946, focused on the Jewish question, Arendt wrote without any apparent sense of incongruity, "We are the sons of our fathers and grandsons of our grandfathers."[20] And even in the 1970s, near the end of her life, she was able to write, and presumably to say out loud in front of a class, "for Kant, the philosopher remains a man like you and me."[21]

In her early adulthood in Berlin, Arendt did publish a short review of a new book on "the contemporary woman-problem." That review criticized the women's movement as having made no advances "on the political fronts, which are still masculine fronts," because the movement moves "only as a unified, undifferentiated whole," without articulating any "concrete goals." A women's movement is politically problematic and bound to remain "abstract," Arendt wrote, if it remains "a movement only for the sake of women," as a youth movement is only on behalf of youth.[22] Young-Bruehl comments: "Arendt was arguing against divorcing women's issues from the larger range of political concerns, just as she later argued against divorcing Jewish issues from national and international political concerns."[23] The parallel is surely correct, yet while Arendt continued to work on Jewish concerns, she never again addressed women's concerns as such. So one cannot quite maintain that in general she treated the one topic *"just as"* she treated the other.

Indeed, as numerous interpreters have pointed out, it is striking that Arendt, so heroically engaged with "the Jewish question" all her life, always refused to address her other pariahdom, "the Woman Problem." Fleeing Jewish pariahdom as a parvenu exception was forbidden, because one must instead fight openly, on principle, in solidarity with fellow pariahs, politically. Fleeing feminine pariahdom as a parvenu exception was also forbidden, but here one may not fight openly, in solidarity with other women, politically. Women must ignore their disadvantages publicly and overcome them privately by extra effort or by circumvention.

Despite her early book review, Arendt told a friend in the 1970s that the woman question had "never interested" her; whenever her own femininity came up in public, she announced firmly that it did not trouble her, was not an issue—in effect, that the topic should never have been raised.[24] Yet there seems to have been something defensive in her tone, as if a hidden temptation were being warded off. During the controversy over her book on Eichmann, for example, Arendt, accused of failing in her duty as "a daughter of" the Jewish people, responded: "The truth is that I have never pretended to be anything else or to be in any way other than I am, and I have never felt tempted in that direction. It would have been like saying that I was a man and not a woman—that is to say, kind of insane.... I have never had the wish to change or disclaim facts of this kind."[25] Never have I even been tempted to become a parvenu!

In her second letter to Jaspers after the war, Arendt explained that she had kept her own surname rather than adopting Blücher's, a practice "quite common here in America when a woman works," a custom she "gladly" adopted both out of "conservatism" and "because I wanted my name to identify me as a Jew."[26]

When Arendt was invited to lecture at Princeton University as the first woman ever selected for the prestigious Christian Gaus seminar, she told an interviewer that she was "not disturbed at all about being a woman professor, because I am quite used to being a woman."[27] But the fact is she *was* disturbed about the Princeton invitation, anxious lest she become a favored exception at the expense of her fellow pariahs. To Kurt Blumenfeld—who had "opened [her] eyes" on the Jewish question—she confided afterward how, when some Princeton professors expressed pleasure at having a woman appear in the series, she felt required to "enlighten ... these *dignified gentlemen*" from the faculty of this most "snobbish" of universities about what an "exception Jew" is, so as to make clear why she was not pleased to be there as an "exception woman."[28]

Bonnie Honig has written that "Arendt's famous reluctance to identify herself as a woman and to address women's issues" should be seen less as "a personal problem of male-identification" than as a political stance of resistance to "a symbolic order that seeks to define, categorize, and stabilize her in terms of one essential, unriven, and always already known identity."[29] Although Arendt was not exactly "reluctant to identify herself as a woman"—almost the opposite was the case when someone brought up the subject—Honig is surely right that her irritated dismissal of the woman question was a mode of resistance to people (not, I think, to a "symbolic order") seeking to impose conventional expectations of what is feminine, not so much on her (the "exceptional woman") as on her more vulnerable fellow pariahs. But useful as that insight is, Honig herself acknowledges that it does not explain the striking difference between Arendt's handling of her two pariahdoms: Jewish and feminine. A mystery remains (7).

Sometimes the issue seems to be duty, the obligation to maintain solidarity with the victims, first imposed on Arendt by her mother in relation to anti-Semitism. At other times, however, particularly in relation to gender, the issue seems to be not duty but pleasure, perhaps because gender is so intimately tied to sexuality and desire. During a discussion of women's liberation at a 1972 editorial board meeting, Arendt scribbled a note to a (male) friend: "The real question to ask is, what will we lose if we win?"[30] Although her meaning is not entirely obvious, it seems likely that Arendt was linking sexual fulfillment and a happy marriage to the maintenance of gender difference.

That surmise is strengthened if one accepts the suggestion of several commentators that Arendt's 1966 portrait of Rosa Luxemburg—her mother's political heroine—contains clues about Arendt herself. Luxemburg's being "self-consciously a woman," Arendt writes in that essay, meant first of all her recognition that she was an "outsider" (the word "pariah" does not appear). It meant recognition, second, of "certain limitations on whatever her ambitions might otherwise have been." And it meant, third, Luxemburg's attraction to Leo Jogiches, whose being "definitely *masculini generis* . . . was of considerable importance to her." The Latin phrase, perhaps token of a slight embarrassment, was one Arendt sometimes applied to her own second husband. Finally, Luxemburg's self-conscious femininity also meant her "distaste for the women's emancipation movement, to which all other women of her generation and political convictions were irresistibly drawn," a distaste Arendt summarizes in the French expression "*Vive la petite différence!*"[31] That expression is the punchline of a slightly risqué joke implying that sexual pleasure depends on maintaining gender difference and thus on established conventions of gender.

One might note also Arendt's remarks on another woman she much admired, Isaak Dinesen, the Baroness Blixen, born Karen Christenze Dinesen, who adopted a male pseudonym when she wrote because of "her firm conviction that it was not very becoming for a woman to be an author, hence a public figure." Dinesen, Arendt adds, "had had her experiences in this matter since her mother had been a suffragette . . . and probably one of those excellent women who will never tempt a man to seduce them" (95).

In Honig's terms, Arendt's stance of recognizing the limitations imposed on feminine ambitions while rejecting public feminism was surely *both* a way to "resist" *and* a "personal problem of . . . identification" for her, but not because she had somehow chosen the wrong (a "male") identification—whether that be condemned as disloyal or inauthentic or both—but because she was deeply and unconsciously conflicted about gender as she was not about Jewishness.

At the conscious level there are problems and conflicts enough facing not just women but all pariahs who seek to enter the public world as citizen peers—problems about identity and classification, desire and duty, individual judgment and convention. Becoming a free, autonomous citizen, Arendt insists, requires realism, the disenchanted recognition both of one's true, unique self and of one's socially ascribed categories. But what, exactly, is the relation between the two?

The difficulties can be brought into focus by a passage from an essay Arendt published in the same year as *The Human Condition,* in which her charge of apolitical abstractness, first articulated in the early review on the woman problem, reappears. Here this charge is leveled against the ideal of world citizenship; yet it is again explicitly—and revealingly—linked to gender. Arendt writes: "Just as men and women can be the same, namely human, only by being absolutely different from each other, so the national of every country can enter [the] world history of humanity only by remaining and clinging stubbornly to what he is. A world citizen . . . would be no less a monster than a hermaphrodite."[32] On one level, this passage says only that world citizenship is apolitical and abstract because it lacks—perhaps in principle cannot have—a practical, institutional arena for action.[33] But on another level the passage says that action and citizenship presuppose a resolute recognition of—indeed, "clinging to"—one's true, concrete identity. The passage points in two opposite directions, revealing a problem. On the one hand, it echoes the many places where Arendt stresses individual human uniqueness, and action as spontaneity—the expression and revelation of that uniqueness, of "who" in particular one is. Indeed, the wording of the passage closely parallels that of one in *The Human Condition* emphasizing that "plurality"—individual uniqueness—is prerequisite to action, "because we are all the same, that is, human, in such a way that nobody is ever the same as anyone else who ever lived, lives, or will live."[34]

Yet, on the other hand, the passage on world citizenship clearly is *not* about clinging to one's unique "who" but about accepting one's various conventional classifications, *what* one is: a "national" of some particular country, a Jew, a woman (179–88, 211, 241–42). The choices available are preexisting and limited, the residual categories being "hermaphrodite" and "monster." On the first reading, the advice to pariahs aspiring to politics is "Be who you uniquely are! Judge for yourself; never mind conventions and what others think." On the second reading, by contrast, the advice is "Maintain solidarity with 'your people'! Acknowledge yourself to be as convention has classified you, and stick with the others so classified." Not only do the two kinds of advice conflict, but both involve problems about who defines the categories. Does the individual always know best who he uniquely is? And if I must accept my public classifications as a woman, a Jew, an American, does that mean I must also accept the conventional stereotypes about femininity, Judaism, and Americanism?

In addition, pariahs who want to act as citizens must consider which aspects of the unique self and of the ascribed categories are suited to political expression. Arendt holds that some matters—love, for example, or moral purity—are inherently private and would be destroyed in public life. Others—the concerns of the *animal laborans* and of *homo faber*—will corrupt and destroy politics if publicly pursued. Pariah peoples are particularly likely to bring with them into politics unsuitable aspects of their selves or their group, both because they lack political experience and because they are likely to have been psychologically damaged by growing up stigmatized. Former slaves who aspire to free citizenship must take special care lest they make public life slavish instead of free. (Of course, the masters are damaged too, and the political life from which they previously excluded the pariahs can't have been genuinely public or free, either, but that is not the issue at the moment.)

So there is a problem about how much, or what aspects, of one's unique self are to be engaged in political action. The abstract rights of man and world citizenship exclude too much of who one is, yet some—inherently private—concerns and all that is "social" must be excluded. If the pariah "translates his status into political terms" and fights for his people, for example, for the "admission of Jews *as Jews* to the ranks of" citizenship, and if he should succeed, would he then be a Jew or a citizen, and who would then be "his people"?[35]

Concerning Jews, Arendt sees and tries to address these problems, even if she is not always fully successful. She sees the Jewish but not the feminine difficulties in being "a man in the street and a Jew at home." She sees the dangers in entering politics without experience of public responsibility, the risk that "formerly oppressed peoples" who come to power may "develop nationalist superiority complexes of their own," yet she does not hesitate to regard the Jewish question as political.[36] Not so the woman problem. It is as if, for Arendt, the very category "woman" were inherently in conflict with politics, were by definition either private or social. Now that is, indeed, part of what being a woman conventionally connotes in a culture such as ours, which tends systematically to confuse personhood, authority, adulthood, and humanness with being male.[37] Yet it surely is not part of what a woman seeking to be a free citizen should "realistically" accept about herself, or about fellow members of her category, and bring with her into public life.

These are clearly issues of classification, of what would today—I think misleadingly—be called "essentialism."[38] They concern whether, when, and how it is ever right to generalize about human beings, including oneself, abstracting from their individual uniqueness and sorting them into conventional categories. Arendt is surely right that no general category can fully capture or do justice to who a particular individual is. Yet without something like generalization, abstracting from particulars, we would be unable to talk at all, to think conceptually, to learn from experience and share what we have learned, to make judgments and pursue justice, let alone to practice politics, philosophy, or political theory. These are difficult issues, to which we shall return briefly in the concluding chapters. For now the point is only that both Jewishness and femininity raise issues of abstraction, the mode of thinking which so attracted Arendt but which she had learned to fear, yet she responded differently in relation to the one category than to the other.

Authority and Gender

Abstraction itself is tied specifically to gender, not just for Arendt personally because of Heidegger and philosophy, but also much more generally in our (and Arendt's) culture. Abstract thinking and tasks involving formal, explicit generalization are stereotypically assigned to men, while concrete and personal concerns are assigned to women. Men are supposed to be objective, rational, detached, to operate in the large-scale, public, rule-governed worlds of science, engineering, mathematics, logic, and law. Women, by contrast, are supposed to take care of particular and personal matters, to attend to the immediate, concrete needs of specific individuals on a face-to-face basis. The attentive, nurturant juggling of urgent particulars that is involved, for example, in managing a household with small children surely requires a kind of implicit generalizing and planning, but precisely one that remains implicit, unarticulated and flexible, ready to adapt at a moment's notice.

By now there exists a considerable scholarly literature arguing that these are not merely conventional role expectations but also correspond to the psychic predilections of many—though not all—men and women reared in our (and Arendt's) cultural system and family patterns.[39] Because we mostly assign the care of infants and small children to women, and insofar as we distinguish adult roles fairly sharply by gender, the psychic tasks involved in maturation are different for boys than for girls. Boys need to differentiate themselves more decisively than do girls from that world of mothers and small children in which almost all of us begin our lives, and to reject more stridently their own occasional yearning to return to that world.

As a result, boys and men tend to feel psychically more threatened by continued connection with femininity, nurturance, need, emotion, and dependence. Girls and women, by contrast, tend to experience psychic security in continued relationship and nurturance; what feels threatening to them is separation, the rupture of connections, rejection, abandonment. Each gender, as Carol Gilligan says, thus tends to mark "as dangerous the [psychic] place which the other defines as safe." For men, adulthood and "gender identity" are threatened by "intimacy," for women, by "separation."[40] One of the characteristic ways for men in our culture to defend themselves against vulnerability and dependence, Gilligan and other writers suggest, is by taking refuge in abstraction. Men tend to seek the protection of distance, generality, rules and rights, formal and impersonal principles. Women instead fear that same, cold abstractness, preferring at all costs to sustain and adjust relationships on an ad hoc basis. Boys learn early, as Seyla Benhabib summarizes Gilligan's point, to adopt the standpoint of "the generalized other," girls to adopt that of "the particular other."[41]

Gilligan's work reaches back indirectly to Jean Piaget's pioneering studies of children's games in Switzerland, which discerned similar patterns. Piaget found that little boys played games characterized by intense competition under elaborate systems of rules, and that working out conflicts over the application of these rules was central to their pleasure in the game. As little boys gradually learned how to play, they also learned how rules are made, changed, and applied and how to settle disputes in an impersonal way, so that the boys could play even with their enemies. Girls, Piaget found, played less formal games and less competitively. If conflict arose, or if it looked as if someone's feelings might be hurt, the girls preferred to abandon the game. Playing mostly with a small number of friends, they developed an empathic attentiveness to feelings but not much experience with handling open conflict or abstracting general principles.[42]

Gilligan speaks accordingly of two competing "voices" in morality: one emphasizing general principles and justice, the other emphasizing personal attention and care, the former more frequent among men, the latter among women. Although it is easy to jump to the conclusion—as numerous interpreters have—that the feminine tendency is more moral, the masculine tendency ruthless or hypocritical, Gilligan holds that a mature morality is the same for all, regardless of gender, that it requires combining principled impartiality with sensitive attention to particular persons and cases. What differs by gender is not morality but characteristic ways of falling short of morality. Morally immature men tend to a defensive, macho pretense at objectivity and impersonal authority, immature women to a reluctance to judge, take a principled stand, or defend their own views in the face of opposition. Reaching morality by different psychic routes, the two genders characteristically find themselves in different places along the way: men too coldly abstracted, women too abjectly adjustable.

Such psychological and gender-related themes, and indeed Arendt's personal life, may at first seem irrelevant to the meaning of the social and its role in *The Human Condition,* but they prove illuminating in at least two ways. The first way is mainly about fathers and authority and speaks to Arendt's use of Tocqueville, Marx, and Heidegger. The second way is mainly about mothers and speaks more directly to the social as Blob and to the structure of Arendt's book.

Paternal Sponsorship

Beginning with fathers and authority, one might now say in terms both of Arendt's personal concerns and of widely shared cultural norms and psychic predilections that in undertaking a general theory of free citizenship, Arendt was venturing to play a boys' game, indeed, to play with the Big Boys on an equal footing. As a woman (and to some extent also as a Jew, particularly in relation to the German academic world), she lacked authority to play.[43] Disqualified on allegedly biological grounds, Arendt surely both rebelled against this unjust dispensation and internalized it. She simultaneously yearned to be in the game, to possess—and prove her possession of—the "masculine" powers of abstraction and authority, feared failure at the game and punishment for her temerity, and rejected the game for its "masculine" abstractness, unreality, and impersonality.

The idea of action in its conceptual triad seemed to offer a way out, but one that was narrow, difficult, risky, and must often have seemed beyond Arendt's reach. Seyla Benhabib rightly observes that in *The Human Condition* Arendt "found her own philosophical voice."[44] I am suggesting, in addition, that at points in the book where she doubted the authority of that voice, she yearned for a sponsoring intellectual father, but of course yearned ambivalently. Her way of securing such sponsorship while avoiding the costs it seemed to entail was to steal it, seize it, appropriate it for herself, rather than maneuver or petition for it like a parvenu, abandoning or hiding her own autonomy. Now, every thinker leans on the ideas of others, consciously or not. I am not accusing Arendt of plagiarism, of claiming credit for ideas not her own, or even of any intent to deceive her readers. In those moments when she despaired of her own powers and helped herself to those of the fathers, she was mainly deceiving not her readers but herself.

Arendt's peculiar, ambivalent treatment of her intellectual authorities, I am suggesting, should be understood as an effort to take from the fathers the authority to join them, without becoming dependent on them. Because that effort originated in self-doubt, partly internalized from cultural mores about gender, abstraction, and ambition, it was fraught with ambivalence and psychic conflict. Because of that ambivalence, her effort mostly escaped Arendt's explicit conscious attention, so that she also failed to think critically about certain intellectual problems that in effect came with the loot she seized, notably the problem of the Blob. These problems show up particularly in the sections of *The Human Condition* where the conceptual triad is displaced by a paralyzing dyad of autonomy-destroying parental figures that permit no third term: the social and the Greeks.

Before turning to this structural observation and the matter of mothers, however, we should note that Arendt's appropriation of masculine intellectual powers worked out differently in relation to the various important authority figures on whom she drew. In relation to Marx, we saw, it meant appropriating something very like his fundamental notion of alienation while denying its existence in Marx and fiercely attacking him for having omitted that notion. In relation to Tocqueville, it meant adopting his view of America, of politics, and of *liberté,* without public acknowledgment. In both cases it may also have meant adopting uncritically their tendency to envision a Blob.

Most striking of all are Arendt's complex debts to and critique of Heidegger's ideas, topics that go far beyond our specific concerns and that fortunately have recently been explored in detail by scholars such as Seyla Benhabib, Jacques Taminiaux, and Dana R. Villa.[45] We have focused in this respect only on *das Man,* together with the *déformation professionelle* Arendt came to think characteristic of philosophy. When the German translation of *The Human Condition* appeared in 1960, Arendt sent Heidegger a copy with a note saying she would have liked to dedicate the book to him, since it "evolved directly from the first Freiburg [Marburg] days and it owes you just about everything in every regard."[46] In the book itself, Heidegger is never mentioned. Whatever degree of authenticity, or indeed sincerity, one ascribes to the note, it surely supports the notion of Heidegger as an ambivalently viewed paternal sponsoring authority for Arendt.

Both Benhabib and Taminiaux show the extent to which Arendt developed (mostly unacknowledged) critiques of some of Heidegger's substantive ideas and how this shaped her own intellectual agenda. Taminiaux adds that what she took from Heidegger most directly and uncritically was certain philosophical methods or devices.[47] Three such Heideggerian rhetorical tools are particularly striking in *The Human Condition,* though at least two of them characterize much of philosophy more generally, and particularly of German philosophy. The first is a focus on certain revelatory concepts. The second is a claim of exclusive access to the original and true meaning of those concepts. The third is invocation specifically of the ancient Greeks as the source of those concepts' true meaning.

It is in *The Human Condition* that all three of these intellectual tools come to characterize Arendt's work, as if the challenge of formulating a general theory drove Arendt to their adoption. Even as she began identifying her work as "political theory," she also came to her specific method of retrieving the "original" meanings of certain crucial concepts, which have "been lost."[48] The rhetorical claim to authority invoked again echoes Heidegger's philosophical stance. Indeed, as suggested in chapter 3, Arendt's hypostasization of "social" may well be part of this Heideggerian manner.[49]

As for invoking the authority of the Greeks, it is as if for the formulation of a general theory, Arendt's own experience—Jewish, feminine, and pariah—was not good enough, not sufficiently dignified, impersonal, and worthy.[50] To render it suitable for the Big Boys' game, that experience had first to be transformed by substituting the Greeks for the Jews and men for a woman. Indeed, given the Greeks' notorious misogyny and competitive heroics, one might regard their role for Arendt as a paternal sponsorship twice over: both in their own masculinism and as an appropriated Heideggerian philosophical device. But it is not easy to sort out such personal, Arendtian elements from the much broader, notorious Grecophilia of the entire German philosophical tradition.[51]

As with respect to Marx and Tocqueville, however, so too with respect to Heidegger: Arendt's invocation of paternal authority is profoundly ambivalent. Though she appropriates Heidegger's way with words, she also holds it in contempt for its self-important dismissal of common sense and ordinary speech. In a private letter from the year in which *The Human Condition* appeared, Arendt criticizes Heidegger for the "indescribably annoying manneredness" of his work, his arrogant and pretentious citing of himself "as though he had written a Biblical text." In Heidegger she recognizes this as an unnecessary defensive mechanism: "he really is a genius . . . why does he need this?"[52]

With respect to the Greeks, Arendt's ambivalence toward her appropriated authority is even more striking. Though she follows Heidegger and German philosophy more generally by invoking the Greek understanding of key concepts, Arendt's Greeks are not exactly Heidegger's or those of the philosophical tradition. Hers are the Greeks of *polis* citizenship, Athenian democracy, and the *bios politikos*, not merely different from but historically ranged in explicit opposition to the contemplative life and the oligarchically allied Athenian philosophers. Thus Arendt uses the ancient Greeks to dignify her own experience and authorize her critique of the way the abstraction game has been played, a critique that, in Gilligan's and Piaget's terms, one would have to call "feminine": the game has been irresponsibly abstracted, insufficiently attentive to the concrete needs, pain, and agency of actual people.

Yet the ancient Greeks also bring with them into her argument their own misogyny, ethnocentrism, and false heroics, partly undermining the argument Arendt introduced them to serve. Explicating and echoing their views on citizenship, Arendt herself sometimes seems to disparage women, the body and its needs, the household and family. This is no mere accident due to carelessness, this chapter has been suggesting, but reflects her own self-disparagement in the theory game, which drives her to seek paternal sponsorship in the first place, however ambivalently. The pattern, then, is viciously circular. That pattern, and the light it sheds on Arendt's peculiar mode of dealing with her intellectual authorities, is the first way in which psychological and gender concerns illuminate the argument of *The Human Condition*—a way connected mainly with fathers and with authority.

Maternal Danger and the Gendered Structure of *The Human Condition*

There is also a second way, connected more with mothers and more directly informative about the social as Blob. From this second perspective, the Greeks are there not despite but precisely because of their patriarchal, misogynist machismo. Despite the historical distance between ancient Greece and modern society, from this perspective the Greeks serve in the symbolic logic of the book to control the Blob, the hidden danger in femininity. But to see how this might be so, one needs first to recognize the extent to which the structure of *The Human Condition* is itself symbolically gendered.

Here we are particularly indebted to Mary Dietz, who has recently explored the book's "provocative gender subtext," meaning not its explicit references to women and family but the underlying "gendered structure" of the argument itself.[53] Dietz shows that what we have noted with respect to various problems Arendt faced in writing *The Human Condition* holds also of gender: the conceptual triad of labor, work, and action offers a liberating way out. It offers a transition beyond the conventional, rigid, dichotomous construction of gender roles, Dietz says, and "displaces the binary of gender" (20). Accordingly, she criticizes both feminist thinkers such as Mary O'Brien and Adrienne Rich, who read Arendt as "phallocentric," as advocating a masculine view, and those such as Nancy Hartsock, who read her as "gynocentric," as drawing her central concepts—such as that of "natality"—from women's experience (23–28). The former, Dietz says, think Arendt favors the public, masculine world of humanly fashioned institutions over the private, feminine world of biology and nature. The latter end up assimilating action, by way of its connection with natality, to labor. Both groups misconstrue as dichotomous an argument that for Arendt is triadic. Action and politics are neither masculine nor feminine in Arendt's book but escape the dichotomization of gender.

There are, indeed, "two concepts that Arendt does relentlessly gender as [respectively] feminine and masculine," Dietz says, but they are not feminine "private" and masculine "public"; they are "labor" and "work." This pair of gendered concepts, however, is part of a triad whose "third concept, action, is existentially superior, as the embodiment of freedom, to both the biological cyclicalities of 'earth's servant,' *animal laborans,* and the means-end fabrications of 'earth's lord and master,' *homo faber.*"[54] About this, it seems to me, Dietz is brilliantly right, as she is about the correspondingly liberating function of the concept of action.

The *animal laborans* is indeed feminine. Explicating the concept of labor, Arendt, unlike any earlier theorist who employs the term, stresses the sense of that word associated with giving birth, an inexorable physiological process, independent of will or intent, usually involving pain and severe effort by the whole body, and "producing" new life.[55]

Even when Arendt turns from labor as birthing to labor as production of food and shelter, she continues to emphasize its connection with the inexorable "life process," and she often speaks of laboring in terms more reminiscent of conventional housework than of agriculture or hunting. She stresses its empty, meaningless repetitiveness (hardly descriptive of giving birth), as people get hungry over and over, the food disappearing almost as soon as it's ready, one meal barely over before preparation for the next must begin. Although Arendt says that "laboring and consuming follow each other so closely that they almost constitute one and the same movement," her imagery suggests not a hungry person preparing and then enjoying food, but the entrapped housewife endlessly feeding others in dutiful, repetitive, self-denying monotony, driven not by her own needs but by those of her helpless dependents.[56]

Besides feeding (and birthing), the *animal laborans* has a second task, which is the "constant, unending fight against the processes of growth and decay through which nature forever invades the human artifice, . . . [through] the monotonous performance of daily repeated chores."[57] The classical myth of Hercules cleaning the Augean stables is misleading, Arendt says, because the daily (feminine) "fight . . . to keep the world clean and prevent its decay" is not in fact like (masculine) heroism. It requires "endurance" rather than "courage," and what makes it "painful is not [its] danger but its relentless repetition." Only in myth, she remarks caustically, does the Augean stable stay clean once the heroic sanitizing task is accomplished.[58]

Like the life of a middle-class housewife, furthermore, particularly in the burgeoning suburbs of the 1950s in America—and like the experience of intense pain in giving birth—labor is isolating, characterized by a "strict and even cruel privacy." Indeed, it is "the most private of all human activities," just as pain is "the most private and least communicable of all" experiences, and therefore forgotten "more quickly and easily than anything else," as is often said (though not by Arendt) about the pain of childbirth.[59] Agriculture, lumbering, ditch-digging, even hunting are by no means inherently isolating activities, as Arendt acknowledges, and she tries to defend her claim about labor by the somewhat strained argument that in joint laboring the "individuals 'labor together as though they were one,'" losing "all awareness of individuality and identity."[60] The images behind this curious claim, I am suggesting, are the pain involved in giving birth and the experience of housewives trapped at home all day with small children.[61]

Work, in Arendt's account, is altogether different. Though it, too, is isolating and privatizing, and though it is less blatantly gendered than labor, Dietz is surely right to read it as symbolically masculine. *Homo faber* is characterized not by helpless entrapment in process but by technical mastery and efficiency, a narrowly focused instrumentalism. Though he, too, "produces . . . in the privacy of isolation" since "there can be hardly anything more alien or even more destructive to workmanship than teamwork," *homo faber*'s isolation is that not of endurance but of mastery, "primarily a mastery of things and material." He needs to be "alone with the 'idea,' the mental image of the thing to be," which he will realize in his product. Work and mastery, Arendt claims, were originally synonymous, which may be why the question of effectiveness is somehow "a masculine question."[62]

Homo faber's goal-oriented instrumentalism and habitual focus on the material world imply "a degradation of all things into means, their loss of intrinsic and independent value." This makes him ruthless both toward other people—contrary to Kantian precepts about the "kingdom of ends"—and toward his materials and the material environment in which he works—"'the earth in general and all forces of nature.'"[63] Although, as Dietz points out, *homo faber* is in some respects helpful to the *animal laborans,* easing the effort involved in life's "sustenance and the pain of giving birth," he is ruthlessly exploitive toward nature and "Earth . . . the Mother."[64] With his "huge arsenal" of tools, which he "uses to erect the [material] world," he seeks to make himself "lord and master of the whole earth," treating nature "as the almost 'worthless material' upon which to work." Thus, an "element of violation and violence is present in all fabrication, and *homo faber,* the creator of the human artifice, has always been a destroyer of nature," whether in "killing a life process," as when a tree is cut down for the carpenter, or in "interrupting one of nature's slower processes," as when minerals are "torn out of the womb of the earth."[65]

Since Arendt consistently genders labor and work as, respectively, feminine and masculine, Dietz argues, an interpreter such as O'Brien, who "poses the problem of human nature as a binary male:female opposition . . . effectively erases Arendt's commitment to a tripartite notion of activities," substituting the dyadic contrast "nature:society."[66] What Dietz herself fails to register, however, is that critics such as O'Brien are not alone in distorting Arendt's triadic scheme into a gendered, dichotomous contrast; Arendt herself does so as well, in the second chapter of *The Human Condition,* where the orderly explication of the conceptual triad is interrupted by the introduction of both the social as Blob and the ancient Greeks.[67] The structure of Arendt's book is not simply and uniformly triadic, but more complex than Dietz acknowledges, in ways that profoundly reflect Arendt's ambivalences about autonomy, ambition, and gender.

The Social as Feminine

That the social is itself gendered for Arendt, and gendered feminine, is most evident where she seems to equate it with labor. In the next chapter we shall see that no such simple equation will do; it is, however, the place to begin. The rise of society, we have seen, means "the rise of the 'household'" and its traditionally feminine concerns "to the public realm," as "housekeeping and all matters pertaining formerly to the private sphere of the family . . . become a 'collective' concern."[68] This rise, however, is also the overturning of paternal control of feminine forces; it means turning those forces loose, letting "the life process . . . into the public realm" (45). Thus, the social *is* "the public organization of the life process itself," which escapes masculine—and thus human—control as the *animal laborans* is "liberated from the restrictions [of] . . . the private realm" (46–47).

But Arendt's notion of society and social concerns was already gendered as feminine long before she hypostasized the adjective and before she came upon the triad of labor, work, and action. The figure of the parvenu greatly resembles the conventionally defined feminine role: abject, deferential, dependent, yet also secretly self-centered, manipulative, and resentful. It is, after all, no accident that Arendt's affair with Heidegger seems in important respects to inform her image of the parvenu. Indeed, as feminist scholarship has indicated, women have almost always and in almost all societies been something like a pariah category, even where they were in certain respects privileged or protected. Women are generally lower in status than men, do not fully count as human persons, are not expected to run things, to lead, to exercise authority (except, of course and importantly, in relation to children). Where women are privileged and honored—say, as the Virgin Mary or the stereotypical beloved Mom who makes apple pie—they are usually in a role safely subordinated to some dominant male figure. In these senses, women, like many pariahs, have the option of becoming parvenus, seeking their individual advantage indirectly by pleasing men, an option that is culturally much encouraged, if not enforced.

Like Arendt's parvenu, then, women are both encouraged to seek and stereotypically seen as seeking individual advantage by subservience to men, in competition rather than solidarity with other women. Like the parvenu, they tend to internalize their pariah status, perceiving the world and themselves through the eyes of supposedly superior others and experiencing difficulty in generalizing and judging for themselves.[69] Like the parvenu, the stereotypical woman is thus passive and dependent in one sense while continually, even obsessively active in another, more indirect, unacknowledged, and manipulative sense. Behind her efforts to accommodate and to please there lies, as Arendt said about the parvenu, an "inevitable but intolerable resentment," which cannot be directly expressed and therefore is partly redirected against the self and fellow pariahs.[70]

But it is not just Arendt's image of the parvenu that suggests the femininity of the social. In ordinary usage, too, society and social matters are multiply classified as women's concerns. Women are stereotypically supposed to take charge of "social life" as hostesses, matchmakers, arrangers of parties, dinners, weddings, as they once were of salons. It is women who are stereotypically supposed to keep track of social relationships—marriages, family feuds, affairs, births, deaths—and to do the unpaid work of soothing feelings and repairing personal connections. Women are the ones expected to enforce social conventions through gossip, upholding norms they neither make nor judge autonomously, in a manner geared mainly to maintaining appearances and avoiding open conflict.

With respect to public life, Denise Riley has traced the extent to which, since the nineteenth century, "social concerns" have been women's special province, not only because social welfare and social services involve nurturance and care but also because what are now called the "helping professions" were among the earliest paid careers open to women.[71] The modern regulatory welfare state, although largely run by men, like other states, not only employs large numbers of women in such roles but is often perceived as symbolically feminine: as nurturing and solicitous by its supporters, as smothering, intrusive, and controlling by its enemies, in a manner reminiscent of Tocqueville's nightmarish "immense protective power" that "would resemble parental authority if, father-like, it tried to prepare its charges for a man's life" but instead (motherlike) "keep[s] them in perpetual childhood."[72]

Finally, *The Human Condition* is one of a number of studies appearing in the 1950s that expressed concern about something variously called "mass society," "mass culture," or simply "the mass," in America or—in accord with "convergence theory"—in the modern world as a whole. These writers and Arendt contributed to a tradition, as Andreas Huyssen has shown in detail, in which the mass had long been gendered, perceived as feminine and dangerously engulfing. Around the turn of the century in particular, "the political, psychological, and aesthetic discourse . . . consistently and obsessively gender[ed] mass culture and the masses as feminine," as "devouring," and as symbolized by "ooze, swamp, and flood." In short, "the fear of the masses in this age of declining liberalism [was] always also a fear of woman, a fear of nature out of control, a fear of the unconscious, of sexuality, of the loss of identity and stable ego boundaries."[73] Helmuth Berking agrees that the mass psychology literature of that period "thematizes 'mass' primarily from the perspective of regression" and "the absence of the subject" in the sense of a responsible agent: "As part of a mass the individual loses his identity, becomes a primitive savage, a mere creature of instinct, proto-human . . . a piece of 'nature.' "[74]

Huyssen and Berking both note that after World War I this explicit gendering of mass society is muted, displaced by themes of technology and of mechanical reproduction gone out of control. But Michael Rogin has pointed out the close connection between the two kinds of imagery in the popular culture of 1950s America, and specifically in the Cold-War and science-fiction motion pictures of that era. These films, he says, are a "register of anxiety," reflecting unconscious fears about "boundary invasion, loss of autonomy, and maternal power."[75] The Cold-War films "construct a Manichaean universe to protect American boundaries from invasion" while in the science-fiction movies "female reproductive power . . . proliferates interchangeable identities" and "biology is out of control," appearing in the form either of "promiscuous, undifferentiated vegetable reproduction" or of "bad mothers" who produce offspring that "lack the stamp of individuality," being mere "interchangeable parts."[76]

Fears of invasion by the insidious Cold-War enemy thus mingle with anxieties about dangerous, resentful housewives and mothers trapped at home in the burgeoning suburbs of this era. Indeed, the suburbs themselves are also seen in such terms; Rogin cites an article from *Esquire* that says they "took root and multiplied almost like a strange, unnatural new life form . . . a social cancer," that there was "something unnatural, menacing, even alien in the bloblike growth of the postwar [su]burbs."[77] What distinguishes Arendt from most mass society theorists is that she explicitly envisions an alternative and insists that it is still within reach: that even in mass society people are not, after all, merely pieces of nature. Mass society theorists are fatalistic, holding that human progress has come to an end, drowned in a sea of sameness and banality. Arendt is a mass society theorist to the extent that she envisions the social as a Blob rather than as a condition that we are even now continually generating. But our entire inquiry in this book is based on the obviously anomalous role that this image of the social plays in Arendt's theorizing.

The Bad Mother

Here we arrive, then, at the social as Blob. Whereas common conventions, ordinary usage, mass-society literature, and 1950s science-fiction link society to femininity in many ways, Arendt's social is not merely feminine but specifically maternal. It is not, to be sure, a nurturing, protective, gentle mother, let alone one who rejoices in her children's gradual maturation toward independence, but an evil, dominating, destructive matriarch constantly seeking to expand her power, to control and infantilize her children, to render them docile and make them behave, until she finally extinguishes their independence altogether, destroying all boundaries and merging the "children" back into a single mass—herself. It is a vision of matriarchal tyranny, of the "bad mother" as she is experienced—according to certain branches of psychoanalytic theory—by infants in those inevitable moments of early life characterized by pain, frustration, distress, and rage.[78]

According to a growing body of scholarship in this genre, the infant does not yet have a delimited, continuing sense of itself, cannot distinguish between self and mother (meaning, of course, the primary caregiver), nor between self and world. It is not even aware yet of continuing, distinct persons and objects, which vanish and return. It cannot yet distinguish between dream or hallucination and reality. Its experience is intensely physical and centers on eating and digestion, thus on the mouth, the belly, and the (mother's) breast, ranging from rapacious devouring to blissful satiation. It has as yet no psychic mechanisms for controlling or filtering the flow of experiences it undergoes and is unable to moderate either external stimuli or inner emotions. Thus, in effect, its waking experience is of a series of fragmented moments, often intensely suffused with affect, in which the momentary self-world-mother mix is sometimes blissfully good-beautiful-happy-omnipotent and sometimes horribly bad-painful-furious-helpless.

Yet the infant's experience is also, from the outset and increasingly as it grows, engaged with relationship and agency, effort and response, recognition, and the beginnings of interaction. As the baby gradually develops a sense of itself as a continuing, distinct being, of its body as separate from other objects, itself as separate from its mother, and both as persons rather than inanimate objects, it makes efforts at initiative and autonomy. Sometimes its body, the world, its mother are responsive, its efforts successful; at other times, inevitably, not. In this negotiation at first the mother presides as the significant counterplayer: sponsor, opponent, and audience. Although initially the infant knows nothing of gender, in due time it will learn that this most central person is a woman.

Later, when the baby can distinguish separate, continuing persons (according to this perhaps too conventional and oversimplified body of theory), the father enters its experience as the second significant other person. For a number of reasons, the father appears as the representative of adulthood and autonomy, while the mother remains that of infancy. Since a separate second other person can appear only at a more developed psychic stage, relations with the father do not reach quite as deep into the baby's psyche, to quite as primitive a level of dependence and fragmentation. Also, the father appears as an alternative to the mother's overwhelming power, another resource. And these tendencies are later reinforced by gender stereotypes, in proportion as the culture defines women as nonpersons, as not fully adult, responsible, desiring actors. For all these reasons the father tends to become both the symbol and the model of access to the larger world outside the family and of autonomous agency.

These psychic mechanisms work out somewhat differently for boys, therefore, than they do for girls, along lines already suggested by our discussion of Gilligan, Piaget, and abstraction. For both boys and girls, however, infantile dependence tends to remain associated with women and specifically mothers, while fathers stand for the possibility of autonomy, albeit at the price of oedipal submission for boys or self-abnegating conventional "femininity" for girls. For all of us, therefore, a return to infancy means being once more in the hands of a gigantic mother, whether she is totally caring and nurturant or as rapaciously devouring as an infant; either way she reabsorbs our individuality. For boys and men, however, that longing and that fear are directed toward a force defined as external, so that the fear can be eased to some extent by controlling actual women. For girls and women the matter is more complicated, because the overwhelming maternal power is more explicitly internal, within the self. Accordingly, it must be controlled or combated either by one's own (remaining) inner resources or else by submitting oneself to the external control of some actual man.

Even someone skeptical of such psychoanalytic ideas about a preverbal time that no adult consciously remembers may nonetheless recognize that in a culture like ours, subjection to feminine power or authority carries different connotations for most people than subjection to masculine power or authority. Being subordinated to a woman tends to arouse echoes of infantilization, humiliation, and helpless dependence. The power of women may be stereotypically conceived as milder and more comforting than that of men, but at a deeper level it is experienced as insidiously dangerous and tyrannical, the more so in proportion as its promise of care and security attracts us. Subjection to the power of men, by contrast, feels more like a step toward independence. To whatever extent our infantile experience remains active in us as adults, or is remobilized in trying circumstances, we all experience the threat to autonomy that can come from a woman as more primitively dangerous than any such threat from a man.[79] Fleeing the danger of engulfing, infantilizing feminine power, we are therefore likely to be tempted by masculine domination as an apparently protective alternative, as Dorothy Dinnerstein says, "a reasonable refuge" from that "earlier and more total tyranny" associated with feminine rule.[80] Masculine authority of course is also resented as restrictive, but never as wholeheartedly, because its removal leaves us psychologically vulnerable once more to the feminine threat, so insidiously powerful because it is half wish, located within ourselves.[81]

It is in terms of the "bad mother" of infantile experience, the dangerous force of chaos associated with femininity, I believe, that one must understand the difference between Arendt's treatment of her two pariahdoms: Jewish and feminine. The threat to individuality, politics, and the world associated with femininity has no counterpart for Arendt associated with Jewishness (though for many anti-Semites it well may, the category "Jew" serving as a symbolic substitute for this feminine power). Arendt encountered her own Jewishness mostly through masculine, quasi-paternal figures: her grandfather and Kurt Blumenfeld. Consequently, I think, Jewishness sorted for her with individuality, politics, and the world, as something precious to be protected against the feminine threat: not masculine so much as beyond the gender dichotomy, and not psychically threatening. Arendt's femininity, by contrast, was a personal problem because it raised unconscious conflicts about controlling the destructive inner force, about whether such control was compatible with self-realization and pleasure or only with self-sacrifice and submission.

The dangerous "bad mother" is illuminating not merely with respect to the difference between Arendt's treatment of Jewishness and femininity, however, but also—and more important—with respect to the social as Blob. "What we call 'society,'" Arendt remarks in *The Human Condition,* is "the facsimile of one superhuman family."[82] This chapter has argued that viewing the social as Blob implies envisioning that family as a single-parent household headed by an altogether dreadful mother. Primitively rapacious like a hungry infant, with whom she is merged, she has, in Arendt's words, "an irresistible tendency to grow, to devour," to "consume" people and "suck [them] into" her undifferentiated "monolithic" mass; she "embraces and controls" them in order to "normalize" them and "make them behave," and she ultimately dissolves the "distinguishing boundaries" that protect the world and our separate individuality.[83] The vision is enough to make anyone yearn for a strong patriarch to domesticate this monster, to force her into the role of selfless caregiver, and to control our own foolish, regressive yearnings toward the blissful merging she deceptively seems to offer.[84]

Symbolically speaking, that is why the social as Blob and the ancient Greeks appear together in *The Human Condition* and why the Greeks' misogynist machismo—so contrary to Arendt's conscious views and intent—is nevertheless underlined, emphasized, and in certain passages almost endorsed. Paternal domination is needed to keep the Blob from getting loose among us; caring and nurturing femininity can be secured only if the primitive bad mother is kept firmly restrained, confined in separate, private units, and rendered submissive both to the paterfamilias and to established norms and conventions.

Action and Autonomy

Both the ancient Greeks and the social as Blob have important positive functions to perform in Arendt's argument, as we have seen. The Greeks authorize and explicate her vision of free citizenship, connecting her concept of action with politics. The social as Blob personifies the post-totalitarian threat, replacing the Nazis as a force mobilizing people to action and prying them loose from their superficial daily concerns. Yet both Greeks and Blob, even as they perform these rhetorical functions, also undermine them, leaving the reader feeling helpless in the grip of superhuman forces. The Greeks are to the social in chapter 2 of *The Human Condition* as men are to women and as *homo faber* is to the *animal laborans* in chapters 1, 3, 4, and 5. But the latter pairs, unlike the former, are part of a trilogy. In chapter 2, the third term, the all-important idea of action, has vanished. Conceived as parents in an imaginary family, the misogynist paternal Greeks and the viciously maternal social as Blob in effect leave no space for a separate, autonomous child, let alone for the shared political freedom that might be enacted by a collectivity of such autonomous individuals. In chapter 2, where politics is represented by the misogynist Greeks and dichotomously juxtaposed to the social, it is assimilated to patriarchal domination instead of to self-realization; its power become the father's rather than our own.[85]

The conceptual triad, and action in particular, by contrast, suggest that there is hope for the child, the real self, to mature into an autonomous, responsible adulthood that simultaneously gratifies the self and serves others. As a third alternative to both the helpless *animal laborans* and ruthless *homo faber*, action is, after all, identified by Arendt with self-disclosure and—in the Dante epigraph to her chapter on action—with self-realization, "mak[ing] patent [the] latent self."[86] Here freedom is within reach for one's real self, as one might be perceived in disenchanted "neighborly" love ("I will that you be"): flawed and fallible, of course, vulnerable and human-all-too-human, yet valuable, dignified, and capable of glory. That is why Arendt says that the heroism associated with politics is not the mythical machismo of ancient Greece but something more like the existential leap into action and public exposure.[87]

Yet though action is self-expression and self-realization, that way of seeing it is still, as Arendt later observed, "perhaps too 'modern,' too self-centered" to capture the idea of the lost treasure.[88] It misses action's other side, its public, political dimension, the crucial difference between action and work. Work, too, especially in the form of craftsmanship and art, is self-expression, but it does not deal with other people, with relationship, with recognition. Action, conducted exclusively in the medium of human relationships, inherently presupposes the existence of other people as fellow actors and peers. Similarly, it inherently implies that institutions, relationships, and rules are humanly created and sustained and thus within our power to alter or replace but also within our responsibility to protect. The lost treasure of the Resistance, after all, had "two interconnected parts," and whereas one of them concerned self-realization (whoever "joined . . . *found* himself"), the other was public and political. Whoever joined became a "challenger," accepting personal responsibility for what the collectivity was doing, and taking initiative, together with others, to found a new "public space . . . where freedom could appear."[89] That is why, also, political action means "taking sides for the world's sake" rather than one's own, yet not as a self-sacrificial duty but "out of gratitude" and love (*amor mundi*), because the world genuinely gratifies.[90] From this perspective, Arendtian politics means, as C. Douglas Lummis says, "the people gathered in the public space, with neither the great paternal Leviathan nor the great maternal society standing over them, but only the empty sky—the people making the power of Leviathan their own again, free to speak, to choose, to act."[91]

Introduced to further Arendt's project of a general theory based on the lost treasure, the Greeks and the social as Blob both tend instead to restore the symbolic impasse that her conceptual triad had helped her to transcend, closing down the possibilities associated with action. The Greeks are not a fully satisfactory example of the free citizenship Arendt had in mind, and the social as Blob is a wholly unrealistic, fearful fantasy. It does not follow, however, that there is no such thing as free citizenship, nor that there is no real, urgent danger facing us. To the possibility of such a danger, seen realistically rather than as a monster from outer space, we now begin to turn, gradually exploring what the threat of the social might be without the Blob (though the Blob itself will receive further attention in chapter 11).

NINE

The Social in *The Human Condition*

Having traced the genealogy of the social as Blob and examined the historical, personal, and intellectual context of *The Human Condition*, we are now ready to ask what the social is in that book, what Arendt means by that phrase. This requires separating the idea of the social from the image of the Blob, for whatever Arendt meant by the phrase, she surely did not intend a monster from outer space. She meant to address what she regarded as an enormously important, urgent, growing problem in the real world of politics and history, where real people live and suffer. We shall return later to the Blob, but for now set it aside to ask, simply: What is the social for Arendt when it is not mystified?

This chapter pursues that question twice, from two different angles: first by trying to map the social onto Arendt's other central concepts, and then, second, by trying to reconcile its two so disparate roots, joined in *The Human Condition* into a single concept: the conformist, or parvenu, social and the economic, or biological, social. To anticipate the results in brief, both approaches lead to the same conclusion: that the social corresponds to none of the ordinary uses or dictionary senses of "society" or "social" but instead greatly resembles what chapter 7 sketched as Marx's fundamental notion of alienation.

The way to begin is by asking how the social, juxtaposed as always for Arendt in a dyadic contrast to politics, maps onto the basic conceptual trilogy that structures *The Human Condition*: labor, work, and action.[1] The question may initially seem trivial and its answer obvious. Indeed, the first few steps are obvious, but after that things become problematic, and their investigation therefore rewarding. Clearly politics—the opposite of the social—sorts with action; they are almost synonyms for Arendt (180, 188). So the social must contrast to action, but how is it related to work and labor? Answering is not easy, because the concept of the social is conspicuously absent from the chapters where labor and work are discussed, and neither labor nor work is mentioned much where the social appears. Instead of labor or work, what appears alongside the social, as action appears alongside politics, is something Arendt calls "behavior." So our question can be reformulated as: How is behavior related to labor and work?

Relating Behavior to the Conceptual Triad

Unfortunately, Arendt never says what "behavior" is, nor does she devote a chapter to it, as she does to each term in her trilogy. What is "decisive" about society, she says, is that it "excludes the possibility of action" and instead "expects from each of its members a certain kind of behavior, imposing innumerable and various rules, all of which tend to 'normalize' its members, to make them behave, to exclude spontaneous action or outstanding achievement."[2] She also equates behavior with "conformism," which suggests that the concept is a successor to that of the parvenu, as action is the successor of the conscious pariah (41–42).

But that is not much help in relating behavior or the social to work and labor. Should one equate behavior with labor and work combined, as the opposite of action? But Arendt argues that work has mostly disappeared from the modern world along with action, leaving only labor, whereas behavior is—like the social—definitely a modern phenomenon. So perhaps one should equate behavior with labor alone. Arendt does say that ours is "a society of laborers" and that, because society now "embraces and controls" us all, behavior has become "the foremost mode of human relationship."[3]

Yet if labor and behavior are the same, why does Arendt introduce the latter term at all? Why not just continue using "labor" throughout? Labor, moreover, is the production of life-sustaining consumption goods through heavy bodily effort, whereas behavior is never said literally to produce anything. People behave, as they act, "with respect to *each other*," not with respect to material objects or substances (42, my emphasis). If behavior is nevertheless in some metaphorical sense productive, as action is, it surely "produces" the same sort of thing as action produces: the web of human relationships. Also, labor concerns the body, biological processes, and natural necessity, but behavior concerns conformity to artificial norms and conventions. Behavior thus presupposes potential choice, the possibility of *mis*behavior, and consequently the absence of determining biological necessity. Accordingly, behavior is not exempt from judgment because driven by necessity, like labor, nor judged by standards of efficiency, like work, nor yet judged like action, "by the criterion of greatness." Instead, at least among "civilized people," it is judged by " 'moral standards' " in the sense of inherited conventions: "the sum total of *mores*" as they have been "solidified by tradition."⁴ Behavior, in other words, like parvenu conduct, is a kind of uncritical self-subjection to unquestioned rules.

So behavior seems in some ways like labor, in some like labor and work combined, in some like action, and in some distinct from all three. In order to sort out this plethora, it helps to return to the ontological question of what sort of reality should be ascribed to these Arendtian categories: are they objective conditions in the world or matters of outlook, attitude, *mentalité*? Sometimes when Arendt says "laborers" she seems to mean a certain class of people, and by "labor" to mean the objective activity of producing food and shelter through bodily exertion. But at other times she uses these words to designate a mode of conduct, a way of doing whatever one does, or even an outlook, so that "labor" is anything done by anyone in a laboring manner or regarded from a labor-ish perspective: *as if* it were exhausting, biologically necessary, and so on.⁵ The same kind of ambiguity haunts Arendt's other central concepts as well.

Only by reading these categories as *mentalités* can one make sense of certain puzzling claims in *The Human Condition*, such as Arendt's assertion that initiative—the basic element of action—"is inherent in *all* human activities," her equation of labor with whatever is "*understood . . . as*" labor, or her casual remark that "of course" a laboring society need not be one in which everyone is a laborer, but only one in which "all members *consider* whatever they do primarily as a way to sustain their own lives and those of their families."⁶

Similarly, much about Arendt's apparent exclusion of economic concerns from politics, so puzzling to her interpreters, makes sense only if one reads "economic" to mean a certain outlook or attitude rather than an objectively identifiable subject matter. For Arendt acknowledges that action and politics mostly and rightly are "concerned with" the sorts of worldly interests we usually identify as economic. Even though action and politics are "directed toward" other people, their "content" is always "exclusively 'objective,' concerned with the matters of the world of things in which men move, which physically lie between them and out of which arise their specific, objective, worldly interests" (182). Indeed, that part of economics we call exchange is *entirely* "in the field of action."⁷ So is the manner in which production is organized, since organization as such "owes its origin to the strictly political sphere of life, to man's capacity to act and to act together in concert."[8] Until modern times, in fact, economics had altogether been regarded as a "part of ethics and politics and based on the assumption that men act with respect to their economic activities as they act in every other respect" (42). Even in modernity "economic man" is really "an acting being"; we moderns have merely stopped recognizing this fact.[9] It is perfectly possible to address what are objectively economic concerns in an appropriately political manner, as for example the early labor movement did in defending "its economic interests" in a manner that amounted to "a full-fledged political battle."[10]

Perhaps, then, behavior and the social should also be read as a *mentalité*—the parvenu way of thinking, seeing, and conducting oneself—applied in whatever people do. Perhaps Arendt should have focused on the adverb instead of hypostasizing the adjective; the social—behavior—would then be anything anyone does or regards in that manner, socially. Sometimes Arendt even suggests that society is not external and objective but inner and psychic. She seems, for example, to endorse what she calls Rousseau's "discovery" that the intrusive society he fears, like the "intimacy of the heart" he wants to protect, cannot be "localized" in any "objective tangible place in the world," that both are "subjective modes of human existence." Yet by the next paragraph, society is again external, making "demands" on people.[11]

Arendt's central concepts cannot be merely *mentalités*, however, since she regards each as appropriate only in certain objectively identifiable contexts and harmful elsewhere. The laboring outlook and mode of conduct are right for repetitive bodily activities necessary to maintain life; the working outlook and mode are right for crafting a world of lasting, humanly fashioned objects; the *mentalité* of action is appropriate where human relationships are at stake. What is destructive is not the laboring or working outlook as such but their "generalization" into contexts where they do not belong.[12] In its home context, each has its own positive value.[13]

Behavior, however, is different. Unlike labor, work, and action, it has no home context of its own, where it is appropriate, justified, necessary, or right. Indeed, Arendt never has anything favorable to say about behavior at all. Apparently its disappearance from our lives would deprive us of nothing worth having. In terms of its objective context, behavior seems like action, since it "produces" only the web of relationships.[14] In terms of outlook and manner, however, it resembles labor: an attitude and mode of conduct that would be suited to constant, driven activity that supports life, combined with a fatalistic helplessness. Behavior thus seems to be Arendt's name for the laboring *mentalité* appearing inappropriately in contexts where action is called for. Behavior is action manqué, the failure to act, opportunities for action missed or denied, an abdication of one's human capacity and responsibility to act.

Unfortunately, this way of reading behavior renders the distinction between behavior and action newly problematic. If behavior is the failure to act, how does one tell it from deliberate *in*action, the considered and responsible decision to do nothing in a particular context, the action of refraining? Is there such a thing as *in*action in Arendt's schema, and how would she classify it? Besides, we know that behavior is by no means equivalent to doing nothing; it often involves obsessive, even frantic activity. And how would Arendt classify *mis*behavior? Is the deliberate violation of social norms sufficient to constitute action?

Though one can find hints here and there, Arendt's writings provide no decisive answer to these questions. Rahel Varnhagen spoke of herself as "doing ... nothing," just "letting life rain upon me," connecting passivity with the parvenu and thus perhaps with behavior.[15] Toward the end of *The Human Condition,* Arendt speaks of the social as threatening, "the deadliest, most sterile passivity history has ever known."[16] In *The Origins of Totalitarianism* we saw suggestions that the mob, like an adolescent rebel, automatically opposed whatever society demanded, which may suggest classifying misbehavior as a kind of (inverted) behavior.[17] In *The Human Condition,* Arendt mentions "non-behavior" as something that society will not "tolerate."[18] There is also one passage mentioning "non-acting" or "abstention from ... human affairs," but in a manner so equivocal that one cannot tell whether Arendt regards them as real possibilities or as an illusion that only "seems" to offer "salvation" from the perils of action (234). Later in her life, commenting on resistance to the Nazis, Arendt wrote that even where "there was no possibility of resistance, ... there existed the possibility of *doing nothing*" or, adopting Otto Kirchheimer's term, the "possibility of '*nonparticipation.*' "[19]

About the difference between behavior and action in general, Arendt says somewhat more. Although both are modes of activity with real consequences in the world, affecting human relationships, they differ in significant ways. Behavior is rule-governed, obedient, conventional, uniform, and status-oriented; action, by contrast, is spontaneous and creative; it involves judging and possibly revising goals, norms, and standards rather than accepting them as given. Behavior is routine, action unpredictable, even heroic. Behavior, like parvenu conduct, is self-referential, but action is for the world's sake; and behavior is isolating, but action is principled and—although based in individual autonomy—oriented toward solidarity with others.

Yet obedience to norms, conformity to conventions, and concern for the opinion of others need not, as such, be behavior. In the right context, any or all of these can be action: for example, obedience to norms jointly self-imposed by an active citizenry, conformity to conventions that one has judged autonomously and found valuable, or respect for the opinions of one's fellow citizens on public issues. Most important, therefore, what distinguishes behavior seems to be that it is thoughtless, mere habit; it involves inauthentically denying one's responsibility for what one is actually doing in the world or for the norms and standards governing one's conduct. Behavior apparently means wearing blinkers, construing not just one's options but one's capacities too narrowly. Action, by contrast, implies a realistic perception and acknowledgment of both self and world, of one's powers and one's situation; it means genuinely, competently taking responsibility for one's conduct, its consequences, and the norms and standards that govern it.

Difficult as the distinction is to draw, and contestable as it always remains, we draw it often enough about our own or other people's conduct. We all sometimes judge, mostly in retrospect, that we or someone else misread a situation and either failed to do what could and should have been done or wasted effort and resources trying to do the impossible. Most of us have at some point had an experience like Arendt's account of those who joined the Resistance: discovering that what had hitherto seemed important was really trivial, that what had seemed out of the question was actually easy, that apparently insurmountable obstacles had been self-imposed.

If one accepts the distinction between action and behavior despite the difficulties in defining it with precision, and if one accepts the reading that behavior is action *manqué,* a failure to act where action is called for, then something similar ought to be true of the social and politics. If the social is the large-scale counterpart to behavior, as politics is to action, then the social must be politics *manqué,* the absence of politics is a context where politics is possible and desirable. Of course, in many situations nothing useful can be done, and in many others nothing needs to be done. Those would not illustrate the social. It would mean actual opportunities for politics missed, denied, or avoided.

The social would thus be Arendt's parvenu writ large, an entire human collectivity's failure to acknowledge its powers and responsibilities. But a collectivity of human beings as one gigantic parvenu is a metaphor. What would it actually look like in the real world? Surely we have not set aside the image of the Blob only to adopt instead an equally metaphorical image of the gigantic parvenu? As a way of demystifying the concept of the social, mapping behavior onto the trilogy of labor, work, and action is not entirely satisfactory. It arrives only at another metaphor, and it is very indirect, proceeding through the notion of behavior, which—after all—corresponds to only half of Arendt's social in *The Human Condition*. The relevance of this entire line of inquiry to the economic or biological social remains unclear.

The Conformist and the Economic Social

Perhaps, then, we should try again by a different approach, focusing directly on the social to see whether its two so disparate versions, springing from such different roots, actually converge, and if so, how. Begin in the terrain where we have already been working, with the conformist or parvenu social. Here the essence of the social seems to lie in classifying people into arbitrary, merely conventional categories, ranking them by their classification, and treating them in accord with that ranking. Because the classification and ranking must be simultaneously both empty of substance and yet taken with the utmost seriousness, the social necessarily implies some sort of pretense or illusion. "What matters" is that each individual be wholly "equate[d] . . . with his rank within the social framework," his category.[20] Historically, this once meant a person's actual rank in a hierarchical class system, but, Arendt says, it continues to be "what matters" socially even after classes disappear in mass society. This is because deference itself implies a kind of ranking: some "they" assumed superior to the likes of "me," whether they be "up there" in an elite or "out there" all around. In mass society, the social is a leveling force, normalizing all into conventional patterns of behavior, but this is merely an extension of what society has always done and meant: forcing people into arbitrary categories. As Arendt would put it later, "no society can properly function without classification, without an arrangement of things and men in classes and prescribed types," because such stereotyping is "necessary" for "social discrimination," which is itself the basic "constituent element of the social realm."[21]

Sometimes Arendt writes as if she opposed classification itself, any and all sorting of human beings into categories, because such stereotyping can never do justice to each individual's "unique and distinct identity."[22] It can tell us only *what* somebody is, but never *who* that person uniquely is.[23] Yet, as we have noted, one must classify if one is to use words at all, and even the most free, politically articulated community will therefore employ general categories as its members discuss issues, formulate policies, enact rules, and interpret principles.

What distinguishes invidious, social classification from useful, political categorization for Arendt is three-fold. First, social categories are arbitrary, formal, empty, devoid of any substantive point or purpose beyond that of sheer classification itself. If they had a substantive utility, people might accept the categorization on its merits, after independent critical judgment, rather than a priori. Such reasoned, critical acceptance can no more illustrate the meaning of the social than obedience can be exemplified by someone happening to do what was commanded because he thinks it a good idea rather than because it was commanded. Conformity to a norm based on such independent judgment is not conformism and does not demonstrate the requisite abdication of one's own powers, the requisite deference to the social "they." The parvenu feels unable to institute norms or even to judge them. Social norms and classifications, one might say, are always and essentially created by someone else. They come—Arendt quotes Kafka—from "above," as something that the individual "receives but does not create."[24]

The "they" that creates the norms and categories, however, as we have seen, is not any real group of actual people but hypothetical, a projection by the parvenu or conformist not acknowledged as such. Social norms are always created and imposed by someone else, someone superior, yet this someone does not really exist. There may be real elites; there surely are real other people; but the social "they" is a myth, constructed out of the parvenu's inauthentic deference: because I cannot make or assess norms and categories myself, the rules *must* come from elsewhere. That is what makes Kafka's metaphor, already cited from one of Arendt's New York essays, so wonderfully apt: "society is a nobody in a dress suit" (82 n.). It is "in a dress suit" because men wear tuxedos only for formal, ceremonial social occasions, and the sartorial details of the dress suit are specified only by tradition, without any functional purpose whatsoever. Society is "in a dress suit" because external forms devoid of meaningful content are all that matters socially, all there is. Unlike political categories, social ones define their members entirely and exhaustively, so the social is best illustrated where inner substance is totally lacking. The stiffly starched shirt-front of the dress suit can in fact stand up by itself, even if it is literally empty. In Kafka's metaphor it contains "a nobody" both because the social man has absented himself, abdicating his powers and individuality, and because the social "they" he claims to obey *is* nobody, is merely hypothetical and projected.

The point is made more explicitly in Arendt's unpublished 1965 lectures, where she says that "the greatest evil" is that "committed by Nobodies," that is, by "human beings who refuse . . . to be persons," who do not think about what they are doing or what they have done. By this refusal they fail "to constitute themselves into somebodies," into "persons."[25]

The idea is also strikingly reminiscent of passages in Kierkegaard, where Arendt is likely to have encountered it well before she found it in Kafka, so that Kierkegaard may be another (very Christian) source of the idea of the social. He calls it "the public" and says it is "a monstrous *nothing* [that] cannot even be represented, because it is an *abstraction.*" It consists of "unreal individuals who never can be united in an actual situation or organization," because people belong to it only at those "moments when they are nothing." Whenever they are their authentic selves, they are no longer part of it. In the modern world, more and more people "aspire to be nothing at all," to merge into "that abstract whole formed . . . by [each participant] becoming a third party (an onlooker)." Yet they are in fact participants whose activities result in concrete consequences, so that their collectivity is not really nothing: it is "a kind of gigantic something, an abstract and deserted void which is everything and nothing."[26]

Social norms, then, are inherently empty and arbitrary, yet they must nevertheless be taken with the utmost, passionate seriousness. If they are to be social, their emptiness and arbitrariness must not be acknowledged as such, for that again would imply judging them autonomously. Social norms must be obsessively pursued and social classifications passionately applied as definitive, not for their substantive content or practical consequences, but because of their supposed source—the always superior "they" to whom deference is due. The social attitude, as we learned in *Rahel Varnhagen,* requires not just outward conformity but "a strenuous effort to love"—to love not the content of the norms but their source, one's social superiors.[27] Deference or obedience aimed at some independent practical purpose does not qualify as social. If, as a member of the Resistance, I worm my way into some high-ranking Nazi's social circle to spy on him, my careful conformity to its norms is not conform*ism*, nor is it social behavior in Arendt's sense. Social behavior, like the refugee's pathological instant "adjustment" to each new country, is not the realistic readiness to do what the situation requires but on the contrary an altogether unrealistic propensity to "adjust in principle to everything and everybody."[28] As for Varnhagen, so more generally in the social, "real" means whatever society acknowledges as real.[29] Social norms and categories must be taken with the utmost seriousness precisely because they cannot be independently assessed or compared with reality. Without them, neither self nor world exists for the parvenu.

This paradoxical combination of arbitrary norms with passionate commitment, third, accounts for the recurrent theme of deception, illusion, hypocrisy, and pretense associated with the conformist, or parvenu, social. We have followed that theme from the parvenu's hypocritical efforts in the salon and the deceptive promises held out to him by society, through the refugee's false optimism and denial of his real condition, to that bourgeois hypocrisy which so repelled various groups in *The Origins of Totalitarianism* as the early bourgeoisie erected a "whole world of fake security, fake culture, and fake life" by publicly "parading" virtues which it not only did not possess but actually "held in contempt," until we arrived at totalitarianism's use of ideology to create an "entirely fictitious world."[30] In the social, the element of pretense or deception has become so pervasive that, in a sense, it disappears. There no longer is any independent reality that anyone can perceive or use as a check on social conventions. Each looks to others, or rather, beyond the real others to some hypothetical "they," to define reality, and—as Arendt wrote to Jaspers during the controversy over her Eichmann book—"each believes what all believe."[31] Utterly isolated and denying their own capacity for initiative and organization, such people cannot act effectively in the world. Instead, they conduct themselves as if they were unindividuated parts of some undifferentiated, gigantic mass and helpless in its grasp. So no one is in charge.

This vision of the parvenu social at first seems altogether unrelated to the other version of the social, which centers neither on status, conventions, and rules nor on false appearances, deception, and hypocrisy, but instead on harsh necessity, biology, and nature: overwhelming physical realities that impose themselves independently of human will or custom. Indeed, this economic, or biological, social, rooted in the "Imperialism" section of *The Origins,* is not even connected with the ordinary meanings of the words "society" and "social" in any obvious way. Yet in *The Human Condition* it has become the more important half of a dual concept, Arendt repeatedly insisting that the social means economics.

Thus she equates "the rise of society" with "the rise of the 'household' (*oikia*) or of economic activities to the public realm" and membership in society with playing a central role in its "all-important economic activities."³² This further connects the social with biology, since household functions are "those related to the maintenance of life" (28). In the household, and thus later in society, people are "driven by their wants and needs," which means by "the driving force [of] life itself." For the same reason, the social connects with labor, since both the productive labor that supplies food and shelter and the reproductive labor by which women give birth are "subject to the same urgency of life" that rules over "the realm of the social" (30–31). Accordingly, society is "the life process itself . . . channeled into the public realm," or the "public organization" of that biological force (45–46). A "social viewpoint" is one taking "nothing into account but the life process" (89).

Rising or channeled into the public realm, this life process is the life of the collectivity, not of individuals. Here "the life of society as a whole, instead of the limited lives of individual men, is considered to be the gigantic subject of the accumulation process" (116). And not just "considered to be"; the collectivity in fact becomes a "monolithic" unity (46). The " 'communist fiction' " invented by the classical economists has "by no means remained an intangible entity" but has been made actual in the world (256). This was accomplished by the industrial revolution, which presupposed the division of labor, which in turn required the emergence of labor from the household, from the "private realm," where it had previously been subject to "restrictions."³³ When society "first entered the public realm," it disguised itself as "an organization of property-owners" seeking protection for their "accumulation of more wealth" (68).

It thus seems indisputable that Arendt is talking about the development of wage labor and a market society, so that a central model for her biological version of the social seems to be the market itself: people so organized that each is arrayed separately and competitively against the rest, yet all affecting each other so that their individual activities result in large-scale consequences that none of them can control or even intentionally influence. These consequences therefore confront them with an absolute necessity even though these individuals, regarded collectively, *are* the market.³⁴

Although primarily and originally economic, this market model of human organization can be applied to all sorts of processes and systems in which "values" are collectively produced by a system of exchange among individuals. Indeed, in a commercial society, ultimately "everything becomes an exchange value, a commodity."³⁵ When standards, norms, or institutions "become entities of exchange" in such a marketlike system, as Arendt put it in an article written while she worked on *The Human Condition,* "the bearer of their 'value' is society," rather than any particular human being "who produces and uses and judges."[36]

This market model of human collectivity does seem close to one familiar use of the word "society," namely "civil society," as that notion is developed in Hegel and Marx and their successors. By "civil society" they mean arrangements in which each pursues his own particular, private good (or that of "his" enterprise or "his" family), treating others only as obstacles or means, in a system of unacknowledged interdependence whose resultants confront them all as an alien, inexorable force.[37] For Hegel, this atomized mass of conflictual activity has to be unified into a harmonious whole by the state, epitomized in a neutral, professional civil service. Marx rejects this account, along with the political economists' "invisible hand" of the market, as a myth of harmony that disguises exploitation. The real good of all without exploitation, he thinks, can be achieved neither by the market nor by the state through its bureaucracy, but only by the "associated producers" jointly regulating their "interchange with Nature," after the revolution.[38]

Arendt accepts neither Marx's nor Hegel's view. She agrees with Marx that bureaucracy and the state are no better solutions than the market, yet she equally rejects Marx's vision of harmonious collective regulation. For her, the social includes not just the shift from *oikia* to market but also centralized control of the market in a sort of "gigantic, nation-wide administration of housekeeping."[39] Gunnar Myrdal's 1953 study, *The Political Element in the Development of Economic Theory,* seems to have exercised a decisive influence on Arendt here. This work, which she calls "brilliant," criticizes proponents of the idea of a "national" or "social economy" (in German, *Volkswirtschaft,* which Myrdal translates somewhat loosely as "collective housekeeping") for falsely assuming that there is a unified entity called "society" that has but a single economic interest, by analogy with "the individual who runs his own or his family household."[40] Neither Myrdal nor Arendt questions whether a family household is itself a "unified entity" with "but a single interest" or whether the other members of "his" family household are not also ("the") individual(s).[41] Myrdal's introduction of the term "housekeeping" for a centrally administered economy may well have connected, for Arendt, with Aristotle's distinction between political and household rule; at any rate, she adopted the expression.

For Arendt, then, bureaucratic administration is no solution to market problems but itself part of the problem. Markets and bureaucracies are fundamentally alike, equally social. In a bureaucracy, understood in Weberian terms as a hierarchical organization based on specialization of function and professional merit, each participant perceives, pursues, and is responsible for only his particular professional task, uncritically accepting instructions from above in all other respects, minding his own business. Bureaucracies deploy large numbers of people for efficiently and undeviatingly carrying out policies that are set and supervised elsewhere and transmitted to the organization by its "head." Like markets, bureaucracies can be highly effective instruments for certain purposes. What neither markets nor bureaucracies can do effectively, however, is set goals, make overall judgments about policy, determine the direction in which a collectivity should move or the principles to which it is to be committed.

Accordingly, Arendt opposes not markets or bureaucracies as such; they are two organizational forms among many. She opposes confining a human collectivity to only this sort of organizational device, and specifically, she opposes substituting them for politics. As a substitute for politics, bureaucracy—that "most social form of government"—means the "complete victory of society," which is to say, being "ruled by an 'invisible hand,' namely, by nobody," just like a market operating by laissez faire. But "rule by nobody is not necessarily no-rule." Indeed, it may be one of the "cruelest and most tyrannical" forms of rule.[42] When they pervade public life and displace politics, bureaucratic and market forms are alike, both equally social and entirely comparable to the flock of parvenus conforming to each other, milling about without human direction.

And yet, not entirely comparable. Markets and bureaucracies are somehow worse, more dangerous, and perhaps even more "social" than the flock of parvenus. As we noted when the economic, or biological, social first appeared as imperialism in *The Origins,* unlike parvenu abdication in favor of some "they," this form of the social involves abdication to a process, to a force that is moving, going somewhere. Economics and biology add to the notion of surrendering oneself an element of irreversibility. Here, if a parvenu should change his mind, he may find that it is too late; things have changed, moved on. Thus, by *The Human Condition,* "one of the outstanding characteristics" of the social is its "*irresistible* tendency to grow."[43] Here as in Marx's Sorcerer's Apprentice story, people use their powers in such selfish or foolish ways that they let loose an evil force they cannot control, a force bent on destroying those powers. They let loose the Blob.

But does that story make sense? Here is the most crucial point for separating the Blob image from the demystified social. In the first place, as we have seen, such a neat chronological separation of free "before" and helplessly determined "after" does not work, because Arendt, like Marx, needs the present moment ("between past and future") to be ambiguous, so that we are both trapped and yet free-to-become-free. Second, the notion of people somehow letting natural necessity or biological process into some space or realm from which these were previously excluded is not easy to translate into less metaphorical terms. It is hard to see how human conduct could effect such a metaphysical transformation. Certainly people sometimes allow some human undertaking—say, a cultivated field—to revert, as we say, to nature. But of course natural necessity, the regularities of physics and biology, governed that land while it was under cultivation just as much as before and afterward. Human activities do not escape natural necessity; in one sense they use it, in another sense they are part of it, and in still another sense it is conceptually irrelevant to them.

Necessity

That is not to deny the logical difficulties inherent in the relationship between human action and nature and between freedom and necessity. Just for starters, there is the confusing bifurcation of meaning in the words "necessary" and "necessity," which are synonymous sometimes with what is inevitable, sometimes with what is needed.[44] Clearly, what someone needs is not inevitably present, will not even inevitably be sought. People do sometimes spurn even what is needed for life itself, whether in a good cause or in a fit of depression. When Arendt is being careful, she hedges her claims to allow for this ambiguity of meaning, speaking only of matters "urged upon" us by necessity or of being driven by "the urges of" necessity, or even of being driven by "*wants and needs.*"[45] Wants, urges, and needs do drive people, but people can also resist them.

At other times, however, Arendt is not so careful, and seems to equate necessity in the sense of needs with the inevitability of natural causation—the laws of physics and biology. Sometimes she just seems downright confused, as in her revelatory treatment of behaviorism, the social scientist's quest for statistical regularities in human behavior. The topic matters, for it is one of Arendt's few and sporadic efforts to link the economic, or biological, to the conformist, or parvenu, social. What appears in the latter as behavior—anxious conformity to empty norms—seems irrelevant to the former, where causal necessity determines outcomes. But behavior*ism is* relevant, since it presupposes precisely the sort of observable regularities over large numbers of cases that characterizes natural science. Both conformist behavior and social-scientific behaviorism concern individuals abstracted from their individuality—observable conduct without effective agency.

What Arendt has to say about behaviorism, however, is deeply inconsistent. The statistical uniformity sought by behaviorism, she first says, "is by no means a harmless scientific ideal" but instead is "the no longer secret political ideal of [our] society" (43). Arendt calls it a political ideal presumably to emphasize that this search for inevitabilities governing human conduct is not itself inevitable but, as she says, "willful," based on an "assumption" that we need not and should not make and on an unacknowledged (though "no longer secret") "aim to *reduce* man . . . to the level of a conditioned and behaving animal" (42, 41, 45; my emphasis). Thus behaviorism is not just blind to human action but committed to replacing it by behavior.

Yet Arendt herself notes as an "unfortunate truth" that "the more people there are, the more likely they are to behave," and the human population is surely growing (43). By the end of *The Human Condition*, she is warning that "the trouble with" social-scientific "theories of behaviorism is not that they are wrong but that they could become true" (322). She means, of course, that people who believe that they are conditioned, behaving particles will not use their capacities for action. But that is *not* enough to make the "theories of behaviorism" *true*, for the unused capacities still exist, as Arendt herself underlines. "Needless to say, modern man" has not lost his human capacities, is not even "on the point of losing them" (323).

That the problem is not the disappearance of human capacities but the failure to use them is fairly obvious in the conformist social. Rahel Varnhagen and refugees with a mania for "adjusting" are social not because they are causally determined but because, although capable of action, they do not act. But the same is also true, though less obvious, in the economic social. Anti-Semitism and racism are destructive in politics not because they somehow "let loose" biology in this "realm" but precisely because they pretend to, presenting as biological and inevitable what is in fact human convention. Imperialism is not a natural growth but on the contrary means adopting as a human policy goal the sort of unlimited growth that sometimes characterizes nature. And the laboring *mentalité* is dangerous not when people face natural necessity but precisely when they don't, when that outlook is "generalized" into contexts where action would be appropriate and possible.

In short, the social—even in its economic, or biological, version—is not the intrusion of causal necessity into human affairs but the conjuring up of what Roberto Mangabeira Unger has called "false necessities."[46] Arendt is not protesting against our generic human helplessness but fighting against illusions of helplessness, the spurious naturalization of matters that are in fact subject to human choice and action. The social resides in the disparity between what people do because they see it as actionable and what they fail to do because they don't so see it: disasters that could have been averted, benefits that could have been achieved, and above all, troubles that people are needlessly inflicting on themselves.[47]

So at the heart of the economic social, which at first seemed utterly unrelated to the issues of false appearance, deception, and hypocrisy that characterize the conformist social, lies a gigantic falsehood, indeed, the very same falsehood as is central to the conformist social: the denial of human agency. Despite all of Arendt's talk about necessity, nature, and process, the real issue is their simulacra: false necessity, spurious naturalization, pretended inevitability, self-imposed helplessness. And this is as true of the economic as of the conformist social.

Institutional Structure

Nevertheless, there is something particularly problematic about the economic social that makes it seem more dangerous and less easy to undo than its conformist version, something that Arendt tried to express by picturing it as a surrender to process, to "necessity in motion."[48] That something, however, is not natural necessity let loose in human affairs, but rather what sociologists call "social structure." In order to avoid confusing it with Arendt's "the social," however, I shall call this feature of human collectivities "institutional structure."

The conformist version of Arendt's social arose as a problem of individual character. Pariahs chose to become parvenus; Arendt summoned them back to conscious pariahdom and to the recognition that the powerful society they sought to mollify was a paper tiger. Yet there also lurked in the background society in a different sense, which wielded real power, making people into pariahs and perhaps even into parvenus. Still, as long as one thought in terms of conformist character, parvenus might change their minds, like Varnhagen at the end of her life, Arendt's fellow inmates at Gurs rejecting a suicide pact, or apolitical intellectuals who joined the Resistance. An individual parvenu has a character problem, but character can change, and the instant it does, the parvenu regains access to his unused capacities.

The conformist individual translates into the social only if one imagines large numbers of them, a whole collectivity made up entirely of parvenus. The economic social, by contrast, was from its first appearance systemic, large-scale, impersonal, collective. It was limitless expansion adopted as a public policy, household production developed into a market, people deployed in a bureaucracy. It was never a problem of character, for systems of human interrelationship have no psyche of their own and no character. Instead of character, what they have is structure: a particular, established "web of relationships," patterns of institutional organization and habitual practice. Now, institutional structure, as Arendt would hasten to stress, is not physical structure; institutions are not buildings. They consist only in the patterned conduct, the relationships, of their participants. Nevertheless they have a certain fixity or inertia of their own, and they can coerce recalcitrant participants. Consequently institutional structure greatly complicates the issues of agency, blame, necessity, and freedom, and thus the possibilities for undoing the social.

The conformist social, conceived as a flock of parvenus, does not appear to be structured; it seems a mass of unrelated particles somehow compressed into an undifferentiated total unity. Indeed, in *The Origins* this was how Arendt saw modern mass society altogether: identical, "atomized" until congealed into a single, "unorganized, structureless mass," like "a sand storm that could cover all parts of the inhabited earth."[49] Totalitarianism, she argued, works to dissolve structure, disorienting and isolating people by keeping everything in flux. By *The Human Condition*, however, and particularly in the economic version of the social, she recognized this pattern of collectivity as itself a form of institutional structure or cluster of such forms—flock, market, bureaucracy—all of which *appear* structureless to their participants, who feel, and therefore conduct their intentional activities, as if they were unrelated, inert atoms caught up helplessly in a Blob. The participants' isolation with respect to their intentional activities leaves them incapable of joint action or power. That is the sense in which Arendt says that "to be isolated is to be deprived of the capacity to act" and that whoever "isolates himself . . . forfeits power and becomes impotent."[50]

Yet it is crucial to recognize that, on Arendt's own account, these are not particles but people, that they are not in fact isolated but structurally interrelated, and that they are not inert but very busy, like the frantic, obsessive parvenu. What they are all busily doing constantly results in the social conditions that constrain them all. So the conformist and the appeaser help sustain oppression, the entrepreneur contributes to market fluctuations, and the bureaucrat "only following orders" makes genocide possible. Various forms of institutional structure can produce and perpetuate a condition *as if* people were inert and isolated particles congealed into a single, "monolithic" unity, which is not a motionless monolith but a moving force constraining them all even though they jointly produce it, because they conduct themselves in ways that preclude their directing or taking charge of it (46). Their conduct constantly produces it; it enforces that conduct. That circularity is the social; they are "driven by a process" that consists in their own conduct (134). In this sense, the social is a particular mode of interrelationship among people, a form of togetherness in which each thinks himself an isolated atom and behaves accordingly, but they in fact generate collective results that include the continual enforcement of such thinking and behavior on each other, and thus their "normalization" into homogeneity. That is why Arendt speaks of them both as isolated atoms and also as congealed together too tightly, into a mass.[51]

For Arendt, this social way of living together stands in sharpest contrast to the political way, in which autonomous and responsible individuals, recognizing their objective interdependence, jointly take such charge of it as human beings can—which of course is never perfect, complete, or lasting. The social kind of "unitedness of many into one is basically antipolitical; it is the very opposite of the togetherness" characterizing political membership.[52] What people do as individuals has joint, large-scale effects in the world insofar as they simply "live together." But when they are politically engaged, they do "not merely live, but act together."[53] So acting together, which Arendt also sometimes calls "co-acting," "concerted action," or—somewhat misleadingly—"acting in concert," cannot simply mean jointly producing large-scale results; the social does that as well.[54] Acting together has to mean something like jointly taking intentional charge of those results, effectively taking responsibility for them. This too involves institutional structure, but it is not social in Arendt's sense.

Because of the systemic nature of institutional structure, individual participants in it may find themselves constrained to behave in certain ways—in order to survive, to keep their dependents alive, or to have any significant effect in the world. And their constrained behavior, in turn, helps to coerce others. This will be true even if they are not by character parvenus, even if a parvenu changes his mind, even if an individual does not believe in what he is doing. Here, by contrast with the conformist social, changing your mind or even your individual conduct is not enough. Here an individual who says "I can't help it. There's nothing else I can do" need not necessarily be inauthentic or hypocritical like the parvenu; he may simply be realistic. "Rule by nobody is not necessarily no-rule," Arendt said.[55] And this was Marx's point, too, in distinguishing his view of the market from Feuerbach's view of the gods: the gods are imaginary beings without independent power, but the market is real, not just humanly imagined but humanly created in fact, and it has genuine coercive power over its participants, even though it consists only in their structured activity.

This is not the intrusion of natural causation or biological necessity into human affairs. People can and sometimes do opt out of institutional structures, though only at great cost, and therefore rarely. But even the individual who opts out is powerless alone to change the structure or to prevent it from continuing to constrain the rest. Viewed collectively, however, these same individuals undoubtedly could change much about what they are collectively doing and forcing on each other. Together with a sufficient number of others, the individual participant can do a lot to alter social structure. Not just any and everything, of course, in just any way; not even a politically articulated free community is omnipotent. As Arendt will put it later, the sphere of politics is always "limited by those things which men cannot change at will."[56] Still, viewed collectively, these individuals could change a lot about what they do, far more than any of them can change alone. The range of what an individual can effect in institutional structure is quite limited; the range of what the collectivity can do is very broad. The collectivity, however, is subject to far greater inertia than the individual. To change institutional structure intentionally, a large number of individuals would have to change their minds and their conduct more or less at the same time, in more or less correlated ways. There is a coordination problem.[57]

So collectively these individuals are and are not helpless. They could change the institutional structure they constantly reproduce by their conduct, and change it intentionally, if only they could (re)organize themselves. What therefore becomes crucial is the capacity to form new relationships, new modes of relationship, people's capacity to innovate institutional structures jointly. That is what Tocqueville called "knowledge of how to combine," or "the art of being free," and what French people rediscovered in forming the Resistance, what Arendt called "action" and would later call "founding."[58] Such joint self-(re)organization, however, is precisely what the social rules out.

So we have arrived a second time and by a different route at the same conclusion as emerged from mapping the social and behavior onto labor, work, and action. The social is Arendt's way of talking about a collectivity of people who, though they are interdependent and active—their doings therefore continually shaping the conditions under which they all live—behave individually in ways that preclude coordinated action, so that they cannot (or at any rate do not) take charge of what they are doing in the world. The ambiguity between "cannot" and "do not" is, as we have noted before, crucial, since Arendt—like Marx and Tocqueville—needs to have it both ways with respect to our present moment: that we are right now both unfree (or there is no real problem) and free-to-become-free (or there is no hope). As Reinhardt says, "read in this way, the social is no longer incapable of politicization; rather, it cries out for it."[59]

Some Difficulties in This Reading

This, I suggest, is what Arendt's social is when not mystified by the imagery of a Blob. In a way, this reading of the social, now attained twice by different routes, is utterly unsurprising—no more than a commonsense interpretation of the idea of a parvenu writ large, with institutional structure paralleling character structure, the social collectivity failing to acknowledge and use its powers as the individual parvenu fails to acknowledge and use his. Yet Arendt never explicitly says anything quite like this, and in several important respects this reading is surprising, indeed, even problematic.

Somewhat surprising, first of all, is that on this reading the social is Arendt's *name* for a particular condition that occurs in human collectivities. Whenever, for whatever reason, a human collectivity is in that condition, we have an instance of the social. Whenever the members of that collectivity, in whatever way, begin to take effective charge of the overall resultants of what they are doing, the social ipso facto disappears. Thus the social precludes politics not causally but logically, by definition. It does not destroy politics, swallow up freedom, wreck both public and private, intrude into some realm, or "substitute behavior for action"; it *is* the absence of action, politics, freedom, public and private from contexts where these would be possible and desirable.[60]

So the social does not do, or cause, or explain anything. It is not an agent, not a Blob. Instead, it is a condition that itself needs to be explained. Why and how have we modern people gotten ourselves into such a fix that we cannot—or at any rate do not—take effective charge of our own conduct on the large scale when it causes us problems? We shall return to that question in a sketchy way in the last chapter.

Meanwhile, there is a second, even more troubling respect in which our reading of the social is surprising and problematic. It seems to run diametrically counter to a basic, repeated Arendtian claim. If the social is people who have no control over the large-scale consequences of what they are doing, then politics is the effort to achieve such control. But Arendt often insists that, precisely in action and politics, consequences *cannot* be controlled, directed, or even foreseen. Our expectation that they might be, she says, derives from the realm of work, where the intended product, *the* work (for example, of art) is the point, and workmanship lies in controlling this outcome. In work, such control is possible because the worker deals only with inanimate materials, not with fellow creators, so that he "remains master of his doings from beginning to end."[61]

Action, by contrast, "produces" only relationships with other actors and creators and does not terminate in any fixed, objective product, so its "*consequences are boundless*," and it "lies altogether outside the category of means and ends."[62] Actions thus do have consequences—"boundless" ones—but the notion of consequences is problematic in relation to action in a way that it is not in relation to work. What, exactly, was done, and with exactly what consequences, are questions always in principle contestable among fellow actors.[63] Actions initiate or change relationships; they "prompt" or "condition"—though they do not "cause"—further actions by others.[64] This means that someone who acts "always becomes 'guilty' of consequences he never intended or even foresaw" and that one can "never . . . foretell with certainty the outcome and end of any action."[65] Subsequent actions both are and are not part of the outcome or consequences of earlier ones, making guilt problematic, which is why Arendt places the word within quotation marks.

These complexities are what prompt Arendt to say that human beings "have never been and never will be able to . . . control reliably" what they "start through action."[66] Nevertheless, she clearly recognizes that actions do have (something like) consequences, of which the actors are (something like) guilty when the consequences do harm. And that implies—logically must imply—that those consequences could have been (to some extent) controlled, directed, or intentionally influenced by the actors. None of Arendt's critiques or strictures would make sense otherwise. If changes in our nonmaterial world bore only a random relationship to our intentions and efforts, if our "actions" simply befell us or popped out of us like hiccups, there could be no such thing as action, no distinction between action and behavior, no way of identifying *this* as "so-and-so's deed." There would be no point in worrying about parvenu scoundrels, about the totalitarian effort to destroy all "consequence and responsibility," about *amor mundi,* unless people can intentionally do something about them.[67]

In countless passages, moreover, Arendt herself referred explicitly to the consequences of action and called on readers to take responsibility for them. She did so in the early New York essays, insisting that "the circumstances under which we live are created by man," so that the evil which people commit "can and must be prevented" by people as well.[68] She was still doing so near the end of her life, as she praised the New Left for its "goals" (another notion that makes no sense unless actions have something like controllable consequences) and its members for their desire to "change things by [their] own efforts" but also criticized them when they seemed insufficiently concerned about "the eventual consequences of [their] demonstrations," those actual, "practical political consequences" for which they bore "direct responsibility."[69]

Our primary concern, however, is not with these early and late writings but with Arendt's concept of the social in *The Human Condition* and her insistence there that the consequences of action cannot be controlled. The problem is whether that insistence can be reconciled with the argument of this chapter about what the social is. Two distinctions are helpful here: first, the difference between Arendt's concern for individual uniqueness and her concern for action, and, second, the distinction between individual action and the politics of a collectivity. Let us take them in turn.

Arendt sees the social as a double threat, endangering both unique individuality and spontaneous action. Clearly these two threats are related, but sometimes individuality matters as prerequisite to action, and at other times action is valued as serving individuality. When Arendt presents individual uniqueness as the ultimate value to which action is a means, worldly consequences seem almost irrelevant. Fellow citizens are an audience before whom the individual actor performs, hoping to do something memorable and achieve immortality through them. Politics is a tool for individual self-realization, and the social is mainly a homogenizing agency.[70] When, instead, Arendt presents action as the real goal, which presupposes individual uniqueness as a means, fellow citizens appear as co-actors rather than audience, and politics is primarily about founding and sustaining our shared world, rather than about oneself. Then the consequences of action—its worldly results—are its real point, and the social means collective impotence. The former perspective tends to emerge when Arendt is explicating the view of the ancient Greeks, with their agonistic, narcissistic emphasis on heroism as immortality. The latter perspective emerges from the Resistance experience.[71] Clearly, our interpretation of the social fits better with the latter than with the former, though even heroism presupposes intentional action. But in any case, the fact that Arendt has dual perspectives here demonstrates that she cannot mean flatly and simply that action has no consequences or that those consequences are altogether beyond intentional human influence.

The second helpful distinction here is that between individual action and political acting together or co-acting. Arendt's insistence that the consequences of action can never be controlled occurs mostly in the context of isolated individual action, suggesting that it is particularly important for the individual agent to recognize that he is not unique or sovereign, not the only one capable of action and thus in control, but one among peers. Individuals need to be reminded that they act into a web of relationships with fellow agents, each of whom is capable of responding in unexpected and creative ways.[72] A politically articulated collectivity, by contrast, though of course it must respect the individuality of its members, does not need reminding of its limitations in quite the same way as the individual agent. Indeed, in joint political action, its members *can* achieve at least a degree of something like control over the consequences of what they do, which is to say that individuals can sometimes do jointly what they cannot do separately. Joining together freely in mutual commitment, people can achieve a certain "limited independence" from that "incalculability of the future" which otherwise characterizes action.

When they are thus conjoined in political action, Arendt says, "sovereignty" and control over what they are doing assume "a certain limited reality."[73]

It is not just that Arendt is ambivalent and ambiguous here, but the topic itself involves an inescapable tension. Action is intentional; it *must* have (something like) consequences that the actor can (to some extent) control, direct, or intentionally influence, or there could be no such thing as action. Yet notions like consequences really do work differently in relation to action than in relation to work on inanimate matter, and the difference does involve the autonomy of one's fellow actors, who share in interpreting one's action and whose interrelationships are the medium in which action takes place.

Perhaps one should take refuge here in Arendt's sometimes carefully qualified phrasing: unable to "control *reliably*," unable to foretell "*with certainty*," achieving only "*a certain, limited* independence" from incalculability, and so on. Or perhaps one should distinguish proximate or "immediate" consequences from more distant ones, the former more controllable than the latter.[74] Or perhaps "control" is simply the wrong word here. Yet each of the available alternatives—influence, direction, guidance, taking charge of, taking care of, seeing to, taking responsibility for—imports its own distinctive and problematic connotations. None is entirely satisfactory.

Surely in both individual life and politics we do effect changes in the world and in our relationships, changes for which we bear, or share, responsibility—always contestable but nevertheless real. And our actions often go wrong; things rarely turn out exactly as we intended. So action and politics are like a series of adjustments, seeking to address perceived problems yet often giving rise to new ones at the same time. Control over consequences is never complete, certain, or beyond dispute, yet something like control—the ability to realize one's intentions in the world—is an indispensable component of action and therefore also of coordinated action, of politics. Indeed, it is what distinguishes action from behavior and politics from the social.

There remains, finally, a third way in which our reading of the social is surprising. Not only does that reading imply that the social explains nothing; not only does it conflict with Arendt's insistence that the consequences of action cannot be controlled; but in addition, the social corresponds to none of the ordinary or dictionary senses of the words "society" and "social." Surprisingly, Arendt's notion of the social does not correlate directly with any of these two words' familiar uses: high or respectable society, the social occasions at which its members gather, the social pages of the newspaper that report their doings, social climbing into their ranks, being a socialite, having a busy social life, attending a social occasion, sociability, one's associates or social circle, an association, social class, social status, social services, social workers, social welfare, social issues, social norms, social diseases, antisocial behavior, social statistics, social science, sociology, or the sociological sense of "society" as meaning (almost) everybody.

Even "civil society," which seems closest to Arendt's notion, also differs from it in important ways, since she strongly rejects both the Hegelian and the Marxist uses of that phrase. Both a Hegelian civil service and the automatic unity she ascribes to Marx's postrevolutionary utopia are social to her. Arendt's use of "the social," moreover, is almost diametrically opposed to the idea of civil society deployed in the recent literature about the collapse of East European Communism.[75] That literature continues the traditional contrast between civil society and the state, although it locates political freedom in the former rather than the latter. Arendt still occasionally used that traditional contrast in *The Origins,* as we saw, but never by the time of *The Human Condition,* and never with that notion of freedom. For her, the opposite of the social is not the state or government but politics and political action, which she understands in ways that are fairly close to what recent writers on Eastern Europe mean by "civil society," or at least to what most interests them about civil society.[76]

No wonder, then, if Arendt's teachings about the social are often misunderstood. Without being aware of it, she gradually worked herself into a highly idiosyncratic use of the phrase, one that was almost bound to mislead readers and that may even sometimes have confused Arendt herself. Her idiosyncratic usage may help to explain her hypostasization of the adjective as well. None of this is intended, however, to suggest that Arendt's deployment of her phrase "the social" is arbitrary or illegitimate. Indeed, we have watched its derivation, step by step, from familiar meanings of "social" and "society," by a series of ordinary semantic projections of a kind that all competent speakers of a language constantly employ in talking, writing, or thinking.[77]

"The social," then, is not a very apt name for the problem Arendt meant to address; yet I know no better one. If the social demystified is a collectivity of people who, for whatever reason—whether because of their character, their institutions, or their ways of thinking—cannot, or at any rate do not, direct or even intentionally influence the large-scale resultants of what they are doing, one might say it is people conducting themselves *as if* they had been swallowed by some Blob that deprived them of their individuality and capacity for initiative, compacted them into an undifferentiated mass. Then the basic question of our study would become: How and why did "*as if* swallowed by a Blob" become, for Arendt, simply and flatly "swallowed by a Blob"? We are almost ready to address that question directly, but one further prior task remains.

It will be useful to look briefly at Arendt's writings, soon after *The Human Condition*, in which there no longer is any Blob, and the word "social," though still centrally important, returns to its adjectival functions. Comparing these writings with *The Human Condition*, in effect, is still another way to investigate the Blob, by noting what difference in the argument results from its excision. The immediate result of removing the Blob, we shall see, is not a more effective and consistent theory but instead something close to theoretical chaos. The works immediately following *The Human Condition*, although highly interesting and important achievements, are also deeply inconsistent—not to say incoherent—at the theoretical level, in precisely that terrain which had previously been occupied by the Blob. If nothing else, the chaos revealed by its excision should help to keep us properly humble in relation to Arendt's failures by showing just how difficult was the task she set herself.

TEN

Excising the Blob

There are indications that soon after completing *The Human Condition* Arendt may have become uneasy about her vision of the social and begun trying to rethink it. Within two years she published an article pointing out that "society" was, after all, just a word, with its own particular history, and there followed in rapid succession two books that readdress familiar Arendtian themes without hypostasizing "social" and virtually without Blob imagery. The hypostasized social never recurred in Arendt's subsequent writings.

That she was troubled about the social is suggested, first of all, by Arendt's publication in 1960 of an article called "Society and Culture," which opened by pointing out that "society" is not a timeless "generic term" but a word whose use "can be dated and described historically." Arendt had mentioned the word's Latin etymology already in *The Human Condition,* only to set it aside and focus on society as a modern phenomenon. Here, having noted that the word has a history, she does not even recur to the Latin but instead declares flatly (and falsely) that the term is "not older than the modern age."[1] Still, the deflationary tone returning "society" to the ranks of ordinary words may be a sign of some rethinking.

The contemporary notion of mass society, which is the main focus of the article, was "historically and conceptually preceded," Arendt says, by that of "good and genteel" society, and all the characteristics now attributed to mass man "first appeared in good society" (198–99) Mass society is simply good society expanded; Arendt quotes Edward Shils: "The mass of the population has become incorporated into society."[2] The origins of good society she locates "probably" in the court of Louis XIV, who reduced the "French nobility to political insignificance by the simple means of gathering them at Versailles, transforming them into courtiers, and making them entertain one another through the intrigues, cabals, and endless gossip which this perpetual party inevitably engendered."[3]

Such fake and politically impotent partying later continued in the "corruption and hypocrisy of the [bourgeois] salons," where all unpleasant realities were viewed "through a veil of 'sweetness and light' " (200, 203). By the nineteenth century, society "had grown so 'polite' that, for instance, during the Irish potato famine," use of the word "potato" was socially unacceptable, and the genteel spoke only of "that root."[4]

All of this is true and supported by the *Oxford English Dictionary*, but very partial, ignoring older meanings of the word in English (let alone its Latin roots), such as society as an association or as the "mode of life of a body of people living together." Omitting these, Arendt makes it seem as if the inclusion of everybody in society were a recent development and as if the only "society" in which they could have been included were the hypocritical "good society" of Versailles and the salons.

Society thus still sorts with hypocrisy for Arendt in this essay, but the revulsion against the social pretentiousness that motivated various groups in *The Origins* is here ascribed to "the artist," whose works the bourgeois philistine wants to use as currency for buying higher social status or "a higher degree of self-esteem . . . than in his own opinion he deserved either by nature or by birth."[5] For artists, good society therefore means "being expelled from reality into a sphere of refined talk where what they did would lose all meaning" (202). This artists' revolt was only one in a series of efforts to shield individuality against the "pressures" of society, but here again Arendt strikes a new note by pointing out that—despite the metaphor—the issue is not external pressures but internal self-discipline. The conformist individual always loses his battle against society because he himself is already "part and parcel of the society" (200). The constrained individuals *are* the constraining society.

The article, however, is at most suggestive of a possible shift in Arendt's thinking. More decisive in this regard are her next two books: *Eichmann in Jerusalem,* published in 1960, and *On Revolution,* in 1962, in which the word "social" has returned to adjectival status, with only a very few passages reminiscent of the Blob. Revisiting familiar Arendtian themes without the social as Blob, these books reveal what that image had hidden from view: considerable theoretical disorder, especially in the areas of agency, responsibility, group categorization, and historical explanation. *On Revolution* mainly addresses large-scale historical events and revisits themes from *The Human Condition;* the Eichmann book focuses primarily on individual guilt and merit, revisiting themes mostly from *The Origins*. The contradictions in *Eichmann* have received considerable critical attention because that book was so controversial; those in

On Revolution have mostly been overlooked, with hostile critics focusing on historical (in)accuracy and friendly interpreters taking the book to be consistent, both internally and with *The Human Condition*. Though the inconsistencies in both books are extensive, however, they are an improvement over the apparent theoretical coherence of *The Human Condition*, achieved at too high a price through the Blob.

Arendt on Eichmann

Shortly after "Society and Culture" appeared, the state of Israel announced that its agents had found Adolf Eichmann in Argentina and that he would be put on trial for his role in the Nazi genocide. Arendt, who was already at work on *On Revolution,* volunteered to cover the trial for *The New Yorker* because, having missed the Nuremberg trials, she felt "an obligation to my past" to see at least one of "these people in the flesh."[6]

When Arendt did see Eichmann, what struck her most forcefully was the mind-boggling discrepancy between the monstrous horrors in which he had played a role and this petty, mediocre, silly man. "Now that the devil himself was in the dock," as she put it, he seemed appallingly ordinary.[7] Indeed, the whole trial, particularly the attorneys, struck her as disappointingly quotidian, wholly inadequate to the magnitude of the crimes, the suffering, the significance of it all: "*stinknormal,* indescribably inferior, worthless."[8] Above all, Eichmann himself was not up to expectations. "Not even uncanny [*unheimlich*]," he struck Arendt as "essentially [*eigendlich*] dumb, and yet somehow not."[9] He was, as "half a dozen psychiatrists" certified, "normal," with the personality—as his own attorney said—of "a common mailman."[10] Most striking was "the undeniable ludicrousness of the man," so inappropriate to the memory of those who had suffered and died. "Everybody could see that this man was not a 'monster,' but it was difficult indeed not to suspect that he was a clown" (54). Utterly taken aback by both the world-historical role and the grandiose pretensions of this silly man, Arendt was "flabbergasted."[11]

Her task as reporter was to think rightly, truthfully, about him, his deeds, and the events of which they formed a part. For of course "the facts of the case, of what Eichmann had done . . . were never in dispute"; the difficulty was calling them by their right names, finding the right names for them.[12] "Technically and organizationally" Eichmann's position in Nazi officialdom had not been very high; he was important only because of his centrality in the extermination of Jews (70). Eichmann had been what Germans came to call a "desk murderer": a bureaucrat who "merely" signed the orders for the transport of Jews to concentration and death camps. He did not personally do the killing; indeed, the actual killing in the camps was often assigned to inmates. As the judgment eventually phrased what Arendt also ratifies as "the truth,"

> the extent to which any one of the many criminals was close to or remote from the actual killer of the victim means nothing, as far as the measure of his responsibility is concerned. On the contrary, in general *the degree of responsibility increases as we draw further away from the man who uses the fatal instrument with his own hands.*[13]

As Arendt presents him, Eichmann was neither an anti-Semite nor a sadist but an ambitious, deferential careerist. He was the son of an accountant, unable to finish high school or the technical school to which he was then sent, "a failure in the eyes of his social class, his family, and hence in his own eyes as well" (28, 33). A traveling salesman for the Vacuum Oil Company, he joined the Nazi Party not out of ideological conviction but in hopes of starting over "from scratch and still mak[ing] a career," but also of somehow merging himself into the heroic grandeur of a world-historical movement, being transported "from a humdrum life without significance and consequence . . . into History" (33).

Eichmann, in short, was a parvenu, diligently obedient in his career, deferential to his social betters, and eager for their approval. By contrast with the many leading Nazis who despised bourgeois respectability, Eichmann "had always been overawed by 'good society.' . . . He did not need to 'close his ears to the voice of conscience,' . . . because his conscience spoke with a 'respectable voice,' with the voice of respectable society around him" (126). And in Nazi Germany, "the whole of respectable society had in one way or another succumbed to Hitler" (295). At the Wannsee Conference in particular, an important turning point in Nazi anti-Semitism and in Eichmann's career, he saw and heard personally what he called " 'the most prominent people . . . the Popes of the Third Reich' . . . vying and fighting with each other for the honor of taking the lead in these 'bloody' matters. 'At that moment, I sensed a kind of Pontius Pilate feeling, for I felt free of all guilt.' *Who was he to judge?* Who was he 'to have [his] own thoughts on the matter?' " (114, emphasis in original).

In addition to his parvenu deference to society, Arendt says, certain other peculiarities of Eichmann's mind particularly suited him to a bureaucratic career under the Nazis. He had no criminal intent; his only motive was "an extraordinary diligence in looking out for his personal advancement.... He *merely*, to put the matter colloquially, *never realized what he was doing*" (287, emphasis in original). This peculiarity of Eichmann's mind, this "sheer thoughtlessness" or "inability to *think*, namely, to think from the standpoint of somebody else" or "to look at anything from the other fellow's point of view," secured him in his parvenu isolation from other people and from "reality as such" (287, 48–49).

Eichmann also displayed a correlated incapacity in the use of words, what Arendt calls his "heroic fight with the German language" (48). Addicted to clichés, he spoke almost exclusively in stock phrases. His mind was "filled to the brim" with such conventional expressions, and when Eichmann did occasionally formulate a thought of his own, he would repeat it endlessly "until it became a cliché" (53, 49). He had one particular stock phrase for each important incident in his life, which had given him "a sense of elation" at the time and which he invariably invoked when speaking about that incident. Often the clichés were ludicrously inappropriate to the occasion; Arendt suggests that for Eichmann, scrupulous rigidity about repeating them exactly replaced any effort to test them against either reality or each other (53–55).

All these characterological and intellectual features made Eichmann an ideal bureaucrat, and particularly an "ideal subject" for the Nazi bureaucracy's rigidly imposed "language rules" (86). As he said during the trial, "Officialese [*Amtssprache*] is my only language" (48). Nazi officialese, however, was not just a professional jargon, nor the polite avoidance of unpleasantness, like referring to the potato only as "that root," but a systematic code of euphemistic circumlocution, in which expressions such as "the final solution" served not just to fool the gullible but to protect the knowledgeable against having to recognize what they were doing.

In sum, Eichmann, a central agent in the commission of monstrous horrors, was himself stunningly ordinary, contemptible, even laughable. As Arendt began to come to terms with this discrepancy, she decided to subtitle her book "A Report on the Banality of Evil" and to close it with "the lesson of the fearsome, word-and-thought-defying *banality of evil*," meaning not that evil as such is banal but rather that the central import of the Eichmann trial lay in the discrepancy between the man and the impact of his conduct in the world.[14] What had initially "flabbergasted" Arendt became the theme of her book.

Commentators have taken her subtitle to mark a simple, singular reversal in her thinking, resulting from her encounter with Eichmann: a shift from the "radical evil" of *The Origins* to "banal evil" in *Eichmann*. The commentators assume that when Arendt went to look at Eichmann "in the flesh" she expected to see radical evil personified, or—as Francis X. Winters puts it—"to look totalitarianism in the face."[15] Finding banality instead, she changed her mind about the nature of evil. Young-Bruehl further suggests that Jaspers, who corresponded with Arendt extensively about these matters, went through a similar shift under her influence. That version of what happened has some foundation, yet it is neither accurate in detail nor adequate as an interpretation.

Arendt surely was taken aback by Eichmann, and reporting on his trial was indeed a transforming experience for her. She called writing the Eichmann book a retroactive cure for something that had ailed her—"somehow a *cura posterior* for me"—and confessed to having written it "in a curious state of euphoria" that left her, even twenty years later, "light-hearted about the whole matter."[16] She even said publicly during the controversy provoked by the book that she had "changed [her] mind" and no longer spoke of radical evil, since evil "possesses neither depth nor any demonic dimension."[17] So Young-Bruehl is right to say that in confronting Eichmann Arendt "freed herself of a long nightmare."[18] The question is what, exactly, that nightmare was, of what ailment she had been cured. Young-Bruehl thinks Arendt was cured of believing in original sin: after Eichmann's banality, Naziism no longer seemed "proof of an original evil element in human nature and hence [was] not an indictment of mankind" (367). But this cannot be quite right.

Arendt's euphoria and her cure involved no simple, singular transformation from original sin to human goodness, nor from radical to banal evil. Instead her encounter with Eichmann was one in a series of shifts within an ongoing ambivalence, and that ambivalence was less about human nature or the nature of evil than it was about the Blob, about thinking about human affairs in terms of some abstract, external, superhuman force. Her cure and euphoria were not unrelated to the fact that this was probably her least abstract and theoretical book, that in writing it she was basically a reporter of testimony and facts. While complaining at the time of desperately "swimming in an enormous amount of material," she added that she was "somehow enjoy[ing] the handling of facts and concrete things."[19]

That Eichmann cannot have effected in Arendt any simple transformation from radical to banal evil should be obvious from the fact that—as we have seen—she *began* her thinking with a recognition of banal evil, in the form of the parvenu, whose conformism feeds the oppression he should be fighting. Eichmann's banality should have come as no surprise to Arendt at all. Already in some New York essays of 1945 and 1946, as we saw, Arendt had interpreted collaboration with the Nazis in terms of anxieties about status and security much like the parvenu's deference. "The real motives which caused people to act as cogs in the mass-murder machine," she wrote then, were not fanaticism and sadism but exaggerated fears of ostracism and unemployment, of being unable to make a living and support their dependents.[20] The "cogs" were "first and foremost job-holders, and good family men," their "docility" deriving from their "normality" (232). "Concerned only with [their] private existence"—with making a living and family duties—and utterly lacking "the classic virtues of civic [action]," they demanded in exchange for their cooperation only that they "be fully exempted from responsibility" for what they did (233, 232). When such a "cog's" job "forces him to murder people[,] he does not regard himself as a murderer, because he has not done it out of inclination but in his professional capacity. Out of sheer passion he would never do harm to a fly" (234). Such anxious refusal of one's own powers and responsibilities has turned twentieth-century reality into a "nightmare," she wrote, and our world will lose its "nightmarish quality" only when people "recognize the human background" of these horrible, seemingly inevitable events, recognize them as deeds "done by men" and thus as preventable through human action.[21]

Even *The Origins of Totalitarianism* was initially intended, as early outlines demonstrate, "to argue against the inevitability of history, and to show that the Nazi catastrophe could have been avoided," as Claudia Roth Pierpont puts it. Arendt intended to show, in particular, that even the victims "bore a significant measure of responsibility for their fate," Pierpont says, not in order to blame the victims nor out of Jewish self-hatred, but on the contrary in order to restore to the surviving victims an awareness of their own powers, agency, and autonomy.[22] To Arendt, "even the awful burden of responsibility was preferable to the humiliation of the helpless victim"; by delivering blame to her own people, she hoped to "deliver control," restoring their access to their own capacities (100). We have seen how, despite these intentions, *The Origins* ended up with a Blob. But even after *The Origins*, when Arendt went to Jerusalem to look at Eichmann for herself, she expected to see not, as Winters supposes, the monstrous face of totalitarianism personified but, as she wrote to Jaspers, a "walking disaster [*Unheil*]" in all its "uncanny nothingness."[23] But then why—about what—was she "flabbergasted"?

Although something like the banality of evil was Arendt's original and lifelong theme, it coexisted from early in her thinking with alternative visions—of Naziism as diabolical and of totalitarianism, and later the social, as a Blob. Even as she was writing articles in the mid-1940s interpreting "cogs in the mass-murder machine" as parvenus, she also wrote to Jaspers that Nazi deeds could not properly be called a (mere) crime, because they really "explode[d] the limits of the law," so that "no punishment is severe enough." That is what "constitutes their monstrousness."[24] This phrasing recurs in *The Origins* and again in *The Human Condition*, both times linked explicitly to the idea of radical evil, an "unpunishable, unforgivable absolute evil which could no longer be understood and explained by the evil motives of . . . human sinfulness."[25]

Arendt, then, was ambivalent. Her entire early orientation against parvenu deference, denial, and romanticism and in favor of realistic neighborly love and political engagement pushed her toward the deflationary "banality" view. But the monstrousness of what the Nazis had done, the scale on which they did it, and above all the horrible suffering of the victims pushed in the opposite direction. In effect, the blood of the victims cried out, demanding something grander, more satanic, more unprecedented than mere banality as an explanation. Just as trivializing or commercializing the holocaust would be an intolerable offense against the victims, so too would any explanation that rendered it ordinary.

Arendt had been one of the fortunate ones, the survivors; even the French camp at Gurs was in no way comparable to the Nazi death factories. So it is likely that her sense of duty owed to the victims—or, as she put it, of her "obligation to my past"—had a significant unconscious component involving issues of the sort discussed in chapter 8. As Young-Bruehl remarks, Arendt had "trouble remembering" what she knew to be true about Eichmann's ordinariness—that "no matter what he does and if he killed ten million people, he is still a clown."[26] She had trouble remembering it, I am suggesting, insofar as it connected for her with an unconscious feeling of her own guilt, relieved first by making totalitarianism diabolical and later by expecting Eichmann to be so as well.

Jaspers had warned Arendt about this in 1946, in response to her letter about how Nazi deeds were more than crimes and beyond punishment. Contrary to Young-Bruehl's suggestion that Jaspers regarded Eichmann simply as a "monster" and was "incredulous" when Arendt first proposed otherwise, the evidence of their correspondence indicates that Jaspers was, like Arendt, ambivalent, and his letters encouraged both poles of her ambivalence.[27] To talk about Nazi offenses as beyond crime and punishment, he warned, inevitably implies "a streak of 'greatness'—

of satanic greatness" in them, which is as wrong as "talk of the 'demonic' in Hitler.... It seems to me that we have to see these things in their total banality, in their sober nullity, because that is how it really was."[28] Arendt at once agreed: "In the way I have expressed this up to now, I come dangerously close to the 'satanic greatness' that I, like you, totally reject." Though she still insisted on the difference between an ordinary murder and the systematic construction of "factories to produce corpses," she concluded: "One thing is certain: all formulations that mythologize the horrible must be resisted, and to the extent that I can't escape such formulations, I haven't understood what actually went on."[29] This was in 1946; when she went on to write *The Origins of Totalitarianism,* despite this "one thing [that was] certain," Arendt apparently could not escape the Blob.

Later, at the time of the trial, Jaspers wrote that because deeds such as Eichmann's "stand outside what is humanly and morally comprehensible," Eichmann himself must have "inhuman personal qualities as well."[30] So Eichmann was a monster to Jaspers, who earlier had also condemned Marx as "an 'evil' person" with "something like" a demon in him.[31] Nevertheless, Jaspers also praised Arendt's notion of the banality of evil and the "wonderful" subtitle of her book and claimed that in it she had spoken "the crucial word against 'radical evil,'" and thus against "gnosis," by teaching that a human being "cannot be a devil."[32]

Jaspers, then, was no help; Arendt had to find her own resolution to their shared ambivalence. Although she probably had begun seeking that resolution by the time of her 1960 article reexamining the concept of society, she found it mainly in coming to terms with Eichmann. His ludicrous banality, which she should have expected but somehow had not, caught her up short and drove her to reexamine those intense, conflicted feelings from which her fantasy of a diabolical Blob had sprung. The result of that effort took something like the following form: in our time, such nullities as Eichmann are so numerous, and are organizationally deployed in such a way, that the large-scale consequences of their banality are monstrous, as if these "walking disasters" of the human species had been taken over by an evil Blob. It is not that all Nazis were banal; Reinhardt Heydrich, for instance, struck Arendt as "absolutely evil."[33] But without the Eichmanns, men such as Heydrich and Hitler would have been virtually powerless. The Eichmanns, not the Heydrichs, are the central problem of our time, and they can be understood, as Jaspers said, only "in their sober nullity," or, as Arendt added, only if one resists all "impulses to mythologize the horrible." Radical evil was the result, not the cause, of banality and parvenu deference. Arendt no longer felt a duty to the victims to diabolize; on the contrary, her duty—now fully in accord with her lifelong teaching about human agency—was to demythologize even the most extreme oppression. She no longer believed in the Blob.

Explanation and Agency

Absent the Blob, however, she was forced to wrestle anew with the problems which that image had hidden from view: the complexities and apparent inconsistencies in our ordinary notions of agency, responsibility, and historical explanation. Images of totalitarianism as Blob would have made Eichmann into one of the victims rather than a criminal deserving death; that would be intolerable, for if Eichmann was not guilty, no one was. Arendt's critique of the prosecution at the trial for presenting Eichmann as part of "anti-Semitism throughout history" and thus as a mere "innocent executor of some mysteriously foreordained destiny" could be applied just as well to her own earlier image of totalitarianism.[34] But even without the Blob, Arendt's simple, concrete task as a reporter seemed equally liable to exonerate Eichmann: *tout comprendre, c'est tout pardonner*. Every time Arendt explained Eichmann's character or motives or made his conduct plausible, she also thereby suggested that he could not have done other than he did, given who he was. Every time she used expressions such as "lack of imagination," "inability to *think*," "incapability for ordinary speech," "perfectly incapable of telling right from wrong," "triggered in him a mechanism that had become completely unalterable," she seemed to imply that he was not to blame.[35] Is a man to be condemned to death for his inabilities and incapacities? That implication was not intended; never for a moment did Arendt mean to exonerate Eichmann.

The difficulties about agency and history in Arendt's book are not confined to Eichmann personally, however. Excising the Blob left behind similar problems regarding other people, whole groups or categories of people. Just as Hitler and Heydrich could never have held great power without the Eichmanns, Eichmann could never have committed his crimes without the collaboration of countless others, without "the almost ubiquitous complicity, which had stretched far beyond the ranks of Party membership" (18). Indeed, "the trouble with Eichmann was precisely that so many were like him, and that the many were neither perverted nor sadistic, that they were, and still are, terribly and terrifyingly normal"

(276). Nazi Germany was pervaded by an "aura of systematic mendacity" that shielded all "against reality and factuality" (52). Such conditions give rise to a "new type of criminal," exemplified by Eichmann but including large sectors of the population, who "commits his crimes under circumstances that make it well-nigh impossible for him to know or to feel that he is doing wrong" (276). Does the "well-nigh" suffice to save the argument from logical trouble?

The most controversial treatment of individual responsibility among categories of people in the Eichmann book is, of course, Arendt's discussion of Jewish collaboration with the Nazis. Arendt accused the prosecution of painting a propaganda picture simultaneously too favorable and too unfavorable to the Jews: too favorable, for instance, in omitting the story of Jewish collaboration; too unfavorable, for instance, in continually asking witnesses why they had not resisted, in order to teach young Israelis the need to fight back. Yet Arendt herself has trouble with praise and blame in relation to her explanation of what happened. She charges that the prosecution, seeking to condemn Eichmann, needed to demonstrate "a clear-cut division between persecutors and victims," but her own theme—how mere banal deference can add up to genocide—requires blurring the distinction, so that the cooperation of some Jews with the Nazis is essential to the story (120). Chronically deferential to established authority, these Jews simply demonstrated the parvenu's usual "dangerous inability . . . to distinguish between friend and foe."[36] When the Nazis established various categories of exemptions to their anti-Semitic policies, Jews competed to qualify. Since, however, "everyone who demanded to have an 'exception' made in his case implicitly recognized the rule," in practice this meant complicity with Nazi policies and signaled "the beginning of the moral collapse of respectable Jewish society" (132, 131).

Arendt's main and most controversial criticism in this regard is directed against the leaders of Jewish communities all over Europe, who "almost without exception, cooperated in one way or another, for one reason or another, with the Nazis" (125). She recognizes that mostly, and particularly in the beginning, these leaders were trying to save lives and minimize suffering, but says that the resulting habits of cooperation made it all too easy for them later "to cross the abyss" between facilitating escape and facilitating deportation to the death camps (11). Had it not been for the Jewish leadership, Arendt maintains, if the Jews had been "unorganized and leaderless, there would have been chaos and plenty of misery, but the total number of victims would hardly have been between four and a half and six million people." She dwells on this matter, she says, only "because it offers the most striking insight into the totality of the moral collapse the Nazis caused in respectable European society" (125). So, on the one hand, Arendt speaks more than once of a "moral collapse," yet in the same sentence, on the other hand, that collapse has a "cause," and its cause is the Nazis, not the Jews.

As with blame, so with merit: one finds confusion. Arendt discusses not merely Jewish collaboration but also Jewish resistance to the Nazis. Resistance occurred, she says, among both Zionist and non-Zionist Jews, and almost exclusively among the young. "Only the very young had been capable of taking 'the decision that we cannot go and be slaughtered like sheep.' "[37] Yet if only the young were capable of resisting, can one fault older Jews for failing to do so? If the Jews of Europe were characteristically unable to tell friend from foe, can one blame them for that inability? If the moral collapse of respectable European society was caused by the Nazis, in what sense was it a *moral* collapse?

Although the text gives some support to critics who charge that Arendt was harder on "her own" people than on the Nazis and Eichmann, the basic difficulty in the argument of *Eichmann in Jerusalem* lies elsewhere, in the multiple incoherences of our ordinary ways of discussing agency, responsibility, and causation in human affairs—incoherences that Arendt cannot avoid but does little to clarify. The strongest evidence that this and not "Jewish self-hatred" is the problem is that Arendt has the same sort of difficulties regarding collaboration and resistance by gentiles.

Although Arendt does briefly discuss various forms of German gentile resistance to the Nazis, only actual efforts to help the Jews as such were directly relevant to the Eichmann trial, and only two such instances were actually mentioned in trial testimony: an army officer who sabotaged documents and a certain Sergeant Anton Schmidt, who helped Jewish partisans in Poland until he was caught and executed. Schmidt's story elicits from Arendt a meditation on "how utterly different everything would be today in this courtroom, in Israel, in Germany, in all of Europe, and perhaps in all countries of the world, if only more such stories could have been told" (231). As an "explanation" of why there were not more such stories, Arendt quotes from a memoir by a German army physician, Peter Bamm, who says that many "decent" German soldiers knew all about the extermination squads slaughtering Jews in eastern Europe and did nothing because "anyone who had seriously protested or done anything about the killing unit would have been arrested within twenty-four hours and would have disappeared," having "sacrificed his life in vain," a sacrifice that, although not "morally meaningless," would have been "practically useless" (231–32). Citing testimony that soldiers selected for the execution squads could request a transfer without risking death, Arendt comments that "decency" as Bamm defines it is no more than social respectability, whose hollowness the story reveals (91, 232).

Bamm's memoir, however, merely articulates what had been a central tenet of Arendt's account of totalitarianism in *The Origins*: that the "totalitarian state lets [causes] its opponents [to] disappear in silent anonymity," thereby making resistance useless in practical terms.[38] Now that the point was made by a German officer, however, and after excision of the Blob from her thinking about the Nazis, Arendt saw its implications in a different light. Where all think like Bamm, none will act like Schmidt, and there will be no "more such stories" as Schmidt's to tell, which would itself be a "practical consequence" of the greatest magnitude. Nazi efforts to make "their opponents 'disappear in silent anonymity' were in vain. . . . One man will always be left alive to tell the story. Hence, nothing can ever be 'practically useless,' at least, not in the long run." The lesson to be drawn, "politically speaking," is that "under conditions of terror most people will comply but *some people will not.*"[39]

The same lesson emerges when Arendt looks at local gentile resistance to—and collaboration with—extermination of the Jews in the various occupied countries: " 'It could happen' in most places but *it did not happen everywhere*" (233, emphasis in original). Arendt seeks to keep alive awareness of the possibility of resistance; but as soon as she tries to say what circumstances facilitate it, explanation threatens to undermine the idea of agency, the very point she wants to make.

She is particularly fascinated by the example of Danish resistance, which is "*sui generis*" and should be "required reading in political science for all students who wish to learn something about the enormous power potential inherent in non-violent action" (171). Danish resistance on behalf of the Jews was prompt, open, principled, and initiated by the king himself. Confronted by that resistance, the Nazis began to back down and modify their policies in Denmark, with some German officials there even sabotaging their orders. Denmark was "the only case we know of in which the Nazis met with *open* native resistance, and the result seems to have been that those exposed to it changed their minds." The vaunted Nazi "toughness" melted away "like butter in the sun" and thus was revealed as a myth behind which lay only "a ruthless desire for conformity at any price." Nazi toughness, like Bamm's "decency," was mere social conformism, but Danish resistance resulted from "an authentically political sense, an inbred comprehension of the requirements and responsibilities of citizenship and independence." Arendt quotes Leni Yahil: "For the Danes ... the Jewish question was a political and not a humanitarian question," presumably meaning that it was a matter of solidarity with Danish Jews as fellow citizens rather than of condescending pity for helpless victims.[40]

But what can Arendt mean by attributing the Danish resistance to an "inbred" political sense, invoking a biological criterion contrary to her basic teaching about political matters? Equally puzzling is why she makes so much of the Danish case as "political," by contrast with that of Bulgaria, which in some ways seems even more impressive by her own criteria. It is true that no witnesses from Bulgaria testified at the trial, yet Arendt does report on Bulgaria and acknowledge that "the same thing happened" there as in Denmark, and it happened in Bulgaria first: facing resistance, German officials there "became unsure of themselves and were no longer reliable" (225, 187).

Indeed, the Bulgarian resistance to anti-Semitic policies arose spontaneously, from below, rather than being instigated by the king, as the German officials supposed and as was the case in Denmark. But this spontaneous popular self-organization, which one might expect Arendt to favor as even more political than the Danes' willingness to follow their monarch's lead, instead seems less political and therefore less exemplary to her because, by contrast with the Danes' "*open* . . . resistance," the Bulgarians saved Jews by "a complicated game of double-dealing and double-crossing, . . . by a tour de force of sheer ingenuity, but they never contested the policy as such" (175, 171, emphasis in original). In Arendt's terms one might say that the Bulgarians pursued a political (principled, solidarity-based) goal by social (unprincipled, double-dealing) means, or at least by mixed means, involving both (political) initiative from below and (social) double-dealing. The ambiguities of that mixture may help explain why Arendt did not discuss Bulgaria at length. Yet the Danish case, too, was ambiguous, since the principled resistance was initiated from above, by the king. That particular violation of her categories, however, may have been (unconsciously) attractive to Arendt as a patriarchal intervention to protect the victims.

Clearly in all this Arendt wants to retain her basic distinction between social and political ways, without having recourse to any Blob. Both ways are modes of human conduct; neither is imposed by any external, satanic power. But this means she must constantly confront something like the familiar conundrum about freedom. She is writing about people most of whom do not use their full capacities for action and responsibility. The question is: Could they have done so? Are they to be blamed? Or did their conduct result from certain conditions that shaped them, which Arendt can describe and explain? As before, she needs to have it both ways, despite their logical incompatibility. Not seeing nor, therefore, addressing the logical problem directly, she vacillates, blaming or praising here, explaining causes and conditions there. It may be that, as critics charge, her way of distributing these elements is not evenhanded: that she tends to blame Jews, praise Danes, explain and thus appear to excuse Eichmann, as she surely never intended to do. But she does none of these consistently, and the real, underlying problem of this book is not some inequity of distribution but the unacknowledged logical difficulties exposed by excision of the Blob.

Revolution and the Social Question

In *Eichmann in Jerusalem* these difficulties are associated primarily with individual conduct, albeit institutionally replicated, and the focus is primarily on the conformist or parvenu social. Large-scale historical explanation and institutional changes remain relatively peripheral. They become central, and attention shifts to the economic, or biological, social, in Arendt's next book, *On Revolution*. In *Eichmann,* the words "society" and "social" are relatively rare, the adjective is never hypostasized, and there is no Blob. But then, *Eichmann* is not a work of abstract theory but a relatively concrete trial report. In *On Revolution,* although there are two intensive passages in which the word "society" is the subject of verbs such as "invade," "overgrow," "impose," "monopolize," and "pervert," tne word "social" remains an adjective throughout. That word does, however, appear in a key phrase often invoked throughout the book: "the social question."[41] That phrase, more idiomatic in French than it is in English, is familiar in the historical literature on the Revolution of 1789 as well as that on the Resistance and postwar France. The meaning of the phrase, Arendt says bluntly, may be "better and more simply" expressed as "the existence of poverty," though we shall see that this is far too simple.[42]

On Revolution compares the French and American Revolutions, investigating why the latter was "so triumphantly successful" and the former "ended in disaster" (56). The answer hinges on the social question. Arendt's criterion for success in a revolution derives from her understanding of what a revolution is, what "revolution" means. A revolution, she argues, is not just any extensive change in institutions, not just any illegal seizure of power, not just any widespread popular violence; revolution must be distinguished from rebellion, putsch, civil war, and coup d'etat. It is based on the human capacity to initiate new relationships and institutions, earlier called conscious pariahdom, spontaneous initiative, action, or politics, but here called "founding," and exercised most extensively and intensively in revolution.[43]

In a revolution, large numbers of people who had been politically inert become actively engaged and start using their capacities for autonomous judgment, initiative, and citizenship. Revolution "set[s] out to abolish" the familiar "distinction between ruler and ruled," previously taken for granted.[44] But a revolution is no mere uprising or rebellion, no matter how widespread. Unless something lasting is created, no real transformation has taken place; revolution implies that a fundamental institutional restructuring is not just imagined or intended, but actually achieved. One can properly speak of revolution "only where change occurs in the sense of a new beginning, where violence is used to constitute an altogether different form of government, to bring about the formation of a new body politic" (35). Thus revolution means founding: the "formation of a new power structure which owes its existence to nothing but the organizational impulses of the people themselves" (257). Part of the success of the American Revolution for Arendt is that it not only did this but called attention to it, came to symbolize it. Thus it gave rise to a new kind of authority—the authority of "the act of foundation itself," the popular "act of constituting" from below.[45]

Not just any popular founding, however, not just any—even lasting and fundamental—new, popularly created institutional structure qualifies as a revolution. The new foundation must also institutionalize the universal human capacity for founding, assuring "the survival of the spirit out of which the act of foundation sprang" (126). The newly founded arrangements, in other words, must perpetuate the "spirit of revolution," its "lost treasure" (215, 221). Arendt quotes Condorcet: "the word 'revolutionary' can be applied only to revolutions whose aim is freedom." This aim also supplies a criterion by which to measure revolutionary success: not just an instant of freedom but the lasting "constitution of a public space where freedom could appear."[46]

That task is paradoxical, since it involves institutionalizing spontaneity, and Arendt acknowledges that "the spirit of revolution contains two elements which to us seem irreconcilable and even contradictory."[47]

The idea of foundation itself implies both the human capacity for innovation *and* success at making the innovation last. These features only seem irreconcilable to us, Arendt maintains, because we have lost our treasure. Regaining access to it, therefore, "must, to a certain extent, consist in the attempt at thinking together and combining meaningfully what our present vocabulary presents to us in terms of opposition and contradiction."[48] Yet Arendt also claims that we have inherited that flawed vocabulary—or at least our dichotomizing way of using it—*from* the great revolutions of the eighteenth century (223).

The problem in *On Revolution* about institutionalizing spontaneity, about somehow "thinking together" these mutually inconsistent ideas, is not new to Arendt's work. In *The Human Condition,* for example, it appears in the tension between action as spontaneity and the need for a preexisting arena to house politics. Like the ancient Greeks, Arendt considers legislation a prerequisite for, rather than a part of, politics, yet also sees the *polis* as "the organization of the people as it arises out of acting and speaking together."[49] What is new in *On Revolution* is not this problem but Arendt's explicit recognition of it as problematic. Previously it was hidden by the social as Blob; now it is recognized, even if not solved. As in *Eichmann,* so in *On Revolution,* mere removal of Blob imagery solves nothing but only reveals the difficulties more clearly. Indeed, even in these works Arendt is only partly aware of these difficulties.

The task in *On Revolution* is even harder than in *Eichmann,* for here the difficulties about individual action are compounded by those concerning human collectivities. *On Revolution,* accordingly, is a profoundly incoherent book, even if full of brilliant insights. Although the study sets out to contrast the success of the American Revolution to the failure of the French Revolution, it provides two conflicting explanations of the latter, eventually concedes that the American Revolution didn't succeed after all, offers three rival explanations of that, and finally claims that it makes no sense to speak of failure or success in such matters, a claim that makes mincemeat of the book's stated purpose.

Arendt says that the "so triumphant . . . success" of the American Revolution lay in its actually having established a lasting body politic and constitution, consciously aimed at perpetuating self-government by the people, albeit in a republican rather than a democratic form. The founders "knew how to build a lasting institution for the formation of public views into the very structure of the republic."[50] The French revolutionaries soon came to insist on national unanimity, partly under the influence of Rousseau's idea of the "general will," but the Americans used the word "people" in the sense of "manyness, of the endless variety of a multitude whose majesty resided in its very plurality."[51] They founded a body politic, rather than surrendering to necessity and to "the people" as an undifferentiated mass, and so the American Revolution never became a process out of human control. It did not, like the French Revolution, "devour its own children."[52] The American founders never abdicated responsibility for what they did. The American "republic was brought into existence by no 'historical necessity' and no organic development, but by a deliberate act: the foundation of freedom."[53]

The French failure was the inverse of this success. Never able to produce a stable constitution, let alone to found freedom, the French Revolution ended in the Terror and in Napoleonic autocracy. This was because it was overwhelmed by "the social question"—by poverty—which "puts men . . . under the absolute dictate of necessity," deflecting the aim of revolution from politics to abundance, to "happiness," and "to the urgency of the life process itself." Arendt quotes Robespierre's last speech: "We shall perish because, in the history of mankind, we missed the moment to found freedom."[54]

But since, in *On Revolution,* this was the doing of no Blob but of human beings, whose fault was the failure?[55] Arendt has two versions of the story. In one, it was the fault, or at least the doing, of the poor, driven by necessity and therefore bringing it with them into politics. "The multitude of the poor and the downtrodden," previously hidden in darkness and shame, now burst into the public realm and began to make history (48) But such people are not fit for the task, because they are driven by "the needs of their bodies," which subject them to "the absolute dictates of necessity" (48, 59–60). Being thus driven, the poor were incapable of founding anything, least of all freedom. When they "invaded the public realm," they could not help but bring "necessity" with them (114).

This meant that they formed "a mass that moves as one body and acts as though possessed of one will" rather than a differentiated body politic, because "the cry for bread will always be uttered in one voice" (94). That cry, moreover, is always and necessarily a cry of rage, "the only form in which misfortune can become active," and rage craves violence; it recognizes no limits and has no patience with institutional arrangements (110). "Their need was violent, and . . . it seemed that only violence could be strong and swift enough to help them" (91). The limits and impartiality of law were "like a mockery" by comparison with these "immense sufferings of the immense majority" (90). As these driven, hungry poor "rushed to the assistance" of the Revolution, they "eventually sent it to its doom" by deflecting its aim from the founding of freedom to "liberation from their masters or from necessity, the great master of their masters" (60, 132). Soon only those leaders could attain power who "surrendered . . . to the 'natural' laws which the masses obeyed, to the forces by which they were driven, and which indeed were the forces of nature herself, the force of elemental necessity" (110).

But Arendt also has another version of the story, in which not the poor but their leaders were at fault. It is true that "the masses of the suffering poor had taken to the streets unbidden," where they became visible in a new way, their suffering "exposed" in public. But these *malheureux* became *enragés* only after their leaders "began to glorify their suffering" in order to mobilize them, opening "the political realm to this pre-political, natural force," so that eventually the leaders themselves were "swept away by it."[56]

As to the motivation of the leaders, Arendt has two accounts (so her second version of the French failure really subdivides into a second and a third). Sometimes what moved the leaders is rage against social hypocrisy; sometimes it is pity for the suffering poor. Either way, however, if the fault lies with the leaders, the "necessity" that doomed the Revolution cannot have been absolute or biological, natural necessity, for the leaders themselves ate well enough; they were only "exposed to the spectacle of the people's sufferings, which they themselves did not share" (75). This spectacle aroused their pity, as social hypocrisy aroused their rage. Neither of these emotions is suited to founding and freedom; being "boundless," they make people impatient of all institutions and limits (89, 92, 100). Arendt quotes Robespierre: "La Republique? La Monarchie? Je ne connais que la question sociale" (56). Whether yielding to pity for the driven poor or to rage against hypocritical conventions and institutions, the leaders of the French Revolution doomed it by trying "to reduce politics to nature" (108).

Arendt, then, is unclear as to whether it was the biologically driven poor or the sentiment-driven leaders who ruined the Revolution, a choice that we may recognize as logically parallel to the problem of real versus false necessity. Sometimes Arendt blames those she thinks driven by biological necessity; sometimes those overwhelmed by pity for the suffering of others; sometimes both; and sometimes no one, as when she says that "the shift of emphasis" in the French Revolution, from founding freedom toward alleviating suffering, "was caused . . . by the course of the Revolution" itself, which seems no explanation at all (76).

Finally, and quite astonishingly in a book that uses terms such as "successful" and "failure," as well as "disaster," "doom," and "deflected," Arendt declares flatly in the middle of the second chapter, titled "The Social Question," that "nothing could be less fair than to take the success of the American Revolution for granted and to sit in judgment over the failure of the men of the French Revolution." Not taking the American success for granted presumably means that it was a great achievement from which we may learn. But not judging the failure? Arendt explains—albeit in a way that seems incompatible with her warning against taking the American success for granted—that praise *or* blame would be inappropriate here because "the reason for [the two Revolutions' respective] success and failure was that the predicament of poverty was absent from the American scene but present everywhere else in the world."[57]

Explaining America

Because the social question—that is, poverty—was absent from America, the revolutionaries there were not deflected from their proper task.

> Since there were no sufferings around them that could have aroused their passions, no overwhelmingly urgent needs that could have tempted them to submit to necessity, no pity to lead them astray from reason, the men of the American Revolution remained men of action from beginning to end.[58]

Men of action? Success and failure? Are such terms appropriate if the social question is objectively determinative of outcomes? The "fatal mistake," Arendt says, is trying "to solve the social question with political means," but avoiding that mistake "is almost impossible when a revolution breaks out under conditions of mass poverty" (112). Does the "almost" save her argument and justify the word "mistake"?

Perhaps she is only saying that the French revolutionaries succumbed to temptations they should have resisted, but we ought not to blame them too much or judge them by the standard of what the Americans achieved, because in America the temptations were minimal. But that does not seem to add up to "*the* reason" for the respective "success *and* failure," and Arendt insists on the latter, stronger claim (68). Once the poor "rushed to the assistance" of the French Revolution, "priority *had to be* given" to their need, "freedom *had to be* surrendered to *necessity*"; it was "*inevitable*" (60, 132; my emphasis). The French Revolution was "*foredoomed*," because in fact no revolution is "*possible* where the masses [are] loaded down with misery" (112, 222, my emphasis). So it is either almost impossible or flatly impossible to have a successful revolution and found freedom in the presence of the social question. What is to blame for the French failure is poverty, and the American success was due to—or at least presupposed—the absence of poverty.

Not so, however. Arendt's account of America is even more confusing than that of France. Immediately after giving "the reason for success" in the American case as the fact "that the predicament of poverty was absent from the American scene," she proceeds to qualify that claim out of existence. First, poverty wasn't absent: there was poverty in America, and people were aware of it. But the American poor were "not miserable . . . were not driven by want." What was absent was not poverty but "misery."[59] But no; there was misery as well as poverty in America, only it was confined to a group of people who did not arouse pity, because they did not count. "Abject and degrading misery was present everywhere in the form of slavery and Negro labor." So, Arendt says, "we" must "remind ourselves that the absence of the social question from the American scene was, after all, quite deceptive."[60] Indeed, she is "tempted" to ask whether the absence of misery among free whites "did not depend to a considerable degree on black labour and black misery" (71). Either way, however, "the social question, whether genuinely absent or only hidden in darkness, was non-existent for all practical purposes" in America (72). What ruins revolutions, then, is not objective conditions of poverty or misery but the *perception* of misery, which perhaps is more likely (but by no means inevitable) where objective misery exists.

But there are still worse complications to come, for Arendt proceeds to show that the American Revolution she herself called "triumphantly successful" did *not* succeed in founding freedom. It founded a lasting state and a constitution, but the institutions it created did not keep alive the spirit of revolution. Indeed, the revolutionary aim of assuring the survival of this treasure "was frustrated almost from the beginning" (56, 126). Arendt has three distinct and partly conflicting accounts of this failure as well: institutional, economic, and ideational.

First, even though the American Revolution successfully founded a polity and a constitution, it did not provide any "lasting institution" to house the revolutionary spirit. While creating institutions for "the formation of public views," it established no public space "for the exercise of precisely those qualities which had been instrumental in building" the republic (228, 232). It provided for representation and allowed for later extension of the suffrage, but it did not establish any "space" where "the people themselves" could "engage in those activities of 'expressing, discussing, and deciding' which in a positive sense are the activities of freedom" (235). So representation displaced the spirit of revolution, and its "machinery could not save the people from lethargy and inattention to public business" (238). Because of "the lack of public spaces to which the people at large would have entrance," America substituted a new, elective "elite" for the "pre-modern elites of birth and wealth" and professional politicians for citizen participation, thereby producing the "obvious inability and conspicuous lack of interest of large parts of the population in political matters as such" (277).

But Arendt also ascribes this lack of interest and failure to participate to a second, different cause: in America, people's energy was differently employed—in making money. The shift in popular concern from public affairs in the eighteenth century to private ones in the twentieth, Arendt says in a passage with echoes of the Blob, "corresponds with great precision to the invasion of the public realm by society." But the continuation of the sentence makes clear that Arendt is now aware that she means *as if* by a Blob: "it is as though the original political principles" that inspired the American Revolution had been "translated into social values" (221). In short, in this second explanation, the fault lies not with the social as Blob but with social values.

The values in question are acquisitiveness, greed, " 'the fatal passion for sudden riches.' "[61] Although she earlier defined the social *question* as meaning poverty, Arendt nevertheless now calls these passions "social," explaining that they were a holdover, in the newly risen middle classes in America, of the poverty they had formerly endured as immigrants. "The poor of yesterday" developed "their own code of behavior" and, having become rich, retained that code and "impos[ed] it on the body politic" (70). So once again real and false necessity blur together, the physical hunger of the poor lingering on as the acquisitiveness of the newly rich. It is all part of the social question: "the bonds of necessity need not be of iron, they can be made of silk" (139) In short, in America as in France, the social question is sometimes a *mentalité,* sometimes not; "necessity" is sometimes false and sometimes real.

Accordingly, Arendt has yet a third explanation of the American failure. Neither wrong institutions nor economic conditions are to blame, but certain wrong ideas, a failure to remember the revolutionary spirit, the lost treasure. That failure "can be traced back to the [original,] fateful failure of post–revolutionary thought" to keep the revolutionary spirit alive by distilling it "into a framework of conceptual notions within which it [could] further exercise itself" (220). The only remedy now is "memory and recollection," the business of poets and theorists (280).

On Revolution is a work of theory, trying again to give people access to the lost treasure, though in a somewhat less abstract way than *The Human Condition* and without resorting to any Blob. Without the Blob, however, Arendt's familiar difficulties about the ontology of society and its power, real and false necessity, action and behavior, being unfree and yet free-to-become-free are patently evident. *On Revolution* is an extraordinarily confusing and confused book, as Arendt struggles to find ways of "thinking together and combining meaningfully" ideas that despite her best efforts continue to seem logically incompatible. Tensions between explanation and blame, individual initiative and social conditions, are everywhere, with no consistent resolution in sight.

It is almost enough to make one dismiss the book—and Arendt as theorist. It is almost enough to make one yearn for a Blob to hide the theoretical chaos. Almost, but not quite. For what Arendt was trying to do remains at least as important today as it was then, and recourse to a Blob is as counterproductive now as it ever was. Understanding our public problems, now as then, requires resisting such mythologizing explanations. But it is no easy task. The chaos revealed in Arendt's theorizing by excision of the Blob is not just Arendt's idiosyncratic failure as a theorist but is also partly inherent in these topics and in our conceptual apparatus for dealing with them. Until we can do the job better, we should be cautious about disparaging Arendt's efforts.

ELEVEN

Why the Blob?

Having split Arendt's concept of the social from its metaphorical figuration as a Blob in order to examine the concept alone in chapter 9, we return now to the metaphor and to our original question: Why did Arendt develop imagery so flagrantly at odds with what she most wanted to say? The genealogical survey of her concept's development, undertaken to answer that question, has not yielded a single, decisive explanation, but it has turned up a number of possible and partial ones. This chapter will review them, starting with some false and trivial leads and concluding with a brief speculation about the nature of political theory.

Begin with hypostasization, a kind of grammatical explanation of why Arendt invented a Blob. In *The Human Condition* she formed a new noun out of the adjective "social." She did so even though the noun "society" was already available, and she did nothing comparable with what was for her the contrasting adjective, "political."[1] Clearly the hypostasization functions somehow as a special marker linking the ordinary lexical meaning of "social" with the generic capacities and connotations of the noun form. Making the adjective available for service as the subject of verbs, hypostasization turns whatever "social" means into an entity, something capable of doing and being done to. The grammatical move, in effect, facilitates or even invites personification, even demonization. But why the hypostasization, especially when there is a noun already in existence?

The most obvious answer suggesting itself is that the adjective must differ in lexical meaning from the existing noun and that its meaning must better suit Arendt's intentions. The ordinary uses of "social" and "society," however, reveal no major difference in meaning. Two minor ones do show up: the first is that the adjective has had, for a couple of centuries, a contrasting term, "antisocial" (as well as the more recent "asocial"), for which there is no corresponding noun. Given the existence of "antisocial," the adjective "social" is likely to emphasize the opposite connotations, its meaning pushed in the direction of *good* behavior, conformity to norms. Those connotations would not be comparably stressed in the meaning of the noun, "society."

The second minor difference in meaning between "society" and "social" is that the noun is conventionally contrasted with "the state," especially when it appears in the phrase "civil society."[2] There is no adjective paralleling "state" in the way that "social" parallels "society," so if one needs an adjectival counterpart of "the state" to contrast with "social," the word "political" seems the most likely choice.[3] Then "social" contrasts to "political" while "society" contrasts to "the state." Now, if—like Max Weber—one equates politics with the state, this hardly matters: the contrast between political and social would match that between the state and society.[4] But Arendt, from early on, long before she gave the topic her explicit attention, used the term "political" in a rather different sense, as we have seen, to mark the way of the conscious pariah, the contrast to the parvenu. That sense of "political," as active engagement with others in the cause of justice, is obviously far from equivalent to the state. For starters, it would not fit a totalitarian or a bureaucratic state at all.

Thus Arendt's central concern from *Rahel Varnhagen* on is indeed better captured by the adjective "social" than by the noun "society," with respect to both of these minor differences in meaning. "Social" is more likely to connote conformist propriety, and it can be opposed to "political" rather than to "the state." Arendt, in effect, could make good use of a noun that connoted what "social" connotes.

It is probably also worth mentioning that hypostasization as such is considerably more common in German than in English, particularly in abstract and philosophical discourse, and we have noted that it was one of Heidegger's rhetorical devices for inducing a contemplative distance from a familiar term. Thus Arendt might have been inclined to hypostasize in proportion as her work reapproached abstraction, philosophy, her own native language, and Heidegger's thought. That she used the device specifically on the term "social" might be connected, as suggested in chapter 8, with the kinship between Arendt's concept and Heidegger's *das Man*, itself an hypostasization.

Nevertheless, the whole topic of hypostasization is mostly a false lead, not a satisfactory answer to the question "Why the Blob?" since Arendt continues to use the ordinary noun, "society," alongside and more or less synonymously with her neologism. To be more precise, the hypostasized adjective appears a total of ten times in *The Human Condition*, three of them being borderline cases of elliptical or quasi-adjectival constructions, such as "not the political sphere but the social." Seven instances is not a very large number, but two of the seven occur in chapter headings, signaling the device's importance. Uses of "society" with some active, Blobbish verb occur about twice that often.[5] Thus hypostasization is better regarded as a symptom than as a source or cause of Arendt's Blob.

The Rhetorical Explanation

Somewhat more promising is a second possible explanation we have encountered, which relates the social as Blob to Arendt's earlier similar figuration of totalitarianism. As chapter 5 noted, explaining the holocaust as the work of some superhuman diabolical force was plausible and even tempting immediately after World War II, particularly for a Jewish refugee, and Arendt succumbed to that temptation despite explicit efforts to resist it. Having once developed that imagery in relation to totalitarianism and won recognition as a scholar by a book centered on that concept so depicted, Arendt might have had strong motives for resorting to the same type of explanation again. After the spectacular success of *The Origins,* in effect, the Blob was a central tool readily available in Arendt's intellectual workshop.

Not only that, but she saw the threat against which *The Human Condition* warns as a direct descendant of totalitarianism, its more "authentic" and dangerous, though possibly less "cruel," form. The rhetorical problem, as chapter 6 noted, was to make this new hidden danger visible and actionable for people, as the danger of Naziism had become only after World War II was fully under way.

Jeffrey C. Isaac has posed with respect to totalitarianism the question we are pursuing with respect to the social: why Arendt "persistently treat[ed it] as an agent, at times even a juggernaut." Isaac's answer is that she did so because this is how "these regimes represent themselves, and are experienced by their supporters and victims."[6] One could claim the same about the social: it too is perceived by those who experience it as an irresistible evil force external to them. Yet whatever merit Isaac's answer may have regarding totalitarianism (and it seems questionable to me even there), as an answer to why Arendt envisioned the social as Blob it is strikingly, and instructively, problematic.

Even with regard to totalitarianism, Arendt's primary teaching concerned the complicity of parvenus, conformists, and apathetically privatized people, the extent to which their collaboration constituted totalitarian power and made possible the holocaust. That teaching would make no sense if totalitarianism were an alien monster and these people merely its victims. In the condition she calls the social, this is even more pointedly the case, because oppressors and victims are the same people. The new, post-totalitarian danger consists precisely in people's feeling helpless in the face of something that they experience as an overwhelming, evil, external force but that in reality results from, consists in, their own conduct. Thus, with respect to the social, the fact that people experience it as a Blob is the *problem* that Arendt's book is intended to address; it *can't* be the solution. People experiencing their own activity as an overwhelming alien force is the disease she wants to diagnose; the mystery is why she succumbs to it herself.

People's failure to see how they are themselves producing their problems nevertheless can serve as a partial explanation for Arendt's Blob, but only by a more indirect route. Even against Naziism, we noted, people were mobilized only when it was almost too late; the French Resistance was formed only after Nazi occupation of France. Against the new, more insidious post-totalitarian danger it must have seemed even more important to mobilize people early, before its debilitating effects could become universal. Yet, as we saw, the mobilizing must not make some new group of people into pariah scapegoats, nor conjure up war and threaten to destroy the earth with nuclear weapons. So the rhetorical problem was how to summon people to urgent action against an enemy that was not some external Evil Empire nor some subversive Enemy Within but instead, as Tocqueville had said long before, a tyranny without a tyrant, a despotism without a despot. The task was to make manifest to people this invisible enemy that was, in some paradoxical sense, they themselves.

Mobilizing people and moving them to action is very hard in the absence of any clearly definable, external enemy to hate and fear. As James Farmer remarked concerning the change in the 1960s civil rights movement after the 1963 march on Washington, "It's difficult to organize around a campaign when you don't have a devil."[7] This is all the more true if the danger is precisely people's own inertia, their immersion in their daily lives, their quotidian ambitions, obligations, anxieties, and distractions. Summoning them from these preoccupations to address a more urgent and important concern requires making the abstract danger visible, tangible, real to them. The social as Blob, chapter 6 suggested, served Arendt rhetorically as such a "devil," a concretely imaginable enemy to fill the same role as the Nazi occupation filled for those who organized and joined the Resistance: to pry them loose from their preoccupation with routine concerns so that they could discover their real options and capacities, their freedom. The Blob was to restore something of the simple, dyadic choice imposed in the wartime years, between Good Guys and Bad Guys, yet without designating any humans as Bad Guys. It was to return people from the confusing and enervating "hardships of the plains" to the clear and bracing "hardships of the mountains," revealing in high profile the new danger hidden by the apparent everyday flatness of the postwar world.[8]

Call this the rhetorical answer to the question "Why the Blob?": this imagery might move people in the right direction. I do not mean to suggest that Arendt herself thought in such manipulative rhetorical terms, or even that she deployed Blob imagery with deliberate intent. On the contrary, it seems to me likely that even when she reexamined her notion of the social and then abandoned Blob imagery and hypostasization after completing *The Human Condition,* she reached only a general sense that something about them was not right for her purposes. While writing the book she was surely not even aware of personifying or demonizing the concept. The point is only that the rhetorical purpose of the book—the need to make vividly real an amorphous, abstract danger of which people were unaware—was in a way served by that personification and demonization.

Of course that purpose was also, as I have argued, directly subverted by this same imagery; the metaphor carries rhetorical *disadvantages* that Arendt must not have noticed, or she would never have used it. Thus a subsidiary question of why Arendt invented a Blob is why she remained unaware that she herself was blatantly doing what she had warned against and had criticized others for doing. That brings us to a fourth partial explanation for the Blob, which one might call the psychological.

The Blob as Regression Fantasy

Psychologically, Arendt was probably blind to the significance and the costs of her Blob imagery for the same reason as she was drawn to that imagery in the first place, which is also central to that imagery's counterproductive rhetorical effects. In psychological terms there seems no doubt that the image of the Blob is a regression fantasy, a fearful vision of what chapter 8 discussed as the "bad mother" of infantile experience. Regression, according to psychoanalytic theory, is a characteristic response to life situations that seem insurmountably difficult, especially those that evoke or intensify unconscious psychic conflicts. At such times people tend to revert in fantasy or in conduct or both to an earlier stage of psychic development.

In less technical terms, all of us yearn from time to time for the security and ease of childhood, to be taken care of by others and relieved of all responsibility, even to crawl back into the original nurturing matrix and disappear. Since childhood and infancy weren't always blissful, however, that yearning and those fantasies also bring with them correlated fears of being once more helpless in the clutches of evil matriarchal power. Along with a fearful, defensive activism not conducive to responsible, creative agency, they tend to produce a yearning for rescue by a masculine power sufficiently fierce to control the dreadful matriarch.

In chapter 8 the focus was on how the Blob as a regression fantasy worked rhetorically to undermine Arendt's purposes, to make readers feel helpless rather than empowered, trapped rather than capable of freedom. Here, however, the issue is why Arendt envisioned such a counterproductive image, and regression may be the psychological answer to that question. Chapters 6 and 8 explored the difficult circumstance in which Arendt wrote *The Human Condition*—both the objective difficulties of what she was trying to do and the psychological conflicts her project aroused. With the discovery of her conceptual triad, Arendt was able to overcome those difficulties and create the book, but the accompanying anxieties, one might say, left their traces in the work, in the form of the Blob and the misogynist Greeks charged with keeping that matriarch under control.

Had Arendt been more sympathetic to depth psychology or to feminism, she might have become explicitly aware of these difficulties and made them part of her investigation, finding some creative way to engage the advantages of Blob imagery without actually conjuring up a Blob. But then again, she might not. A superficial dip into psychology might even have heightened the inner tension and made it impossible for her to write her book.

Though the Blob may be tempting as a rhetorical device, and though it may be psychologically a regression fantasy, it is not merely either of these things. More interesting explanations remain to be considered. Arendt, we have noted, was not alone in her vision. Not only Marx and Tocqueville, who may have influenced her imagery directly, but also numerous other highly regarded modern political theorists have invoked one or another form of Blobbish imagery, many of them—like Arendt—despite having explicitly warned against such ways of thinking. Although it is certainly possible that all of these thinkers, too, were tempted by the apparent rhetorical advantages of the imagery and blinded to the disadvantages by unconscious psychic conflicts, one does begin to suspect that something more may be going on, something related to the problem that all of these thinkers were trying to address or even to their shared enterprise of political theory as such. If that were so, then investigating the Blob might bear significance beyond Arendt studies, perhaps even beyond critical commentary on political theory. Our own thinking about our political or social problems might be vulnerable to Blob imagery, too, and our quest for solutions misguided by such obscuring fantasies.

Dangerous Abstraction

What makes these thinkers' conjuring up of a Blob so strikingly paradoxical are their explicit warnings against what they then go on to do, and their attacks on other thinkers for having done it. To be more precise, what they mostly warn against and criticize is abstraction, or perhaps some special kind or degree of abstraction. So we too must consider abstraction as a possible explanation for the Blob, even if their warning did not succeed in protecting these thinkers against it.

Arendt's explicit opposition to abstraction as somehow contrary to or destructive of politics, we noted, dates back at least to her early critique of the women's movement, later echoed in her condemnation of the ideal of world citizenship. "Abstract" here seemed to mean impractical, unrealistic, thus in political terms not really serious. We have suggested that this criticism was anchored for Arendt personally in her experience with Heidegger, and specifically in her way of explaining his Naziism to herself without altogether condemning him: philosophy's characteristic *déformation professionelle*. Feeling that she herself had nearly succumbed to disaster because of her own ambition toward philosophy and her related attraction to Heidegger, Arendt was convinced when she left Germany that it was "a matter of this profession, of intellectuality" as such, and so she vowed "never again [to] touch" such abstract enterprises.[9]

In Rahel Varnhagen's introspective romanticism Arendt found a very similar dissociated abstraction from the real world and the real, pariah self. In *The Origins* she found it again in "social" anti-Semitism, with its stereotype of "the 'Jew in general,' the 'Jew everywhere and nowhere,' " unrelated to any actual experience, a mode of abstraction that became genocidal once it was applied as public policy.[10]

By the time she was working on *The Human Condition*, Arendt saw this same *déformation* not just in philosophers but also in historians, whose concern with the past, thus with matters that "could not even be grasped by the mind if they had not come to some kind of an end," makes it "only natural" for them to abstract. Focused on endings rather than beginnings, as philosophers focus on mortality rather than natality, historians tend to miss the human creative capacity altogether, "to see an end (and doom) everywhere."[11] In *The Human Condition* the same critique is applied also, albeit without the word "abstraction" or the phrase "*déformation professionelle*," to behavioral and statistical social scientists, whose quest for general laws of behavior amounts to a "willful obliteration" of their own purported subject matter: human affairs.[12] What is centrally characteristic of human beings is culture—historically developed civilization—created by action and sustained by human conduct. For Arendt, the single most important thing to understand about human beings is our capacity for action, which she thought is always and necessarily individual. An "abstraction" such as "mankind . . . never can become an active agent" (184).

All of these intellectual deformations—the distortions of action and misunderstandings of human affairs characteristic of philosophy, history, and social science—Arendt found concentrated in Marx, who ascribed intentions and initiative to abstractions such as the proletariat and the bourgeoisie, to the human species, and specifically to "society," which she says he construed as a "collective subject" with a single interest and a unified "life process" (256). Focused on this "life of society as a whole, instead of the limited lives of individual men," Marx saw agency only in large-scale "forces" that allegedly "inform, move, and direct" society (116, 321).

Yet Marx himself, as we noted, had issued much the same warning as Arendt, and had criticized others much as she criticizes him, cautioning that "what is to be avoided above all is the re-establishing of 'Society' as an abstraction *vis-à-vis* the individual."[13] Marx himself condemned the kind of "reification [*Verdinglichung*] of social relationships" whereby abstract concepts such as the classical economists' "trinity formula" of capital, land, and labor are "autonomized" into an "enchanted and inverted world in which Monsieur le Capital and Madame la Terre do their ghost-walking as social characters."[14] Marx himself attacked the "fetishism of commodities," in which "a definite social relation between [people] assumes, in their eyes, the fantastic form of a relation between things," so that the producers experience "the social character" of their *Arbeit* only as if it were a relationship between their products, independent of the producers themselves.[15] "The life-process of society," Marx said, using the very phrase Arendt criticizes, cannot be seen realistically, in unmystified form, until it is recognized and treated "as production by freely associated human beings," which is to say, by individuals engaged in what Arendt called action, "consciously regulat[ing it] in accordance with a settled plan" (327).

Above all, Marx attacked Hegel and "German philosophy which descends from heaven to earth," because it starts from concepts, ideas, and "phantoms formed in the human brain" instead of starting, as he and Engels did, from "real individuals, their activity and the material conditions under which they live," factual matters that can "be verified in a purely empirical way" (154, 149). If, unlike Hegel, one starts from "real premises from which abstraction can only be made in the imagination," Marx said, notions such as "morality, religion, metaphysics, all the rest of ideology . . . no longer retain their semblance of independence," and agency is returned to its real locus, "real, active human beings," which is to say, "definite individuals."[16]

Yet Hegel, whose abstractness Marx thus criticizes and who indeed invented that arch-Blob, the "world spirit," himself attacked some of his predecessors on charges much the same as those Marx brought against him and Arendt against Marx. He accused them of an abstract "formalism" based on mere "feeling and intuition," of hoping to "palm off" their "rapturous haziness" of empty abstractions as knowledge and as profound insight. They write, he said, as if uttering the abstract phrase "all animals" were equivalent to knowing—and doing—zoology.[17]

Hegel, Marx, and Arendt form a sequence of similar criticism. Their shared violation of their own strictures might therefore have resulted from the sequential influence of each on his successor and critic. But we have seen that Tocqueville, who—though he surely influenced Arendt—was no part of *this* sequence, displayed the same pattern: he too both warned against and himself engaged in Blobbish abstraction. "An abstract word," he said, "is like a box with a false bottom; you may put in it what ideas you please and take them out again unobserved."[18] In a democratic age, in particular, people develop "a taste, and often a passion, for . . . generic terms and abstract words" to compensate for their feelings of individual helplessness (481). Each, comparing himself to all of his fellows together and feeling "overwhelmed by a sense of his insignificance and weakness," tends to "personify these abstractions and make them act like real men" (435, 481). Historians in democratic ages cater to this craving, ascribing agency to "great general causes" rather than to people, or explaining human affairs in terms of "the nature of races, the physical character of the country, or the spirit of civilization" (494). Thus they present their readers "with the sight of the world moving without anyone moving it," tempting them "to believe that this movement is not voluntary" but instead obeys "some superior dominating force" (495). Such a sight, therefore, "does not serve to preserve human *liberté*" but instead robs people of their "faculty of modifying their own lot and make[s] them depend either on an inflexible providence or on a kind of blind fatality" (495–96).

God, Tocqueville said, does not resort to abstractions. He "has no need of general ideas," for he can survey "distinctly and simultaneously all mankind and each single man" (437, 704). For human beings, however, there is a necessary trade-off: discerning the larger pattern requires losing the particular details. So the "abundance of abstract terms in the language of democracy . . . both widens the scope of thought and clouds it" (482). It is, Tocqueville says, like leaving a city and looking back on it from a nearby hill. Suddenly "the city's outline is easier to see, and for the first time [one] grasps its shape," but one also "loses sight of" the people, loses the concrete, embodied individual (408).

But Tocqueville applies this simile *to himself* as theorist, in summing up the rich detail of volume 1. He claims that precisely in this new, democratic age God, or at any rate "providence," has given people a light by which to discern "the first causes in the fate of nations," and that is why he sought in America the abstract "shape of democracy itself," whose "universal and permanent" advance was a "sure sign" of God's will (32, 19, 12). Indeed, humans must "do all [they] can to enter into understanding of this divine view of the world" and to "consider and judge the affairs of men" from God's point of view (704). Tocqueville himself is doing this as he observes democracy being furthered as much by those who oppose as by those who favor it, all of them "blind instruments in the hands of God" (12).

Indeed, like the thinkers he criticizes, Tocqueville often writes about "irresistible" developments "imposed by Providence," to which people are "fated," "inevitable" outcomes to which they are "doomed," and "force[s] beyond human control" that carry people along "regardless of [their] desires" (12, 338, 326, 245). He explains America in terms of the country's physical characteristics, the nature of races, and the spirit of the first European settlers' civilization.[19] He also insists that in a democratic age, "general causes" in fact explain more than does the influence of particular individuals, so the historians "are right in attaching much importance to" the former (495). That is not to say Tocqueville is a fatalist, of course; on the contrary, he tries to distinguish those developments that could and should be changed from those that could not.[20] Like Arendt after him, he seeks a way of generalizing and abstracting that does not deny individuality or blind people to the very possibility of action and politics.

Unlike Hegel, Marx, and Arendt, however, Tocqueville is self-consciously aware of the paradoxicality of his task: that he himself is a historian in a democratic age and shares its "passion" for abstraction: "I can best illustrate my meaning by my own example. I have often used the word 'equality' in an absolute sense, and several times have even personified it" (481–82). This pattern of thought, then, is most striking in Tocqueville, because he criticizes not only other thinkers but also himself for mystifying human agency by personifying abstractions, yet by his own admission also continues to do so.

In a way, none of this should be surprising. As we noted in chapter 8, one cannot talk, write, or think conceptually at all without generalizing and thus abstracting; the problem cannot be abstraction as such. Both Tocqueville and Marx, indeed, try to distinguish between kinds of abstractions or ways of abstracting: the helpful and the harmful. Sometimes the distinction seems to be a matter of degree: the danger lies in excessive abstractness, the hubristic desire to escape one's concrete, human particularity and see from God's perspective. Yet these thinkers also agree that there is danger in excessive concreteness as well, in an excessively narrow focus on the personal, particular, and local: the failure to see the forest for the trees. Tocqueville, Marx, and Hegel are, after all, theorists, as is Arendt herself. Despite her critique of abstraction, she summons us to the "second reversal" from action back into thought, to "think what we are doing." And she surely holds that the parvenu, the bureaucrat, the housewife, the *animal laborans* and *homo faber* all take too narrow a view of themselves and their situations; they are mired in particularity. So, too, Tocqueville persists in talking about equality, democracy, and providence, trying to reveal the larger pattern in which people are linked even as they imagine themselves isolated; and Marx never gives up his youthful fantasy that the proletariat might find "its *intellectual* weapons in philosophy"—his philosophy—so that the "lightning" of his thought might "penetrate deeply into [the] virgin soil of the people."[21]

At other times the distinction between helpful and harmful abstraction seems to be a matter less of degree than of content. The danger is *empty* abstractions, by contrast to what one might call "full" ones, rich in empirical content. Tocqueville says that helpful generalization "results from the slow, detailed, and conscientious labor of the mind," while harmful abstractions are those formed hastily from first impressions and producing "only very superficial and uncertain notions."[22] Hegel's remark about the fool who thinks that saying "all animals" is doing zoology suggests a similar division, and Marx is doubtless drawing on his Hegelian education in a dense, almost inscrutable methodological passage about abstraction in an introductory section of the *Grundrisse*.

A concept such as "the population," he says there, remains just "an abstraction" unless one considers the classes that compose that population. "These classes in turn are an empty phrase" unless one is "familiar with the elements on which they rest," such as wage labor, capital, and the like. "These latter in turn presuppose exchange, division of labor, prices, etc." So one must distinguish between the empty, ignorant, "chaotic conception [*Vorstellung*] of the whole" and the "rich totality of many determinations and relations" in the real world that fills the empty abstraction for someone who knows what he is talking about.[23] The distinction between empty and "full" abstractions seems, then, to depend less on the particular abstraction invoked than on how it is used and understood in specific situations.

One begins to wonder what, exactly, abstraction is, and whether the term has any meaning at all. Etymologically the word derives from the Latin *trahere*, "to draw or pull," and *ab-*, "away from." To abstract is to draw away from something, gaining the perspective of distance, or to draw out some particular aspect of reality for specific attention, ignoring the rest. The dictionary mentions three more specific senses of the term: drawing away from matter (abstract versus concrete), from practice (in the abstract versus in practice), and from the varying details of particular cases or examples in order to generalize about their shared features.

At first it may seem that all words, words as such, are abstract, since their use presupposes recurrence; but, as Thomas Hobbes already pointed out, we call only those terms "abstract" that we use for talking *about* abstractions.[24] This, however, presupposes a distinction in what we talk about in the world, between abstract and not abstract. We consider, say, "injustice" an abstract concept and, say, "cow" a concrete one. Yet though a particular cow may be concrete, the idea of cows seems every bit as abstract as that of injustice, and today one is likely to see more concrete instances of the latter than of the former. And what of the herd of cows? Surely the herd is as concrete, and as abstract, as the cow, the tree as concrete and as abstract as the forest.[25]

For all four of these thinkers, the real complexities only begin when one is talking about human affairs, where agency and responsibility may be at stake: not the herd or the forest, but various human collectivities and large-scale phenomena in human affairs. What worries Marx, Tocqueville, Arendt, and I suspect even Hegel, is how to express the larger picture—which we need—without losing the very idea of human agency. All of these thinkers want to show us the larger picture of our human reality, so that we may know better what to do.

Arendt, we noted, remarks that an "abstraction" such as "mankind ... can never become an active agent."[26] Yet of course she, like the rest of us, talks about such matters as Germany invading Belgium, the attitude of the German people toward their own past, and what the Catholic Church offered to people, not to mention the activities she ascribes to labor, action, politics, freedom, the polis, bureaucracy, imperialism, and so on. And then there is the social as Blob. Are some of these abstractions, and others not?

It is simply not true that abstractions cannot be agents or do things. We speak not only of human collectivities but even of inanimate objects and conditions as doing things: the wind knocked down that tree; invention of the mechanical cotton picker led to widespread rural unemployment; famine drastically reduced the population. Indeed, there are things that *only* certain human collectivities can do: declare war, for example, or declare a dividend. Of course, when we say that Germany invaded Belgium or that America declared war, we are usually prepared to translate those claims into other, more specific ones: this or that regime issued orders, these or those members of the legislature voted, these or those men wearing uniforms marched or drove from this spot to that, and so on. But one must not suppose that only the latter form expresses what really happened, because it is more "concrete." There are times, to be sure, when one gets at the truth by forcing a translation from "Germany declared war" to more specific claims about who voted how, who collaborated or resisted, who marched from where to where, and so on. But there are also times when one gets at the truth in the opposite way, by forcing a translation from "some men just marched from this point to that" into "the United States has invaded Cambodia." It is as deceitful to call a demonstration a riot as to call a riot a demonstration. There is no way to tell, in general and in advance, what will be a euphemism and which will be the brute facts in a particular case.[27]

Abstraction may be necessary for personifying or demonizing, but it is not by itself sufficient to bring on the Blob. One does indeed need to refer to a collectivity in order to ascribe agency to it, but there is nothing wrong with ascribing agency to collectivities as such. It is all a matter of knowing when that is appropriate and realistic, when a metaphor, a euphemism, or an illusion. So abstraction is relevant to explaining Arendt's Blob but is not by itself an explanation.

The Pervasiveness of Paradox

Let us, then, try a different but related tack: the role of paradox. Surely one of the most striking features of our genealogy of the social as Blob is how often it came up against paradoxical or problematic concepts, many of them not confined to Arendt's thought but appearing also in that of Marx, Tocqueville, or other theorists.[28]

Just to review, we have encountered the problematic ontology of society and of the reality of its power; the dangerous temptation to extrapolate the idea of society until it tautologically includes everything that anyone does; the conflicting meanings of "individual," "individuality," and "individualism"; the conflicting meanings of "necessary" and "necessity"; the conflicting meanings of "nature" and "natural" in relation to human affairs; the difficulties about large-scale explanation, blame, and responsibility so striking in *Eichmann* and *On Revolution*; and the many paradoxes connected with Arendt's interrelated concepts of action, politics, founding, and freedom. These last included whether these concepts are objective categories in the world or matters of outlook and attitude; whether these phenomena have causes or even preconditions, for instance, whether politics requires a preexisting arena; whether action has consequences and produces anything; whether it is purposive and taken in pursuit of interests; how action is related to the body and its needs, and politics to economics; whether and how one can teach freedom to those who have not experienced it.

All of these conundrums are directly related to, if not conjoined in, the central paradox we repeatedly encountered—of how to express concretely the idea of a collectivity of people by their own conduct rendering themselves helpless to deal effectively with problems resulting from that conduct. Such people are, we noted, paradoxically not free yet free-to-become-free, thus free after all. They are getting in their own way. Can such claims make sense and characterize a real condition? Perhaps these paradoxes indicate only the incoherence of Arendt's concept of the social, or even some personal obsession with conundrums on my part, like Gilbert and Sullivan's modern major-general with his "pretty taste for paradox." It would be tempting so to dismiss the matter, were it not for the way the real world seems to keep presenting evidence that something like this problem is actually going on. Perhaps the difficulties of reaching a coherent account of it result from the kind of problem it is, or even from the nature of Arendt's enterprise, political theory itself.

Arendt's concept of the social, we have observed, concerns not absolute but spurious necessity, not our inability to change what cannot be changed but the gap between what we do accomplish and what we might have accomplished in dealing with our problems. Behavior is action *manqué,* and the social is the lack of politics where politics could and should be. So the idea of the social is inherently tied to that of missed alternatives, unrealized possibilities, what we can do, or what we could do if circumstances were changed.

Now, "can" and "could" are notoriously tricky words, vitally useful in our daily interactions but a philosophical nightmare.[29] Their use always seems to presuppose an unlimited number of implicit "if's," counterfactual or hypothetical assumptions, often involving further "can's" and "could's" that are equally problematic. Given enough "if's," including some wildly unrealistic ones, everything is possible. Yet in the event, only one of the many possibilities actually happens. So it will seem in retrospect as if the other "possibilities" were never "really" possible after all. In the terrain between the apparently infinite possibilities licensed by "if's" and the singular actual outcome, one might say, "can" and "can't" range about, accompanied by the even more elusive "could" and "couldn't." These words are heavily context-dependent, instruments of commitment as much as or more than they are neutral labels for an objective state of affairs.

The difficulties are great enough with respect to an individual. Suppose that I have a bad habit, or a character flaw, or an addiction. Can I stop? "You can if you want to enough," admonishes the reformer. "She can if she has sufficient ego strength," comments the psychologist. "She can if placed in a favorable supportive environment," adds the sociologist. "God willing," murmurs the preacher. And we know that, in practical terms, it all depends.

If this is hard to generalize or theorize about with respect to individuals, it is doubly difficult with respect to human collectivities and the sorts of questions that come up in politics and history, where the issue is not just whether I or he can or cannot do something but whether we or they can. Here we must deal not just with the problematic "can" and "could" but also with the problematic "we" or "they," "Germany" or "America," "Jews" or "women," "the state" or "society." What we can do depends on who we are—how many, how determined, how wealthy or powerful, how resourceful and well organized—but also on who they are that might oppose us or deflect our doing. And the membership and strength of both "we" and "they" may shift with each redefinition of problems, goals, means, and possibilities, as some join and others depart, some are discouraged and others engaged, and so on.

Perhaps, then, Arendt envisions the social as a Blob because of the logical or conceptual difficulties of articulating the problem she thinks we face—which we nevertheless cannot dismiss as illusory or as a mere construct of logic. The problem of the social is so resistant to coherent articulation, one might say, because it lies at the intersection of "can" and "we," thus of two of the most persistent, pervasive, and intractable issues in the whole history of philosophy: the issue often referred to as "free will" and that which I shall call "micro-macro," meaning the relationship of parts and wholes, particular and general, individual and collective.[30] When one tries to theorize about human affairs, these two sets of conundrums together create logical complexities of such intricacy as almost to defy analysis, though all the terms involved seem to function well enough in ordinary, everyday communication in context. In *The Human Condition*, I am suggesting, the social as Blob both expresses and disguises these logical complexities.

Political Theory

But the difficulty is not Arendt's alone. Not merely her concept of the social is located at the intersection of these two conundrums; the enterprise of political theory itself inhabits this terrain. As theory, it aims to be abstract, general, contemplative, to strive for the God's-eye view and perceive the whole. Yet it aims also to be about politics and thus must get the nature of politics right. Politics, too, is concerned with the large-scale, with the affairs, institutions, and policies of the whole collectivity. But in politics, that large-scale unity must be constantly (re)constructed, (re)negotiated, (re)enacted out of the conflicting particular views, needs, interests, and commitments of the citizenry. Politics is necessitated as well as made possible by the combination of both these aspects: the diverse distinct citizens in conflict and their interrelationships and interdependence, which create common problems and necessitate common policies. Theorizing is an activity mostly carried out by individual thinkers, envisioning the whole by themselves. But if it is to be about politics, it must envision a whole whose unity is enacted, continually (re)created by diverse agents, out of both their existing interdependence *and* their existing conflicts. Political theory seeks to provide the larger picture—a perspicuous overview—of an activity whose central premise is agency—both individual and collective.[31]

Thus political theory has to engage both the free will conundrum and the micro-macro conundrum at every turn: it is about, and addressed to, people who are and are not parts of a unitary whole, who are (or could be) actively testing the limits of what they can and cannot do, individually and collectively, trying to address their problems in a way that will let them continue to be a (sort of a) whole together. So the political theorist is forever in the paradoxical position of telling people unchangeable truths about what they are doing, in hopes of getting them to change what they are doing. Bound to talk about collectivities and the large scale, yet bound to talk about conflicting, distinct individual agents; bound to tell people how things inescapably are, yet aiming thereby to help them change things for the better, political theory is perpetually vulnerable, as it were, to attacks of the Blob. It flirts with twin dangers: utopian irrelevance, on the one hand, as if absolutely *anything* were possible here and now, and the immoral and apolitical presentation of people as inanimate objects or instinct-driven animals, on the other hand, as if *nothing* were possible for us, the future already determined.

Each political theorist and each tradition of thought or movement within that enterprise has its own way of juggling these interrelated conundrums, or sometimes of experimenting with various ways, as Arendt conjures up a Blob in a work mainly devoted to explicating free political agency.

It was while writing *The Human Condition* that Arendt began referring, first to the topic of her book and soon thereafter to her own vocation, as "political theory." Some notion of what that phrase meant to her at the time emerges from a 1954 essay in which she spoke of the need, at long last, to direct the contemplative gaze of traditional philosophy onto this-worldly, human concerns, and thus onto politics, without the traditional prejudice of philosophers against that activity, "to grant the realm of human affairs that *thaumadzein,* that wonder at what is as it is, which, according to Plato and Aristotle, is the beginning of all philosophy." If we are to recover our lost treasure by making this century's second reversal, from thoughtless activity back into thought, the traditional philosophical "wondering and hence questioning impulse must now (i.e., contrary to the teachings of the ancients) directly grasp the realm of human affairs and human deeds" and thus specifically "the political realm . . . [and] the center of politics—man as an acting being."[32]

That, Arendt thought, was what being a political theorist meant: using what she had learned from and still shared with Heidegger in a better way than he had used it, a way free of the professional thinker's *déformation.* Thus it meant assuming for herself the mantle of authority, simultaneously both inheriting and rejecting the tradition, including Heidegger, who had himself appropriated the tradition's authority in an ambivalent way; the tradition, in any case, was no longer available in its traditional form. To do political theory thus meant "to think against the tradition while using its own conceptual tools," which is what Arendt said in her 1953 Gauss lectures—not, however, about her own work or Heidegger's but about what Marx had "tried desperately" to do, "not unlike Kierkegaard and Nietzsche." Our traditional philosophical way of thinking about human collectivities "began when Plato discovered that it is somehow inherent in the philosophical experience to turn away from the common world of human affairs; it ended when nothing was left of this experience but the opposition of thinking and acting, which, depriving thought of reality and action of sense, makes both meaningless."[33] Arendt thus undertook to join Marx, Kierkegaard, Nietzsche, and Heidegger, but in a way that would not end in "self-defeat" and would serve rather than deny action and politics.[34]

That undertaking, however, left her increasingly entangled in the twin conundrums of free will and micro-macro. Like Marx and Tocqueville before her, Arendt made considerable effort to address these conundrums explicitly or to rule them out of her enterprise. Like Marx, she sometimes tried to frame them chronologically. But where Marx theorized about a determined past and an altogether free future, leaving the present in doubt, Arendt theorized about the menace of a determined future brought about by some wrong actions taken—or right actions neglected—in a presumably free past, leaving the present equally problematic. Where Marx focused on collectivities in the past and expected the flowering of individuality within collective harmony in the future, Arendt focused on individuality in the past and tried to contrast the sort of collectivity freely enacted by individuals with the modern, monolithic, individuality-destroying social.

Like Tocqueville, Arendt also sometimes tried to sort out these conundrums through spatial metaphors. Striving to keep people "using their free will" and to resist the "doctrine of fatality," Tocqueville envisioned a sacred enclosure: "Providence has, in truth, drawn a predestined circle around each man beyond which he cannot pass; but within those vast limits man is strong and free, and so are peoples."[35] Arendt speaks less expansively of an "island of freedom" in a "surrounding sea of necessity," or of "oases in a desert."[36] She also, more generally, strives to distinguish her paradoxically interrelated central categories by assigning each to a different "sphere" or "realm," whose boundaries she then polices and whose internal consistency she takes for granted, sorting freedom here, necessity there, action here, behavior there, as indeed the metaphors suggest. A sphere, after all, comprises a certain volume of continuous space; things are either inside it or outside. A realm comprises a certain contiguous territory subject to a single monarch; you are either inside the jurisdiction or outside.[37] But words, concepts, do not function like that. They do indeed have precise meanings that can be established but not a uniform "inside" of the meaning, clearly distinguishable from an excluded "outside," nor a border that can be policed. The various senses of a word often have incompatible implications, so the supposed "inside" is not fully coherent, and the word's problematic semantic connections and contrasts, which are not boundaries or borders, need to be explicitly investigated, not forbidden.[38]

Take Arendt's way of dealing with the micro-macro conundrum, which is by focusing on the distinction—which is indeed important—between two contrasting forms of human collectivity: the political form, in which unique, autonomous individuals join together freely in a collectivity of which they together take charge, and the social form, in which isolated but identical, helpless units are compressed into a monolithic mass by a force they experience as external and of which they cannot take charge. Arendt does not acknowledge and probably does not see the extent to which each of these forms is bound to the other by the micro-macro conundrum, though of course she knows that unique, autonomous political agents become such by being raised in some particular culture— so that they are always already parts of preexisting collectivities—and that the helpless units behaving themselves in the social are still human and have not lost their capacities for autonomous judgment and action.

With respect to the free will conundrum, in most of Arendt's work she takes a similarly polemical, boundary-policing stance: the only real or true freedom is participation in shared self-government; all other interpretations of the concept are illegitimate or derivative, distractions from the political one.[39] The free will question, in particular, she construes narrowly as focused on an inner something called "the will" and whether it is "free." In that sense the issue is, as she points out, invented by philosophers only after political freedom had disappeared from the ancient world. She does not acknowledge, and probably does not see, the extent to which her own teachings about political freedom depend on the free will conundrum more broadly construed, how the very idea of action presupposes something like free will, and how her distinction between freedom and necessity is another version of the same conundrum. She herself, moreover, continues to use the word "freedom," in a variety of ordinary ways at odds with her own definition, to mean not just action in concert but the capacity to begin something new, actually beginning something new, the right to move about physically in the world, the ability to move about physically in the world, the absence of constraining commitments or obligations, and the openness of possibilities available before one acts.[40]

Toward the end of her life, Arendt acknowledged explicitly that the word "freedom" has multiple legitimate senses, and made her own effort to address the free will conundrum.[41] Even then, however, she did not give any account of how the various senses of freedom fit together into one concept, and even after a book-length exploration of the issue, she was still left with the same conundrum: a mysterious "abyss of freedom" separating the causally determined past from a future open to present action, a "hiatus" that remained "somehow opaque" (195, 207, 204–5, 216–17).

The fact is that despite Arendt's efforts and those of Marx, Tocqueville, and others to solve or escape these conundrums, they cannot be resolved or escaped. They are, in Arendt's own words, "dilemmas which permit of no solution," built right into our ways of talking and thinking about human affairs.[42] They characterize not merely certain ambiguous or troublesome words that might be reformed or abolished but whole networks of concepts and structural features of language as well. Nor are they confined to any particular language, such as English, or language family, such as Indo-European.[43] Of course, each language and each culture configures these conceptual regions differently; that is part of what makes their investigation so difficult. But I, at least, cannot imagine a human culture in which people are never in any sense recognized as agents, never praised or blamed or held responsible, never admonished, advised, commanded; but I equally cannot imagine a culture that never identifies something like the causal antecedents or consequences of what people do, in which no one ever considers how to get someone else to do something, or what is likely to happen if someone does this rather than that. Similarly, I cannot imagine a culture in which particular individuals are never recognized as this person rather than that one, nor a language that lacks all general categories.

Now, what one can and cannot imagine is a risky criterion; reality is constantly surpassing our wretched imaginations. Still, I am convinced that both something like agency and something like causal necessity, both something like particularity and something like generality, must be assumed, and assumed *together,* despite their apparent logical incompatibility. Neither assigning them to separate conceptual compartments nor choosing resolutely between them is any help at all.

Dialectical Thinking

That does not mean, however, that no help is available. Though such fundamental conundrums are inescapable, there are better and worse ways of living with them, thinking about them. For starters, it helps to recognize that such basic philosophical conundrums share a characteristic pattern or schema: two equal and opposite absolute generalizations confront each other in what one might call the "heavens" of philosophical abstraction, unrelated to any particular, concrete context where one person actually needs to say something to another. For example, "Really, strictly speaking, all actions have causal antecedents" and "Really, strictly speaking, everyone is capable of spontaneous innovation at every moment"; or again, "Really, strictly speaking, there are only particular individuals" and "Really, strictly speaking, all so-called particulars are parts and products of larger wholes, all individuals shaped by some culture." Each of the opposed claims by itself can seem convincing, since each is extrapolated logically from aspects of a word's meaning, features of how we actually use that word. Yet they are obviously incompatible.[44]

Although choosing between them can seem of the greatest importance, the fact is that it would make no practical difference, since even if one or the other is true, we would still need to draw (something like) the distinctions we ordinarily draw in particular, practical contexts, for example, between what was "your fault" and what you "couldn't help" or whether my lack of a job is my personal failure or is due to widespread unemployment. Although the two opposed absolute generalizations endlessly confront each other in the "heavens," in short, life goes on here on the "earth" of our ordinary engagements and transactions, where we know well enough how to operate with the terms and structures of our language in particular contexts. Thus, not only do the heavenly claims conflict with each other, but both together also conflict with our ordinary earthly ways of talking and drawing distinctions, as is marked by the expression in the above examples: "Really, strictly speaking. . . ."

The fact that both heavenly claims conflict with the way we ordinarily talk does not refute the claims, nor does it prove that we should leave our ordinary usage and practices uncriticized and untheorized. They are full of inconsistencies, shot though with a heritage of past ignorance, illusions, denial, ideology, and euphemism, to which we remain captive unless we examine them critically for ourselves, which is why Socrates kept asking his pesky questions. But our efforts to theorize or generalize critically are always liable to go awry by sliding into one or the other— or both—of the heavenly generalizations and remaining there, which is no help for criticism, reform, or even comprehension of what is going on.

Though one cannot escape or resolve basic philosophical conundrums, what one can achieve is a perspicuous overview of the existing, partly incoherent pattern of these relationships. With respect to particular words, one can find in the patterns of ordinary, earthly usage the basis for both of the conflicting heavenly extrapolations and what each of them omits. More generally, what is most helpful in securing the perspicuous overview is a way of thinking that I persist in wanting to call "dialectical," despite the considerable freight of special meanings that word has acquired in the history of philosophy, much of which I do not intend. By dialectical thinking I mean a way of living with ambiguity and inconsistency that permits intellectual comprehension and mastery without resolving the tensions. Thinking dialectically means theorizing, as Jessica Benjamin puts it, "in ways that allow competing ideas to be entertained simultaneously . . . accepting the paradoxes that can arise from an ability to identify with more than one perspective. To accept paradox is to contain rather than resolve contradictions, to sustain tension between elements heretofore defined as antithetical."[45] Contrary to the usual way of reading Hegel, this sort of intellectual mastery of tensions without resolving them seems to me the most promising interpretation of his notion of dialectical synthesis and of that vexing, untranslatable German verb for what the synthesis does, *aufheben*. The difficulty is to distinguish this necessary and desirable sort of living with contradiction from common confusion and incoherence, thoughtlessness, vacillation, and unwillingness to commit oneself in action.

Dialectical thinking is particularly needed in relation to basic philosophical conundrums such as the two we have been discussing, where the relevant concepts (such as individuality and collectivity) are simultaneously both interdependent and incompatible *and* where the relevant phenomena in the world are similarly interdependent, simultaneously both mutually enhancing *and* conflicting (as, for example, are personal liberty and participation in collective self-government).

This is precisely the sort of terrain in which political theory works. So, for example, in Arendtian terms, the social and free politics are simultaneously two rival heavenly ways of *looking at* human affairs and two rival earthly ways of *conducting* human affairs, and of course, how people look at things and how they conduct themselves are profoundly interrelated, but not in any simple, one-to-one correlation. So delineating publicly what has to be accepted as given from what is to be done is no easy task, and political theory is itself inherently in tension. Politics is practical, "the art of the possible," but theorizing means reconceptualization, questioning the existing framework of assumptions so that new possibilities can emerge. Yet the possibilities must be political and therefore practical. The value of the heavenly abstractions, seen dialectically, is that they loosen the grip of existing assumptions on our thinking, but the earthly practicalities, however reconceptualized, remain the test of what counts as political possibility.

That is why Tocqueville thought that "nowadays the need is to keep men interested in theory" yet insisted that people's theorizing must also be tied to "daily, practical attention" to public affairs.[46] It is also why Arendt sought a mode of theorizing that neither succumbs, through its abstractness, to the *animal laborans*' fatalism, which for so many in our time "has become the major experience of their lives," nor partakes of *homo faber*'s ruthlessness and the ideological illusion—characteristic of totalitarianism—"that everything is possible if one knows how to organize the masses for it."[47] Dialectical thinking, in effect, allows political theory to keep the conundrums of heavenly abstraction in view and put them to use in getting on with the business of revising existing earthly arrangements.

Thus, although dialectical thinking as such "leaves everything as it is," as Wittgenstein famously said about philosophy, it can serve as a preparation equally for accepting the inevitable or for deciding what to do and acting.[48] Like a skilled dancer or what equestrians call a "collected" horse, a dialectical thinker is intellectually ready at each moment to move off gracefully in whatever direction seems appropriate. Thus such thinking implies a balanced readiness to translate back and forth as needed between the perspective of the spectator and that of the actor, between causation and agency, between large-scale collective conditions and individual experience and options, between abstract principles and particular applications. In short, it is a way of using the intellect in the service of life rather than as an escape from reality, of abstracting to the large-scale, long-range view without losing touch with oneself in one's particularity or other people in theirs.

These are obviously my formulations, not Arendt's, though her theorizing is one of the main sources from which I have fashioned them, and I regard them as very much in the spirit of her effort to focus philosophy's traditional *thaumadzein* on politics and on "the center of politics—man as an acting being."[49]

Arendt's explicit arguments dance tantalizingly around these ideas without quite articulating them, half suggesting, half rejecting the dialectical possibility. Thus, despite her lifelong hostility to both Hegelian and Marxist dialectics, she argued toward the end of her life that real thinking—thinking in the sense of thoughtfulness rather than mere brain-cell activity—"is dialectical," but then immediately explained that she meant only that such thinking "proceeds in the form of a silent dialogue," which makes the thinker (want to be) consistent. Someone lacking this inner dialogue—as Arendt thought Eichmann did—"will not mind contradicting himself."[50] Arendt's notion of good dialectical thinking thus seems to stress consistency, by contrast with my stress on living with inconsistency. Arendt saw that at the "very center" of the work of "the great authors" one finds "fundamental and flagrant contradictions" such as are rarely encountered in second-rate thinkers, yet the context in which she says this is a sustained critique of Marx's inconsistency.[51]

She did not even consider the possibility that seems so clearly implicit in the passage: that the fundamental and flagrant contradictions are what make the authors great rather than second-rate, for example, because the fundamental truths they teach us actually are contradictory. Then again, Arendt condemned technocrats who begin by "forcing the choices into mutually exclusive dilemmas," whereas "reality never presents us with anything so neat," but she also saw that in relation to a certain kind of dilemma that permits no "solution" our real need is for "thinking together and combining meaningfully" ideas that are in mutual "opposition and contradiction."[52]

It would surely be useful to have a better account of these difficult matters, so troubling in the enterprise of political theory. The point to be made here, however, is only that one fairly important answer to the question of why Arendt envisioned the social as a Blob in *The Human Condition* is that coherent realistic theorizing about human affairs in a way that takes account of the large scale and yet is true to the nature of action and politics is extremely difficult, so that the seductive power of metaphor is very strong. The Blob both expresses and hides the difficulties.

That is the last in the series of possible explanations for Arendt's surprising way of envisioning the social that this chapter has reviewed: hypostasization, the prior appearance of totalitarianism as a Blob, the vision's rhetorical advantages, its psychological role as a regression fantasy, the significance of abstraction, and finally the explanation in terms of paradox, which one might want to call the logical or conceptual explanation. Any or all of these might lead one to dismiss not only the Blob—which Arendt herself surely would have recognized in retrospect as a mystification that interfered with understanding—but also the entire problem of the social. If it cannot be coherently expressed, one is likely to feel, then it cannot be a real problem, but only a figment of the overheated imagination, a logical confusion, a psychological projection, or a misguided rhetorical device. There is no real problem of the social; no need to worry.

Maybe so. But I believe it would be a serious mistake to dismiss the problem Arendt was trying to address as one dismisses its infelicitous appearance as Blob. If something like the social, although not a Blob, is a real and urgent problem, in one sense addressing that problem is no part of the project of this book, but in another sense it is surely the whole point. So the last chapter must at least try to look at the real-world problem against which Arendt meant to warn, without either mythologizing it or falling captive to the paralyzing philosophical conundrums that haunt political theory. Only by avoiding such false difficulties can we get a clearer view of the real political difficulties, and opportunities, we face.

TWELVE

Rethinking "the Social"

The account of Arendt's concept of the social, its provenance, its meaning, and how she came to envision it as a Blob is completed, but in a sense the most significant work only begins here. If the problem she intended her concept to address is real and anywhere near as important and urgent as she thought, we desperately need better ways of thinking about it and dealing with it. That surely is the real point, the job that needs doing.

Unfortunately, it is not a job I can do. Had I been able to diagnose and prescribe for what ails us, *that* is the book I would have written. All that this concluding chapter can offer instead is the barest sketch of an overview of some ways of approaching the problem of the social without invoking a Blob. I take that effort to be in the spirit of Arendt's enterprise, resisting all "formulations . . . that mythologize" so that we may understand what is really going on.[1]

The aim of this chapter thus being radically different from what has gone before, the tone too must change, for at this point we get down to matters on which I have no special expertise or authority and cannot muster textual evidence (except when I occasionally cite Arendt's views). Now we get down to you and me, Dear Reader, and what we are to do. You live here too; you know as much as I do about how things are with us, what we are doing. We meet here as potential citizens of a free republic, which we must project if it is to exist.

Perhaps, Dear Reader, you do not believe that we are about to be swallowed by an extraterrestrial monster. Neither do I. Nor did Arendt. Perhaps you do not even think that we are in imminent danger of permanently losing the human capacities for action and autonomous judgment. Neither do I; nor did Arendt. We might well be on the verge of doing some irreversible physical or chemical harm to our ecosystem, even of rendering the earth uninhabitable, and that possibility does make the problem of the social even more urgent. But the social as such—if we are to think about it without mythologizing—is not some imminent irreversible metaphysical change of state. It is better—more plausibly and more usefully—regarded as a matter of degree, a condition that can increase or lessen, but which for some time now has been increasing at an accelerating rate. That way of thinking about it gives quite enough cause for alarm.

The social unmythologized, chapter 9 concluded, should be understood as the absence of politics where politics belongs, a condition in which a collectivity of people—for whatever reason—cannot (or at any rate do not) effectively take charge of the overall resultants of what they are severally doing. The large-scale outcomes of their activities happen as if independent of any human agency, as if these people had been swallowed by some Blob. That chapter also noted that "the social" is not a particularly apt name for this condition, given its remoteness from the ordinary meanings of "society" and "social." Still, for coherence and for lack of a better term, I continue to use Arendt's phrase. Abandoning Blob imagery, one might say: there surely have been times and places in history when collectivities of people did relatively well at jointly taking charge of what their activities engendered, and other times and places when they did so poorly, or failed utterly to do so. It is surely worth asking what made the difference, worth trying in effect to specify for our time the "for whatever reason" in our interpretation of the social. The job of this chapter, then, is to inquire what it might be about us now—our arrangements, our ways of conducting ourselves, the sorts of people we are, how we think—that keeps continually enhancing the social.

It does seem to me that we are in fact increasingly, maybe more than ever before in human history, jointly bringing about disasters for ourselves and each other, knowing that we are doing so, yet somehow unable to stop. More and more the conditions under which we live are the resultants of human activity, and more and more they seem to constrain, cripple, impoverish, and destroy millions of human lives, while we stand by—or rather, sit in front of our television sets or our computers—wringing our hands and blaming each other. Some try to do this or that about it, of course, but seem only to make things worse.

Though there is no Blob, there is a very real problem of what Arendt called the social, and we are it. Is that good news or bad? If we are the problem, surely we must also be the solution. We are getting in our own way, the opening chapter said, and asked if that expression even makes sense. When predicated of an individual, such expressions usually refer either to clumsiness or to unconscious conflict and ambivalence. Those ideas are problematic enough, but what might be their unmythologized counterparts in relation to a human collectivity? Any effort to answer that question is bound to get entangled in the conceptual complexities discussed in chapter 11, of "can" and "could" and "we." The whole topic of the social—our collective ineffectuality—forms an almost impenetrable thicket of assumptions, prejudices, ignorance, guesswork, projections, irrelevancies, conceptual conundrums, and logical tangles that boggles the mind. The thicket had best be avoided, but it lies squarely in the way of any effort to deal with our condition without mythologizing it, so we cannot avoid it.

This chapter will not trace a path through that thicket, either theoretically or practically. The most it can offer is a crude map of several paths leading into the brush, each of which, however, leaves us still entangled. Though distinct paths approaching the thicket from different directions, once inside, they twist and turn confusingly and repeatedly intersect, so that it is hard to keep track of which path one is following, let alone which direction might eventually bring one out on the far side of the tangle. Arendt had ideas to contribute along each of these paths, particularly in works prior and subsequent to *The Human Condition,* and this chapter draws on them, but she is by no means the only, and not always the best, source of ideas here, so one should also try to think beyond her in the service of her goal.

To speak less metaphorically, this chapter takes up four distinct, even competing, yet interrelated ways of analyzing the "for whatever reason" in our interpretation of the social. There is, first of all, what we shall call the institutional path, entering the thicket of the social from the direction of organizational structures, large-scale patterns of interpersonal relationship and conduct. Maybe we are collectively ineffectual because of the institutional forms that predominate among us. Maybe we have got ourselves organized in ways that are so unwieldy or otherwise unsuitable as to make effective concerted action almost impossible.

There is, second, what we shall call the characterological approach, entering the thicket from the side of personal conduct and individual psychology. Maybe we are becoming, have become, are raising our children to be the sort of people who are not suited to action, particularly to joint action with others, people who do not want to act, do not know how to go about it, are inept at it.

There is, third, what we shall call the ideational path, entering the thicket from the direction of thought: concepts, frameworks of assumptions, patterns of ideas, *Weltanschauung, mentalité.* Maybe we have developed ways of thinking about human affairs, about ourselves and other people, about history and politics, that blind us to our real capacities or to the real sources of our troubles, or that systematically distort things in ways that keep us from acting effectively together.

Finally the chapter will also consider a path of a different kind, which we shall call the "Just do it!" path into the thicket of the social. Entering the brush from the direction of agency and responsibility, initiative and solidarity, and with primary focus on what is to be done, this path offers neither a rival diagnosis nor a rival prescription but instead an indispensable supplement to any remedies proposed along the other paths. Not coincidentally, this approach also provides a convenient opportunity to honor once more, in conclusion, Arendt's distinctive and most valuable contribution to contemporary political theory.

Institutions and Organization

Begin, then, with the *institutional* path into the thicket of the social, the approach that is most salient in *The Human Condition*. Arendt, we saw, singled out two organizational forms as particularly characteristic of the social: markets (economics let loose from the *oikia*) and bureaucracies (the "most social form of government"). Looking around our world, it seems to me that people are indeed increasingly organized into one or the other or some combination of these two forms. Except perhaps in personal relations, which are increasingly circumscribed, virtually the only institutional arrangements we know are—to borrow Oliver Williamson's title—markets and hierarchies.[2] Despairing of the human ability to arrange our affairs deliberately, we cleave to the market, hoping that it will produce impersonally what we cannot achieve directly. When the market in fact produces trouble instead, we try to remedy the damage through administrative measures, which is to say, through bureaucratic regulation. When bureaucratic regulation fails and chokes us, we return without much hope to laissez-faire. So we practice competitive acquisitiveness on the one side and managerialism on the other.

Should one add the Internet and the ghostly "relationships" of virtual reality as a distinct, newly emerging institutional form of comparable significance? Although a little more will be said about this shortly, the potential of the Internet as an empowering and liberating tool seems to me far outweighed by its technobiological, depersonalizing, distracting, and isolating aspects. People already politicized and actively, autonomously engaged in public life could take advantage of its facilities, but it is as unlikely to invite or incite people into action, let alone into public responsibility, as either markets or bureaucracies.

As Arendt saw, these two institutional forms, usually contrasted, have much in common where they are pervasive; they might, as Reinhardt remarks, be "better thought of as Siamese twins."[3] Both isolate people from each other in the sense of requiring each to mind his own business, leaving overall outcomes to someone else, while at the same time both connect people in ways they do not perceive and cannot intentionally direct. To be sure, we are accustomed to think of bureaucracy in just the opposite way, as a really efficient way of organizing large numbers of people to accomplish a specified purpose or policy, directed from the apex of the bureaucratic pyramid. Functioning according to this model, bureaucracies surely have their uses, as indeed do markets and the new electronic systems of communication. But this is not how bureaucracies function among us.

Our bureaucracies, as Arendt suggests, are like onions rather than pyramids: they would work just the same if no one was at their "head." Those nominally in charge and setting policy are the most isolated from reality and dependent on their organizational system for information. Because of the huge size and complex interconnections of these institutions and their pervasiveness among us, they generate enormous inertia. They are, it is often said, "centralized," but this is not really right: their interconnections are ubiquitous, but there is no center. Arendt noted in the 1960s that "centralization, under the impact of bigness, turn[s] out to be counterproductive," which accounts for the "growing, world-wide resentment against bigness as such."[4] Yet that resentment does not produce any alternative arrangements.

This may sound like a claim that no one has power or privilege among us, that none is to blame for what is going wrong, or that we are all equally powerful and equally guilty. But that is neither Arendt's intent nor mine. The notion that no one has power is the Blob vision; the notion that all have equal power Arendt explicitly rejected.[5] Power is another deeply problematic concept. First off, the blatant and increasing inequalities of privilege must not be confused with power. People can be helpless beneficiaries as well as helpless victims. Second, our problem is not immobility but inertia, not the absence of change or movement but the inability to redirect it or to influence its direction intentionally. Things are getting done, all right, and we all feel their impact, feel ourselves subjected to something like power. The question is whether it really is *power,* that is, whether anyone is wielding it purposefully to accomplish what in fact happens.

It seems obvious to me that what C. Wright Mills argued in the 1950s is now even more true: some among us have far more power than others, in the sense that they make decisions with enormous consequences for large numbers of other people, for example, hiring or firing thousands.[6] Yet these decisions are mostly market-driven and, as Mills himself pointed out, the power to make them is institutional, resulting from these people's positions in "the major hierarchies and organizations of modern society" (4). That means, first, that the decisions can only be made in the direction of our general, inertial drift, not contrary to it; the decision makers cannot do whatever they please.[7] Second, it means that they are dependent on others for advice and information, as well as for the execution of those decisions. So these decision makers have power only as long as everyone else keeps on doing more or less what they now do. Mills concluded his argument for the existence of a power elite by urging that we hold them "accountable for a decisive range of the historical events" we experience (27). But if only those at the institutional apexes have power, it is not clear how the rest of us could hold them accountable in any meaningful, effective sense. If we could, isn't the power already ours, theirs only by our indulgence?

The conundrum is familiar.[8] We could, *if:* for example, if we had different institutions, if we reorganized ourselves. Though both markets and bureaucracies have their uses, neither form is suited to joint deliberation about public affairs. So where these are the only institutional forms available, there is likely to be little deliberation, little concern for public affairs, little free citizenship, little chance of people jointly taking charge of what they are collectively but separately doing.

In a world like ours, organized institutionally like ours, even relatively well-intentioned, conventionally thoughtless people just trying to get on with their lives can play a role in monstrous horrors. That is Arendt's "banality of evil." Each merely looks the other way, be it ambitiously and acquisitively, anxiously, resentfully, cynically, or apathetically. Put anyone into such an institutional structure, and he would have to behave as an isolate, leaving responsibility for the whole to hypothetical others, in order to function effectively. Those who fail or refuse to do so will be expelled from membership, fired from jobs, avoided by other people; they will not be promoted, preferred, respected, nominated, or elected. The consequences of nonconformity are either openly punitive or therapeutically disciplinary.

So pervasive are such institutions among us that we can scarcely imagine any significant alternatives. Arendt called the significant alternative "politics," but she did not mean the institutions that we designate as political as they now operate. These she saw as simply replicating market competition or administrative management or both. What we call policy is made by technical "problem-solvers" to whom the rest of us defer; what we call political parties are bureaucratically managed "instruments through which the power of the people is curtailed and controlled"; politics is "a profession and a career" for a few and of no concern to the rest; representation and elections "in fact become oligarchic government," as the relationship between representative and constituents "is transformed into that between seller and buyer" and deliberation over public issues is replaced by the "obvious phoniness" of image-making, message-sending, and credibility.[9]

Neither in our governmental institutions nor in any others of significance, official or unofficial, are there arrangements that might encourage action and provide ordinary people "an opportunity to engage in those activities of 'expressing, discussing, and deciding' which in a positive sense are the activities of freedom."[10] As to what sorts of institutions would do this, however, Arendt is for the most part distressingly vague, speaking only of public "spaces" or "arenas," and though she does call for the institutionalization of freedom, she also acknowledges that it seems an inherently "contradictory" undertaking.[11]

Perhaps because of this paradoxicality, Arendt was, on the whole, not much interested in institutional arrangements, in this respect more like Marx than like Tocqueville. Her one specific institutional enthusiasm was for what she called "the council system," a kind of "power structure" she saw as spontaneously created from below by "the people themselves" in one after another of modern revolutions and uprisings.[12] Like Thomas Jefferson and Tocqueville, Arendt thought that on the basis of such participatory local "elementary republics" one might erect "an entirely new form of government," a genuinely free and political "council-state."[13] As Isaac and Reinhardt point out, Arendt imagined such councils not as alternatives but as an invigorating, politicizing complement to familiar institutions of representation and federation.[14] Like Tocqueville, she thought that in local, face-to-face participation citizens might acquire the experience of freedom—that "public spirit" and awareness of their own effectiveness in transacting public affairs—which they could then apply also in their more remote and impersonal institutional memberships.

Clearly, to fulfill this function, such local bodies must be small and accessible to all who want to participate, but they must also have something meaningful to do and must have or be able to acquire sufficient power to make a real difference in matters that affect the participants' lives. Mere sociability is not the point, nor can mere debating societies provide the appropriate experience. So the question becomes whether and how these requirements can be met in our world.

Structural Conditions

Here we come up against a number of broader structural arrangements, perhaps better called conditions than institutions, which are profoundly resistant to policy intervention and appear to set limits to what is institutionally possible. I mean arrangements such as the global economy, the dizzying growth of world population, and increasingly elaborate technology. Although Arendt had things to say about each of these, she never subjected them to any sustained analysis. Nor, of course, can we do so here. Again a survey must suffice; but then, we all already know something of these matters.

It was evident to Arendt by the 1950s that the world had undergone a drastic "economic and geographic shrinkage" so that market fluctuations now "tend to become world-wide phenomena."[15] She also perceived the "catastrophic decline of the nation-state system," which left states no longer able to assure either domestic sovereignty or international justice.[16] She did not quite put the two together into what seems to me the heart of the problem: that economic, market-oriented, and bureaucratically organized structures of power have gone global, surpassing many nation-states in their size and resources and exceeding the reach of any existing political (or even potentially political) institutional forum where people might address the dislocations that result from the operations of these apolitical structures.[17] So it's not just that no one is taking responsibility for the whole; there is a serious problem about what "the whole" now is. As several of Arendt's most astute commentators have pointed out, the state is both too big and too small for the job: too big to serve as an effective primary forum for participatory citizenship and too small to be effectively self-governing in the face of such internationalized private power and systemic drift.[18] "Think globally, act locally" is all very well as far as it goes, but if the locally felt problems are globally generated, local action may not be meaningful or empowering.

It seems to me that while drifting in the social we have formed a world of international corporations, trusts, banks, and other institutions that locate their production units wherever labor is cheap and subservient and the tax laws are favorable. The leading executives and major owners of these organizations travel about the globe; they and their families have multiple residences in agreeable locations in various countries, well protected by security forces and paraphernalia. They have no special stake in any particular country.[19] At the same time, at the other end of the economic scale are huge numbers of unemployed, underemployed, and landless people, driven by hunger and need to wherever work is available, migrating—whether legally or illegally—in hope of feeding themselves and their dependents, and experiencing a degree of "uprootedness and superfluousness" beyond anything that even the prescient Arendt envisioned.[20] There is no work for them, though much needs to be done; without access to work, they cannot live. So they, too, are importantly internationalized, though a certain number of them will find employment in one or another army, police force, or security agency, whether "public" or "private," and a large proportion of the rest will become inmates in the prisons, camps, and other facilities these employees administer.

Even if one rejects Arendt's conviction that a genuinely political world government is inherently impossible ("abstract"), so that any global organization is bound to be social and to "signify a threat to freedom," it is difficult against such background conditions to envision participatory local councils combined federally into some global institutional network that facilitates political freedom.[21]

Meanwhile—and not unrelated—there are too many of us humans now on this earth, and our numbers grow daily at an incredible rate. Arendt thought that "large numbers of people, crowded together, develop an almost irresistible tendency to despotism," which is to say that population pressure is powerfully conducive to the social. "The more people there are, the more likely they are to behave."[22] Our numbers deplete resources, crowd the land, destroy habitat and species, and subject everyone to constant stress by crowding. Must we hope for war, famine, and the new diseases to correct the balance and return us to conditions less productive of "contempt for the value of human life" and more conducive to action in concert?[23]

Third, there is our ever more complex, sophisticated, and rapidly changing technology, almost guaranteed to produce narrowly focused expertise among the technicians and resentful acquiescence among the rest of us. We struggle, of course, to control and use that technology for solving some of our problems, but in the process it constantly generates new and often worse ones, and we all become daily more dependent on it.[24] In particular, new developments in communication and computers, as well as in genetics, are transforming lives, institutions, and character everywhere in ways no one can yet fully foresee. Despite "the simple fact that technological 'progress' is leading in so many instances straight into disaster," as Arendt said, we allow it to follow its own supposedly "inexorable laws, compelling us" in turn.[25]

A global economy without political direction, a burgeoning population that strains resources and crowds facilities, a technology traveling its own trajectory—it is truly a daunting list of conditions underlying our institutional systems of bureaucracies and markets and obstructing any effort to reduce the social. Yet even these structural conditions are continually reproduced only by human activity. They are not inherent inevitabilities. The joint-stock, limited-liability corporation, for example, is a human creation, sustained only by what we are continually doing.[26]

The point of all this, as I said earlier, Dear Reader, is not so much whether Arendt saw the details of our institutional situation aright, or whether I do, but that we need to reconsider our institutional forms and structural conditions with a view to reducing the social and enlarging the possibilities for freedom. We need to seek out, invent, and cultivate organizational modes—official and unofficial, large and small—that politicize people and encourage their participation in the active shaping of their shared public life: institutions that facilitate creative initiatives from below and encourage not just the expression of ordinary people's views, as in interactive television or public opinion polls, but widespread deliberation about public affairs that connects public policy to what really matters to people and that lets them experience themselves jointly improving the shared public conditions that limit their personal choices.

Psychology and Character

There are, however, also other ways to approach the thicket of the social, besides the institutional path. In a world structured almost entirely into markets and bureaucracies, we noted, anyone would have to function as part of the social if he hopes to have any individual success or influence. But that observation could also be inverted. How an institution actually functions, as distinct from its formal rules, depends mostly on the kind of people in it. An institution, after all, is not a building or a bus, into and out of which people move. In a central sense, the institution *is* the conduct—the habitual, structured conduct—of people "in" it. And though an isolated deviant individual may indeed be utterly helpless to change the institution, if a sufficient number of those in it share that deviancy, the institution will certainly change, will already *be* changed.

The social is not only an external pressure on the individual who strives to be autonomous but also an internal barrier to autonomy; it is "invasive" as much as "pervasive," as Reinhardt says.[27] Perhaps, then, the right way to understand the prevalence of the social among us is in terms of what we are like, what sort of people we have become, in terms of individual psychology. As a courtesy to Arendt's strong aversion to depth psychology, however, let us use a more old-fashioned term, and speak of the *characterological* path into the thicket. Arendt herself in the 1970s related American political freedom to our "national character," though she put the phrase in quotation marks; and despite her rejection of psychology, she actually had a lot to say about what sort of people tend to behave socially and what sort are more suited to free citizenship.[28]

Her primary image of the character structure that promotes the social was, of course, the parvenu: the outsider seeking to get by or get ahead as an individual exception by pleasing or deceiving some "they" projected as superior. We traced the gradual expansion of this idea to include refugees who "adjust in principle to everything and everybody," selfless agents of imperialism, cowardly or selfish collaborators, ambitious or deferential bureaucrats, privatized romantics, abstracted philosophers and social scientists, and above all the conformists of mass society. In all of these forms the syndrome was a matter of character: not a readiness to make necessary, realistic adjustments but a predilection for needless, irrational, surplus deference, resulting from a too narrowly self-centered perspective that neglects both solidarity and one's own real capacities.

Arendt was not alone in suggesting that Americans are becoming people of this kind. Indeed, the year before *The Origins of Totalitarianism* appeared, her friend David Riesman and his associates published a study that found a similar pattern of character increasingly pervasive in America. They called it the "other-directed" personality and distinguished it from the character both of people who orient themselves by a traditional code ("tradition-directed") and of those who orient themselves autonomously by their own inner standards ("inner-directed"). If the latter might be said metaphorically to have a psychic gyroscope that holds them steady whatever those around them may be doing, Riesman and his associates wrote, the "other-directed" might be said to have instead an inner radar set, constantly sounding out the behavior and attitudes of those around them and adjusting accordingly.[29]

More recently, Riesman's diagnosis has been strikingly supported by Stanley Milgram's well-known finding that a very large proportion of his experimental subjects were willing—contrary to their own prior expectations—to inflict (what they took to be) severe pain and mortal risk on (what they took to be) innocent others, in obedience to the authority of (what they took to be) scientists engaged in research.[30]

Such people are probably susceptible to recruitment in authoritarian cults or mass movements led by some ruthlessly selfish or power-mad criminal types, but in Arendt's view that is no longer the greatest danger, for open ruthlessness and bold selfishness are themselves disappearing. Just as *homo faber*'s utilitarian efficiency has been displaced by the *animal laborans*' fatalistic routine, there will be no more "mob" to lead the mass; a bureaucracy formed like an onion rather than a pyramid needs no leader, and those near the center are the most out of touch with reality. The problem now is not the Hitlers or the Heydrichs but the Eichmanns of the world: banal, timid, thoughtless.

Now, Arendt may well have underestimated the staying power of openly criminal exploitation, but it surely is true that without a lot of conformists to carry out their orders, the boldly exploitative criminals constitute far less of a danger. Nor are the old-fashioned ruthless exploiters any better material than the conformists for free citizenship. Arendt may also have underestimated the importance of the parvenu's hidden rage, the component in the conformist's character that Nietzsche discussed so brilliantly as *ressentiment*. She certainly recognized the parvenu's "inevitable but intolerable resentment," the sadistic underlying counterpart to his characteristic masochistic self-denial and self-disparagement.[31] She saw also how a "vehement yearning for violence" is the "natural reaction of those whom society has tried to cheat of their strength." In relation to totalitarianism she noted how this yearning and this resentment prepared recruits for mass movements—people seeking "access to history even [or especially?] at the price of destruction."[32] But in relation to the social, perhaps because she ascribed all agency to it as Blob, she did not discuss the role of *ressentiment*.

Nor did she theorize in any systematic way about what sort of character structure might be conducive to freedom. Her remarks on the topic are scattered and cryptic, often in the form of striking quotations or epigraphs. Their systematic explication would take at least another chapter; only a brief overview is possible here.

The central desirable character trait she discusses is courage—not the exceptional heroism of an Achilles, or even the desperate boldness involved in joining a resistance movement, but the simple, quotidian gumption to "leave one's private hiding place" and speak or act in public, "disclosing and exposing" oneself to strangers.[33] Courage "is the political virtue par excellence," but it is a courage contrasting less to cowardice than to anxiety.[34] Citizenship requires that kind of boldness "not because of the particular dangers that lurk" in the public world but because to enter politics one must leave behind one's personal "worries and anxieties"—about being accepted or valuable, or making a living—because in politics the "primary concern is ... always for the world," not oneself.[35] That, we noted, is why people who "joined the Resistance, *found*" themselves, discovered that they could do without their anxieties and their habitual defenses against those anxieties.[36] Political engagement thus facilitates, but also requires, what Lummis has called the "sorting out of our true needs from those that are the maimed consequences of ... fear and envy," often enhanced in our time by the "professional needs-manufacturers."[37]

Action and freedom presuppose at least enough self-respect so that there are some indignities or inequities to which one will not stoop, no matter what the cost, and at least enough self-confidence to imagine the possibility that one's own direct initiative might succeed in the world, that one might, at least sometimes, be "able to change things by one's own efforts" directly and openly, rather than by indirect manipulation of the powerful.[38] Because action means initiative in relation to people rather than objects, furthermore, it requires sufficient trust in oneself and other people to allow open engagement with them, sufficient courage not just for risking oneself but also for putting others at risk, for leading, organizing, exercising personal authority "to enlist the help, the co-acting" of others.[39]

None of this, of course, is to be confused with recklessness or ruthlessness or hubris. The requisite "self-confidence ... has nothing to do with arrogance," just as a realistic respect for other people's views should not be confused with conformism.[40] Accordingly, a second cluster of character traits serving free citizenship centers on solidarity and responsibility: due concern for the welfare of others and of the world. Action and politics require not the narrowly focused, ruthless technical efficiency of *homo faber* but a kind of initiative that recognizes limits and commitments to other people.

With respect to the world, this means understanding that one is "partly responsible for the order of things" even though one did not choose or create that order, just as the conscious pariah takes responsibility for himself even though he did not choose or create himself, may even be "the product of an unjust dispensation." Taking on such responsibility for the world, for preserving what is valuable in it, for changing what is wrong, and for creating better arrangements is part of growing up. The conscious pariah, we saw, "renounce[s] the comfortable protection of nature," of carefree childhood, in order to "come to grips with the world of men and women."[41] Indeed, one might think of children as, in a way, like pariahs. Not that they are despised or deliberately excluded, of course, but they are unavoidably newcomers and outsiders, gradually initiated into the humanly enacted world. For the child, however, something like the parvenu role is appropriate: the significant adults in the child's life do have almost total power over it, and they are the sources of its norms and standards. There is nothing wrong with the child's wanting to please them, to be accepted and valued by them, to become like them.

But childhood comes to an end. From this perspective, Arendt's parvenu and conformist look rather like overgrown children, still trying too hard to be (or to seem) "good" and mistaking officials, elites, experts, the *Führer*, or public opinion for benevolent (or credulous) parents. So one might say that free citizenship is facilitated by growing up.

Arendt speaks of it as a renunciation and a duty, an obligation of adults toward the young. But she also recognizes it as a fulfillment, both because it is a realization of one's own powers and because the world serves our needs and desires. Carefree, childish dependence on nature is all very well in fair weather but leaves one helpless in foul. Human civilizations are the record of (flawed) human efforts to fashion shelter against foul weather, shelter that Arendt calls "the world."[42] Growing up means both developing one's capacities and, as a corollary, accepting one's responsibility for the competent maintenance and improvement of that inherited world. It is a self-realization; Arendt quotes Dante in the epigraph to her chapter on action in *The Human Condition*: "in action the being of the doer is somehow intensified, [so that] delight necessarily follows."[43] And growing up serves self-interest as well; everyone needs shelter, and the world and the earth that require our care also genuinely gratify. Not the adult—the conscious pariah—but the childish parvenu is out of touch with self, world, truth, and reality and sacrifices the "simple pleasures" of nature.

The adult capacity for agency, Arendt therefore says, is grounded in gratitude and love, in recognizing that however corrupt, flawed, and unjust the inherited world may be, it is also the source of pleasure and fulfillment, of one's own powers, and of the very standards by which one condemns its injustice and corruption. Responsibility for the world, which "stands always at the center of politics," rests on *amor mundi,* on "lov[ing] the world enough to take care of it." Arendt wrote that in 1958, when, as she said, she herself had only recently "begun truly to love the world."[44] Not that she had earlier been selfish and only now become dutiful, but rather she had moved from an overly dutiful and somewhat fanatical rebellion on behalf of the victims against those in charge of the unjust world to a more nuanced recognition of her own continuing stake in that world and her own share in being "in charge."

That is why she took our greatest danger to be alienation from the world and the earth: those who feel they have no stake in the world are unlikely to love it, and would just as soon see it all go smash. Yet we all have a stake in the world, because even the most excluded and deprived, even the most rebellious and critical, spring from that world. The acceptance of world and self that underlies maturation into competent, responsible agency is akin to the "neighborly love" Arendt found in Augustine. It is akin also to that "second birth, in which we confirm and take upon our selves the naked fact of our original physical appearance," and of our psychic appearance as well, of the person we have become, capable of agency.[45] Like Nietzsche's *amor fati,* this sort of acceptance, ratification, even love of world and self, just as they are, must not be confused with conservatism, complacency, or a commitment to leaving things unchanged. On the contrary, realistic acceptance and appreciation of what is, are prerequisite to effective action for preserving what is valuable, resisting what is unjust, and founding better arrangements for the future. An infant is helpless; growing up into agency does not mean giving up, or giving in.

Responsibility toward other people follows a somewhat different logic than responsibility for the world, because people—unlike the world—are themselves capable of action and judgment, so that a primary element in caring for them is recognizing them as peers capable of caring for themselves. That requirement is reflected in any number of Arendtian themes, for example, her stress on individual uniqueness. Essential to free action is the capacity to recognize human "plurality"—the diverse "manyness" of the people—and one's own membership in that plurality.[46] Each sees and judges the world from a distinct perspective; each is an independent source of initiative; each has something to contribute, therefore, but also is a potential source of conflict. So free citizenship presupposes the ambiguous dual awareness that one is—as a human adult—inescapably "in charge" and responsible, yet never in charge alone, not sovereign, but merely one among many others whom one must take into account, because only together with them can one be free or self-governing.[47]

The same theme also informs Arendt's distinction between pity and solidarity as two modes of response to other people's suffering. In the first mode, the one who pities is fundamentally interested only in himself, his own uncomfortable response to another's suffering. What she calls "pity" is self-centered and driven by passion, and therefore recognizes no limits, easily becoming ruthless toward those considered responsible for the suffering and condescending or managerial toward the sufferers. What Arendt calls "solidarity," by contrast, "that solidarity which is the political basis of the republic," means making common cause with the sufferers as one's peers without losing track of one's own separateness from them or confusing their suffering with one's own. Solidarity means genuinely recognizing them as autonomous agents, no matter how victimized and in need of help.[48]

Free citizenship, then, is facilitated by the capacity to relate to others in this balanced way—responsive to their needs but respectful of their capacities, empathic but without merger, attentive to their perspective without surrendering one's own judgment. That capacity is crucial for politics because it underlies both the mutuality requisite between fellow citizens and the genuine but limited conflict essential to political freedom. The free citizen must be capable of reciprocal relations with peers some of whom are threateningly different from himself, by contrast with the fatal tendency of the privileged to stereotype those they exclude (" 'The Jew' in general") and of the victims to huddle together and avoid confrontation, preferring "as far as possible to deal only with people with whom they cannot come into conflict."[49] Free citizenship presupposes the ability to fight—openly, seriously, with commitment, and about things that really matter—without fanaticism, without seeking to exterminate one's opponents. That ability contrasts both to the ruthlessness of *homo faber*, ready to eliminate whatever stands in his way (including people), and the spinelessness of the *animal laborans* and of the parvenu, so anxious to accommodate that he cannot bear open disagreement.

Arendt may not have given enough attention to this theme of vigorous but limited conflict, of contestation in mutuality, taken as central to politics by Machiavelli and to morality by Nietzsche. But in terms of individual character traits inhibiting or conducive to action, she certainly recognized the parvenu's anxiety, hidden resentment, and masochistic attachment to victimhood, and by contrast the value of what she—partly following Sorel—called the capacity for "fighting without hatred and 'without the spirit of revenge.'"[50]

Time: Being "Entirely (in the) Present"

That spirit had for Arendt, as it did for Machiavelli, Nietzsche, and Freud, all of whom valued it, an importantly chronological aspect. Action and citizenship are facilitated by the capacity for timeliness, avoiding nostalgia and revenge, as well as utopian dreams of some future world. As the epigraph to the preface of the first edition of *The Origins of Totalitarianism*, Arendt adopted a line from Jaspers:

> *Weder dem Vergangenen anheimfallen noch dem Zukünftigen.*
> *Es kommt darauf an, ganz gegenwärtig zu sein.*
> [To fall prey neither to the past nor to the future.
> What matters is to be entirely (in the) present.]

The point of the epigraph, the preface makes clear, is the unprecedented newness of totalitarianism, which cannot be comprehended by categories inherited from the past, nor avoided by fantasies about a different future, but must be confronted here and now by new, autonomous, realistic thought.[51] That becomes a continuing Arendtian theme: our loss of the tradition of "Western" thought, the opportunities for autonomous thinking that this loss might provide, and the central importance of realism—of seeing reality truly, undistorted by outdated theories or irrelevant fantasies. We shall return to that theme when we take up thinking, on the next path into the thicket of the social. But the theme has characterological aspects as well.

By the time Arendt chose "between past and future" as the title for the volume of essays that followed *The Human Condition,* the present moment had become for her a "gap," a "small non-time-space in the very heart of time," which was the locus not just of realistic, undistorted thought but also, crucially, of action. This gap provides the only possible "ground on which [to] stand" in order to act, "insert[ing one]self between an infinite past and an infinite future." Her essays, Arendt said in the preface, concern "how to move in this gap."[52] Action is, by definition, neither determined by a causal chain from the past (since action is spontaneity) nor justifiable with technical certainty as the means to some future end (since action always enters the web of relationships, so that its outcome is never fully in the agent's control).[53] If one looks at the world in terms of causal processes in time, then the present moment, and action, disappear. The idea has roots in, appears to be a secularized version of a theme in Jewish mysticism discussed by Arendt's friend Walter Benjamin: that every moment is a sacred "now" through which the Messiah might appear.[54] But it takes a kind of courage and a certain liberating distance from one's own past to live in that "now" and take advantage of its opportunities (for example, to walk out of an internment camp, contrary to the rules, with "only a toothbrush").

Characterologically, then, Arendt suggests, free citizenship is hampered by parvenu conformism, resentment, and revenge and facilitated by courage, responsibility, and the capacity for being (in the) present, for realistic initiative. On the whole, there is nothing startling or particularly innovative in these suggestions. As she remarked about Sorel, "the new values turn out to be not very new."[55] They have parallels in the thought of moralists from Socrates and Augustine to Nietzsche and Freud. In any case, with respect to character as with respect to institutions, what matters is less whether Arendt's ideas are new or true, or whether mine are, than that we should think about character—our own and other people's—in relation to the problem of the social.

We need to inquire whether we might be becoming, and forming, the sort of people who cannot act, who lack the desire or the requisite skills and traits for action, particularly for action in concert with others. If so, we urgently need to think also about how to turn this trend around, what it might take to develop—in ourselves, in each other, in our children—a character structure more conducive to political engagement and freedom. Is it a matter of child-rearing patterns and family arrangements? Is it about economic security and opportunity, or about work patterns that provide greater experience of autonomy? Is it about schooling, leisure activities, media, or some altogether different and less commonly cited institution?

As one formulates such questions on the characterological path into the thicket of the social, however, one realizes that there has been an intersection. With topics such as family patterns, media, economic security, we are back on the institutional path; one cannot think about promoting large-scale character change without thinking institutionally. Yet we are back on that path, as it were, at a different point from any we had reached before; it does not look entirely familiar. For there is no guarantee that institutions which might help develop the right sort of character for freedom are the same as—or even compatible with—institutions more directly conducive to free politics itself. It becomes evident that, to think the matter through, one would have to re-travel both paths repeatedly, relating what one finds on each to the other.

Thought, Ideas, Conceptual Frameworks

Besides, there are still other approaches to the social. Both institutional arrangements and character are mediated by thinking, and it may be that the problem of the social is best approached in terms of our ideas and assumptions, how we conceive of human affairs. Perhaps there is something about our intellectual framework, our conceptual system, our outlook that promotes the social. Maybe even courageous, responsible people in institutions eminently suited to concerted action would conduct themselves as we do if they thought as we do. Call this the *ideational* path into the thicket.

This surely was one of Arendt's most persistent themes. Though she was modest—even pessimistic—about the likely effects of her own writings, thinking is what she urged on people, from her early ratification of Kafka's view of thought as the pariah's "new weapon" through her late engagement with "the life of the mind." In *The Human Condition*, while holding that "not ideas but events change the world," she identified thoughtlessness as one of "the outstanding characteristics of our time" and claimed to be proposing "nothing more than [that we should] think what we are doing."[56] Later, however, Arendt claimed that she became interested in thinking only after her encounter with Eichmann, the epitome of our time's "sheer thoughtlessness."[57] It is not obvious how one might decide whether one era is more thoughtless than another, or indeed what "thoughtlessness" really means. Clearly it does not mean—here or ever—a literal absence of brain activity, but instead suggests some sort of inadequate or misguided mode of thinking. So the question is what modes of thinking are conducive to the social, and what modes might facilitate freedom.

In *The Human Condition* Arendt briefly glosses thoughtlessness as meaning "heedless recklessness or hopeless confusion or complacent repetition of 'truths' which have become trivial and empty."[58] With respect to Eichmann, she offers a somewhat different trilogy, interpreting his thoughtlessness as, first, an inability "to think from the standpoint of somebody else"; second, an inability to think critically for himself, which left him dependent utterly on "the voice of respectable society around him"; and, third, a "remoteness from reality," especially from the reality of his own conduct: he "*merely,* to put the matter colloquially, *never realized what he was doing.*"[59]

The two trilogies overlap but do not coincide. "Heedless recklessness," as in the retrospective apology "I just didn't think," seems parallel to Eichmann's remoteness from reality, which made him unable even in retrospect to appreciate what he had done. "Hopeless confusion" might include imprecision in language—a topic to which we shall return shortly—but is surely broader, a baffled "I just don't know *what* to think," reminiscent of the disorientation that Arendt said totalitarian governments induce by keeping everything in constant flux. The "complacent repetition" of clichés corresponds to Eichmann's uncritical dependence on "the voice of society" and to Arendt's portrait of the parvenu. All of these are also related to not seeing things from anyone else's point of view, whether out of a failure to listen, or a lack of empathy, or sheer abstraction. For it is only in conversation with concrete others, listening to and appreciating their perspective on our shared world, Arendt says, that we can sort out reality from both idiosyncratic fantasy and projected conventions.

To each of these ideational failures or disabilities, Arendt juxtaposed an alternative, a way of thinking more suited to action and politics. As a remedy for inability to put oneself in another person's place, she proposed training "one's imagination to go visiting."[60] This is a matter not (merely) of empathy, for one must not abandon but must precisely seek objectivity, as in the distinction between pity and solidarity discussed on the characterological path. One must remember that one's imagination is *only* visiting, not occupying, the other's place. Thinking that is appropriate to freedom must be neither oblivious to nor passionately driven by other people's pain.

Putting oneself in another's shoes ("Think how *you* would feel...") is, of course, the most ancient and fundamental precept of morality, but Arendt seeks to extend and adapt it to politics in a more impersonal form, which she calls "representative thinking," links to Kant's "enlarged mentality," which makes judgment possible, and identifies as the "hallmark" of political thinking.[61]

One's political opinion or judgment is valid, she says, in proportion as one has succeeded in making other people's standpoints "present to [one's] mind." This is neither mere identification with the other people's feelings nor adoption of their actual opinions, but imagining "how *I* would feel and think if I were in their place."[62] Arendt is not very clear, however, about how this mental activity articulates with conduct. There are difficulties both about how representative thinking relates to actual political deliberation with fellow citizens and about how its results are supposed to affect one's activity. There is, after all, a significant gap between the precept "Think how you would feel . . ." and the more demanding moral maxim "*Do* unto others. . . ." Can there be a mode of thinking that would be the general, political counterpart of the latter maxim?

A related ambiguity haunts Arendt's second prescription against thoughtlessness: her remedy for the failure to think autonomously. Following Lessing, she calls it *Selbstdenken,* translated literally in *Rahel Varnhagen* as "self-thinking" but later more felicitously as "independent thinking for oneself."[63] *Selbstdenken* is particularly important in modernity, because the tradition that guided the thought of Europeans around the globe since ancient times is no longer available to us. "Tradition itself has become part of the past."[64] Insofar as it has not brought thoughtlessness and clichéd repetition of traditional formulas, now empty, the loss presents an opportunity for radical *Selbstdenken,* for an autonomy and creativity in thinking comparable to action in conduct. The loss of tradition thus "could be an advantage, promoting a new kind of thinking that . . . move[s] freely without crutches over unfamiliar terrain." We have noted that Arendt regarded herself as engaged in this task, following Marx, Nietzsche, and Kierkegaard, whose efforts "ended in self-defeat."[65] Arendt called this possibility "*denken ohne Geländer,*" thinking without banisters, or without railings for guidance and support.[66]

She also called it "critical thinking" and explicitly contrasted it both to Eichmann's deference toward society and to that chameleonlike modern adaptability in thinking which produces shifts in public opinion so sudden and so widespread as to suggest "that everybody was fast asleep when [they] occurred."[67] *Selbstdenken* is supposed to keep one awake and in touch with reality; and yet Arendt also says that reality is what everyone sees, each from his own, distinct perspective, so that establishing what is real requires checking one's own perceptions against those of others. Political thinking requires "common sense"—by contrast with romantic dreams and philosophical abstraction—yet must resist conformism to public opinion and clichés. Arendt does nothing to resolve these tensions, but she is surely right that thinking as a free citizen does include these apparently incompatible requirements: forming and following one's own judgment, and yet listening to and respecting the opinions of one's fellow citizens.

Arendt's most central and persistent remedy for all the forms of thoughtlessness, however, is realism, which we already encountered as a characterological trait. Her persistent quest for realism began in the neighborly love of her dissertation and her revulsion against Heidegger's professional blindness. It continued in her critique of Varnhagen's parvenu and romantic illusions and in her fascination in *The Origins* with bourgeois hypocrisy and those repelled by it. It informed her attack in *The Human Condition* on the blindness to reality of *homo faber,* the *animal laborans,* and Marx, and it culminated in the diagnosis that in modernity "thought and reality have parted company," leaving the former empty and our conduct thoughtless.[68]

Most striking of all is what Arendt says about ideological illusions—deliberately imposed policies of unreality to which those who impose them eventually themselves fall victim. The topic is central to totalitarianism, which so disorients people and makes them doubt their own capacity to perceive reality that they become desperate for the security apparently offered by ideology's "entirely fictitious world." The same "aura of systematic mendacity" and widespread "practice of self-deception" formed the background for Eichmann's thoughtlessness.[69] Still later the theme became central to Arendt's diagnosis of America in the era of the Vietnam War—not, of course, as totalitarian, but as exemplifying the post-totalitarian threat of the social.

Arendt depicted Americans as living in a "defactualized world," in which genuine, substantive interests and goals had been almost entirely displaced by the imposition and frantic defense of various "images" and "messages." It was becoming our world of impression management, public relations, scenarios, spin-doctors, sound-bytes, deniability, and credibility; already "image-making [had become] global policy."[70] Surrounded by technocrats—by "scientifically minded brain trusters in the councils of government," who "do not *think*" or "judge" or perceive reality but only "calculate"—and shielded from the real world by layer upon layer of onionlike bureaucracy, the president at the center, supposed wielder of enormous power, is the one most "likely to be an ideal victim of complete manipulation" (108, 37, 9, emphasis in original).

Although the Vietnam War and even the Cold War are long past, it seems to me that the conditions Arendt thus describes have only gotten worse, particularly with the advent of various kinds of "virtual reality" provided by the communications and computer industries, by docudramas and infomercials, and indeed by the whole experience of watching television, playing video games, engaging in computer simulation, and "visiting sites" on the world wide web, activities that children now begin before they can even walk or talk. As Marshall McLuhan presciently argued, the problem is not primarily the content of the new media, nor the opportunity they offer for widespread indoctrination and deception, but the role that watching and "interacting" with them plays in our lives, how it shapes us: "the medium is the message."[71]

Indeed, as Andrew Ross has argued, the content is sometimes rebellious and critical, just as the plethora of television channels and the capabilities of the Internet could in principle be used for purposes of Arendtian politicization, but the effect of these media themselves in people's lives and thinking seems to me stronger and more pervasive than any such messages or uses. Even Ross acknowledges that despite those sitcoms and talk shows that express popular disrespect for experts and officials, the narratives somehow work to reinforce their authority: "In the end, doctors and professors and patriarchs know best."[72] True, people are not taken in, but they behave as though they were.

Václav Havel called it "liv[ing] within a lie." People are not required to believe the lie, but only to live as if they did, for by doing that they "confirm the system, fulfill the system, make the system, are the system."[73] But Arendt suggested that "lie" is a notion inappropriate to the kind of disorientation induced in our world, where cynicism is not just compatible with but actively stimulates deference, withdrawal, and resentful conformity.[74] Virtual reality displaces the very possibility of reality, so that character, institutions, and thought are all shaped in directions that serve the social. As Benhabib remarks, "radio talk shows have not encouraged public deliberation," and it seems to me that even those who think themselves actively engaged against "the system" too often end up fighting merely symbolic battles, diligently enforcing "correct" forms of expression rather than any more substantive changes.[75]

Much of what Arendt called hopeless confusion, it seems to me, has to do with living our lives as if in a virtual rather than the real world, continually refusing our own perceptions and judgments to the contrary. Since this way of thinking greatly interferes with effective action, conditions in the real world get worse, and the gap between thought and reality widens, necessitating ever more illusion. We have much practice in what one is supposed to say (and to refrain from saying), little practice in formulating in words what we really feel or observe. We learn how to "shine it on," how to sound like an expert, how to sound agreeable and uncontroversial, and even how to protest in standardized ways. We do not learn how to tell it like it is, how to bear witness, let alone how to deliberate seriously with others about what really troubles us or them, in a way that might eventuate in shared action. From childhood on, in virtually all our institutions, we reward euphemism, salesmanship, slogans, and we punish and suppress truth-telling, originality, thoughtfulness.

So we continually cultivate ways of (not) thinking that induce the social. What Arendt suggests would instead promote free citizenship is a tough-minded, open-eyed readiness to perceive and judge reality for oneself, in terms of concrete experience and independent, critical theorizing. Understanding what is going on requires an "unpremeditated attentive facing up to . . . reality," swayed neither by personal escapism into a private dream world nor by conformism to public opinion.[76] Such courageous realism is not to be confused with a cynical or behavioralist reductionism in which principles and commitments are dismissed as unreal, nor with a skeptical or deconstructionist denial of objective reality itself. On the contrary, Arendt's realism is like that of Machiavelli "at his best," neither cynical nor hortatory, tough-minded about human weakness and fallibility and about the limits that true necessity sets for politics, yet recognizing the tangible, crucially important achievements of human history. Action, freedom, and justice are as real for her as greed, cowardice, and selfishness, or as bread and air, barbed wire and bombs.[77]

The Lost Treasure

That brings us to the second half of Arendt's account of how our thinking furthers the social: the void in what we think *about*. Besides being thoughtless, we lack the very ideas of action, of politics, of freedom. We use those words, but only as empty clichés, in hortatory and manipulative ways or cynical and reductionist ones. These ideas are not serious for us, not actionable. So our thinking promotes the social also because we cannot even imagine a real alternative. Action and freedom are our lost treasure: forgotten, inadequately articulated, never theorized systematically, desperately difficult to convey to people who lack the relevant experiences.

To restore access to these ideas, Arendt employed several methodological devices, which also illuminate the sort of thinking that encourages free citizenship. The first of these devices is what she called "pearl diving," dredging up from the depths of the past the lost meaning of some crucial term. As the term, which had become a cliché, is restored to lively, actionable meaning, it is like a precious gem, refracting light on contemporary realities we had missed. Arendt quoted Shakespeare's *Tempest*: "Full fathom five thy father lies. . . ."[78] She was trying, she said, "to discover the real origins of traditional concepts in order to distill from them anew their original spirit which has so sadly evaporated from the very key words of political language—such as freedom and justice, authority and reason, responsibility and virtue, power and glory—leaving behind empty shells."[79]

Most words, however, do not have an identifiable "real origin" nor any "original meaning" that scholarship can recover. Linguists simply trace a word's ancestry back from one language to another until the evidence runs out. Furthermore, Arendt never made clear why the earlier meanings of words should be authoritative for us, and indeed for some words, such as "society" and "revolution," she preferred the modern to the earlier meaning.

Arendt's "pearl diving" thus remains ambiguous. It can be understood in two distinct ways, with radically different implications for thinking and the social: as authoritative scholarly research or as a mode of empowerment accessible to everyone. On the first reading, Arendt is one more expert, a scholar of ancient languages who teaches the rest of us what a word "originally" meant and therefore still ought to mean, issuing an authoritative definition to which we are expected to submit. As chapter 8 suggested, Arendt is particularly drawn to this mode of presenting her work when she doubts her own authority and wants to fend off any possible objections in advance. Paradoxically, this way of explicating the lost treasure actually teaches unthinking deference, and thus is likely to promote the social.

On the second reading, however, what is to be retrieved is not a word's original meaning but, as in the passage quoted above, its "original spirit," which I take to mean the spirit of origins, the creative capacity of speakers, employed in a word's "origin" but also in every subsequent extension of its meaning. A word, as Arendt wrote late in her life, "*is something like a frozen thought that thinking must unfreeze.*"[80] Young-Bruehl reports that Arendt also sometimes called her enterprise "conceptual analysis," a phrase suggesting that it involves not a historical but a contemporary investigation, within the capabilities of any thoughtful person.[81] Etymological information can sometimes help, as can a knowledge of history that reveals the real political struggles, with real winners and losers, which shaped the meanings of words that we inherit. But ultimately the task of unfreezing meanings must be accomplished by each speaker for himself, by "a kind of pondering reflection" that, as Arendt notes, produces neither definitions nor any other "results" and yet can deeply alter one's relationship to one's own language, so that, for example, "somebody who had pondered the meaning of 'house' might make his own look better."[82]

In this sense a "lost" aspect of meaning is valuable insofar as it is not (really) lost but still preserved in the implicit regularities of our own contemporary language—regularities we observe in our speaking but of which we may well lack conscious awareness. The missing aspect of meaning thus is not lost so much as neglected, hidden, suppressed, whether by personal neurosis or by widely shared ideology, and kept hidden by thoughtlessness. That we all have such tacit knowledge which we practice but cannot easily make explicit is a commonplace of both linguistics and psychoanalysis. When such knowledge is brought to awareness, it becomes available to active, intentional use or critique. So atrophied powers are invigorated and we gain access to "lost" parts of ourselves and our world.

Thus it is not because ancient Greek is somehow better or more authoritative than modern English that we benefit from attending to the meaning of *polis*, as we might from discovering the meaning of some revealing Chinese or Shoshone concept, but because, as Arendt says, "the Greek *polis* will continue to exist at the bottom of our political existence—that is, at the bottom of the sea—for as long as use the word 'politics,'" or (one might add) words such as "policy," "police," "polite," and so on.[83] As noted in chapter 11, Arendt was not entirely clear about this, but she was surely right to maintain simultaneously both that in language "the past is contained ineradicably" and also that (aspects of) meaning get "lost" and their recovery can constitute a "treasure."[84] Here what ratifies the value of recovered meaning is the authority not of the scholar but of the individual speaker; "pearl diving" in this sense involves not the deference but the autonomous judgment of ordinary people, and thus facilitates not the social but free citizenship.

Arendt's second device for restoring the ideas of agency and politics was what she called "storytelling," the narration of some particular, concrete life or deed. By contrast with the empty abstractness of philosophy, large-scale historiography, and social science, storytelling invites the listener or reader to identify with the hero and thus to share vicariously in an agent's experience instead of adopting "the standpoint of the spectator."[85]

As one of the epigraphs to the chapter on action in *The Human Condition*, Arendt chose a line by Isaak Dinesen: "All sorrows can be borne if you put them into a story or tell a story about them."[86] She praised storytelling because it reveals "meaning without committing the error of trying to define it," brings about consent to and "reconciliation with things as they really are," allows "a specific content" or particular "individual experiences [to be] generalized without being falsified," and conveys—as generalization never can—who a particular individual uniquely is.[87] In an unpublished paper delivered at the annual meeting of the American Political Science Association in 1960, Arendt even referred to her own work as "my old-fashioned storytelling."[88]

It should not be surprising, then, that she has recently been widely interpreted as fundamentally a storyteller herself—an interpretation that to me nevertheless seems untenable.[89] One difficulty is that although stories can indeed reconcile us to reality, they can also function in the opposite way, as an escape and a distraction. The Blob, after all, is a fiction. Our problem of the social does not seem to be diminished by people's intense engagement in television dramas or their fascination with public figures' private lives. The Arendt who so praised storytelling also warned against this pervasive interest in personal matters and noted that stories can foster withdrawal into a "dreamland."[90] Even as she praised storytelling for reconciling people to "things as they really are," she also interpreted a line from Dinesen—"Be loyal to the story"—as meaning "Be loyal to life, *don't create fiction* but accept what life is giving you" (97, my emphasis). At the minimum, then, reading Arendt as basically a storyteller would require some accounting of her committed realism. It may be possible to reconcile the idea of storytelling with the precept "don't create fiction," but it is not easy.[91]

The real difficulty in interpreting Arendt as a storyteller, however, is that—to put it bluntly—that was not what she did. Much as she admired Dinesen and enjoyed telling stories to her friends and students, Arendt's writing did not take the form of tales, novels, plays, or (published) poetry. Certainly she narrated some lives, notably those of Varnhagen and Eichmann, as well as those of some thinkers on whom she wrote interpretive essays. Certainly she enriched her political theorizing with illustrative stories, quotations from plays and poetry, references to mythology, and imaginative metaphors, as all great political theorists have done. She also made extensive use of history, which can be construed as a kind of narration.

Still, it seems obvious to me that Arendt's major works are not themselves stories but, as she said, political theory. She did indeed, as chapters 6 and 8 argue, seek a way of abstracting that allows the experience of individual action to be "generalized without being falsified," as storytelling also does. She did indeed, as Lisa Jane Disch says, want theory "grounded . . . in experience."[92] In her unpublished APSA paper Arendt remarked that "no matter how abstract our theories may sound . . . , there are incidents and stories behind them which, at least for ourselves, contain as in a nutshell the full meaning of whatever we have to say."[93] But clearly she did not conclude from this wise observation that there is no need to theorize, that one might do better simply to narrate the relevant incident and forget the theory.

Pearl diving and storytelling were among Arendt's tools, but they were not her primary work. Her main device for restoring access to the lost treasure was neither etymology nor narration but, quite simply, explicit theorizing about that treasure, its nature, the reasons for its loss, and the possibility of its recovery. Unlike her friend Walter Benjamin, from whom the idea of pearl diving derived and who engaged in it because "he was not much interested in theories," Arendt believed that explicit theorizing was needed, particularly in our time, when "the concrete and the general . . . have parted company."[94] More of the concrete by itself is not enough, not even stories of concrete action. What we need is a rejoining of concrete and general, local and large-scale, commitment and prediction. The problem is reconciling these logically incompatible perspectives into a single, realistic understanding of oneself in the world, oneself in relation to other people.

Thus we might add to Arendt's list of modes of thought conducive to free citizenship the dialectical thinking briefly introduced in chapter 11: thought that is able to entertain competing perspectives in an intellectual ordering that does not obliterate their tension. Indeed, one might develop Arendt's notions of representative thinking, opinion, and judgment along such lines.

Like pearl diving in the sense of investigating one's own concepts and like storytelling, political theorizing too is an activity of which all are capable. Not that everyone can or should write books, of course, but theorizing—that is, formulating generalizations from one's own experience and thinking critically about inherited assumptions—is within everyone's reach. Arendt endorsed Jaspers's wholly unprofessional outlook on philosophizing, which echoes Socrates: "Both philosophy and politics concern everyone."[95] And so once again it comes back to us, Dear Reader, and to the task of thinking about our thinking: whether the social might be an increasing problem because of what or how we (don't) think. Perhaps we have trained ourselves and each other *not* to think, because if we did we might have to change the way we lead our lives. Perhaps we think in such abstracted, pseudo-objective ways that we cannot even imagine what we most lack. If so, we need to find modes of thought more conducive to action and politics: ways of keeping our abstractions connected to common sense and to ourselves, ways of becoming more reflective and critical, ways of imagining ourselves as agents and of putting ourselves in the place of even distant or obnoxious others without losing track of our real selves, ways of facing up to reality, no matter how unpleasant.

These, then, are three fundamentally different approaches to the social: institutional, characterological, and ideational. Yet we have already seen how interdependent they are, that the paths intersect. Institutions are simply widespread, stable patterns of individual conduct, which depends on character; both institutions and character depend on thinking. Thinking is shaped by experience, which is channeled by institutional practice. These are distinct aspects of a single, continuous reality. So even as we seek institutions, or character patterns, or ideas conducive to action and politics, we must also examine any policy suggested along one path for its potential consequences for the other paths. What is likely to be the institutional effect of a proposed change in ideas? How well do institutional changes to facilitate political action fit with those that might promote courageous and responsible character? There are likely to be some trade-offs and hard choices, and how we go about things may matter as much as—may even be inseparable from—what we set out to do.

The formidable array of conditions conducive to the social—from the global economy, population pressure, and high technology, through conformism and resentful victimhood, to our paralyzing cynicism and hopelessness—are enough to make anyone yearn for rescue by some superhuman force. It may seem that the only way to get what we are doing back under some degree of control is through a wise and benevolent world dictator, efficiently deploying the rest of us as robots. But that yearning is, of course, part of the social: the paternal rescue fantasy corresponding to the maternal Blob. Not only are such fantasies of an isolated "strong man" who will shape the rest of us as one shapes "other 'material'" illusions, as Arendt says, but in yearning for them we mistake the nature of our problem.[96] The social is not a condition of inert immobility, nor an inability to produce collective consequences. We are very much in motion, already interrelated, as if organized by a Blob, and daily producing global consequences. So not just any collaborative activity will be what we need.

One might even argue that we should do less rather than more, that our frantic activism and craving for mastery are among the sources of the social, and that the remedy lies in letting things be, simplifying, disengaging. But disengaging from one's place and time is no easy matter; everything depends on what constitutes letting be or simplification. One cannot just stop doing, period; one needs something else to do instead; and if the doing less or otherwise is to have any significant effect, it must be widely shared, organized. In short, even doing less or refusing mastery must take the form of concerted action if it is to help us.

Although the social means a collectivity not taking charge of what it is doing, it also and more fundamentally means the absence of politics where politics could and should be. The alternative is not just movement—not even coordinated movement—but shared self-government, public freedom. Even if a benevolent world dictator commanding perfect obedience were a realistic possibility, he could not restore *our* action, *our* taking charge, nor could he bestow freedom on us.

The Fourth Path: "Just Do It!"

The depressing sense of hopelessness that results from examining the array of conditions in our lives conducive to the social and inhibiting free citizenship is partly an artifact of the way we have been examining those conditions. There is something else to be said, something so far omitted from consideration, not exactly an additional fact or condition but another perspective on what we have seen: a fourth and final path into the thicket of the social. It would be ironic indeed if a study criticizing Arendt for having mystified the social were to end with only the three unmystified approaches we have examined, for each and all of them still miss what is most valuable in her theorizing. Stopping with these three paths would amount to throwing out Arendt's achievement along with her unfortunate Blob. So we must add one more approach, akin to the outlook of existentialism, which we shall call the path of "Just do it!"

We have been discussing the lost ideas of action, politics, and freedom, but discussing them in the same manner as we discussed institutional arrangements and character structure: as possible explanations for the social, suggesting possible remedial policies. These are certainly relevant to politics, but they still lack the existential impetus that might carry us across the conceptual gap between the spectator's outlook and that of the engaged citizen. A political approach must include not just thinking *about* action but thinking *as* an actor: not as a hypothetical world dictator magically imposing an ideal policy but as one free citizen among others, whose joint commitment and effort will be required for accomplishing the right sort of changes.

The fourth approach to the problem of the social, then, is not one more rival explanation or policy prescription but more like an essential supplement to any and all of the other approaches, more about how they are to be employed than an alternative to them. If one puts the perspective of the agent at the center, then the only "explanation" of the social one needs or can have is that we aren't (yet) doing anything to diminish it. And the only "policy" that can help bring about free politics is to start enacting it. As an explanation of how we are getting in our own way and as a prescription for what we should do, this obviously is not much help. As a way of persuading people to act and use their capacities, it is just about useless. Yet as a supplement to explanations and policy suggestions it is essential, if our goal is free politics or diminishing the social. For this fourth approach reminds us that whatever we may learn along the other paths will have to be enacted by and among people, not imposed on inanimate material or cattle, because this particular goal can only be achieved by enlisting people's action, inducing their own free citizenship. Action, as Arendt insists, has no causes. That is a logical or conceptual point: to look on human conduct from the perspective of agency is to see (some of) that conduct as *originating* in the agent "whose" action it is, so that he deserves the credit or the blame, unlike a storm, a chemical process, or the movements of a puppet. That is why she says that, from the perspective of explanation and policy prescription, action always "looks like a miracle."[97] The agent is by definition an unmoved mover, the inexplicable origin of something uncaused, even though we know that from a different perspective action does not exist and that every apparent action also has a causal history and an intended goal. If politics is concerted action, then, the kind of "taking charge" it involves will be very different from *homo faber*'s efficient technical mastery of materials. The basic political question remains "What shall we do?" and both the "do" and the "we" are always problematic, contestable, continually being (re)constituted.

Approaching the social by the fourth path reminds us that the various conditions discovered along the other paths are, singly and in combination, neither necessary nor sufficient to displace the social or assure free politics, though they can indeed facilitate or hinder, invite or discourage, aid or inhibit. They are not necessary because the social is a matter of degree, not a metaphysical transformation, and the human capacities for action and judgment cannot be lost. We learn that truth from the Resistance; we learn it from popular rebellions and revolutions; we learn it from social movements; we learn it from the story of Anton Schmidt: action can never be ruled out. Whether one inquires conceptually—about the meaning of agency—or historically—about past times and places where previously apolitical people in large numbers have begun to engage actively in a concerted effort to direct their shared fate—the result is the same: there can be no absolute prerequisite to freedom. We are always already free-to-become-free. Or at least, since there is no guarantee of success, we are always already free-to-begin-moving-toward-freedom, free-to-enlarge-the-degree-of-our-freedom, both individually and collectively. A public arena already institutionalized may facilitate action, but concerted action can also create arenas. Courage and responsibility may be conducive to action, but often we only discover our real capacities in action. Awareness of what action and freedom really are may help, but one of the best ways to gain such awareness is through experiencing them.

Similarly, no set of facilitating conditions is sufficient to produce action or assure free citizenship. No conceptualization or theorizing can guarantee their remembrance; no institutions can assure their continuation; no type of character suffices to make people free agents, because freedom is not something that can be caused, given, or imposed. It has to be taken, chosen, exercised, enacted, if it is to exist at all. Nothing can guarantee its coming into existence except doing it; nothing can make it endure except continuing to do it.

These matters are too often discussed today in terms of "resistance" and "identity," located in "civil society," and contrasted to government and politics.[98] Though Arendt began from Jewish identity and resistance to the Nazis, it seems to me that she was right to move beyond them toward a more general theory of active citizenship and to identify such citizenship with politics. Resistance to unjust power is surely important, and there may be need for it in any collectivity. But it retains a conceptual division between "they," who have power and are guilty, and ourselves, who resist their initiatives but are not in charge. The problem of the social, however, is that people *are* power without *having* it, that even the "powerful," whose decisions affect hundreds of thousands, are unable to alter the inertial drift as long as everyone keeps doing as we now do.

One may have to begin with resistance, but it is not the goal, is not enough. Seeking to force "them" to change "their" government and policy does not yet recognize that government and policy as (potentially and properly) ours, everyone's concern. And though, under conditions of the social, the beginnings of free action are very likely to take place outside of the formal institutions of government, thus in "civil society," they surely are political if they aim at redirecting, taking some charge of the collectivity. When, as Tocqueville said of France in the 1830s, the officially political institutions of government are devoid of "political life itself," so that in them all is "languor, impotence, stagnation, and boredom," then it may happen that elsewhere, among those excluded or withdrawn, "political life beg[ins] to make itself manifest."[99] Such unofficial political life is not merely resistance—negative or defensive—but instead, as Char said about the French Resistance, "a public realm" where free citizens address the real "affairs of the country."[100] Thus Arendt was right to insist, with Tocqueville, that what we need is politicization, the arousal of now subjected, withdrawn, or irresponsible people to their own real capacities, needs, and responsibilities. Politicization here implies neither increased managerial intrusion into people's personal lives nor dutiful submission to official authorities, but, on the contrary, responsible and effective participation in self-government that addresses people's real troubles and needs.

Reviewing the conditions of our world along any of the first three paths into the thicket of the social, we noted, can be discouraging, suggesting that we have become entrapped in a vicious cycle. The conditions we would need for escaping it are precisely what we lack: institutions reflect character, character reflects ideas, ideas emerge out of praxis, everything depends on everything else, and here we are, deep in the social. The fourth path into the thicket reminds us that, precisely because everything depends on everything else and because freedom has no absolute preconditions, any step in the right direction—be it institutional, characterological, or ideational—can have further, widening effects, enlarging the space for freedom. Where one steps forward, others may follow. Where one speaks the truth, others may recognize it and take heart to do the same. The only place to begin is where we are, and there are a hundred ways of beginning, as Arendt says, "almost any time and anywhere," because action "is the one activity which *constitutes*" our public, shared world.[101] Once we do begin, moreover, we may find others already under way, may discover all sorts of organizations and movements—be they about ecology, feminism, disarmament, torture, human rights, or nuclear power—movements locally generated but aimed at public responsibility and power.

Too hortatory and idealistic? Out of keeping with this book's stress on dialectical balance and on the seriousness of the problem of the social? Yes, of course. But that is because we have been pursuing the fourth path in isolation, when it is actually an essential supplement to the others. Blind activism is no help—no more than impotent thought. Political action requires realism, responsibility, thoughtfulness about conditions and trends, possibilities and policies, ends and means, and only then does it also require something more. Though Arendt calls action a miracle, if you wait for your own action to befall you, it will not; you have to just do it. Others may or may not join you. Your action and the others may or may not succeed in extending freedom rather than furthering the social. There are no guarantees. But who will do it if we do not? Reversing our present drift into the social is everyone's task, and one we must do together. That follows from recognizing that the social is not a Blob. The task is not slaying an alien monster but reconstituting ourselves: reorganizing institutions, reforming character, contesting ideas. That may not be easy, but it can never become impossible. We are depressingly the problem; we are encouragingly the solution.

Now, to say that the social is no Blob and that we could at any time begin reappropriating our freedom is not to say that we *will* do so. Myself, I'm a pessimist; have been all my life. Still, one mustn't let one's pessimism interfere with doing what one can. Above all, I think, we must not abandon the project, the effort, the hope. It's up to us; that means you and me, Dear Reader. Here we are, in the social. What do you say?

Notes

Chapter One

1. Hannah Arendt, *The Human Condition* (1974).
2. Dagmar Barnouw, *Visible Spaces: Hannah Arendt and the German-Jewish Experience* (1990), p. 22. Actually the Barnouw passage refers to Arendt's view of mass culture, which is not quite the same thing as the social.
3. Arendt, *Human Condition,* pp. 323, 5.
4. *The Blob* (1958), a Paramount release of a Jack H. Harris production, directed by Irvin S. Yeaworthy, screenplay by Theodore Simonson and Kate Phillips. Other films of this genre in the period include *Attack of the Crab Monsters* (1957), an Allied Artists release of a Roger Corman production (he also directed); *Attack of the Fifty-Foot Woman* (1958), an Allied Artists release of a Bernard Woolner production, directed by Bernard N. Hertz; *The Brain Eaters* (1958), an American International release of an Edwin Nelson production, directed by Bruno Ve Sota; *The Brain from Planet Arous* (1958), a Favorite Films release of a Jacques Marquette production, presented by Howco International, directed by Nathan Hertz; *The Creeping Unknown* (1956), a United Artists release of an Anthony Hinds production, directed by Val Guest; *The Creature from the Black Lagoon* (1954), a Universal release of a William Alland production, directed by Jack Arnold; *The Creature Walks Among Us* (1956), a Universal release of a William Alland production, directed by John Sherwood; *The H-Man* (1959), a Columbia release of a Toho production, produced by Tamoyuki Tanaka, directed by Inoshire Honda; *Invaders from Mars* (1953), a Twentieth Century Fox release of an Edward L. Alperson production, directed by William Cameron Menzies; *The Invasion of the Body Snatchers* (1956), an Allied release of a Walter Wanger production, directed by Don Siegel; *The Invisible Invaders* (1959), a United Artists release of a Premium Pictures presentation, produced by Robert E. Kent, directed by Edward L. Cahn; *It Came from Outer Space* (1953), a Universal release of a William Alland production, directed by Jack Arnold; *It Came from Beneath the Sea* (1955), a Columbia release of a Charles H. Schneer (Clover) production, directed by Robert Gordon; *The Mysterians* (1959), a Metro release of a Toho production, produced by Tamoyuki Tanaka, directed by Inoshire Honda; *Rodan* (1957), a DCA (Japan) distribution of a Toho production, produced by Tamoyuki Tanaka, directed by Inoshire Honda; *The Thing* (1951), an RKO release of a Howard Hawks production, directed by Christian Nyby; *The Thing from Another World* (1951), an RKO (B & W) release of a Howard Hawks production,

directed by Christian Nyby; *This Island Earth* (1955), a Universal release of a William Alland production, directed by Joseph Newman; and *The War of the Worlds* (1953), a Paramount release of a George Pal production, directed by Byron Haskin.

5. Naomi R. Goldenberg, *Returning Words to Flesh* (1990); Susan Sontag, "The Imagination of Disaster" (1986); Michael Paul Rogin, "*Kiss Me Deadly*" (1987). See also Andrew Ross, *No Respect* (1989).

6. Goldenberg, *Returning*, pp. 8–10. See also Sontag, "Imagination," pp. 215, 219–24; Rogin, "*Kiss Me*," pp. 258, 264–66.

7. Goldenberg, *Returning*, pp. 7–8, 14–15; Sontag, "Imagination," pp. 224–25; Rogin, "*Kiss Me*," pp. 238, 262.

8. Sontag, "Imagination," pp. 224–25; Goldenberg, *Returning*, p. 9; Rogin, "*Kiss Me*," p. 263.

9. Rogin, "*Kiss Me*," pp. 239, 265. This is also the theme of Andrew Griffin, "Sympathy for the Werewolf" (1984), pp. 646–51.

10. Goldenberg, *Returning*, p. 9. See also Sontag, "Imagination," pp. 215, 219, 224–25; Griffin, "Sympathy," pp. 649–51.

11. Arendt, *Human Condition*, p. 2.

12. This being a study of Arendt's use of the words "society" and "social," I have tried not to use these words at all in my own substantive arguments, in order to avoid confusion. Occasionally I use "culture" instead, in the anthropological sense of that word; more often I substitute the phrase "human collectivity," which seems slightly more neutral and general than "community," "group," "polity," or other such terms.

13. For a recent example, see Bernard Yack, *The Longing for Total Revolution* (1992).

14. Thomas Hobbes, *Leviathan* (1978), p. 19.

15. On saying "we," consult Elisabeth V. Spelman, *Inessential Woman* (1988), chap. 3: "Simone de Beauvoir: Just Who Does She Think 'We' Is?" pp. 57–79; Herbert Speigelberg, "On the Right to Say 'We' " (1973).

16. Georg Lukács, *History and Class Consciousness* (1971).

17. Max Horkheimer and Theodore W. Adorno, *Dialectic of Enlightenment* (1972), p. 29. See also pp. 32–36.

18. Franz Kafka, "A Little Fable," in *Franz Kafka: His Complete Stories* (1948), p. 445; Hanna Fenichel Pitkin, "Rethinking Reification" (1987), p. 263.

19. Arendt, *Human Condition*, p. 3.

20. Ibid., pp. 23, 27–28. See also Hannah Arendt, *Between Past and Future* (1969), p. 199. The social, thus, is one of those concepts—like revolution but unlike politics, the public, and freedom—whose "original" or "earliest" meaning does not govern its "true" meaning for Arendt.

21. Arendt, *Human Condition*, p. 33. See also pp. 38, 43, 56.

22. Ibid., p. 46. See also pp. 29, 45.

23. Ibid., p. 46. See also p. 45.

24. Ibid., p. 44 n. Arendt is quoting Gunnar Myrdal, *The Political Element in the Development of Economic Theory* (1953), pp. 194–95.

25. Arendt, *Human Condition*, p. 40.

26. Ibid., pp. 257, 38. See also pp. 59, 61.

27. Ibid., pp. 209, 31, 126. But cf. the ambiguous "it is frequently said that ... ," p. 126; "last stage," p. 40; "final stage," pp. 45, 60; and particularly p. 134.

28. Margaret Canovan, *The Political Thought of Hannah Arendt* (1974).

29. Elisabeth Young-Bruehl, *Hannah Arendt* (1982); Elzbieta Ettinger, *Hannah Arendt Martin Heidegger* (1995); Hannah Arendt, *The Jew as Pariah* (1978). Canovan does not significantly extend her analysis of the social in her more recent *Hannah Arendt: A Reinterpretation of her Political Thought* (1992), pp. 116–22.

30. Young-Bruehl, *Hannah Arendt*; Judith N. Shklar, "Hannah Arendt as Pariah" (1983), 65–77; Ann M. Lane, "The Feminism of Hannah Arendt" (1983), 101–17; Elisabeth Young-Bruehl, "From the Pariah's Point of View," in *Mind and the Body Politic* (1989); Barnouw, *Visible Spaces*; Jennifer Ring, "The Pariah as Hero" (1991), 433–52; Jacques Taminiaux, *La fille de Thrace et le penseur professionel* (1992); Lisa Jane Disch, *Hannah Arendt and the Limits of Philosophy* (1994); Ettinger, *Hannah Arendt*; Bonnie Honig, ed., *Feminist Interpretations of Hannah Arendt* (1995); Dana R. Villa, *Arendt and Heidegger* (1996); Seyla Benhabib, *The Reluctant Modernism of Hannah Arendt* (1996); Larry May and Jerome Kohn, eds., *Hannah Arendt: Twenty Years Later* (1996); Richard J. Bernstein, *Hannah Arendt and the Jewish Question* (1996).

31. Benhabib, *Reluctant Modernism*, pp. 23, 29.

Chapter Two

1. Hannah Arendt, *Rahel Varnhagen* (1974), pp. xiii, xx; Elisabeth Young Bruehl, *Hannah Arendt* (1982), pp. 91, 299.

2. Arendt, *Rahel Varnhagen*, p. 3. Heinrich Schnee has pointed out that Arendt suppressed the closing lines of Varnhagen's deathbed speech, lines in which she identified herself with the suffering of Jesus, said she felt he was her brother, admired the suffering of Mary, remarking that it would have been beyond her own strength to bear, and asked God to forgive her weakness. Heinrich Schnee, review of *Rahel Varnhagen* (1960), 458–59. The suppressed passsage does indeed show that Varnhagen did not regret or revoke her conversion, but Arendt was surely right that in the end Varnhagen was no longer a parvenu. She accepted and affirmed as a "nexus of destiny" *both* her Jewish birth *and* her conversion, undertaken originally for parvenu reasons but no longer so held. There may be other inaccuracies or distortions in Arendt's account of Varnhagen as well. Compare Heidi Thomann Tewarson, *Rahel Levin Varnhagen* (1988).

3. Arendt, *Rahel Varnhagen*, p. 3. Compare Young-Bruehl, *Hannah Arendt*, p. 86.

4. Arendt, *Rahel Varnhagen*, p. 3.

5. The terms "pariah" and "parvenu" used in this context are borrowed from Bernard Lazare, *Job's Dungheap* (1948), a collection of his essays that Arendt edited and for which she wrote a brief introductory biography of Lazare. See Hannah Arendt, *The Jew as Pariah* (1978), p. 32.

6. Arendt, *Rahel Varnhagen*, p. 199.

7. Richard J. Bernstein, *Hannah Arendt and the Jewish Question* (1996), p. 33.

8. Arendt, *Rahel Varnhagen*, p. 7.

9. Gisela T. Kaplan, "Hannah Arendt: The Life of a Jewish Woman" (1989), p. 78; Arendt, *Rahel Varnhagen*, p. 201.
10. Arendt, *Rahel Varnhagen*, p. 213.
11. Ibid., p. 220. See also p. 85.
12. Arendt, *Jew as Pariah*, p. 107.
13. Ibid., p. 87; Arendt, *Rahel Varnhagen*, p. 224.
14. Arendt, *Rahel Varnhagen*, p. 216.
15. Ibid., p. 25. See also pp. 9, 224.
16. Ibid., pp. 217–18. See also p. 13.
17. Ibid., p. 225. See also p. 205.
18. Ibid., p. 23. See also p. 177; Arendt, *Jew as Pariah*, p. 82.
19. Arendt, *Rahel Varnhagen*, p. 177.
20. Ibid., pp. 117, 209, 208. It therefore seems to me misleading to regard the salons, as Benhabib does, as a "public sphere"; they were, rather, as she also says, a "social space"; Seyla Benhabib, *The Reluctant Modernism of Hannah Arendt* (1996), pp. 14–15, 29.
21. Arendt, *Rahel Varnhagen*, p. 213.
22. Ibid., p. 222. Compare pp. 7, 30 on the possibility of a "political" alternative.
23. Ibid., pp. 201, 215, 224, emphasis in original. Varnhagen wanted "to be esteemed as a peer" *of the aristocrats,* to be sure, not of all her fellow-citizens equally; indeed, she wanted to be "a princess." One could argue that in fact citizen equality and mutuality were what she needed, and thus "really" wanted, but Arendt would have scorned such psychologizing.
24. Ibid., pp. 222–23. Bracketed insertions in Varnhagen's text are by Arendt.
25. Ibid., p. 94. See also p. xvi.
26. For an example of the latter sense, see ibid., p. 33: "*mauvais société.*"
27. Ibid., pp. 222–23. This is the only passage in *Rahel Varnhagen* juxtaposing society to the state—a contrast which might seem to parallel that between the parvenu strategy and "political struggle . . . the other possibility" but does not, as we shall see; ibid., pp. 7, 177.

Chapter Three
1. Hannah Arendt, *Rahel Varnhagen* (1974), pp. xv, xvi.
2. See chapter 2, note 2.
3. Hannah Arendt, *Men in Dark Times* (1969), p. 98.
4. Arendt, *Rahel Varnhagen*, p. xviii.
5. Hannah Arendt, *Essays in Understanding, 1930–1954* (1994), p. 6; Günter Gaus, *Zur Person* (1964), p. 19; Jeanette M. Baron, "Hannah Arendt: Personal Reflections" (1980), p. 58.
6. Arendt, *Essays*, p. 8; my translation from Gaus, *Zur Person*, p. 20.
7. Arendt, *Essays*, pp. 6–7; my translation from Gaus, *Zur Person*, pp. 19–20.
8. Arendt, *Essays*, p. 8; my translation from Gaus, *Zur Person*, p. 21.
9. Elisabeth Young-Bruehl, *Hannah Arendt* (1982), pp. 33–34; Wolfgang Heuer, *Hannah Arendt* (1987), p. 15.
10. Elzbieta Ettinger, *Hannah Arendt Martin Heidegger* (1995), p. 103.

11. Young-Bruehl, *Hannah Arendt*, p. 23.
12. Ettinger, *Hannah Arendt*, p. 2.
13. Young-Bruehl, *Hannah Arendt*, p. 14.
14. Heuer, *Hannah Arendt*, p. 13. See also Arendt, *Essays*, p. 17; Gaus, *Zur Person*, p. 28. Concerning the absence of prejudices, cf. also Arendt's remarks on Rosa Luxemburg's childhood and "Jewish family background": Arendt, *Men in Dark Times*, p. 41.
15. Heuer, *Hannah Arendt*, p. 21; Arendt, *Essays*, pp. 2–3, my translation from Heuer, *Hannah Arendt*, p. 16; Young-Bruehl, *Hannah Arendt*, pp. 272–73. The denial of interest in the woman question is all the more striking because Arendt early published a review of a book on that topic. See chapter 8, note 22, below.
16. Heuer, *Hannah Arendt*, p. 7; Young-Bruehl, *Hannah Arendt*, pp. 27–28; Gaus, *Zur Person*, p. 20; Arendt, *Essays*, p. 7.
17. Ettinger, *Hannah Arendt*, p. 18.
18. Arendt, *The Jew as Pariah* (1978), pp. 241, 245–46.
19. Gaus, *Zur Person*, p. 21; Arendt, *Essays*, p. 8; Heuer, *Hannah Arendt*, p. 17.
20. Hannah Arendt, "Martin Heidegger at Eighty" (1971), p. 51.
21. Heuer, *Hannah Arendt*, p. 7.
22. Ettinger, *Hannah Arendt*, p. 14.
23. Heuer, *Hannah Arendt*, p. 20; Young-Bruehl, *Hannah Arendt*, p. 50; Friedrich Georg Friedmann, *Hannah Arendt* (1985), p. 114.
24. Ettinger, *Hannah Arendt*, p. 17.
25. Ibid., p. 30. Apparently not recognizing the source of these lines, which Arendt of course quoted in German, Ettinger translates them back into very prosaic English.
26. Young-Bruehl, *Hannah Arendt*, p. 463.
27. Arendt, *Essays*, p. 22; Gaus, *Zur Person*, p. 31. See also the much earlier letter (March 25, 1947) to Jaspers; *Hannah Arendt Karl Jaspers Correspondence, 1926–1969* (1992), trans. Robert and Rita Kimber, p. 79; *Hannah Arendt Karl Jaspers Briefwechsel, 1926–1969* (1985), p. 116. I have sometimes used the Kimber translation, sometimes done my own. For the reader's convenience I cite page references in both, using *Correspondence* and *Briefwechsel* as the short titles from here on.
28. Young-Bruehl, *Hannah Arendt*, p. 46.
29. Heuer, *Hannah Arendt*, p. 50, quoting a letter to Blücher, March 1, 1950; Ettinger, *Hannah Arendt*, p. 28, quoting a letter to Kurt Blumenfeld, February 8, 1950.
30. Arendt and Jaspers, *Correspondence*, p. 142; *Briefwechsel*, p. 178; to Jaspers, September 29, 1949.
31. Arendt and Jaspers, *Correspondence*, p. 457; *Briefwechsel*, p. 494; to Jaspers, November 1, 1961.
32. Young-Bruehl, *Hannah Arendt*, pp. 75–76, 218–219; Heuer, *Hannah Arendt*, pp. 23–25; Hannah Arendt, "What Is Existence Philosophy?" (1946), pp. 34–56.
33. Hannah Arendt, *Love and Saint Augustine* (1996), pp. 28, 39, 94–95,

98–100. The original dissertation was published in Berlin in 1929 by J. Springer. An English translation prepared by E. B. Ashton in 1963 was subsequently revised by Arendt.

34. Ibid., p. 97, and pp. 94–98, passim.

35. Ibid., p. 93. See also p. 67.

36. Ettinger, *Hannah Arendt*, p. 30; Hannah Arendt, *The Origins of Totalitarianism* (1973), p. 301; Hannah Arendt, *Willing* (vol. 2 of *The Life of the Mind* [1978]), pp. 104, 136, 144.

37. Heuer, *Hannah Arendt*, p. 25; Karl Jaspers, *Provokationen: Gespräche und Interviews* (1969), p. 120. Gordon A. Craig says that the Varnhagen study was intended to become Arendt's *Habilitationschrift*, the research project prerequisite to a teaching post at a German university, but his only support for this claim is that in 1966 Arendt applied for compensation from Germany as a victim of Nazi persecution on the basis that the Nazis' coming to power had interrupted her career as an academic. Jaspers supported the application with an affidavit stating that she had completed the basic requirements for habilitation, and her application was eventually approved. Gordon A. Craig, "Letters on Dark Times" (1993), p. 10. See also Dagmar Barnouw, *Visible Spaces* (1990), p. 30. Whatever Arendt's intentions when she began the Varnhagen study, the difficulties her first husband encountered in his effort at habilitation, partly due to anti-Semitism, must have apprised her of the obstacles in her way in 1933, if she was not already aware of them in 1929 or 1930. Young-Bruehl, *Hannah Arendt*, pp. 56, 77, 80–81; Arendt and Jaspers, *Correspondence*, pp. 7, 14; *Briefwechsel*, pp. 43, 50; to Jaspers, July 24, 1929, Jaspers to Arendt, November 16, 1931. Compare also Arendt's view of Rosa Luxemburg as leaving academic life after completing her dissertation because "she couldn't stand the injustice *within the world.*" Melvin A. Hill, ed., *Hannah Arendt* (1979), p. 311.

38. Young-Bruehl, *Hannah Arendt*, pp. 56, 77.

39. Ibid., pp. 67–71, 77–78; Ettinger, *Hannah Arendt*, p. 27.

40. Ettinger, *Hannah Arendt*, p. 75.

41. Young-Bruehl, *Hannah Arendt*, p. 79.

42. Arendt, *Essays*, pp. 10–11; Gaus, *Zur Person*, p. 23.

43. Arendt, *Essays*, p. 9; my translation from Gaus, *Zur Person*, p. 21.

44. Her choice of topic may have been influenced by the fact that her friend Hans Jonas, also a Jew, was writing on Augustine; Young-Bruehl, *Hannah Arendt*, pp. 59, 66. Arendt's teachers, Heidegger, Jaspers, and Romano Guardini, had all written on Augustine as well; Patrick Boyle, S.J., "Elusive Neighborliness" (1987), p. 84.

45. Arendt, *Essays*, p. 4; Gaus, *Zur Person*, p. 17.

46. Young-Bruehl, *Hannah Arendt*, pp. 70–71, 91, 98–99; Arendt and Jaspers, *Correspondence*, p. 197; *Briefwechsel*, p. 234; to Jaspers, September 7, 1952. Hannah Arendt and Kurt Blumenfeld, —*in keinen Besitz verwurzelt: Die Korrespondenz/Hannah Arendt, Kurt Blumenfeld* (1995), pp. 97–98, Arendt to Blumenfeld, May 24, 1954.

47. Arendt, *Essays*, p. 10; my translation from Gaus, *Zur Person*, p. 22. Young-Bruehl, *Hannah Arendt*, p. 108. Note that "four years prior" means 1929, the year in which Arendt began work on Varnhagen.

48. Arendt, *Essays*, p. 10; my translation from Gaus, *Zur Person*, p. 20.
49. Heuer, *Hannah Arendt*, pp. 29–30; Arendt, *Essays*, p. 5, my translation from Gaus, *Zur Person*, pp. 17–18; Hill, *Hannah Arendt*, p. 306.
50. Heuer, *Hannah Arendt*, p. 28; Young-Bruehl, *Hannah Arendt*, pp. 59–62, 69; Philippe Lacoue-Labarthe, *Heidegger, Art, and Politics* (1990), pp. 19, 25, 25 n, 124; Friedmann, *Hannah Arendt*, p. 115.
51. Arendt, *Essays*, pp. 10–11; Gaus, *Zur Person*, p. 22.
52. Arendt, *Essays*, p. 11; my translation from Gaus, *Zur Person*, p. 23.
53. Arendt, "Martin Heidegger at Eighty," p. 54; Hannah Arendt, *Lectures on Kant's Political Philosophy* (1982), p. 22.
54. Young-Bruehl, *Hannah Arendt*, pp. 304, 443. See also p. 327.
55. Erich Heller, *The Importance of Nietzsche* (1988), p. 159.
56. Arendt, *Essays*, pp. 11, 14–15, my translation from Gaus, *Zur Person*, pp. 23, 25; Arendt, *Rahel Varnhagen*, p. 10; Young-Bruehl, *Hannah Arendt*, pp. 57, 88.
57. Arendt, *Essays*, p. 11; my translation from Gaus, *Zur Person*, p. 23.
58. Heuer, *Hannah Arendt*, pp. 27, 18, emphasis in original; Young-Bruehl, *Hannah Arendt*, pp. 109, 119. Later Arendt modified the precept; Arendt, *Men in Dark Times*, pp. 17–18.
59. Hannah Arendt, *Jew as Pariah* (1978), p. 89; Arendt, *Essays*, p. 12; my translation from Gaus, *Zur Person*, p. 23.
60. Young-Bruehl, *Hannah Arendt*, pp. 124 ff.
61. Ettinger, *Hannah Arendt*, pp. 34–35.
62. Martin Heidegger, *Being and Time* (1962), sec. 27, pp. 163–68. For general analyses of Arendt's use and critique of Heideggerian ideas, see particularly Jacques Taminiaux, *La fille de Thrace et le penseur professionel* (1992), and Dana R. Villa, *Arendt and Heidegger* (1996).
63. Heidegger, *Being and Time*, p. 164. Note that the capitalization of "Others" is the translator's; in German all nouns are capitalized. Arendt's view is not entirely fair to Heidegger, who does say that *das Man* "can become concrete in various ways in history," p. 167. Hubert L. Dreyfus says that Heidegger began to think historically, about the distinctive characteristics of our time, precisely in the early 1930s; Hubert L. Dreyfus, "Heidegger and Foucault on the Ordering of Things," unpublished essay, p. 9. On some of the difficulties of *das Man*, see Hubert L. Dreyfus, *Being-in-the-World* (1991), chap. 8.
64. Arendt, "What Is Existence Philosophy?" pp. 46–47.
65. Arendt, *Essays*, p. 32. See also p. 35.

Chapter Four

1. Hannah Arendt, *The Jew as Pariah* (1978), p. 82 n. 3. The former image is from Kafka and is discussed further in the text at note 11, below.
2. Elisabeth Young-Bruehl, *Hannah Arendt* (1982), p. 160; Arendt, *Jew as Pariah*, p. 59.
3. Personal communication to Sara M. Shumer.
4. Arendt, *Jew as Pariah*, pp. 59–60. Compare Hannah Arendt and Kurt Blumenfeld, *—in keinen Besitz verwurzelt: Die Korrespondenz/Hannah Arendt, Kurt Blumenfeld* (1995), p. 62, Arendt to Blumenfeld, August 6, 1952.

5. Young-Bruehl, *Hannah Arendt*, pp. 153–55, quoting a letter by Arendt to *Midstream* magazine (1962), p. 87.
6. Arendt, *Jew as Pariah*, pp. 76, 60.
7. Ibid., pp. 77–78. The first phrase Arendt quotes from Bernard Lazare, *Job's Dungheap* (1948), p. 66; see also pp. 44, 65, 85.
8. Young-Bruehl, *Hannah Arendt*, p. 120.
9. Arendt, *Jew as Pariah*, p. 60.
10. Hannah Arendt, *The Human Condition* (1974), p. 41.
11. Arendt, *Jew as Pariah*, p. 82.
12. Sara Mayhew Shumer has spoken of this as "alienated power": "Arendt: Power/Alienated Power" (1990). See also C. Douglas Lummis, *Radical Democracy* (1996), p. 40. For a different view see Paul Thomas, *Alien Politics* (1994); and for a more Blobbish account consult Michel Foucault, *Power/Knowledge: Selected Interviews and Other Writings* (1980).
13. Arendt, *Jew as Pariah*, pp. 76–77.
14. Hannah Arendt, *Rahel Varnhagen* (1974), p. 222.
15. Arendt, *Jew as Pariah*, p. 90.
16. Concerning Chaplin, see ibid., p. 69 n. 1.
17. The category here also includes accepting a limited ghetto or bohemian life, "calmly enjoying the freedom and untouchability of outcasts": ibid., p. 90. Note also p. 82, "a society of pariahs."
18. Arendt, *Rahel Varnhagen*, p. 4.
19. Arendt, *Jew as Pariah*, p. 76.
20. Arendt, *Rahel Varnhagen*, p. 120.
21. Arendt, *Jew as Pariah*, p. 150.
22. See Hanna Pitkin, "Slippery Bentham" (1990), esp. pp. 117–18.
23. Hannah Arendt, *Men in Dark Times* (1969), p. 17; Arendt, *Jew as Pariah*, pp. 125, 148; Hannah Arendt, *The Origins of Totalitarianism* (1973), p. xv; Young-Bruehl, *Hannah Arendt*, pp. 109, 124; Melvin A. Hill, ed., *Hannah Arendt* (1979), p. 334.
24. Arendt, *Jew as Pariah*, pp. 76–77, 128.
25. For an excellent real-world examination of such problems of Jewish identity under Naziism, see Kenneth Jacobson, *Embattled Selves* (1994).
26. Arendt, *Jew as Pariah*, p. 128.
27. Young-Bruehl, *Hannah Arendt*, pp. 171, 173, 179, 183, 224–33; Richard J. Bernstein, *Hannah Arendt* (1996), pp. 109–22.
28. Arendt, *Jew as Pariah*, p. 186.
29. For example, ibid., p. 90.

Chapter Five
1. On the genealogy of the concept of totalitarianism before Arendt, see Jeffrey C. Isaac, *Arendt, Camus, and Modern Rebellion* (1992), pp. 39–42. On the centrality of the holocaust for *The Origins*, see also Seyla Benhabib, *The Reluctant Modernism of Hannah Arendt* (1996), pp. 64–65. On the late addition of the Soviet Union to *The Origins*, see Margaret Canovan, *Hannah Arendt* (1992),

pp. 17–23; Richard J. Bernstein, *Hannah Arendt and the Jewish Question* (1996), pp. 197–98 n. 4.

2. Hannah Arendt, *On Revolution* (1977), p. 113; my emphasis.

3. Hannah Arendt, *The Origins of Totalitarianism* (1973), p. 66.

4. Arendt clearly derives this understanding of the motive for anti-Semitism from what she calls Alexis de Tocqueville's "great discovery" in *The Old Regime and the French Revolution* about the resentment generated by privilege unaccompanied by function; ibid., p. 4.

5. Elisabeth Young-Bruehl, *Hannah Arendt* (1982), pp. 179–80, quoting from Hannah Arendt, "Can the Jewish-Arab Question Be Solved?"

6. Arendt, *Origins*, pp. 54, 301.

7. Ibid., pp. 68, 80, 81. See also p. 72.

8. Ibid., p. 83. See also p. 66.

9. Ibid., p. 61. In the crucial chapter on Continental imperialism, however, Arendt blames this on the pan-movements instead; ibid., p. 229.

10. Ibid., p. 81. But cf. also p. 55, where Arendt claims that in Europe social anti-Semitism "had little influence on the rise of political antisemitism."

11. Hannah Arendt, *Rahel Varnhagen* (1974), pp. 217, 213, 210.

12. For Kant's distinction, see Immanuel Kant, *Critique of Pure Reason* (1990), pp. 252–56, 299–317; Immanuel Kant, *Critique of Judgment* (1987), pp. 9–12; Immanuel Kant, *Foundation of the Metaphysics of Morals* (1959), pp. 55–56.

13. Arendt, *Origins*, p. 455, does recognize the paradox that "man's 'nature' is only 'human' insofar as it opens up to man the possibility of becoming something highly unnatural, that is, a man."

14. Ibid., pp. 125, 137. Later Arendt will argue that the idea of process itself derives from human action, but in *The Origins* it clearly stands for the opposite of action, the inhuman natural. Compare Hannah Arendt, *The Human Condition* (1974), pp. 232–33; Hannah Arendt, *Between Past and Future* (1969), p. 168.

15. Arendt, *Origins*, p. 125.

16. Ibid., p. 192. Arendt evidently has Africa in mind, and her own prejudices clearly show through these passages. It is obvious that her intent is to combat all racism; nevertheless, she simply shares the European prejudice against so-called primitive cultures as somehow less cultured or more natural—in a pejorative sense—than the European.

17. Arendt, *Human Condition*, p. 40. Like the principle of expansion, unobjectionable in economics but deadly as a political aim, administrative hierarchy and efficiency are desirable for certain purposes. The problem arises only with bureaucracy "as a form of government," a substitute for politics; *Origins*, p. 216.

18. Arendt, *Origins*, p. 214.

19. Ibid., p. 216. For convenience and clarity I have melded what Arendt says about these two groups, although she in fact speaks sometimes only of one or the other of them, sometimes of both together. I detect no important difference in her argument about the two.

20. Ibid., p. 218. See also p. 211.

21. Ibid., p. 196. Arendt's complex use of "nation" and "nationalism" in this book deserves a study in its own right. See esp. pp. 125–26, 227–31.

22. Ibid., p. 193, quoting C. W. de Kiewiet, *A History of South Africa, Social and Economic* (1941), p. 19.

23. Arendt, *Origins*, p. 194.

24. Ibid., pp. 107, 10, 189. But cf. p. 337, where the mob is "the underworld *of* the bourgeois class" (my emphasis).

25. Ibid., p. 150. See also p. 326.

26. Ibid., p. 351. Note that Arendt herself invokes adolescent rebellion, pp. 107, 155.

27. Ibid., pp. 151, 206, 189, quoting Carl Peters (possibly the model for Conrad's Mr. Kurtz in *The Heart of Darkness*) from Paul Ritter, *Kolonien im deutschen Schrifttum* (1936), preface.

28. Arendt, *Origins*, pp. 331, 354. See also p. 108 and cf. p. 201, where Arendt finds a "mob element among the Jewish people."

29. Ibid., pp. 10, 317, 326–27, 337, 351. But cf. pp. 156–57, where the "mass" seem to be "a mob."

30. Ibid., p. 317. Note the unusual use of "social."

31. Ibid., p. 311. See also pp. 317, 326.

32. Ibid., p. 315. See also p. 318.

33. Ibid., pp. 138, 150. It is important to recognize that in tracing totalitarianism's "origins," Arendt emphatically does not mean to invoke causation in history, at least not in the sense of "causes that inevitably lead to certain effects"; Hannah Arendt, "Totalitarianism" (1958), p. 1, quoted in Bernstein, *Hannah Arendt*, p. 133. See also Hannah Arendt, *Essays in Understanding, 1930–1954* (1994), p. 319. Nevertheless, Arendt herself of course sometimes speaks of historical events as "caused by" something (e.g., Hannah Arendt, *The Jew as Pariah* [1978], p. 137, Arendt, *On Revolution*, p. 76), though surely without meaning to imply inevitability. See also chapter 10, n. 57, below.

34. Arendt, *Origins*, p. 169; the passage concerns specifically the German bourgeoisie. Compare Arendt, *Rahel Varnhagen*, p. 180: the "customs, habits and values of the nobles dominated bourgeois society."

35. Arendt, *Origins*, p. 338. See also pp. 156, 334.

36. Ibid., p. 333. See also pp. 331, 335, 337.

37. Wolfgang Heuer, *Hannah Arendt* (1987), p. 49.

38. Arendt, *Origins*, p. 460.

39. Ibid., p. 445. See also pp. 411, 417.

40. Ibid., p. 404. So totalitarianism must not be confused with authoritarianism; they involve "diametrically opposed" principles. Ibid.

41. Ibid., p. 366. See also p. 376.

42. Ibid., pp. 396, 399. See also p. 400.

43. Ibid., pp. 402, 430; Arendt, *Between Past and Future*, pp. 99–100.

44. Arendt, *Origins*, p. 447.

45. Ibid., p. 348. See also pp. 412, 362.

46. Ibid., pp. 61, 229. See also p. 472.

47. Ibid., p. 438, quoting David Rousset without further identifying the source, presumably *Les Jours de notre mort* (Paris, 1947); my translation. Arendt

says that ideology means spinning out "the logic of an idea" and that, though it pretends to scientific certainty, it is not really "a body of statements about something that *is*." Instead, it projects a goal too abstract to be attainable; thus ideology means commitment to endless "process" for its own sake. Ibid., p. 469.

48. Ibid., p. 438. Compare Young-Bruehl, *Hannah Arendt,* pp. 204, 206, quoting Arendt's unpublished December 10, 1948, draft "Memo: Research Project on Concentration Camps."

49. Arendt, *Origins,* p. 458.

50. Ibid., p. 438. See also p. 455.

51. Ibid., p. 452. See also p. 447.

52. Ibid., p. 457. See also pp. 412, 427, 458.

53. Ibid., p. 459. The idea of radical evil reappears in *The Human Condition,* but it is no longer identified with the threat we face now, "the social"; Arendt, *Human Condition,* p. 241.

54. Arendt, *Origins,* p. 443.

55. Arendt, "Totalitarianism," p. 1, cited in Bernstein, *Hannah Arendt,* p. 133.

56. Compare Hannah Arendt, *Was ist Politik?* (1993), pp. 14–15.

Chapter Six

1. In 1952 Arendt applied in these terms for a Guggenheim grant; Elisabeth Young-Bruehl, *Hannah Arendt* (1982), pp. 276–79.

2. Jeffrey C. Isaac, *Arendt, Camus, and Modern Rebellion* (1992), pp. 38–44; Margaret Canovan, *Hannah Arendt* (1992), pp. 19–23.

3. For example, Zbigniew Brzezinski and Samuel P. Huntington, *Political Power USA/USSR* (1964); William Walter Rostow, *The Stages of Economic Growth* (1960).

4. Young-Bruehl, *Hannah Arendt,* pp. 164–66.

5. Hanna Arendt and Karl Jaspers, *Correspondence* (1992), pp. 30–31; *Briefwechsel,* (1985), pp. 66–67; to Jaspers, January 29, 1946. The italicized phrase is in English in the original.

6. Hannah Arendt, *The Jew as Pariah* (1978), p. 158.

7. Arendt and Jaspers, *Correspondence,* p. 30; *Briefwechsel,* p. 66; to Jaspers, January 29, 1946. Later Arendt would argue that precisely because America lacked a shared ethnicity and heritage, it was all the more free, held together only "through the strength of mutual promises." Hannah Arendt, *Crises of the Republic* (1972), p. 87.

8. Arendt and Jaspers, *Correspondence,* p. 31; *Briefwechsel,* p. 67; to Jaspers, January 29, 1946. See also Young-Bruehl, *Hannah Arendt,* pp. 209–10.

9. Arendt and Jaspers, *Correspondence,* p. 137; *Briefwechsel,* p. 173; to Jaspers, June 3, 1949. By 1963 Arendt thought that "fear of revolution has been the hidden *leitmotif* of postwar American foreign policy"; Hannah Arendt, *On Revolution* (1977), p. 217.

10. Young-Bruehl, *Hannah Arendt,* pp. 274–75.

11. Arendt and Jaspers, *Correspondence,* pp. 210–11; *Briefwechsel,* pp. 246–47; to Jaspers, May 13, 1953.

12. Arendt and Jaspers, *Correspondence,* p. 215; *Briefwechsel,* p. 251; to

Jaspers, May 13, 1953. The italicized phrase is in English in the original. See also Hannah Arendt, *Was ist Politik?* (1933), p. 133.

13. Young-Bruehl, *Hannah Arendt,* p. 280; Hannah Arendt, "Europe and America: Dream and Nightmare" (1954), pp. 551–54; Hannah Arendt, "Europe and America: Europe and the Atom Bomb" (1954), pp. 578–80; Hannah Arendt, "The Threat of Conformism" (1954), pp. 607–10.

14. Arendt, "Threat of Conformism," p. 609.

15. Ibid.; Arendt and Jaspers, *Correspondence,* pp. 211, 213, 249; *Briefwechsel,* pp. 247, 249, 285; to Jaspers, May 13, 1953, October 6, 1954.

16. Arendt and Jaspers, *Correspondence,* p. 249; *Briefwechsel,* p. 285; to Jaspers, October 6, 1954.

17. Arendt and Jaspers, *Correspondence,* pp. 235–36; *Briefwechsel,* p. 272; to Jaspers, December 21, 1953.

18. Arendt and Jaspers, *Correspondence,* pp. 263–64; *Briefwechsel,* pp. 300–301; to Jaspers, August 6, 1955.

19. Young-Bruehl, *Hannah Arendt,* p. 171.

20. Arendt, *Jew as Pariah,* pp. 148, 183. Compare Arendt's critique of Jean-Paul Sartre, *The Origins of Totalitarianism* (1973), p. xv.

21. Young-Bruehl, *Hannah Arendt,* p. 183, quoting Hannah Arendt, "Can the Jewish-Arab Question Be Solved?" Arendt vigorously opposed the Herut Party of Menachim Begin as racist and mystifying; Young-Bruehl, *Hannah Arendt,* p. 232.

22. Arendt, *Jew as Pariah,* p. 193.

23. Young-Bruehl, *Hannah Arendt,* p. 229. These phrases are included among passages Young-Bruehl quotes from Arendt's "To Save the Jewish Homeland" but do not appear in the published article.

24. Arendt, *Jew as Pariah,* pp. 181.

25. Arendt, *Origins,* p. 290.

26. Young-Bruehl, *Hannah Arendt,* p. 298, quoting a letter to Blücher, November 5, 1956.

27. Young-Bruehl uses this phrase as the subtitle of her biography. Arendt and Jaspers, *Correspondence,* p. 264; *Briefwechsel,* p. 301; to Jaspers, August 6, 1955.

28. Hannah Arendt, *The Human Condition* (1974), p. 6. See also Arendt, *Was ist Politik?* pp. 14, 29–31, 70–71, 85, 124.

29. Young-Bruehl, *Hannah Arendt,* p. 212.

30. The exact date of the preface is not known to me.

31. Hannah Arendt, *Between Past and Future* (1969), p. 3. On the importance to Arendt of her own brief clandestine anti-Nazi activity, see Hannah Arendt, *Essays in Understanding, 1930–1954* (1994), p. 5; Günter Gauss, *Zur Person* (1964), p. 18.

32. See, e.g., Gregory D. Sumner, *Dwight MacDonald and the politics Circle* (1996), p. 64; Jean-Paul Sartre, "The Republic of Silence" (1947), pp. 498–500.

33. Arendt, *Essays,* p. 14; Gauss, *Zur Person,* p. 25. Compare Hannah Arendt and Kurt Blumenfeld, *Korrespondenz* (1995), p. 43, Arendt to Blumenfeld, July 19, 1947, and Hannah Arendt, "Introduction," J. Glenn Gray, *The*

Warriors (1967), p. xii, in which Arendt repeats what Gray reports that a Frenchwoman told him after the war: "Anything is better than to have nothing at all happen day after day. You know that I do not love war or want it to return. But at least it made me feel alive, as I have not felt alive before or since." Gray's book is the best treatment of men's nostalgia for war known to me.

34. Arendt, *Between Past and Future*, p. 3.
35. Compare Sartre, "Republic," pp. 488–89.
36. Arendt, *Between Past and Future*, p. 4. See also Sartre, "Republic," p. 488.
37. Arendt, *Between Past and Future*, p. 4.
38. Ibid., p. 151, my emphasis. See also p. 167. The passage is from Shakespeare's *Julius Caesar*, 2.1.
39. Sumner, *Dwight MacDonald*, pp. 64–65, 69, 81; Isaac, *Arendt*, pp. 17, 179. But note that for other members of the *politics* circle such participatory councils were "social," not political, despite the journal's title; Sumner, *Dwight MacDonald*, pp. 28, 32, 172–73.
40. Sumner, *Dwight MacDonald*, pp. 74, 76, 79.
41. Arendt, *Between Past and Future*, p. 27.
42. Ibid., pp. 5–6. Its name, of course, is "freedom," but we no longer understand the meaning of that word, especially its "public" nature; ibid., pp. 149–51.
43. Compare Hannah Arendt, *Men in Dark Times* (1969), p. 30, on the limitations of groups consisting only of the like-minded.
44. Arendt, *Human Condition*, p. 2.
45. See Isaac, *Arendt*, on parallels between Arendt and Camus in this respect, and Sumner, *Dwight MacDonald*, p. 79.
46. Young-Bruehl, *Hannah Arendt*, p. 263, from Bertold Brecht, "Wahrnehmung" (1949).
47. This view is an alternative to the views of those such as Canovan, who argue that Arendt neglected normal politics and "the ordinary business of government," and those such as Isaac, who think her politics entirely a matter of resistance; Margaret Canovan, "The Contradictions of Hannah Arendt's Political Thought" (1978), p. 19; Jeffrey C. Isaac, "Oases in the Desert: Hannah Arendt on Democratic Politics" (1994), pp. 156–67.

Chapter Seven

1. Seyla Benhabib, *The Reluctant Modernism of Hannah Arendt* (1996); Jacques Taminiaux, *La Fille de Thrace et le penseur professionel* (1992); Dana R. Villa, *Arendt and Heidegger* (1996).
2. Suzanne D. Jacobitti, "Individualism and Political Community" (1991), p. 586 n. 3. Jacobitti presents a thorough and insightful comparison of these two theorists' views to which I am much indebted.
3. Hannah Arendt, *The Origins of Totalitarianism* (1973), p. 316, where "America, the classical land of equality of condition . . . , knows less of the modern psychology of masses than perhaps any other country," seems a particularly striking locus for a *Democracy in America* reference if the book had been lively in Arendt's mind. Benhabib says that Arendt "was indebted to" *Democracy in*

America for certain observations in *The Origins* but cites no evidence for this debt; Benhabib, *Reluctant Modernism,* p. 70.

4. Alexis de Tocqueville, *Democracy in America* (1969), pp. 18–19, 50, 196, 503, 506. But America was also "in an exceptional situation," precluding easy transfer of its experience to Europe (p. 455), a point discussed further below.

5. Ibid., pp. 9, 12, 196. See also p. 704.

6. Ibid., pp. 9, 12, 18, 50, 57, 163, 196, 245, 503, 705.

7. Ibid., pp. 697, 702. I leave *liberté* untranslated because of the complexities disguised by the choice a translator must make between "freedom" and "liberty," a choice that was later assigned great importance by Arendt. See my "Are Freedom and Liberty Twins?"

8. Tocqueville, *Democracy,* p. 667. See also pp. 18–19, 196, 245, 671, 695, 702.

9. The systematic difference between volumes 1 and 2 was first called to my attention by Sara Mayhew Shumer. The classical source is Seymour Drescher, "Tocqueville's Two *Démocraties.*"

10. Tocqueville, *Democracy,* p. 95.

11. The former phrase is in ibid., vol. 1, pp. 240, 290; the latter is in vol. 2, p. 517. See also pp. 514, 522; Roger Boesche, *The Strange Liberalism of Alexis de Tocqueville* (1987), p. 126, on Tocqueville's use of the verb *s'associer;* and Mark Reinhardt, *The Art of Being Free* (1997).

12. Tocqueville, *Democracy,* p. 513.

13. Ibid., pp. 263, 285–86. See also pp. 161, 238, 523–24.

14. Ibid., p. 690. See also pp. 645, 667, 689, and Drescher, "Tocqueville's Two *Démocraties,*" p. 202.

15. Tocqueville, *Democracy,* pp. 691, 693. Compare Hannah Arendt, *Crises of the Republic* (1972), p. 178.

16. Tocqueville, *Democracy,* p. 691.

17. Ibid., p. 439. See also pp. 430, 433.

18. Ibid., p. 692. Henry Reeve's translation of *tutélaire* as "tutelary" rather than "protective," as Lawrence has it, seems preferable.

19. Ibid., p. 693. But cf. pp. 668–69, where the anonymous power seems to be "the state." By the time of *The Old Regime,* Tocqueville speaks of this power mainly as "the state," but in a context where he is characterizing not actual developments but the thought of the Economists before 1789. They sought a sovereign power, he says, that "theoretically" resided in the people, but the people were to be an "undiscriminated mass" of individuals "almost exactly alike and unconditionally equal," so that the mass would have been "carefully deprived of any means of controlling or even supervising the activities of the government"; Alexis de Tocqueville, *The Old Regime and the French Revolution* (1955), p. 163. See also pp. 158–62.

20. Tocqueville, *Democracy,* pp. 692–93, 645. See also pp. 614, 638, 670.

21. Compare ibid., pp. 254–56, with pp. 435, 643. But see also pp. 448–49, where public opinion is still associated with "the majority," even in vol. 2. See also pp. 692–93.

22. Ibid., p. 513. See also pp. 667–68.

23. Ibid., pp. 511–12, 522–23, 263.

24. Ibid., pp. 161, 455, 534, 639, 555–58. See also pp. 444, 448, 546, 671, 685.

25. Gustave de Beaumont and Alexis de Tocqueville, *On the Penitentiary System in the United States* (1964), pp. 58–59. See also Thomas L. Dumm, *Democracy and Punishment* (1987), pp. 128–40.

26. Beaumont and Tocqueville, *Penitentiary System*, p. 60.

27. Tocqueville, *Democracy*, p. 195.

28. Ibid., pp. 522, 524, 645. See also p. 521.

29. Ibid., pp. 455–56. The passage concerns intellectual and artistic activity, but the point and the problem are more general.

30. Tocqueville, *Old Regime*, p. 169. See also Tocqueville, *Democracy*, p. 540. Practical experience, however, could enlarge private to public purposes; ibid., pp. 512, 515–17, 522, 525–28, 540.

31. Hannah Arendt, *On Revolution*, (1977), p. 137.

32. Reinhardt, *Art*, pp. 59–89.

33. Tocqueville, *Democracy*, p. 444.

34. Ibid., pp. 291–92. See also pp. 434, 449.

35. Ibid., p. 292. See also p. 449.

36. Ibid., p. 291. See also p. 590.

37. Ibid., pp. 602, 593. Even when the father's house was wealthy and on the civilized eastern seaboard and the husband's was a primitive cabin on the frontier, Tocqueville found the wife "sad but resolute"; ibid., p. 594.

38. Ibid., pp. 361, 363, 342–43, 341. But note that Tocqueville took the Spanish and the English to be distinct "races"; ibid., p. 409. See also Reinhardt, *Art*, p. 196 n. 17.

39. Reinhardt, *Art*, p. 65.

40. For favorable references to Marx, see Hannah Arendt, *The Human Condition* (1974), pp. 44, 159, and perhaps 93. There are also various references to his having been right on some particular point. See also Arendt, *On Revolution*, pp. 54, 61, 69.

41. Elisabeth Young-Bruehl, *Hannah Arendt* (1982), p. 276, quoting from Hannah Arendt, "Project: Totalitarian Elements of Marxism" (ca. winter 1952), to Guggenheim Foundation, Library of Congress.

42. Hanna Arendt and Karl Jaspers, *Correspondence* (1992), pp. 186–87, 205; *Briefwechsel*, (1985), pp. 222–23, 241; Jaspers to Blücher, July 21, 1952, Jaspers to Arendt, Dec. 29, 1952.

43. Karl Marx and Friedrich Engels, *The Marx-Engels Reader* (1979), pp. 134–35, emphasis in original.

44. Melvin A. Hill, ed., *Hannah Arendt* (1979), p. 334; Young-Bruehl, *Hannah Arendt*, pp. 9, 27–28; Hannah Arendt, *Essays in Understanding, 1930–1954* (1994), p. 7; Günter Gauss, *Zur Person* (1964), p. 20.

45. Young-Bruehl, *Hannah Arendt*, pp. 164, 171, 234–36.

46. Arendt and Jaspers, *Correspondence*, p. 205; *Briefwechsel*, p. 241; Jaspers to Arendt, Dec. 29, 1952. Although this passage is actually from a letter written almost two years later than Arendt's "defense" of Marx to Jaspers, quot-

ing it first here seems permissible, since Arendt's letter of defense makes clear that she is responding to an earlier criticism of Marx by Jaspers, presumably Jaspers to Arendt, April 20, 1950; Arendt and Jaspers, *Correspondence*, p. 149; *Briefwechsel*, p. 185. Note that Jaspers ascribes "something analogous to" the "demonic" to Marx despite having himself earlier warned against ascribing "satanic greatness" to the Nazis or a " 'demonic' element to Hitler"; Arendt and Jaspers, *Correspondence*, p. 62; *Briefwechsel*, p. 99; Jaspers to Arendt, October 19, 1946.

47. Arendt and Jaspers, *Correspondence*, p. 160; *Briefwechsel*, p. 196; to Jaspers, December 25, 1950.

48. Arendt and Jaspers, *Correspondence*, p. 163; *Briefwechsel*, p. 199; Jaspers to Arendt, January 7, 1951.

49. Arendt and Jaspers, *Correspondence*, p. 167; *Briefwechsel*, p. 203; to Jaspers, March 4, 1951.

50. Ibid.

51. Arendt and Jaspers, *Correspondence*, pp. 186–87; *Briefwechsel*, pp. 222–23; Jaspers to Blücher, July 21, 1952.

52. Arendt and Jaspers, *Correspondence*, p. 216; *Briefwechsel*, p. 252; to Jaspers, May 13, 1953.

53. Hannah Arendt, *Between Past and Future* (1969), p. 17. See also p. 21.

54. Arendt, *Essays*, p. 445.

55. Arendt and Jaspers, *Correspondence*, p. 137; *Briefwechsel*, p. 173; to Jaspers, June 3, 1949.

56. Arendt, *Human Condition*, p. 79, quoting Benjamin Constant, "De la liberté des anciens comparée a celle des modernes" (1819), reprinted in *Cours de politique constitutionelle* (1872), 2:549.

57. Young-Bruehl, *Hannah Arendt*, p. 277; Arendt, *Human Condition*, p, 79, quoting John Locke, *Second Treatise of Civil Government*, sec. 26.

58. Arendt, *Human Condition*, p. 80.

59. Making is a matter of skill and know-how, whereas doing depends on character, virtue, and (practical) wisdom; making has a goal or purpose outside itself (the object made), whereas doing is its own end or goal; accordingly, the former is assessed by the quality of the object made, the latter by the excellence displayed in the activity itself, so that a workman who does a bad job intentionally is less to be condemned than one who does so from incompetence, whereas in action the person who does wrong intentionally is worse than the one who just doesn't know any better. Aristotle, *Nicomachean Ethics*, 1140 a 1–1140 b 30. Arendt thought that Aristotle did not hold to this distinction consistently; Arendt, *Human Condition*, p. 196. See also pp. 5, 19, 25.

60. Arendt, *Human Condition*, pp. 93, 86, 101.

61. Ibid., pp. 108, 111, 98. See also pp. 255, 321.

62. Ibid., pp. 89, 255. See also pp. 103, 108, 117; Arendt, *On Revolution*, p. 64.

63. Arendt, *Human Condition*, p. 108.

64. Ibid., p. 135. See also pp. 94, 116–17, 137, 321.

65. Ibid., p. 183. See also Arendt, *Between Past and Future*, pp. 30, 32, 77; Arendt, *On Revolution*, pp. 62–64, 250, 255–58.

66. Arendt, *Human Condition,* p. 104, quoting Marx's phrases from *Das Kapital,* 3:873. See also Arendt, *Human Condition,* pp. 87 n, 105; Arendt, *Between Past and Future,* pp. 18, 24–25.

67. Arendt, *Human Condition,* p. 81. Arendt also notes that *Werk* designates the product but not that it designates *only* the product, never the process. There are various other compound nouns on the *Werk-* root, but they correspond more to "craftsman" than to "worker." So for most purposes, *Arbeit* and *Arbeiter* must serve for both "labor" or "laborer" and "work" or "worker," except where "work" is meant in the sense of product. Thus *arbeitslos* translates "out of work," *überarbeitet* translates "overworked," *Arbeiterklasse* translates "working class," and so on.

68. So if anyone was obsessed with labor here, it would have had to be Engels, the translator, not Marx himself, who had little choice about which word to use. But there is nothing wrong with Engels's translation of Marx's *Arbeit.*

69. Arendt, *Human Condition,* pp. 101–2, 306. Nor does it make much sense to claim that Marx's aim was for "the distinction between labor and work [to] have completely disappeared." Ibid., p. 89. See also Arendt, *Between Past and Future,* pp. 18, 24.

70. Marx and Engels, *Marx-Engels Reader,* pp. 71–78. He mentions the *Arbeiter*'s alienation from the product (pp. 71–73) and from the process of production (pp. 73–75), then enumerates four other forms: alienation from nature, from self, from the species, and from other people (pp. 74–78). Philip Birger Hansen is the only Arendt commentator known to me who remarks that she gets Marx wrong on this point, and he does not elaborate. Philip Birger Hansen, *Hannah Arendt* (1993), pp. 37–38.

71. Georg Lukács, *History* (1971); Hanna Fenichel Pitkin, "Rethinking Reification" (1987). There are problems about translating *Entäusserung* and *Entfremdung,* Marx's and Hegel's two words in the same semantic region as the English "alienation." Some translators use "alienation" for the one German word, others for the other, and there are good reasons for either usage. *Entäusserung* is related to *aussen,* which means "outside"; so it means "outering," externalization, projection. *Entfremdung* is related to *fremd,* meaning "foreign" or "strange"; so it means "foreignization," estrangement. But the former term is used in German for alienation of property, the latter for alienation of affections. For a thoughtful discussion, see Martin Milligan, "Translator's Note on Terminology," in Karl Marx, *Economic and Philosophical Manuscripts* of 1844 (n.d.), pp. 10–13.

72. Marx and Engels, *Marx-Engels Reader,* p. 76, emphasis in original. Where Tucker translates "man," with its problematic gendered connotations, Marx of course used *Mensch,* the German word for human being, which is not the same as the word for male human being, *Mann.*

73. Ibid. See also pp. 128–29, 137, 150, 157.

74. Ibid., pp. 76, 85. See also pp. 78, 83, 86.

75. Ibid., p. 92, emphasis in original. See also pp. 78, 85–89, 154, 158; with respect to pleasures see esp. pp. 51, 83–84.

76. Ibid. See also pp. 34–36, 46, 52, 70–73, 87, 93, 223.

77. Karl Marx, *Karl Marx: Selected Writings* (1977), p. 166. See also Marx and Engels, *Marx-Engels Reader,* pp. 43–45, 157, and cf. ibid., p. 136.
78. Marx and Engels, *Marx-Engels Reader,* p. 478.
79. Ibid., p. 93, emphasis in original. See also pp. 71, 160, 292, 376.
80. "Increasingly paradoxical" because it is not clear whether early humans were less dominated by their dependence on nature than they now are by their dependence on money, the market, and each other, or more dominated, or equally dominated. What makes the latter kind of domination and dependence different is that it is collectively self-imposed: nothing constrains us but what we collectively are doing, so that if we could stop . . . . Thus, the proletariat is constituted not by "*naturally existing* poverty, but [by] poverty *artificially produced*"; ibid., p. 64, emphasis in original. The paradox—not helplessness as such—is what makes alienation; ibid., p. 100.
81. Ibid., pp. 72, 163, 100, emphasis in original. See also pp. 71, 292; Marx, *Karl Marx: Selected Writings,* pp. 115, 118; chapter 4, note 12, above.
82. Marx and Engels, *Marx-Engels Reader,* pp. 333–34, 359.
83. Arendt, *Human Condition,* p. 104. See also Arendt, *Between Past and Future,* p. 24. Arendt quotes Marx in German as saying, in *The German Ideology,* that the communist revolution removes, does away with, or sets aside [*beseitigt*] *Arbeit* (Karl Marx, *Die Deutsche Ideologie* in *Gesamtausgabe,* pt. 1, 3:59, quoted by Arendt, *Human Condition,* p. 104 n; see Marx and Engels, *Marx-Engels Reader,* pp. 193, 200). Marx does say that—once—but that locution must surely be read in the light of the other passage she also quotes, where he says *Arbeit* must be *aufgehoben*—that famous word from Hegelian dialectics that means something both ended *and* preserved, because transformed (Marx, *Deutsche Ideologie,* p. 185, quoted in Arendt, *Human Condition,* p. 87 n). One might also cite the *1844 Manuscripts,* where Marx says that in communism, "The category of *Arbeiter* is not done away with, but extended to all men" (Marx and Engels, *Marx-Engels Reader,* p. 82).

Marx does say that in communist society, life will no longer "begin for the [*Arbeiter*] where [*Arbeit*] ceases" (Karl Marx, "Wage Labor and Capital," p. 77, quoted in Arendt, *Human Condition,* p. 89 n). But the context makes perfectly clear that Marx is saying *Arbeit* should be fulfilling rather than debilitating, by contrast with life under capitalism, where people's fulfillment (such as it is) begins only when they get off work. He clearly is not saying that communism will make even leisure-time activities debilitating (Marx and Engels, *Marx-Engels Reader,* p. 205). Marx emphatically does not say, as Arendt claims, that "only when labor is abolished can the 'realm of freedom' supplant 'the realm of necessity.' " The famous passage from vol. 3 of *Capital* that Arendt cites (twice) in support clearly says that freedom begins not where *Arbeit* leaves off but where *that sort of Arbeit* which is "*determined* through want and external utility ceases" (Marx, *Kapital,* vol. 3, in *Marx-Engels Gesamtausgabe,* pt. 2 [1933], p. 873, quoted in Arendt, *Human Condition,* pp. 104, 87 n). Arendt's translation of the passage (p. 104) is correct, better than Tucker's (Marx and Engels, *Marx-Engels Reader,* p. 441), but on p. 87 n. she conveniently elides the modifying clause.
84. Marx and Engels, *Marx-Engels Reader,* pp. 441, 193.
85. Ibid., p. 197. The bracketed insertion is Tucker's.

86. Ibid., pp. 20–21, emphasis in original. Later, of course, Marx begins using the word "democracy" to mean "so-called 'democracy'" and no longer praises it; e.g., ibid., pp. 160–61.

87. Ibid., pp. 197, 223. Marx is thus one of the theorists who translate *zoon politikon* as "social animal," neglecting the distinction that Arendt stresses.

88. Ibid., pp. 160, 163, 398, 413–15, 491, 531.

89. Arendt, *Human Condition*, p. 133. See also p. 131 n; Arendt, *Between Past and Future*, p. 19.

90. Arendt, *Human Condition*, pp. 256–57.

91. Ibid., pp. 111, 209. Perhaps we are only "almost" a laboring society, in the "final stage" of its development; see pp. 31, 45–46, 126, 134. Perhaps Arendt would argue that Marx's false claim was self-fulfilling once people believed it (see also Arendt, *Origins*, p. 349). But such an argument encounters logical difficulties, since the fact that something happens does not prove, even in retrospect, that it was inevitable, like a natural law.

92. Arendt, *Human Condition*, pp. 209–10. The chain of connection is obscure because spread over two pages of dense text, but Arendt seems to be saying that world alienation is greatest in a consumer society, which is the last and most social stage of a laboring society, because people relate only through the market, and even there relate only to the goods exchanged, not to the other people with whom they exchange. This utter isolation and lack of human relationship (which thus *is* world alienation) is what Marx "denounced as . . . dehumanization and self-alienation."

93. Although Arendt sometimes uses the word "world" in the familiar, vaguely totalizing way to mean "everything," for the most part she distinguishes between the earth, or nature, on the one hand, and the world—in the sense of all that is produced, altered, or sustained "exclusively" by human activity—on the other; ibid., pp. 9, 52, 134, 204. Thus, whereas "earth alienation" means thinking and conducting oneself as if one were not of this earth but instead had some hypothetical location in outer space, or nowhere at all (ibid., pp. 1–2, 250–51, 262, 264), "world alienation" is about "flight from" the material culture of humanly made or altered objects and substances and the nonmaterial culture of humanly sustained relationships, institutions, customs, mores, concepts, and civilization in general (ibid., pp. 209–10, 252–57, 264, 301, 308). It can take the form of introspection, abstraction, loss of contact with common sense, or regression from responsibility for the maintenance of the world (ibid., pp. 9, 22, 52, 182–83, 198, 254, 272, 284, 300, 312, 320–21; on the last theme, see also Arendt, *Between Past and Future*, p. 196; Hannah Arendt, *Men in Dark Times* [1969], pp. 4, 7–8, 14, 16, 18–19). It includes the sort of total individual isolation and loss of relationships that leaves people helpless to direct the overall resultants of what they are separately doing, which Arendt calls "the social" and which, this chapter argues, corresponds to Marx's central notion of alienation. At the extreme of the social, we "no longer live in a world at all" (Arendt, *Human Condition*, p. 134). Marx's theory includes no elaboration of anything like the Arendtian idea of "world" (but cf. Marx and Engels, *Marx-Engels Reader*, pp. 87, 92, 136, 326, and particularly 145, the eleventh thesis on Feuerbach).

Seyla Benhabib has noted the debt Arendt's concept of world owes to

Heidegger's, but for Heidegger the world means only humanly produced or altered material objects; Benhabib, *Reluctant Modernism,* p. 108; see also pp. xxviii, 50–56, 104–18. Arendt's account is confusing because inconsistent; sometimes she uses "world" in Heidegger's way (e.g., Arendt, *Human Condition,* pp. 2, 7, 252–57); sometimes to mean only intangible culture, the web of relationships (e.g., ibid., p. 198); and often explicitly to mean both together (e.g., ibid., pp. 22, 52, 182).

94. Arendt, *Origins,* p. 455. See also Marx and Engels, *Marx-Engels Reader,* p. 157, where human life "since the dawn of civilization" appears as "a double relationship," always both "natural" and "social." See also p. 77 in chapter 5, above, on the concept of nature and the natural.

95. Marx and Engels, *Marx-Engels Reader,* p. 86; the capitalization of "Society" is Tucker's; in German all nouns are capitalized.

96. Ibid., p. 321. Marx emphasizes the false, fetishistic nature of their claims on pp. 327, 421, seems to endorse such (or comparable) claims on pp. 323, 335, 413, 422–23.

97. Ludwig Feuerbach, *The Essence of Christianity* (1957).

98. Marx and Engels, *Marx-Engels Reader,* pp. 53–54, 68–70, 72, 143–45. Hence "the criticism of religion is the premise of all criticism"; p. 53. In the earliest writings the humanly created god is money; pp. 50, 52, 93, 103–4. But from *The German Ideology* onward, the gods are the market, capital, and commodities; pp. 163, 292, 319, 321, 376, 422.

99. For Marx, it turns out, the bourgeois political economists were "fetishists" and mystifiers not because they said the market had power and that its regularities functioned *like* natural laws, but because they presented the market and its regularities *as* natural laws, as "a self-evident necessity imposed by Nature," and therefore as not just necessary but eternally necessary, like the law of gravity. Even Marx himself says that the market "*at present* imposes itself *after the manner of* an overpowering natural law," but it is not, and its hitherto necessary laws are now or are about to become changeable; ibid., pp. 327, 413, my emphasis. See also pp. 225, 421; Pitkin, "Rethinking Reification," pp. 270, 279.

100. Marx and Engels, *Marx-Engels Reader,* p. 164. See also pp. 85, 99, 323; cf. pp. 60, 65.

101. About why this revolution will differ fundamentally from all previous revolutions in history, Marx says remarkably little. See ibid., pp. 64, 193, 438, 482, 518, 597.

102. Along the lines, e.g., of Hill, *Hannah Arendt,* p. 335: "Marx did not understand . . . what power really is . . . this strictly political thing." Marx of course would argue that there is no point in preaching to people about what they should strive to do; but how does one distinguish useless preaching from useful scientific teaching in this area? For some of Marx's explicit pronouncements on "politics," see Marx and Engels, *Marx-Engels Reader,* pp. 481, 490, 508, 518–20, 523, 538, 606, 634–35. In later writings, Arendt adopts the familiar—but I think ultimately unhelpful—distinction between a political, "young" Marx and a disappointed, determinist, "old" Marx after 1848; Arendt, *Between Past and Future,* pp. 30, 39; but cf. p. 24. Arendt, *On Revolution,* pp. 61–65.

Chapter Eight

1. Hanna Arendt, *The Human Condition* (1974), pp. 100–101.
2. Ibid., p. 154. The status of art in Arendt's scheme is problematic, since it usually involves material objects, yet surely does express the artist's self and create meaning; see pp. 82 n, 127, 167–69, 184, 210–12, 323.
3. Ibid., p. 23. See also pp. 7, 175, 188, 220, 234.
4. Hannah Arendt, *On Revolution* (1977), pp. 29, 34–36, 41, 126, 203–4, 216, 222–23, 234; Alexis de Tocqueville, *Democracy in America* (1969), p. 240; see also pp. 95, 517, 522.
5. Hannah Arendt, *Willing* (vol. 2 of *The Life of the Mind* [1978]), p. 32, quoting Henri Bergson, *La Penseé et le mouvant* (Paris, 1950), p. 10.
6. Hanna Arendt and Karl Jaspers, *Correspondence* (1992), p. 264; *Briefwechsel* (1985), p. 301; to Jaspers, August 6, 1955. Hannah Arendt, *Essays in Understanding, 1930–1954* (1994), p. 1; Günter Gaus, *Zur Person* (1964), p. 15.
7. Arendt, *Human Condition*, p. 5.
8. Hannah Arendt, *Between Past and Future* (1969), p. 9. This way of presenting the argument oversimplifies, as Arendt also identifies the first turn, to action, with existentialism; ibid., p. 8.
9. Arendt and Jaspers, *Correspondence*, p. 80; *Briefwechsel*, p. 116; to Jaspers, March 25, 1947. Elisabeth Young-Bruehl, *Hannah Arendt* (1982), pp. 25–26.
10. Young-Bruehl, *Hannah Arendt*, pp. 149, 171. Arendt and Jaspers, *Correspondence*, pp. 79–80; *Briefwechsel*, p. 116; to Jaspers, March 25, 1947.
11. Young-Bruehl, *Hannah Arendt*, pp. 150, 171, 234.
12. Arendt and Jaspers, *Correspondence*, p. 79; *Briefwechsel*, p. 116; to Jaspers, March 25, 1947.
13. Young-Bruehl, *Hannah Arendt*, pp. 235–37.
14. Ibid., pp. 246–48; Elzbieta Ettinger, *Hannah Arendt* (1995), pp. 100–102.
15. Ettinger, *Hannah Arendt*, p. 101.
16. Arendt and Jaspers, *Correspondence*, p. 264; *Briefwechsel*, p. 301; to Jaspers, August 6, 1955. Arendt, *Human Condition*, p. 2; see also pp. 231, 324. Hannah Arendt, *Men in Dark Times* (1969), p. 22. On the difference between world and earth, see chapter 7, note 93, above.
17. Hannah Arendt, *Rahel Varnhagen* (1974), p. xviii.
18. Young-Bruehl, *Hannah Arendt*, pp. 230 (quoting an unpublished letter to Judah L. Magnes, August 3, 1948), 238. Arendt, *Essays*, pp. 2–3; my translation from Gaus, *Zur Person*, p. 16. Compare also Arendt's reliance on a friend as spokeswoman in organizing inmates at Gurs, chapter 4, text at n. 3.
19. Young-Bruehl, *Hannah Arendt*, p. 238.
20. Hannah Arendt, *The Jew as Pariah* (1978), p. 108.
21. Hannah Arendt, *Lectures on Kant's Political Philosophy* (1982), p. 28. Note that in German the word here would be *Mensch*, which means "human being" but not specifically "a male."
22. The review, appearing in *Die Gesellschaft* (1932), pp. 177–79, of Alice Rühle-Gerstel, *Das Frauenproblem der Gegenwart: Eine psychologische Bilanz*, is

reprinted in English under the title "On the Emancipation of Women" in Arendt, *Essays,* pp. 66–68. The quoted passages are on p. 66.

23. Young-Bruehl, *Hannah Arendt,* p. 97.

24. Wolfgang Heuer, *Hannah Arendt* (1987), p. 21, quoting a letter to C. Koonz/R. Breidenthal, March 8, 1972.

25. Arendt, *Jew as Pariah,* p. 246.

26. Arendt and Jaspers, *Correspondence,* p. 29; *Briefwechsel,* p. 65; to Jaspers, January 29, 1946.

27. Young-Bruehl, *Hannah Arendt,* p. 273, quoting Arendt's obituary, *New York Times,* December 5, 1975.

28. Hannah Arendt and Kurt Blumenfeld, *Korrespondenz* (1995), p. 94, Arendt to Blumenfeld, November 16, 1953. In the original German text, the words here italicized were in English.

29. Bonnie Honig, *Feminist Interpretations of Hannah Arendt* (1995), p. 4.

30. Young-Bruehl, *Hannah Arendt,* p. 513 n. 54.

31. Arendt, *Men in Dark Times,* pp. 44–45.

32. Ibid., p. 89. See also Arendt, *Human Condition,* p. 257; Arendt, *Men in Dark Times,* pp. 16–17; and the much earlier Arendt, *Jew as Pariah,* p. 75.

33. Compare Hannah Arendt, *The Origins of Totalitarianism* (1978), p. 291. See also Arendt, *Human Condition,* comparing pp. 63–64, 194, which suggest that an arena is prerequisite to action, with pp. 195, 197, 198, which suggest, to the contrary, that it is created by action.

34. Arendt, *Human Condition,* p. 8. The "who" vs. "what" distinction is originally from Augustine; ibid., p. 10 n. 2. See also pp. 175, 178–80, 186, 241.

35. Arendt, *Jew as Pariah,* pp. 77, 68, emphasis in original.

36. Arendt, *Origins,* p. 67; Arendt, *Jew as Pariah,* p. 186. On the Jews' lack of political experience, see Arendt, *Origins,* pp. 83, 117–18, 120, 225, 241, 243, 296–97.

37. Hanna Fenichel Pitkin, *Fortune Is a Woman* (1984), p. 8.

38. For example, Elisabeth V. Spelman, *Inessential Woman* (1988); Denise Riley, *"Am I That Name?"* (1988); Diana Fuss, *Essentially Speaking* (1989).

39. "Many—though not all" is important because of what Gene Marine, an early male convert to feminism, called "Jo Freeman's rule" in honor of Jo Freeman, a psychologist and feminist writer. In her essay "Growing up Girlish" (*trans/action* [November–December 1970]), Freeman pointed out that psychological studies comparing men and women or boys and girls usually result in generalizations that apply to about two-thirds of those tested, which are then written up as characteristically "masculine" or "feminine." Marine remarks, "One-third is one hell of a large minority"; Gene Marine, *A Male Guide to Women's Liberation* (1972), pp. 46–47. The literature to which I refer includes Dorothy Dinnerstein, *The Mermaid and the Minotaur* (1976); Carol Gilligan, *In a Different Voice* (1982); Nancy Chodorow, *The Reproduction of Mothering* (1978); Jessica Benjamin, *The Bonds of Love* (1988). See also Janine Chassequet-Smirgel, ed., *Female Sexuality* (1970); Susan Griffin, *Pornography and Silence* (1981).

40. Gilligan, *In a Different Voice,* pp. 62, 8; see also pp. 42, 51, 157.

Benjamin, *Bonds of Love*, pp. 76, 170, 184–86, 189. See also Nancy Chodorow, "Gender, Relation, and Difference in Psychoanalytic Perspective" (1980).

41. Seyla Benhabib, "The Generalized and the Concrete Other: The Kohlberg-Gilligan Controversy and Feminist Theory," in Seyla Benhabib and Drucilla Cornell, eds., *Feminism as Critique* (1987), p. 86. The former term is from George Herbert Mead, *Mind, Self, and Society* (1955), p. 154, though Benhabib explains that she uses it in a somewhat different sense than Mead does.

42. Jean Piaget, *The Moral Judgment of the Child* (1965), pp. 42–50, 65–76.

43. Arendt, *Men in Dark Times*, p. 177. Unbaptized Jews had been barred from a university career in Germany until after World War I. On the importance to Arendt of the traditional exclusion of women from intellectual life in Judaism, see Jennifer Ring, *The Political Consequences of Thinking* (1997). Compare also Dagmar Barnouw, *Visible Spaces* (1990), pp. 225–26.

44. Seyla Benhabib, *The Reluctant Modernism of Hannah Arendt* (1996), p. 103.

45. Ibid., esp. pp. xxiv–xxviii, 53–54, 104–5, 111, 115; Jacques Taminiaux, *La Fille de Thrace et le penseur professionel* (1992); Dana R. Villa, *Arendt and Heidegger* (1996).

46. Ettinger, *Hannah Arendt*, p. 114. Ettinger cites no source on this page. She explains that she has substituted the word "Marburg" for what she reports was "Freiburg" in the original note, calling Arendt's error "a telling mistake"; Marburg is where Arendt studied with Heidegger, Freiburg where he moved when he ended their affair.

47. Taminiaux, *Fille*, p. 41.

48. Arendt, *Human Condition*, p. 23. See also pp. 32–33, 38, 41. A similar argument is adumbrated in *Origins*, p. 54, but only in passing and only with respect to the concept of equality.

49. See chapter 3, above, notes 62, 63.

50. See Arendt, *Jew as Pariah*, p. 60, where "we refugees" do not "feel entitled to Jewish solidarity."

51. See Eliza Marion Butler, *The Tyranny of Greece over Germany* (1958).

52. Young-Bruehl, *Hannah Arendt*, pp. 304–5, quoting a letter to Kurt Blumenfeld, December 16, 1957. See also Arendt and Jaspers, *Correspondence*, p. 142; *Briefwechsel*, p. 178; to Jaspers, September 29, 1949.

53. Mary Dietz, "Feminist Receptions of Hannah Arendt" (1995), pp. 29, 46 n. 80. Dietz draws the second phrase from Susan Okin ("Reason and Feeling in Thinking about Justice," in *Feminism and Political Theory* [1990], ed. Cass Sunstein, p. 15).

54. Dietz, "Feminist Receptions," p. 29. See also pp. 30, 31. Arendt, *Human Condition*, p. 139 for the internal quotations, though the actual wording there is "the servant of nature and the earth" and "lord and master of the whole earth"; see also p. 157. At the quoted passage Arendt uses the masculine pronoun for the *animal laborans*, which elsewhere is mostly an "it" (but cf. also ibid., p. 112, where both "it" and "his" appear as pronouns for the *animal* in the same sentence).

55. Arendt, *Human Condition*, p. 88. See also pp. 30, 62–63, 71, 106–

7, 115–17. This aspect of birth should not be confused with Arendt's notion of "natality," which she associates with action, not labor. "Natality" Arendt derives from Augustine's view that human beings were created by God (not birthed by a mother!) "so that a beginning might be made," which she reads as referring to the human capacity for initiative. Hannah Arendt, *Love and Saint Augustine* (1966), p. 51; Arendt, *Origins*, p. 479; Arendt, *Human Condition*, pp. 9, 176–77, 247; Arendt, *On Revolution*, p. 211; Arendt, *Willing* (vol. 2 of *Life of the Mind*), pp. 109–10, 217. Later Arendt herself acknowledged that "none of the properties of [the distinctively human kind of] creativity is adequately expressed by metaphors drawn from the life process. To beget and give birth are no more creative than to die is annihilating; they are but different phases of the same, ever-recurring cycle" (Hannah Arendt, *Crises of the Republic* [1972], p. 179). *Giving* birth is labor, and *being* born is not an activity at all. It is, moreover, a characteristic of all mammals, and thus hardly suitable as a metaphor for a distinctively human capacity. Nevertheless, birth is of course a traditional symbol for new beginnings, particularly in Christian theology, where it takes the form either of Jesus' miraculous birth from a virgin or of the "second birth" of conversion (or baptism). Arendt explicitly adopts the latter metaphor for the moment of action, "in which we confirm and take upon ourselves the naked fact of our original physical appearance" on earth (Arendt, *Human Condition*, p. 176). Compare Arendt's dissertation, concerning how Augustine thinks freely chosen membership can replace the given (discussed in chapter 3, above), and Lazare's demand that the pariah take responsibility for his own origins (Arendt, *Jew as Pariah*, p. 77). She attempts to rationalize the metaphor by invoking the Greek distinction between *bios*, the individual human life, and *zoe*, the phenomenon of life in general (Arendt, *Human Condition*, pp. 96–97), but the question is whether both begin with birth, or whether "birth" means the same in both forms of "life." It seems to me that in Arendt's as well as the traditional uses, the metaphor is systematically misleading.

56. Arendt, *Human Condition*, p. 100. Note also that in an essay published while she worked on *The Human Condition* that refers to Vladimir Lenin's remark in *Anti-Dühring* about a postrevolutionary world in which "administration . . . has become so simplified that every cook is qualified to take over its machinery," Arendt uses a feminine pronoun for the cook and adds, "Obviously under such circumstances the whole business of politics . . . could be of interest only to a cook" (Arendt, *Between Past and Future*, pp. 19–20).

57. Arendt, *Human Condition*, p. 100.

58. Ibid., p. 101. On the idea that routine, repetitive tasks of cleaning and repair are particularly seen as feminine responsibilities, see Pat Mainardi, "The Politics of Housework" (1982).

59. Arendt, *Human Condition*, pp. 117, 112, 50–51.

60. Ibid., p. 213, quoting Viktor von Weizsäcker, "Zum Begriff der Arbeit," in *Festschrift für Alfred Weber* (1948), pp. 739–40.

61. Even giving birth is not inherently an isolating experience, as Mary O'Brien points out; Mary O'Brien, *The Politics of Reproduction* (1981), pp. 9–10.

62. Arendt, *Human Condition*, pp. 163, 161; Arendt, *Essays*, p. 3; Gaus,

Zur Person, p. 16. In Gilligan's terms, one might construe an author's concern for the effects of her writing as feminine, insofar as it is a concern for human relationships, but Arendt clearly heard the question, posed to her about her own writing by a male interviewer, as instrumentalist, and hence as based on the outlook of *Homo faber,* and masculine. Recall also Arendt's review of a book on the woman question, where she identified the effective "pursuit of concrete goals" with "the men's front," although at that time she still classified politics dichotomously, as masculine; see note 22, above.

63. Arendt, *Human Condition,* p. 156, quoting Marx, *Das Kapital* 3 *(Marx-Engels Gesamtausgabe,* pt. 2, [Zurich, 1933]), p. 698.

64. Dietz, "Feminist Receptions," p. 30; Arendt, *Human Condition,* pp. 121, 2.

65. Arendt, *Human Condition,* pp. 139, 155, quoting a source she does not name. See also p. 228. Note that mining and lumbering are thus classed as work, not labor, their "violence" attributed to *homo faber;* cf. pp. 100, 103.

66. Dietz, "Feminist Receptions," p. 24.

67. Arendt's dyad, unlike O'Brien's, however, classes society together with nature in opposition to politics, rather than contrasting society to nature.

68. Arendt, *Human Condition,* p. 33 (quoting Gunnar Myrdal, *The Political Element in the Development of Economic Theory* [1953], p. 140).

69. For example, Catherine MacKinnon, *Toward a Feminist Theory of the State* (1989); Catherine MacKinnon, *Feminism Unmodified* (1987); Simone de Beauvoir, *The Second Sex* (1973); Elaine Marks and Isabel de Courtrivon, eds., *New French Feminisms* (1981); Luce Irigaray, *This Sex Which Is Not One* (1985); Gayle Rubin, "The Traffic in Women" (1975), pp. 157–210.

70. Arendt, *Rahel Varnhagen,* p. 199.

71. Riley, *"Am I That Name?"* chap. 3. Prostitution, often called "the oldest profession," might be similarly classified as   helping" or caregiving, and thus social (as in "social disease"), though hardly as hypocritical or oriented toward status.

72. Tocqueville, *Democracy,* p. 692.

73. Andreas Huyssen, "Mass Culture as Woman" (1986), pp. 47, 52–53. See also pp. 47–55, passim, and Andrew Ross, *No Respect* (1989), p. 45.

74. Helmuth Berking, "Mythos und Politik" (1984), pp. 35–41.

75. Michael Rogin, *"Kiss Me Deadly"* (1987), pp. 238, 242. See also p. 258.

76. Ibid., pp. 245, 264–65. See also Andrew Griffin, "Sympathy for the Werewolf" (1984), pp. 649–51.

77. Rogin, *"Kiss Me Deadly,"* p. 26; Ron Rosen, "The House That Levitt Built" (1983), p. 380.

78. The following six paragraphs are based particularly on Benjamin, *Bonds of Love,* Jessica Benjamin, *Like Subjects, Love Objects* (1995), and Dinnerstein, *Mermaid,* but they also owe much to Chodorow, *Reproduction,* and of course to the classics: Melanie Klein, *Envy and Gratitude* (1990); D. W. Winnicott, *The Child, the Family, and the Outside World* (1964); D. W. Winnicott, *The Maturational Process and the Facilitating Environment* (1965); D. W. Winnicott, *Playing and Reality* (1974). See also John Bowlby, *Attachment* (1971); Joseph

Lichtenberg, *Psychoanalysis and Infant Research* (1983); Daniel Stern, *The Interpersonal World of the Infant* (1985).
79. Dinnerstein, *Mermaid,* p. 112.
80. Ibid., p. 187; Benjamin, *Bonds of Love,* p. 206.
81. Dinnerstein, *Mermaid,.* p. 175.
82. Arendt, *Human Condition,* p. 29. See also p. 39.
83. Ibid., pp. 45, 132, 46, 41, 40, 126.
84. I am grateful to Bonnie Honig for initially bringing this point to my attention.
85. As she was completing *The Human Condition,* Arendt began to turn her attention explicitly to the concept of authority itself, and a few years later she located its origins not in Greece but in ancient Rome, a culture considerably more patriarchal—though no more misogynist—than the ancient Greek (Hannah Arendt, "Authority in the Twentieth Century," *Review of Politics* 18 [October 1956]: 403–17; followed by Hannah Arendt, "What Was Authority?" in *Authority,* ed. Carl Friedrich [Cambridge: Harvard University Press, 1959], later reprinted in Arendt, *Between Past and Future*). For the Romans, authority was always derived from the forefathers and tied to the one, singular, original founding of the city of Rome, by contrast to the Greeks, for whom founding a new polis was "an almost commonplace experience" (Arendt, *Between Past and Future,* p. 121; see also pp. 120, 122). Psychologically speaking, assigning the patriarchal role of controlling dangerous feminine force to the Romans would leave the Greeks available as better symbols for Arendt's understanding of action and politics. Still, invoking them as a sponsoring authority for her ideas would continue to raise ambivalence, and their misogyny would remain problematic. In the event, Arendt found a new historical symbol for her idea; instead of a revised, less authoritarian and patriarchal version of the ancient Greeks, she began using the American "founding fathers" to represent a founding whose authority was not patriarchically mystified (Arendt, *Between Past and Future,* p. 140; Arendt, *On Revolution,* p. 204; see also pp. 193, 213–14).
86. Arendt, *Human Condition,* pp. 175, 180–85.
87. Ibid., p. 186. See also p. 36.
88. Arendt, *On Revolution,* p. 281. See also Arendt, *Human Condition,* p. 194.
89. Arendt, *Between Past and Future,* p. 4.
90. Arendt, *Men in Dark Times,* pp. 7–8; Arendt and Jaspers, *Correspondence,* p. 264; *Briefwechsel,* p. 301; to Jaspers, August 6, 1955.
91. C. Douglas Lummis, *Radical Democracy* (1996), p. 27. Lummis is referring to "radical democracy," which may not be the right phrase for Arendtian politics; see Mark Reinhardt, *The Art of Being Free* (1997), pp. 162–66.

Chapter Nine
1. Even the basic contrast of social and political gets shaggy around the edges as we learn that the social has its own characteristic "political form in the nation-state," its own "form of government" in bureaucracy, and even its own characteristic, albeit "perverted," version of " 'acting together' " in lobbying and

pressure politics; Hannah Arendt, *The Human Condition* (1974), pp. 28, 40, 203. See also pp. 29, 45.

2. Ibid., p. 40. See also p. 45.

3. Ibid., pp. 126, 41. See also pp. 219, 322. Actually, what Arendt says on p. 126 is, "It frequently said that" ours is a "consumer society," which "is only another way of saying that" it is a society of laborers; but she continues in a manner strongly suggesting that she herself shares this view.

4. Ibid., pp. 205, 245. Note the internal quotation marks that Arendt puts around "moral standards," rightly suggesting that this is so-called, merely conventional, rather than true morality.

5. See ibid., p. 82 on "the *homo faber* mentality" and Hanna Fenichel Pitkin, "Justice: On Relating Private and Public" (1981), p. 342. See also Melvin A. Hill, ed., *Hannah Arendt* (1979), p. 318; Seyla Benhabib, *The Reluctant Modernism of Hannah Arendt* (1996), pp. 139, 141, 145, 172.

6. Arendt, *Human Condition*, pp. 9, 89, 46, my emphasis.

7. Ibid., p. 209. See also p. 214.

8. Ibid., p. 123. See also pp. 47, 87–88.

9. Ibid., p. 185. See also Hannah Arendt, *On Revolution* (1977), pp. 244, 271; Hannah Arendt, *The Jew as Pariah* (1978), pp. 201–3; Hill, *Hannah Arendt*, pp. 317–20. And see C. Douglas Lummis, *Radical Democracy* (1996), pp. 46, 56: "The economy is . . . political, but pretends not to be," a way of "depoliticizing political power."

10. Arendt, *Human Condition*, p. 219.

11. Ibid., p. 39. Benhabib holds that "the only tenable and productive way of distinguishing the social from the political is in the light of attitudinal orientations"; Benhabib, *Reluctant Modernism*, p. 141. This interpretation, however, then leads her to conclude that the distinction "is untenable"; ibid., p. 172.

12. Arendt, *Human Condition*, p. 157.

13. On labor, ibid., pp. 108, 120; on work, pp. 52, 94, 137.

14. Perhaps it also "produces 'stories,' " as action does. Since behavior is by definition not distinctive, it may not generate any story worth telling, yet Arendt says "*every* individual life . . . can eventually be told as a story," presumably including the life of even the most banal behaving conformist, e.g., Eichmann; Arendt, *Human Condition*, p. 184, my emphasis.

15. Hannah Arendt, *Rahel Varnhagen* (1974), p. xvi. See also p. 94. The topic of guilt by inaction is discussed in Hannah Arendt, "Collective Responsibility," in James W. Bernauer, *Amor Mundi* (1987), pp. 43–45. See also Hannah Arendt, *Eichmann in Jerusalem* (1965), pp. 91, 233, 247; Hannah Arendt, "Thinking and Moral Considerations: A Lecture" (1971), pp. 417–46.

16. Arendt, *Human Condition*, p. 322.

17. Hanna Arendt, *The Origins of Totalitarianism* (1978), pp. 314, 317, 331.

18. Arendt, *Human Condition*, p. 43.

19. Arendt, *Jew as Pariah*, pp. 248–49.

20. Arendt, *Human Condition*, p. 41.

21. Hannah Arendt, *Men in Dark Times*, p. 155. This essay, on Walter

Benjamin, was first published in *The New Yorker* in 1968 as "Walter Benjamin: 1892–1940."

22. Arendt, *Human Condition*, p. 180. See also pp. 176, 178, 213–14.

23. Ibid., pp. 10, 177–81, 186, 211, 241–42.

24. Arendt, *Jew as Pariah*, p. 87. The Kafka passage allows a reading that implies reference to God, though Arendt's use of it does not.

25. Richard J. Bernstein, *Hannah Arendt* (1996), p. 195 n. 21, citing Arendt's unpublished lectures "Some Questions of Moral Philosophy" in the Arendt Archives, Library of Congress.

26. Søren Kierkegaard, *The Present Age* (1962), pp. 60–64, emphasis in original.

27. Arendt, *Rahel Varnhagen*, p. 199.

28. Arendt, *Jew as Pariah*, p. 63.

29. Arendt, *Rahel Varnhagen*, p. 177.

30. Arendt, *Origins*, pp. 328, 334, 362.

31. Hannah Arendt and Karl Jaspers, *Correspondence* (1992), p. 523; *Briefswechsel* (1985), p. 559; to Jaspers, October 20, 1963.

32. Arendt, *Human Condition*, pp. 33, 218.

33. Ibid., p. 47. See also pp. 87–88.

34. On social value as equivalent to "exchange value" on the market, see Hannah Arendt, *Between Past and Future* (1969), p. 33; and Hannah Arendt and Kurt Blumenfeld, *Korrespondenz* (1995), p. 93, Arendt to Blumenfeld, November 16, 1953. One suspects here the influence of Karl Polanyi's *The Great Transformation* (1957), which first appeared in 1944, but though Polanyi was a European refugee who came to America, I have come across no direct evidence that Arendt knew him or read his work. Polanyi's discussion of the rise of the "self-regulating market system" in the nineteenth century greatly resembles Arendt's account of the rise of society. Polanyi, however, opposes what he calls "society" to this self-regulating market system; pp. 3, 71, 186. Prior to the nineteenth century, he maintains, not economic gain but all sorts of "social" motives governed human conduct; pp. 30, 46, 57, 67, 153, 250. Nevertheless Polanyi also says that the new market system led to a new way of conceiving society: as a natural phenomenon "subject to laws" comparable to those of physics or biology; p. 125. Social dislocations resulting from market fluctuations called people's attention to "their own collective being," and from then on "naturalism haunted" their thinking about public affairs; pp. 84, 126. Sometimes Polanyi even speaks of this not as a new way of thinking about society but as "the emergence of society in a new and distinctive sense," and in one chapter title flatly as "the discovery of society"; pp. 84, 103, 111. Polanyi thus is another example of the ambiguities concerning the ontology of society we have seen in Arendt, Marx, and Tocqueville.

35. Arendt, *Human Condition*, p. 165. See also Arendt, *On Revolution*, p. 221.

36. Arendt, *Between Past and Future*, pp. 32–33. This essay was first published in 1954 but is based on a series of 1953 lectures. See also Arendt, *Human Condition*, pp. 164–66.

37. On the concept of civil society in Hegel, see Georg Wilhelm Friedrich Hegel, *Philosophy of Right* (1967), pp. 110, 122–23, 189, 266–67. For the same

in Marx, see Karl Marx and Friedrich Engels, *Marx-Engels Reader* (1979), pp. 26–52, 101, 163, 222.

38. Marx and Engels, *Marx-Engels Reader*, p. 441; the capitalization is the translator's.

39. Arendt, *Human Condition*, p. 28.

40. Ibid., pp. 44 n. 36, 28, 29 n. 13, 33 n. 24. See also p. 165 n. 37.

41. But cf. ibid., pp. 8 n. 1, 39–40, 72 n. 80, where Arendt does see this as a problem.

42. Ibid., pp. 40, 44–45. See also Arendt, *Eichmann*, p. 189; Hannah Arendt, *Crises of the Republic* (1972), p. 29, where she borrows Tocqueville's phrase, "tyranny without a tyrant."

43. Arendt, *Human Condition*, p. 45, my emphasis.

44. The meaning of both "necessity" and "necessary" is sufficiently bifurcated that the *Oxford English Dictionary* groups their various senses (each assigned an arabic numeral) into two broad "branches" (each assigned a roman numeral). (Actually, there are three branches, but the third is minor and obsolete.)

45. Arendt, *Human Condition*, pp. 117, 135, 30, my emphasis. For other passages on necessity (not in the index), see pp. 7, 13, 25, 30–32, 64–65, 72–73, 83, 87, 97–99, 111, 115–17, 119, 177, 234, 255, 317.

46. Roberto Mangabeira Unger, *False Necessity* (1987). See also Margaret Canovan, *Hannah Arendt* (1992), p. 23 on "pseudo-natural processes."

47. Arendt, *Between Past and Future*, p. 170: "It is disaster, not salvation, which always happens automatically and therefore always must appear to be irresistible."

48. Arendt, *On Revolution*, p. 113.

49. Arendt, *Origins*, pp. 317, 315, 478. See also p. 318.

50. Arendt, *Human Condition*, pp. 188, 201.

51. Ibid., pp. 39–40, 46, 52–53, 182, 214. See also Arendt, *Between Past and Future*, pp. 89–90; Arendt, *Origins*, pp. 465–66; Arendt, *On Revolution*, pp. 86, 93–94, 107, 175.

52. Arendt, *Human Condition*, p. 214. Note that in this passage the social unitedness also contrasts to "commercial" relations among people who are "unequal"; pp. 214–15.

53. Ibid., pp. 246, 123. As Arendt will later put it, this turns "a more or less accidental proximity into a political institution"; Arendt, *On Revolution*, p. 267. It is the public counterpart to Augustine's Christian, who turns the given into the chosen by freely choosing it, but even more like the conscious pariah, who ratifies his situation even though it is the product of an unjust dispensation, in order to fight against that dispensation effectively in solidarity with other pariahs. See also Hannah Arendt, *Was ist Politik?* (1933), p. 36.

54. Arendt, *Human Condition*, pp. 123, 162, 189, 198, 200, 203, 208. Note, however, that all action is, in a sense, interaction or co-action, even if not intentionally coordinated; Hill, *Hannah Arendt*, pp. 305, 310. See also Benhabib, *Reluctant Modernism*, p. 111. The phrase "action in concert" may be misleading insofar as it implies a conductor, a composer, and a score; but perhaps if one thinks of a jazz concert, it will serve. Arendt quotes the phrase from Edmund Burke, *Upon Party*, 2nd ed. (London, 1850), in *Origins*, pp. 254, 474; but it is

also found in (the English translation of) Gustave de Beaumont and Alexis de Tocqueville, *Penitentiary System* (1964), p. 60.

55. Arendt, *Human Condition*, p. 40.

56. Arendt, *Between Past and Future*, pp. 263–64.

57. This theme is of course central particularly to social contract theory, though the fantasy of starting over from scratch, all at once, is older still, as in Socrates' proposal in *The Republic* to rusticate all adults and raise the children right. For a more fashionable version, cf. Thomas C. Schelling, *Micromotives and Macrobehavior* (1978).

58. Alexis de Tocqueville, *Democracy in America* (1969), pp. 517, 240; Arendt, *On Revolution*, pp. 35, 92, 161, 204.

59. Mark Reinhardt, *The Art of Being Free* (1997), p. 156; but cf. p. 158, where the social "also can be understood to be among the primary instruments through which *politics* in our time is carried out" (emphasis in original).

60. Arendt, *Human Condition*, p. 45.

61. Ibid., p. 220. See also Arendt, *Between Past and Future*, p. 78; Hannah Arendt, *Essays in Understanding, 1930–1954* (1994), p. 3.

62. Arendt, *Human Condition*, pp. 190, 207, my emphasis. See also pp. 144, 234.

63. Hence the importance of "representative thinking"; ibid., pp. 57–58; Arendt, *Between Past and Future*, p. 241; Hannah Arendt, *Lectures on Kant's Political Philosophy* (1982), pp. 42–47, 62–77. See also Behabib, *Reluctant Modernism*, p. 113.

64. Arendt, *Human Condition*, pp. 9–11, 177, 184, 190, 233.

65. Ibid., p. 233. See also Arendt, *Crises*, p. 106.

66. Arendt, *Human Condition*, pp. 232–33. Any number of Arendtian teachings seem to hang from this peg. It is the reason why we cannot " 'make' something in the realm of human affairs—'make' institutions or laws, for instance, as we make tables and chairs," nor "make" history; p. 188; see also pp. 185–86, 228. It is why recognizing one's fellow citizens as peers is crucial. It is why Arendt thinks that politics is not aimed primarily at legislation or even policy-making; pp. 26, 32–33, 63, 189, 194, 196, 225. And it underlies her critique of Plato; pp. 20–21, 225–26, 228, 230.

67. Arendt, *Origins*, pp. 445, 457.

68. Arendt, *Jew as Pariah*, pp. 108, 174. See also Arendt, *Rahel Varnhagen*, p. 10; Arendt, *Origins*, p. 480; Arendt, *Human Condition*, pp. 184, 190.

69. Arendt, *Crises*, pp. 201–2, 227–28.

70. Arendt, *Human Condition*, pp. 41, 175–80, 184, 194, 197–98, 206, 220; Arendt, *Origins*, pp. 438, 454–55; Arendt, *Between Past and Future*, pp. 171, 263; Arendt, *On Revolution*, pp. 108, 119; Arendt, *Crises*, pp. 202–3. Even seen from this perspective of individual self-realization, action "has consequences," but these can be "consciously aim[ed]" at only if one is willing to accept a "premature death"; Arendt, *Human Condition*, pp. 183, 193.

71. See particularly Arendt, *Human Condition*, p. 194; Arendt, *On Revolution*, p. 281.

72. Arendt, *Human Condition*, pp. 190–91, 233–34.

73. Ibid., p. 245. But cf. p. 190, where the "consequences" of *both* individual and concerted action are "boundless."

74. For example, ibid., p. 184 (my emphasis).

75. For recent concern with civil society, see Jean Cohen and Andrew Arato, eds., *Civil Society and Political Theory* (1992); Pierre Clastres, *Society against the State* (1977); Steven M. De Lue, *Political Thinking, Political Theory, and Civil Society* (1997); Ernest Gellner, *Conditions of Liberty* (1994); John Keane, *Democracy and Civil Society*, (1988); John Keane, ed., *Civil Society and the State* (1988); Adam B. Seligman, *The Idea of Civil Society* (1992); H. Gordon Skilling and Paul Wilson, eds., *Civic Freedom in Central Europe* (1991); Keith Tester, *Civil Society* (1992).

76. Arendt's views thus resemble and yet differ profoundly from those in this "civil society" literature in ways that recapitulate the relationship of her thinking in the 1950s to the ideas of Nicola Chiaromonte and others of her friends and associates in the circle around Dwight Macdonald and the journal *politics*. See chapter 6, note 39, above.

77. Hanna Fenichel Pitkin, *Wittgenstein and Justice* (1972), pp. 61–63, 78.

Chapter Ten

1. Hannah Arendt, *Between Past and Future* (1969), p. 199, where the article is reprinted under the title "The Crisis in Culture: Its Social and Its Political Significance."

2. Ibid., p. 198, quoting Edward Shils, "Mass Society and Its Culture," *Daedalus* (spring 1960). See also ibid., p. 200.

3. Arendt, *Between Past and Future*, p. 199.

4. Ibid., p. 202, quoting G. M. Young, *Victorian England: Portrait of an Age* (New York, 1954).

5. Arendt, *Between Past and Future*, p. 204.

6. Elisabeth Young-Bruehl, *Hannah Arendt* (1982), pp. 328–29.

7. Hannah Arendt, *Eichmann in Jerusalem* (1965), p. 42.

8. Young-Bruehl, *Hannah Arendt*, p. 331, quoting Arendt to Blücher, April 20, 1961, Library of Congress.

9. Young-Bruehl, *Hannah Arendt*, pp. 329–30, quoting Arendt to Blücher, April 15, 1961, Library of Congress, and Arendt to Jaspers, December 29, 1963. The latter letter is not included in the Arendt-Jaspers published correspondence but referenced as "not among the literary remains"; Hannah Arendt and Karl Jaspers, *Correspondence* (1992), p. 777.

10. Arendt, *Eichmann*, pp. 25, 145.

11. Young-Bruehl, *Hannah Arendt*, pp. 330, 331, quoting Arendt to Blücher, April 20, 1961, Library of Congress.

12. Arendt, *Eichmann*, p. 90.

13. Ibid., pp. 246–47, Arendt's emphasis. See also pp. 22–23.

14. Ibid., p. 252, emphasis in original. See also Hannah Arendt, "Thinking and Moral Considerations: A Lecture" (1971), p. 417.

15. Francis X. Winters, "The Banality of Virtue," in James W. Bernauer, ed., *Amor Mundi* (1987), p. 188.

16. Young-Bruehl, *Hannah Arendt*, p. 374, quoting Arendt to Herr Meier-Cronomeyer (July 18, 1963, Library of Congress), 337; Hannah Arendt and Mary McCarthy, *Between Friends* (1995), p. 168.

17. Hannah Arendt, *The Jew as Pariah* (1978), pp. 250–51.

18. Young-Bruehl, *Hannah Arendt*, p. 367. Young-Bruehl thus reads "radical evil" to mean to Arendt something like evil that is fundamental and deep-seated in human beings, as when she invokes Freud's "death instinct," p. 370, but I read it to mean evil that transcends the human.

19. Brightman, *Between Friends*, p. 131, Arendt to McCarthy, May 20, 1962.

20. Arendt, *Jew as Pariah*, p. 231. Later Arendt would not have spoken of motives as "causes."

21. Ibid., p. 174. See also Hannah Arendt, *Essays in Understanding, 1930–1954* (1994), p. 134.

22. Claudia Roth Pierpont, "Hearts and Minds," review of Brightman, *Between Friends, The New Yorker.* 20 March 1995, 98.

23. Arendt and Jaspers, *Correspondence*, pp. 409–10; *Briefwechsel*, p. 446; to Jaspers, December 2, 1960.

24. Arendt and Jaspers, *Correspondence*, p. 54; *Briefwechsel*, p. 90; to Jaspers, August 17, 1946.

25. Hannah Arendt, *The Origins of Totalitarianism* (1973), p. 459. See also Hannah Arendt, *The Human Condition* (1974), p. 241.

26. Young-Bruehl, *Hannah Arendt*, p. 331, citing a 1973 interview with Roger Ererra, excerpted for *The New York Review of Books* 26 (October 1978): 18.

27. Young-Bruehl, *Hannah Arendt*, p. 330. For a thoughtful treatment of their correspondence about Eichmann, cf. Richard J. Bernstein, *Hannah Arendt* (1996), pp. 147–53.

28. Arendt and Jaspers, *Correspondence*, p. 62; *Briefwechsel*, p. 99; Jaspers to Arendt, October 19, 1946. The editors suggest that this might have been the source of Arendt's subtitle; Arendt and Jaspers, *Correspondence*, p. 702; *Briefwechsel*, p. 736. But Jaspers himself writes later that a friend told him Blücher had suggested the subtitle; Arendt and Jaspers, *Correspondence*, p. 542; *Briefwechsel*, p. 578; Jaspers to Arendt, December 13, 1963.

29. Arendt and Jaspers, *Correspondence*, p. 69; *Briefwechsel*, p. 106; to Jaspers, December 17, 1946.

30. Arendt and Jaspers, *Correspondence*, pp. 410, 439; *Briefwechsel*, pp. 447, 476; Jaspers to Arendt, December 14, 1960 (the *Correspondence* dates this letter December 12), June 8, 1961.

31. Arendt and Jaspers, *Correspondence*, p. 62; *Briefwechsel*, p. 99; Jaspers to Arendt, October 19, 1946.

32. Arendt and Jaspers, *Correspondence*, pp. 542, 525; *Briefwechsel*, pp. 578, 561; Jaspers to Arendt, December 13, 1963, October 22, 1963. But note that Disch finds Arendt's "for-publication voice sound[ing] polemical and

idiosyncratic" already in *The Origins*; Lisa Jane Disch, *Hannah Arendt and the Limits of Philosophy* (1994), p. 123.

33. Young-Bruehl, *Hannah Arendt*, p. 370.

34. Arendt, *Eichmann*, p. 19. See also pp. 211, 253.

35. Ibid., pp. 287, 49, 86, 26, 50, emphasis in original. See also pp. 48, 114, 126, 295. Arendt rightly rejects the French saying as a "popular misrepresentation" (Arendt, *Essays*, p. 308), but there surely is a logical problem about explanation and agency.

36. Ibid., p. 11. See also p. 43.

37. Ibid., p. 12. See also p. 122.

38. Ibid., p. 232; Arendt, *Origins*, pp. 452, 459.

39. Arendt, *Eichmann*, p. 232–33, emphasis in original.

40. Ibid., pp. 175, 179. See also p. 180.

41. Hannah Arendt, *On Revolution* (1977), pp. 105, 221. See also p. 114, where "necessity invade[s]" the political realm. Arendt already used the phrase "the social question" in the essay "Society and Culture" (1960), discussed at the outset of this chapter.

42. Arendt, *On Revolution*, p. 60.

43. The term "foundation" does occur in Arendt, *Origins*, p. 138.

44. Arendt, *On Revolution*, p. 237.

45. Ibid., pp. 196, 204. See also pp. 198–99, 214.

46. Ibid., pp. 29 (quoting Condorcet, *Sur le sens du mot révolutionnaire*, Oeuvres [1847–49], vol. 12), 255.

47. Arendt, *On Revolution*, pp. 222–23. As Reinhardt points out, "to institutionalize means both to establish and to confine"; Mark Reinhardt, *The Art of Being Free* (1997), p. 21.

48. Arendt, *On Revolution*, p. 224.

49. Arendt, *Human Condition*, p. 198. See also pp. 63, 194–95, and Arendt, *Between Past and Future*, p. 3, on formation of the Resistance.

50. Arendt, *On Revolution*, pp. 10, 228.

51. Ibid., pp. 76, 93. See also pp. 270, 279.

52. Ibid., p. 44; note the Blobbish metaphor—not Arendt's invention, of course, but that of "Verginaud, the great orator of the Gironde"; ibid., p. 49.

53. Ibid., p. 216. See also p. 92.

54. Ibid., pp. 60–61. See also p. 111. Note that the "happiness" to which the French Revolution was deflected is "private," not the "public happiness" of political participation; p. 128; cf. pp. 56, 246, and Arendt, *Human Condition*, p. 134, where "only the *animal laborans* . . . has ever demanded to be 'happy.'"

55. The Blob is perhaps not wholly gone. Arendt does still contrast human relations "whose principle is freedom" to a different "sphere of life whose principle is necessity" and suggest that mistakes in the former sphere can release a dangerous "force" from the latter into the former sphere, a force "*experienced as* superhuman." Is that force absolute or spurious necessity? "The less we are doing ourselves, the less active we are, the more forcefully will this biological process assert itself." Arendt, *On Revolution*, pp. 274, 105, 110–11, 181, 59, my emphasis.

56. Ibid., pp. 111, 181. See also pp. 110–12.

57. Ibid., p. 68. No doubt Arendt would have maintained with respect to both *Eichmann* and *On Revolution*, as she did with respect to *The Origins*, that she never intended a causal explanation, at least not in the sense of "causes that inevitably lead to certain effects"; Bernstein, *Hannah Arendt*, p. 54 (quoting Arendt, "Totalitarianism," *Meridian* 2, no. 2 [Fall 1958], p. 1). As she wrote in 1954, causality "is an altogether alien and falsifying category in the historical sciences," for a historical event "can never be deduced" from "its own past"; Arendt, *Essays*, p. 319; see also Arendt, *Human Condition*, pp. 188, 228, 252; Arendt, *On Revolution*, pp. 52, 55, 113. Her attempt to replace causation with "crystallization" in response to a critic only adds to the confusion, since crystallization, being a physical process, clearly is a matter of causal necessity; cf. Bernstein, *Hannah Arendt*, p. 51, citing Arendt's response to a review of *The Origins* in *Review of Politics* 15 (January 1953): 68–85, pp. 77–78. Nor can the difficulty be avoided by eschewing words such as "causality" and "inevitably" when discussing human affairs, nor by insisting that, although natural phenomena have causes, historical actions are explained by reasons—the agent's reasons for doing what he did. Indeed, Arendt herself uses both "cause" and "reason" in passages quoted above in ways that violate such strictures. The question still remains whether particular historical actors, or human beings in general, could or could not—given their situation, who they specifically were, what they knew, and so on—have done other than they did. As Arendt later observed, the very idea of action requires that the agent "could also have left undone what he actually did"; Hannah Arendt, *Willing* (vol. 2 of *The Life of the Mind* [1978]), p. 5; see also pp. 6, 26, 29, 210. Even this formulation, however, fails to distinguish action from behavior. We shall return to this difficult topic in chapter 11.

58. Arendt, *On Revolution*, p. 95.

59. Ibid., p. 68. See also Young-Bruehl, *Hannah Arendt*, p. 388.

60. Arendt, *On Revolution*, p. 70.

61. Ibid., p. 137 (quoting Judge Pendleton in Niles, *Principles and Acts of the Revolution* [1822], p. 210).

Chapter Eleven

1. Arendt's followers and critics do tend to say—and to ascribe to her—"the political." Thus, e.g., Alan Ryan, "Dangerous Liaison," p. 26; Richard J. Bernstein, *Hannah Arendt* (1996), pp. 10, 17, 106; Richard J. Bernstein, *Philosophical Profiles* (1986), pp. 238, 248; Seyla Benhabib, *The Reluctant Modernism of Hannah Arendt* (1996), p. 139; Claude Lefort, *Democracy and Political Theory* (1988); James Miller, "The Pathos of Novelty," in Melvin A Hill, ed., *Hannah Arendt* (1979), p. 200; Sheldon S. Wolin, "Hannah Arendt: Democracy and the Political," in Reuben Garner, ed., *The Realm of Humanitas* (1990), pp. 167–86; and Hanna Fenichel Pitkin, "Justice" (1981), p. 334. See also Sheldon S. Wolin, *Politics and Vision* (1960), pp. 286–94, 362–68, 414–34, where, however, Arendt is not mentioned.

2. For Hobbes and even for Adam Ferguson, civil society more or less coin-

cided with the state, both together contrasting to an uncivil, anarchic state of nature. The distinction is central in Hegel and in the early writings of Marx.

3. There are, of course, "statist," "governmental," and "legal," but the first has a radically different and specialized meaning, and either of the others would be an even worse choice than the noun "state" for capturing what Arendt wants to advocate as the opposite of "social," for reasons the rest of the paragraph explains. "Society" *can* also be juxtaposed to "politics," instead of to "the state," but the result would not be an idiomatic, familiar contrast.

4. Hans H. Gerth and C. Wright Mills, trs. and eds., *From Max Weber: Essays in Sociology* (1946), pp. 77–78.

5. For "the social," see Hannah Arendt, *The Human Condition* (1974), pp. 38, 68 (chapter titles); 31, 39 (twice); and marginal instances at 33, 38 (twice), 43. For the two occurrences of "the political," see pp. 38, 43. For "society" with active verbs or Blobbish implications, see pp. 39 (twice), 40 (twice), 41 (twice), 45 (three times), 59, 68.

6. Jeffrey C. Isaac, *Arendt* (1992), p. 63.

7. Quoted in Fred Powledge, *Free at Last?* (1991), p. 547.

8. Elisabeth Young-Bruehl, *Hannah Arendt* (1982), p. 263, epigraph from Bertold Brecht, "Wahrnehmungen" (1949).

9. Hannah Arendt, *Essays in Understanding, 1930–1954* (1994), p. 11; my translation from Günter Gaus, *Zur Person* (1964), p. 23.

10. Hannah Arendt, *The Origins of Totalitarianism* (1978), p. 87.

11. Arendt, *Essays*, p. 320 ("Understanding and Politics," first published 1954), where the phrase is actually used. See also Hannah Arendt, *On Revolution* (1977), p. 52, where it is not.

12. Arendt, *Human Condition*, p. 42. See also Hannah Arendt, *Eichmann in Jerusalem* (1965), p. 297.

13. Karl Marx and Friedrich Engels, *The Marx-Engels Reader* (1979), p. 86, emphasis in original. The capitalization is the translator's.

14. Tom Bottomore, ed., *A Dictionary of Marxist Thought* (1983), p. 311, quoting Marx, *Das Kapital*, 3, 48:411.

15. Marx and Engels, *Marx-Engels Reader*, pp. 319–21.

16. Ibid., pp. 149, 154–55. See also p. 3.

17. Georg Wilhelm Friedrich Hegel, *Phenomenology* (1977), pp. 4, 6, 9, 11. Hegel has a lot more to say on this subject, but it would take us too far afield.

18. Alexis de Tocqueville, *Democracy in America* (1969), p. 482.

19. For example, ibid., pp. 30–33, 51, 279, 282, 341, 674–75.

20. Ibid., pp. 196, 245, 496, 671, 695, 702, 705.

21. Marx and Engels, *Marx-Engels Reader*, p. 65, emphasis in original.

22. Tocqueville, *Democracy*, p. 440.

23. Marx and Engels, *Marx-Engels Reader*, p. 237. Compare Paul Ziff, *Semantic Analysis* (1960), pp. 234, 221.

24. Thomas Hobbes, *Leviathan* (1978), pt. 1, chap. 4, p. 38.

25. Stanley Cavell writes: "If you are walking with a child [in New York City] and she looks up to you, puzzled, and asks, 'Where is Manhattan?,' you may feel you ought to be able to *point* to something, and yet at the same time

feel there is nothing to point to; and so fling out your arms and look around vaguely and say, 'All of this is Manhattan,' and sense that your answer hasn't been a very satisfactory one. Is, then, Manhattan *hard* to point to? [Too abstract?] But if you were approaching La Guardia Airport on a night flight from Boston, then just as the plane banked for its approach, you could poke your finger against the window and, your interest focused on the dense scattering of lights, say 'There's Manhattan'; so could you point to Manhattan on a map." Stanley Cavell, *The Claim of Reason* (1979), p. 74.

26. Arendt, *Human Condition*, p. 184.

27. Compare G. E. M. Anscombe, "On Brute Facts" (1958), pp. 69–72.

28. Again, Canovan pioneered here, with her 1978 article, but she still sees Arendt's contradictions simply as "defects"; Margaret Canovan, "The Contradictions of Hannah Arendt's Political Thought," p. 23. See also Benhabib, *Reluctant Modernism*, p. 118.

29. This and the following paragraph are slightly revised from Hanna Fenichel Pitkin, "Rethinking Reification" (1987), pp. 283–84. Recommended there for further reading is John L. Austin, "Ifs and Cans," in his *Philosophical Papers* (1961).

30. Will it help, or will it only add complications, to point out that the conundrum about free will corresponds to the third of Kant's "Antinomies of Pure Reason" and that the conundrum of micro-macro is at least closely related to the second antinomy? Immanuel Kant, *Critique of Pure Reason* (1987), pp. 246–56, 302–17.

31. In this respect political theorists and perhaps political scientists are worse off than sociologists. The latter do have to wrestle with the problem of reconciling—as they often put it—"structure" with "agency" or even "action," but in fact they mostly engage only the micro-macro conundrum, because sociology mostly studies patterns in learned human conduct that are produced *unintentionally*—what Arendt calls "the social."

32. Arendt, *Essays,* pp. 445, 433.

33. Hannah Arendt, *Between Past and Future* (1969), p. 25, a revised version of her Gauss lectures.

34. Ibid., p. 35. Compare Hannah Arendt, *Willing* (vol. 2 of *The Life of the Mind* [1978]), p. 216.

35. Tocqueville, *Democracy,* pp. 694, 496, 705. See also p. 702.

36. Arendt, *On Revolution,* pp. 275–76. See also Arendt, *Human Condition,* p. 237.

37. The German word translated as "realm" in Arendt's thought, however, is not *Reich,* but *Bereich,* which is less powerfully metaphorical than "realm." See, e.g., Hannah Arendt, *Was ist Politik?* (1933), p. 19.

38. This, I think, and not some kind of "essentialism," as Benhabib and Isaac suggest, is what accounts for Arendt's sometimes so frustrating way of deploying her central concepts; Benhabib, *Reluctant Modernism,* p. 123; Isaac, *Arendt,* p. 230. The charge of essentialism seems to me unclear, the term not well suited to what authors who use it seem to have in mind. Words do and do not have essences, depending on what one means; "*essence* is expressed by grammar," Wittgenstein says (Ludwig Wittgenstein, *Philosophical Investigations* [1968],

par. 371); see also Hanna Fenichel Pitkin, *Wittgenstein and Justice* (1972), pp. 84–85, 89–93, 116–21. The problem is not that Arendt "conflates conceptual distinctions with social processes, ontological analysis with institutional and historical descriptions" (Benhabib, *Reluctant Modernism*, p. 124), for these are, unavoidably, connected. What, for instance, politics has looked like historically cannot be separated from what "politics" means or what politics is "ontologically," for our notion of these latter will determine what, in history, we look at and describe. Instead, the difficulty is that Arendt assumes concepts to be internally consistent, so that if she has identified one feature of a given concept in one context, it can reliably be expected to show up in all other contexts where that concept appears as well. Thus, if a woman in labor is isolated in her pain, then labor as such is always painful and isolating.

39. Arendt, *Between Past and Future*, pp. 145–46, 157, 163–65; Arendt, *Willing*, pp. 5, 33, 199.

40. On action in concert, see Arendt, *On Revolution*, p. 218; Arendt, *Willing*, p. 201; Arendt, *Between Past and Future*, pp. 146, 148–49. On capacity to innovate, see Arendt, *Between Past and Future*, p. 167. On actually innovating, see Arendt, *Between Past and Future*, pp. 153, 165. On moving about in the world, see Arendt, *Between Past and Future*, p. 148. On absence of obligations, see Arendt, *Human Condition*, p. 245. On possibilities terminated by action, see Arendt, *Willing*, p. 141. See also Arendt, *Was ist Politik?* pp. 34–5, 51.

41. Arendt, *Willing*, pp. 32, 198–99, 203.

42. Arendt, *On Revolution*, p. 237.

43. Compare Kant, *Critique of Pure Reason*, pp. 239, 284, 286, 299–302, 308–14.

44. Compare Pitkin, *Wittgenstein*, pp. 85–98.

45. Jessica Benjamin, *Like Subjects, Love Objects* (1995), pp. 4, 10.

46. Tocqueville, *Democracy*, pp. 464, 442. See also p. 481.

47. Arendt, *Origins*, p. vii.

48. Wittgenstein, *Philosophical Investigations*, par. 124.

49. Arendt, *Essays*, p. 433.

50. Hannah Arendt, *Thinking* (vol. 1 of *Life of the Mind*), pp. 187, 191. See also pp. 3–5, 185–92 passim; Arendt, *Eichmann*, pp. 49, 55.

51. Arendt, *Human Condition*, pp. 104–5.

52. Hannah Arendt, *Crises of the Republic* (1972), p. 12; Arendt, *On Revolution*, p. 224.

Chapter Twelve

1. Hanna Arendt and Karl Jaspers, *Correspondence* (1992), p. 69; *Briefwechsel* (1985), p. 106; to Jaspers, December 17, 1946.

2. Oliver Williamson, *Markets and Hierarchies* (1975).

3. Mark Reinhardt, *The Art of Being Free* (1997), p. 55.

4. Hannah Arendt, *Crises of the Republic* (1972), pp. 181–82.

5. Hannah Arendt, *Eichmann in Jerusalem* (1965), p. 278; Hanna Arendt, *The Jew as Pariah* (1978), pp. 229–30; Melvin A. Hill, ed., *Hannah Arendt* (1979), p. 302.

6. C. Wright Mills, *The Power Elite* (1956), pp. 3–5.

7. Compare ibid., p. 9: "By the powerful we mean, of course, those who are able to realize their will, even if others resist it."

8. The best brief introduction to it in terms of power and blame is Diane Nash's comment on the Montgomery, Alabama, bus boycott, where residents with black or dark brown skin succeeded in forcing an end to segregated seating on the city's buses. "When Montgomery blacks decided that there weren't going to be segregated buses any more, there were segregated busses no more. It didn't take *any* change on the parts of whites.... So then you ask yourself the question, 'Well, who was segregating the buses all this time?'" And then Nash adds the complication: the "thin line between what's known as 'blaming the victim' and identifying appropriate responsibility ... [in order] to withdraw your participation"; Fred Powledge, *Free at Last?* (1991), pp. 232–33.

9. Arendt, *Crises*, p. 9, quoting Neil Sheehan, in *The Pentagon Papers*, as published by *The New York Times* (New York, 1971), p. xiv; Hannah Arendt, *On Revolution* (1977), pp. 269–71, 276–77. See also Arendt, *Crises*, pp. 11, 17–18, 36–42; Arendt, *On Revolution*, pp. 69, 143, 226–27, 234–40, 268, 272.

10. Arendt, *On Revolution*, p. 235, quoting Thomas Jefferson, letter to Samuel Kercheval, July 12, 1816. See also Arendt, *Crises*, p. 232.

11. Arendt, *On Revolution*, p. 223.

12. Arendt, *Crises*, p. 231; Arendt, *On Revolution*, pp. 249, 257. See also Arendt, *Crises*, p. 124; Arendt, *On Revolution*, pp. 240, 244, 246, 249–57; Hannah Arendt, *The Origins of Totalitarianism* (1978), pp. 497–500; Hannah Arendt, *The Human Condition* (1974), p. 216.

13. Arendt, *On Revolution*, p. 249; Arendt, *Crises*, pp. 231, 233. See also Arendt, *On Revolution*, pp. 166, 249–56; Arendt, *Jew as Pariah*, pp. 191–92, 217, 221–22; Hannah Arendt, *Was ist Politik?* (1933), p. 68.

14. Jeffrey C. Isaac, "Oases in the Desert" (1994), pp. 156, 160, 165; Reinhardt, *Art*, pp. 57, 161–66.

15. Arendt, *Human Condition*, p. 257. See also p. 250.

16. Arendt, *Jew as Pariah*, pp. 161, 141.

17. Arendt's views on the relationship between politics and economics are much misunderstood but also very obscure. She is not a liberal in the sense of believing that political equality justifies economic inequality or that it is wholly independent of citizens' economic status. She is a critic both of the laissez-faire market and of an administered economy—communist, socialist, or welfare. But she never really specifies a viable alternative. She clearly does believe that we must take political charge of any undesirable consequences produced by the operations of the market, as—for example—the Jewish leadership in Palestine should have made policy to prevent the development of distinct Jewish and Arab economies that kept the two peoples separated; Arendt, *Jew as Pariah*, pp. 201–3, 222. She writes in favor of private property, yet believes that freedom is possible under the "rather inhuman conditions of modern production" only if "a decent amount of property is available to every human being." But this must somehow be accomplished without "expropriating"; Hill, *Hannah Arendt*, p. 320. She does not explain how, nor what she means by "available." She distinguishes between property and wealth, the former meaning a privately owned, small piece of the world,

the latter, ownership of the means of production that other people must use to keep themselves and their families alive, and thus implying a process of accumulation that uproots people and destroys private property; Arendt, *Human Condition*, pp. 61, 67–69, 110, 252–57. "What is important" for political freedom "is not the more or less enterprising spirit of private businessmen but the fences around the houses and gardens of citizens"; ibid., p. 72.

18. Jeffrey C. Isaac, *Arendt* (1992), pp. 226, 255; Reinhardt, *Art*, pp. 55–56; C. Douglas Lummis, *Radical Democracy* (1996), chap. 2.

19. See, e.g., Robert B. Reich, *The Work of Nations* (1992), pts. 1 and 2; Richard J. Barnet and Ronald E. Muller, *Global Reach* (1974).

20. Arendt, *Origins*, p. 475.

21. Hannah Arendt, *Essays in Understanding, 1930–1954* (1994), p. 436. See also Arendt, *Jew as Pariah*, p. 75; Arendt, *Human Condition*, p. 257; Hannah Arendt, *Men in Dark Times* (1969), p. 89; Hannah Arendt, *Lectures on Kant's Political Philosophy* (1982), p. 44.

22. Arendt, *Human Condition*, p. 43.

23. Arendt, *Origins*, p. 311.

24. The classic source here is Jacques Ellul, *The Technological Society* (1964). See also Langdon Winner, *Autonomous Technology* (1977).

25. Arendt, *Crises*, pp. 118, 183.

26. Compare James S. Coleman, *Power and the Structure of Society* (1974).

27. Reinhardt, *Art*, p. 81. See also Alexis de Tocqueville, *Democracy in America* (1969), p. 255.

28. Arendt, *Crises*, p. 46.

29. David Riesman, Nathan Glazer, and Reuel Denny, *The Lonely Crowd* (1964), pp. 5–25. Arendt and Riesman worked together in connection with Judah Magnes's support group for the Ikhud Party in Palestine; Elisabeth Young-Bruehl, *Hannah Arendt* (1982), pp. 227–30. Riesman read *The Origins of Totalitarianism* in manuscript form, and he wanted Arendt to contribute a chapter to what eventually became *The Lonely Crowd*; ibid., pp. 251–52.

30. Stanley Milgram, *Obedience to Authority* (1974).

31. Hannah Arendt, *Rahel Varnhagen* (1974), p. 199.

32. Arendt, *Human Condition*, pp. 203–4. Arendt, *Origins*, p. 332; see also pp. 189, 206, 314, 351, 384, 454. Arendt, *Men in Dark Times*, p. 11. Arendt, *Eichmann*, pp. 33–34.

33. Arendt, *Human Condition*, p. 186. See also p. 36.

34. Ibid., p. 36. See also Arendt, *Was ist Politik?* p. 45.

35. Hannah Arendt, "Freedom and Politics" (1961), p. 199. See also Arendt, *Jew as Pariah*, pp. 89, 231–32; Arendt, *Human Condition*, p. 254; Arendt, *Crises*, pp. 60–61.

36. Hannah Arendt, *Between Past and Future* (1969), p. 4, quoting René Char.

37. Lummis, *Radical Democracy*, pp. 77–78.

38. Arendt, *Crises*, p. 202. See also p. 118.

39. Arendt, *Human Condition*, p. 189. Compare Lummis, *Radical De-*

mocracy, pp. 143–54; Robert D. Putnam, *Making Democracy Work* (1993), esp. chap. 6; Edward C. Banfield, *The Moral Basis of a Backward Society* (1958); Diego Gambetta, ed., *Trust* (1988).

40. Hannah Arendt, "Reflections (W. H. Auden)," *The New Yorker* (January 20, 1975), p. 39, quoted in Elisabeth Young-Bruehl, *Mind and the Body Politic* (1989), p. 5. See also Arendt, *Human Condition,* p. 191.

41. Arendt, *Jew as Pariah,* p. 77. See also Arendt, *Rahel Varnhagen,* p. 4; Arendt, *Between Past and Future,* p. 196; Arendt, *Men in Dark Times,* pp. 14, 16.

42. Compare chapter 7, note 93, above.

43. Arendt, *Human Condition,* p. 175. As the rest of the epigraph shows, Dante, unlike Arendt, meant all activity, including that due to "natural necessity."

44. Arendt, *Was ist Politik?* p. 24; Arendt, *Between Past and Future,* p. 196; Arendt and Jaspers, *Correspondence,* p. 264; *Briefwechsel,* p. 301; to Jaspers, August 6, 1955. See also Arendt, *Men in Dark Times,* pp. 14, 16–17, 22.

45. Arendt, *Human Condition,* pp. 176–77.

46. Ibid., pp. 7–8; Arendt, *On Revolution,* p. 93, and pp. 85–98, passim. Arendt, *Men in Dark Times,* pp. 24–25; Arendt, *Origins,* pp. 300–302.

47. "Neither a beast nor a god," Aristotle might have said. Arendt says: "Neither *animal laborans* nor *homo faber.*"

48. Arendt and Jaspers, *Correspondence,* p. 54; *Briefwechsel,* p. 91; to Jaspers, August 17, 1946. Arendt, *On Revolution,* pp. 85–89, 92.

49. Arendt, *Origins,* p. 61; Arendt, *Men in Dark Times,* p. 30. See also Arendt, *Jew as Pariah,* pp. 71, 90; Arendt, *Was ist Politik?* p. 64. Compare Seyla Benhabib, *The Reluctant Modernism of Hannah Arendt* (1996), p. 196; Jessica Benjamin, *Like Subjects, Love Objects* (1995), pp. 23, 90.

50. Arendt, *Crises,* p. 167, quoting Georges Sorel, *Reflections on Violence* (1906). Compare Hanna Fenichel Pitkin, *Fortune Is a Woman* (1984), pp. 90–93, 297–301.

51. Arendt, *Origins,* pp. vii, ix. Compare Arendt, *Men in Dark Times,* p. 101.

52. Arendt, *Between Past and Future,* pp. 13–14. See also pp. 11–12, 15; Arendt, *Human Condition,* pp. 176–77.

53. Arendt, *Human Condition,* pp. 9–11, 95, 177, 183, 233, 241.

54. In the winter of 1939–40, still in Paris, Arendt and Blücher spent many hours with Benjamin discussing Gershom Scholem's book *Major Trends of Jewish Mysticism,* which speaks of the seventeenth-century Sabbatian movement. In a 1948 essay Arendt called this movement "the last great Jewish political activity," the only example of mysticism being "able to bring about a great political movement and to translate itself directly into real popular action"; Hannah Arendt, "Jewish History, Revised" (1948), pp. 34, 38. Benjamin wrote, in an essay included in a volume edited by Arendt, that this Jewish mysticism involved an understanding of time as "filled by the presence of the Now [*Jetztzeit*]," a conviction that "every second of time [is] the strait gate through which the Messiah might enter." Benjamin used the idea to combat both deterministic historicism in general and Marxist dialectical materialism, which he saw as efforts to guarantee the

future and thus as the sort of "soothsaying" that Judaism prohibits; Walter Benjamin, *Illuminations* (1961), pp. 261, 264. But "the now" is already "outside time" in Arendt's dissertation; Hannah Arendt, *Love and Saint Augustine* (1966), p. 15. And there are clear echoes of Nietzsche as well; Arendt, *Thinking* (vol. 1 of *Life of the Mind*), p. 204.

55. Arendt, *Crises,* p. 167.

56. Arendt, *Human Condition,* pp. 273, 5. See also Arendt, *Essays,* p. 3; Günter Gaus, *Zur Person* (1964), pp. 16–17; Hill, *Hannah Arendt,* pp. 304–5, 309; Arendt, *Men in Dark Times,* p. 10, on Lessing; Arendt, *Jew as Pariah,* p. 83; Arendt, *Between Past and Future,* pp. 9, 13.

57. Arendt, *Thinking,* pp. 3–6; Arendt, *Eichmann,* pp. 287–88.

58. Arendt, *Human Condition,* p. 5.

59. Arendt, *Eichmann,* pp. 49, 126, 287–88, emphasis in original. See also p. 114.

60. Arendt, *Lectures on Kant,* p. 43.

61. Arendt, *Between Past and Future,* pp. 220–21, 241–42; Arendt, *Human Condition,* pp. 50, 57–58, 199; Arendt, *Lectures on Kant,* p. 43.

62. Arendt, *Between Past and Future,* p. 241, my emphasis.

63. Arendt, *Rahel Varnhagen,* p. 9; Arendt, *Men in Dark Times,* p. 8.

64. Stan Spyros Draenos, "Thinking Without a Ground," in Hill, *Hannah Arendt,* p. 218, quoting from a letter by Arendt in *The New York Review of Books* (January 1, 1970).

65. Arendt, *Men in Dark Times,* p. 10; Arendt, *Between Past and Future,* p. 31.

66. Hill, *Hannah Arendt,* p. 336.

67. Arendt, *Lectures on Kant,* pp. 42–43; Arendt, *Eichmann,* p. 126; Arendt, *Thinking,* p. 177.

68. Arendt, *Between Past and Future,* p. 6.

69. Arendt, *Origins,* p. 362; Arendt, *Eichmann,* p. 52.

70. Arendt, *Crises,* pp. 21, 18. See also pp. 11, 17, 20, 35, 37–39, 42.

71. Marshall McLuhan, *Understanding Media* (1964). Before McLuhan there was H. A. Innis, *The Bias of Communication* (1950).

72. Andrew Ross, *No Respect* (1989), p. 3.

73. Václav Havel et al., *The Power of the Powerless* (1985), p. 31, emphasis removed. See also pp. 27–28, 30.

74. See Arendt, *Origins,* pp. 314, 351, 384; Arendt, *Men in Dark Times,* p. 11; Joan Didion, *Salvador* (1983), p. 67.

75. Benhabib, *Reluctant Modernism,* p. 205. This is not to deny that symbolic expression has substantive consequences, but only to suggest that these do not justify its regulation, that regulation of expression is not an effective way to combat these consequences.

76. Arendt, *Origins,* p. viii.

77. Compare Pitkin, *Fortune,* pp. 286, 308–9; Isaac, *Arendt,* p. 229.

78. Arendt, *Thinking,* p. 212; Arendt, *Men in Dark Times,* pp. 193–206. The idea derives from Arendt's friend Walter Benjamin, but is also strikingly reminiscent both of Heidegger's way of philosophizing (as Arendt notes) and of her account of what made him such an exciting teacher, who drew students from all

parts of Germany ("the cultural treasures of the past, believed to be dead, are being made to speak . . ."); Arendt, *Men in Dark Times*, p. 201; Hannah Arendt, "Martin Heidegger at Eighty" (1971), p. 51. The Shakespearean metaphor is striking psychologically—among other ways—for Arendt comments on "Those are pearls that were his eyes" by saying that the pearl diver "cut[s] out" the father's eyes; Arendt, *Men in Dark Times*, p. 196; see also p. 193 on Benjamin's own metaphor of "robbers."

79. Arendt, *Between Past and Future*, p. 15; Young-Bruehl, *Hannah Arendt*, p. 318.

80. Arendt, *Thinking*, p. 171, emphasis in original.

81. Young-Bruehl, *Hannah Arendt*, p. 318.

82. Arendt, *Thinking*, p. 171.

83. Arendt, *Men in Dark Times*, p. 204. See also Arendt, *Was ist Politik?* p. 36; cf. Dagmar Barnouw, *Visible Spaces* (1990), p. 209; and John L. Austin, *Philosophical Papers* (1961), p. 149, on "trailing clouds of etymology."

84. Arendt, *Men in Dark Times*, p. 204.

85. Arendt, *On Revolution*, p. 52.

86. Arendt, *Human Condition*, p. 175. See also Arendt, *Men in Dark Times*, p. 104.

87. Arendt, *Men in Dark Times*, p. 105; Arendt, *Rahel Varnhagen*, pp. 114–15; Arendt, *Human Condition*, pp. 178–79, 184.

88. Hannah Arendt, "Action and the Pursuit of Happiness," lecture delivered at the annual convention of the American Political Science Association, 1960, quoted in Hill, *Hannah Arendt*, p. 296, and in Lisa Jane Disch, *Hannah Arendt* (1994), p. 107.

89. For example, Benhabib, *Reluctant Modernism*, p. 87. See also p. 91; Disch, *Hannah Arendt*, p. 139; Hill, "The Fictions of Mankind and Stories of Men," in his *Hannah Arendt*, pp. 275–99; Young-Bruehl, "Hannah Arendt's Storytelling," in *Mind*, pp. 1–6; Seyla Benhabib, "Hannah Arendt and the Redemptive Power of Narrative" (1990), pp. 167–96; David Luban, "Explaining Dark Times" (1983), pp. 215–47.

90. Arendt, *Men in Dark Times*, p. 101.

91. Commentators who attempt to do this include Barnouw, *Visible Spaces*, esp. chap. 5; Hill, *Hannah Arendt*, p. 298; Ronald Beiner, *What's the Matter with Liberalism?* (1992), p. 12.

92. Disch, *Hannah Arendt*, p. 128.

93. Arendt, "Action," quoted in ibid., p. 1, and in Hill, *Hannah Arendt*, p. 296. See also Arendt, *Between Past and Future*, p. 14, and particularly Hill, *Hannah Arendt*, p. 306, where we learn that "metaphysical fallacies," too, are grounded "in some experience," so that a grounding in experience is no guarantee of truth or realism.

94. Arendt, *Men in Dark Times*, p. 165; Arendt, *Between Past and Future*, p. 64. See also ibid., p. 6; Arendt, *Human Condition*, p. 3.

95. Arendt, *Men in Dark Times*, p. 74. See also Hill, *Hannah Arendt*, p. 303.

96. Arendt, *Human Condition*, p. 188.

97. Ibid., p. 246. Compare Albert Camus, *The Rebel* (1956), p. 13; Havel, *Power*, p. 39.

98. See particularly Isaac, *Arendt*; Isaac, "Oases"; Reinhardt, *Art*, esp. chap. 5; Bonnie Honig, *Feminist Interpretations of Hannah Arendt* (1995), pp. 135–66, 313–35; Michel Foucault, "The Subject and Power" (1983).

99. Alexis de Tocqueville, *Recollections* (1959), pp. 7–8.

100. Arendt, *Between Past and Future*, p. 3, quoting René Char.

101. Arendt, *Human Condition*, p. 198, my emphasis. See also Reinhardt, *Art*, pp. 33, 57, 144, 194 n. 88; and cf. p. 158.

Bibliography

Anscombe, G. E. M. "On Brute Facts." *Analysis* 18 (January 1958): 69–72.
Arendt, Hannah. *Between Past and Future: Six Exercises in Political Thought.* Cleveland and New York: World, 1969.
———. *Crises of the Republic.* New York: Harcourt Brace Jovanovich, 1972.
———. *Eichmann in Jerusalem: A Report on the Banality of Evil.* New York: Penguin, 1965.
———. *Essays in Understanding, 1930–1954.* Ed. Jerome Kohn. New York, San Diego, and London: Harcourt Brace, 1994.
———. "Europe and America: Dream and Nightmare." *Commonweal* 60 (September 10, 1954): 551–54.
———. "Europe and America: Europe and the Atom Bomb." *Commonweal* 60 (September 17, 1954): 578–80.
———. "Freedom and Politics." In *Freedom and Serfdom,* ed. Albert Hunold. Dordrecht, Holland: D. Reidel, 1961.
———. *The Human Condition.* Chicago: University of Chicago Press, 1974.
———. "Introduction." In *The Warriors,* by J. Glenn Gray. New York, Evanston, and London: Harper and Row, 1967.
———. *The Jew as Pariah: Jewish Identity and Politics in the Modern Age.* Ed. Ron H. Feldman. New York: Grove, 1978.
———. "Jewish History, Revised." *Jewish Frontier* 15 (March 1948): 34–38.
———. *Lectures on Kant's Political Philosophy.* Ed. Ronald Beiner. Chicago: University of Chicago Press, 1982.
———. *The Life of the Mind.* New York: Harcourt Brace Jovanovich, 1978.
———. *Love and Saint Augustine.* Ed. Joanna V. Scott and Judith C. Stark. Chicago and London: University of Chicago Press, 1966.
———. "Martin Heidegger at Eighty." *New York Review of Books* 17 (October 21, 1971): 50–54.
———. *Men in Dark Times.* New York: Harcourt, Brace and World, 1969.
———. *On Revolution.* New York: Penguin, 1977.
———. *The Origins of Totalitarianism.* New York: Harcourt Brace Jovanovich, 1973.
———. *Rahel Varnhagen: The Life of a Jewish Woman.* Trans. Richard and Clara Winston. New York: Harcourt Brace Jovanovich, 1974.
———. "Thinking and Moral Considerations: A Lecture." *Social Research* 38 (fall 1971): 417–46.

———. "The Threat of Conformism." *Commonweal* 60 (September 24, 1954): 607–10.

———. *Was ist Politik? Fragmente aus dem Nachlass.* Ed. Ursula Ludz. Munich and Zurich: Piper, 1933.

Arendt, Hannah, and Kurt Blumenfeld. *Hannah Arendt Kurt Blumenfeld "In keinem Besitz verwurzelt": Die Korrespondenz.* Ed. Ingeborg Nordmann and Iris Pilling. Hamburg: Rotbuch Verlag, 1995.

Arendt, Hannah, and Karl Jaspers. *Hannah Arendt Karl Jaspers Briefwechsel, 1926–1969.* Ed. Lotte Köhler and Hans Sanes. Munich: Piper, 1985.

———. *Hannah Arendt Karl Jaspers Correspondence, 1926–1969.* Ed. Lotte Kohler and Hans Sanes, trans. Robert Kimber and Rita Kimber. New York: Harcourt Brace Jovanovich, 1992.

Arendt, Hannah, and Mary McCarthy. *Between Friends: The Correspondence of Hannah Arendt and Mary McCarthy, 1949–1975.* Ed. Carol Brightman. New York: Harcourt Brace Jovanovich, 1995.

Austin, John L. *Philosophical Papers.* Oxford: Clarendon, 1961.

Banfield, Edward C. *The Moral Basis of a Backward Society.* Chicago: Free Press, 1958.

Barnet, Richard J., and Ronald E. Muller. *Global Reach: The Power of the Multinational Corporations.* New York: Simon and Shuster, 1974.

Barnouw, Dagmar. *Visible Spaces: Hannah Arendt and the German-Jewish Experience.* Baltimore and London: Johns Hopkins University Press, 1990.

Baron, Jeanette M. "Hannah Arendt: Personal Reflections." *Response* 39 (1980): 58–63.

Beaumont, Gustave de, and Alexis de Tocqueville. *On the Penitentiary System in the United States and Its Application to France.* Carbondale and Edwardsville: Southern Illinois University Press, 1964.

Beauvoir, Simone de. *The Second Sex.* New York: Vintage, 1973.

Beiner, Ronald. *What's the Matter with Liberalism?* Berkeley, Los Angeles, and London: University of California Press, 1992.

Benhabib, Seyla. "Hannah Arendt and the Redemptive Power of Narrative," *Social Research* 57 (spring 1990): 167–96.

———. *The Reluctant Modernism of Hannah Arendt.* Thousand Oaks, London, and New Delhi: Sage, 1996.

Benhabib, Seyla, and Drucilla Cornell, eds. *Feminism as Critique.* Minneapolis: University of Minnesota Press, 1987.

Benjamin, Jessica. *The Bonds of Love: Psychoanalysis, Feminism, and the Problem of Domination.* New York: Pantheon, 1988.

———. *Like Subjects, Love Objects.* New Haven and London: Yale University Press, 1995.

Benjamin, Walter. *Illuminations.* Ed. and with an introduction by Hannah Arendt. New York: Schocken, 1973.

Berking, Helmuth. "Mythos und Politik: Von der historischen Semantik des Massenbegriffs." *Aesthetik und Communikation* 56 (November 1984): 35–41.

Bernauer, James W., S.J., ed. *Amor Mundi: Explorations in the Faith and Thought of Hannah Arendt.* Boston, Dordrecht, and Lancaster: Martinus Nijhoff, 1987.

Bernstein, Richard J. *Hannah Arendt and the Jewish Question.* Cambridge: MIT Press, 1996.
———. *Philosophical Profiles: Essays in a Pragmatic Mode.* Philadelphia: University of Pennsylvania Press, 1986.
Boesche, Roger. *The Strange Liberalism of Alexis de Tocqueville.* Ithaca: Cornell University Press, 1987.
Bottomore, Tom, ed. *A Dictionary of Marxist Thought.* Cambridge: Harvard University Press, 1983.
Bowlby, John. *Attachment.* London: Penguin, 1971.
Bradshaw, Leah. *Acting and Thinking: The Political Thought of Hannah Arendt.* Toronto: University of Toronto Press, 1989.
Brzezinski, Zbigniew, and Samuel P. Huntington. *Political Power USA/USSR.* New York: Viking, 1964.
Butler, Eliza Marion. *The Tyranny of Greece over Germany: A Study of the Influence Exercised by Greek Art and Poetry.* Boston: Beacon, 1958.
Camus, Albert. *The Rebel.* New York: Vintage, 1956.
Canovan, Margaret. "The Contradictions of Hannah Arendt's Political Thought." *Political Theory* 6 (February 1978): 5–26.
———. *Hannah Arendt: A Reinterpretation of Her Political Thought.* Cambridge: Cambridge University Press, 1992.
———. *The Political Thought of Hannah Arendt.* New York and London: Harcourt Brace and Jovanovich, 1974.
Cavell, Stanley. *The Claim of Reason: Wittgenstein, Skepticism, Morality, and Tragedy.* Oxford: Clarendon, 1979.
Chassequet-Smirgel, Janine, ed. *Female Sexuality.* Ann Arbor: University of Michigan Press, 1970.
Chodorow, Nancy. "Gender, Relation, and Difference in Psychoanalytic Perspective." In *The Future of Difference,* ed. Hester Eisenstein and Alice Jardine. Boston: G. K. Hall, 1980.
———. *The Reproduction of Mothering: Psychoanalysis and the Sociology of Gender.* Berkeley: University of California Press, 1978.
Clastres, Pierre. *Society against the State.* Trans. Robert Hurley. New York: Urizen, 1977.
Cohen, Jean, and Andrew Arato, eds. *Civil Society and Political Theory.* Cambridge: MIT Press, 1992.
Coleman, James S. *Power and the Structure of Society.* New York: W. W. Norton, 1974.
Craig, Gordon A. "Letters on Dark Times." *New York Review of Books* 40 (May 13, 1993): 10–14.
De Lue, Steven M. *Political Thinking, Political Theory, and Civil Society.* Boston: Allen and Bacon, 1997.
D'Entrèves, Maurizio Passerin. *The Political Philosophy of Hannah Arendt.* London: Routledge, 1994.
Didion, Joan. *Salvador.* New York: Simon and Shuster, 1983.
Dietz, Mary. "Feminist Receptions of Hannah Arendt." In *Feminist Interpretations of Hannah Arendt,* ed. Bonnie Honig. University Park, Pa.: Pennsylvania State University Press, 1995.

———. "Hannah Arendt and Feminist Politics." In *Feminist Interpretations and Political Theory,* ed. Molly Shanley and Carole Pateman. Oxford: Polity, 1991.

Dinnerstein, Dorothy. *The Mermaid and the Minotaur: Sexual Arrangements and the Human Malaise.* New York: Harper and Row, 1976.

Disch, Lisa Jane. *Hannah Arendt and the Limits of Philosophy.* Ithaca and London: Cornell University Press, 1994.

Dossa, Shiraz. *The Public Realm and the Public Self: The Political Theory of Hannah Arendt.* Waterloo, Ont.: Wilfred Laurier University Press, 1989.

Drescher, Seymour. "Tocqueville's Two *Démocraties.*" *Journal of the History of Ideas* 25 (1964): 201–16.

Dreyfus, Hubert L. *Being-in-the-World: A Commentary on Heidegger's Being and Time, Division I.* Cambridge, Mass., and London: MIT Press, 1991.

———. "Heidegger and Foucault on the Ordering of Things." Unpublished paper.

Dumm, Thomas L. *Democracy and Punishment: Disciplinary Origins of the United States.* Madison: University of Wisconsin Press, 1987.

Ellul, Jacques. *The Technological Society.* Trans. John Wilkinson. New York: Vintage, 1964.

Ettinger, Elzbieta. *Hannah Arendt Martin Heidegger.* New Haven and London: Yale University Press, 1995.

Ferguson, Adam. *Essays on the History of Civil Society.* Ed. Fania Oz-Salzberger. Cambridge: Cambridge University Press, 1996.

Feuerbach, Ludwig. *The Essence of Christianity.* Trans. George Eliot. New York, Evanston, and London: Harper and Row, 1957.

Foucault, Michel. *Power/Knowledge: Selected Interviews and Other Writings, 1972–1977.* Ed. Colin Gordon. New York: Pantheon, 1980.

———. "The Subject and Power." In *Michel Foucault: Beyond Structuralism and Hermeneutics,* ed. Hubert Dreyfus and Paul Rabinow. Chicago: University of Chicago Press, 1983.

Friedmann, Friedrich Georg. *Hannah Arendt: Eine deutsche Jüdin im Zeitalter des Totalitarismus.* Munich and Zurich: Piper, 1985.

Fuss, Diana. *Essentially Speaking: Feminism, Nature, and Difference.* New York and London: Routledge, 1989.

Gambetta, Diego, ed. *Trust: Making and Breaking Cooperative Relations.* Oxford: Blackwell, 1988.

Garner, Reuben. *The Realm of Humanitas: Responses to the Writings of Hannah Arendt.* New York, Bern, Frankfurt am Main, and Paris: Peter Lang, 1990.

Gaus, Günter. *Zur Person: Porträts in Frage und Antwort.* Munich: Feder, 1964.

Gellner, Ernest. *Conditions of Liberty: Civil Society and the State.* New York: Penguin, 1994.

Gerth, Hans, and C. Wright Mills, trans. and eds. *From Max Weber: Essays in Sociology.* New York: Oxford University Press, 1946.

Gilligan, Carol. *In a Different Voice: Psychological Theory and Women's Development.* Cambridge, Mass., and London: Harvard University Press, 1982.

Goldenberg, Naomi R. *Returning Words to Flesh: Feminism, Psychoanalysis, and the Resurrection of the Body.* Boston: Beacon, 1990.

Gottsegen, Michael S. *The Political Thought of Hannah Arendt*. Albany: SUNY Press, 1993.
Griffin, Andrew. "Sympathy for the Werewolf." In *The Borzoi College Reader*, ed. Charles Muscatine and Melanie Griffith. 5th ed. New York: Knopf, 1984.
Griffin, Susan. *Pornography and Silence: Culture's Revenge against Nature*. New York: Harper and Row, 1981.
Hansen, Philip Birger. *Hannah Arendt*. Cambridge: Polity Press, 1993.
Havel, Václav, et al. *The Power of the Powerless*. Ed. John Keane. Armonk, N.Y.: M. E. Sharpe, 1985.
Hegel, Georg Wilhelm Friedrich. *Hegel's Phenomenology of Spirit*. Trans. A. V. Miller. Oxford, New York, Toronto, and Melbourne: Oxford University Press, 1977.
———.*Philosophy of Right*. Trans. T. M. Knox. London, Oxford, and New York: Oxford University Press, 1967.
Heidegger, Martin. *Being and Time*. Trans. John Macquarrie and Edward Robinson. New York and Evanston: Harper and Row, 1962.
Heller, Erich. *The Importance of Nietzsche*. Chicago and London: University of Chicago Press, 1988.
Hertz, Deborah. "Hannah Arendt's Rahel Varnhagen." In *German Women in the Nineteenth Century: A Social History*, ed. John C. Font. New York: Holmes and Meier, 1984.
Heuer, Wolfgang. *Hannah Arendt*. Hamburg: Rowohlt, 1987.
Hill, Melvin A., ed. *Hannah Arendt: The Recovery of the Public World*. New York: St. Martin's, 1979.
Hinchman, Lewis P., and Sandra K. Hinchman, eds. *Hannah Arendt: Critical Essays*. Albany: SUNY Press, 1993.
Hobbes, Thomas. *Leviathan, of the Matter, Forme and Power of a Commonwealth Ecclesiastical or Civil*. Ed. Michael Oakeshott. New York: Collier, 1978.
Honig, Bonnie, ed. *Feminist Interpretations of Hannah Arendt*. University Park: Pennsylvania State University Press, 1995.
Horkheimer, Max, and Theodor W. Adorno. *Dialectic of Enlightenment*. New York: Herder and Herder, 1972.
Huyssen, Andreas. *After the Great Divide: Modernism, Mass Culture, Postmodernism*. Bloomington and Indianapolis: Indiana University Press, 1986.
Innis, H. A. *The Bias of Communication*. Toronto: University of Toronto Press, 1950.
Irigaray, Luce. *This Sex Which Is Not One*. Trans. Catherine Porter with Carolyn Burke. Ithaca: Cornell University Press, 1985.
Isaac, Jeffrey C. *Arendt, Camus, and Modern Rebellion*. New Haven and London: Yale University Press, 1992.
———. "Oases in the Desert: Hannah Arendt on Democratic Politics." *American Political Science Review* 88 (March 1994): 156–68.
Jacobitti, Suzanne D. "Individualism and Political Community: Arendt and Tocqueville on the Current Debate in Liberalism." *Polity* 23 (summer 1991): 585–604.

Jacobson, Kenneth. *Embattled Selves.* New York: Atlantic Monthly, 1994.
Jaspers, Karl. *Provokationen: Gespräche und Interviews.* Ed. Hans Saner. Munich: Piper, 1969.
Kafka, Franz. *Franz Kafka: His Complete Stories.* Ed. Nahum N. Glazer. New York: Schocken, 1948.
Kant, Immanuel. *Critique of Judgment.* Trans. Werner S. Pluhar. Indianapolis: Hackett, 1987.
———. *Critique of Pure Reason.* Trans. J. M. D. Meiklejohn. Buffalo: Prometheus, 1990.
———. *Foundation of the Metaphysics of Morals.* Trans. Lewis White Beck. Indianapolis, New York, and Kansas City: Bobbs-Merrill, 1959.
Kaplan, Gisela T. "Hannah Arendt: The Life of a Jewish Woman." In *Hannah Arendt: Thinking, Judging, Freedom,* ed. Gisela T. Kaplan and Olive S. Kessler. Sydney: Allen and Unwin, 1989.
Kateb, George. *Hannah Arendt: Politics, Conscience, Evil.* Totowa, N.J.: Rowman and Allanheld, 1984.
Keane, John. *Democracy and Civil Society: On the Predicaments of European Socialism, the Prospects for Democracy, and the Problem of Controlling Social and Political Power.* London and New York: Verso, 1988.
———, ed. *Civil Society and the State.* London and New York: Verso, 1988.
Kierkegaard, Søren. *The Present Age.* Trans. Alexander Dru. New York: Harper and Row, 1962.
Klein, Melanie. *Envy and Gratitude.* New York: Basic Books, 1990.
Lacoue-Labarthe, Philippe. *Heidegger, Art, and Politics.* Trans. Chris Turner. New York and London: Basil Blackwell, 1990.
Lane, Ann M. "The Feminism of Hannah Arendt." *democracy* 3 (summer 1983): 101–17.
Lazare, Bernard. *Job's Dungheap: Essays on Jewish Nationalism and Social Revolution.* Trans. Harry Loren Binsse with a preface by Hannah Arendt. New York: Schocken, 1948.
Lefort, Claude. *Democracy and Political Theory.* Trans. David Macey. Minneapolis: University of Minnesota Press, 1988.
Lichtenberg, Joseph. *Psychoanalysis and Infant Research.* Hillsdale, N.J.: Analytic, 1983.
Luban, David. "Explaining Dark Times: Hannah Arendt's Theory of Theory." *Social Research* 50 (spring 1983): 215–247.
Lukács, Georg. *History and Class Consciousness: Studies in Marxist Dialectics.* Trans. Rodney Livingstone. London: Merlin, 1971.
Lummis, C. Douglas *Radical Democracy.* Ithaca and London: Cornell University Press, 1996.
MacKinnon, Catherine. *Feminism Unmodified: Discourses on Life and Law.* Cambridge: Harvard University Press, 1987.
———. *Toward a Feminist Theory of the State.* Cambridge: Harvard University Press, 1989.
Mainardi, Pat. "The Politics of Housework." In *The Politics of Housework,* ed. Ellen Malos. London: Allison and Busby; New York: Schocken, 1982.

Marine, Gene. *A Male Guide to Women's Liberation*. New York, Chicago, and San Francisco: Holt, Rinehart, and Winston, 1972.
Marks, Elaine, and Isabel de Courtrivon, eds. *New French Feminisms*. New York: Schocken, 1981.
Marx, Karl. *Economic and Philosophical Manuscripts of 1844*. Trans. Martin Milligan. Moscow: Foreign Language Publishing House, n.d.
———. *Karl Marx: Selected Writings*. Ed. David McLellan. Oxford: Oxford University Press, 1977.
Marx, Karl, and Friedrich Engels. *The Marx-Engels Reader*. Ed. Robert C. Tucker. 2d ed. New York: W. W. Norton, 1979.
May, Larry, and Jerome Kohn, eds. *Hannah Arendt: Twenty Years Later*. Cambridge, Mass., and London: MIT Press, 1996.
McLuhan, Marshall. *Understanding Media: The Extensions of Man*. New York: New American Library, 1964.
Mead, George Herbert. *Mind, Self, and Society: From the Standpoint of a Social Behaviorist*. Ed. Charles W. Morris. Chicago: University of Chicago Press, 1955.
Milgram, Stanley. *Obedience to Authority: An Experimental Approach*. New York: Harper and Row, 1974.
Mills, C. Wright. *The Power Elite*. New York: Oxford University Press, 1956.
Minnich, Elizabeth. "Hannah Arendt: Thinking as We Are." In *Between Women*, ed. Carol Asher, Luise De Salvo, and Sara Ruddick. Boston: Beacon, 1990.
O'Brien, Mary. *The Politics of Reproduction*. Boston, London, and Henley: Routledge and Kegan Paul, 1981.
Parekh, Birku. *Hannah Arendt and the Search for a New Political Philosophy*. London: Macmillan, 1981.
Piaget, Jean. *The Moral Judgment of the Child*. Trans. Marjorie Gabain. New York: Free Press, 1965.
Pitkin, Hanna Fenichel. "Are Freedom and Liberty Twins?" *Political Theory* 16 (November 1988): 523–52.
———. *Fortune Is a Woman: Gender and Politics in the Thought of Niccoló Machiavelli*. Berkeley, Los Angeles, and London: University of California Press, 1984.
———. "Justice: On Relating Private and Public." *Political Theory* 9 (August 1981): 327–52.
———. "Rethinking Reification." *Theory and Society* 16 (1987): 263–93.
———. "Slippery Bentham." *Political Theory* 18 (February 1990): 104–31.
———. *Wittgenstein and Justice*. Berkeley, Los Angeles, and London: University of California Press, 1972.
Polanyi, Karl. *The Great Transformation*. Boston: Beacon, 1957.
Powledge, Fred. *Free at Last? The Civil Rights Movement and the People Who Made It*. Boston, Toronto, and London: Little, Brown, 1991.
Putnam, Robert D. *Making Democracy Work: Civic Traditions in Modern Italy*. Princeton: Princeton University Press, 1993.
Reich, Robert B. *The Work of Nations: Preparing Ourselves for 21st Century Capitalism*. New York: Random House, 1992.

Reinhardt, Mark. *The Art of Being Free: Taking Liberties with Tocqueville, Marx, and Arendt*. Ithaca and London: Cornell University Press, 1997.
Riesman, David, Nathan Glazer, and Reuel Denney. *The Lonely Crowd: A Study of the Changing American Character*. New Haven and London: Yale University Press, 1964.
Riley, Denise. *"Am I That Name?" Feminism and the Category of "Women" in History*. Minneapolis: University of Minnesota Press, 1988.
Ring, Jennifer. "The Pariah as Hero: Hannah Arendt's Political Actor." *Political Theory* 19 (August 1991): 433–52.
———. *The Political Consequences of Thinking: Gender and Judaism in the Work of Hannah Arendt*. Albany: SUNY Press, 1997.
Rogin, Michael. "*Kiss Me Deadly:* Communism, Motherhood, and Cold War Movies." In *Ronald Reagan, the Movie and Other Episodes in Political Demonology*. Berkeley, Los Angeles, and London: University of California Press, 1987.
Rosen, Ron. "The House That Levitt Built." *Esquire*, December 1983, 378–90.
Ross, Andrew. *No Respect: Intellectuals and Popular Culture*. New York and London: Routledge, 1989.
Rostow, William Walter. *The Stages of Economic Growth*. Cambridge: Cambridge University Press, 1960.
Rubin, Gayle. "The Traffic in Women: Notes on the 'Political Economy' of Sex." In *Toward an Anthropology of Women*, ed. Rayna R. Reiter. New York: Monthly Review Press, 1975.
Ryan, Alan. "Dangerous Liaison." *New York Review of Books* 42 (January 11, 1996): 22–26.
Sartre, Jean-Paul. "The Republic of Silence." In *The Republic of Silence*. Ed. A. J. Liebling. New York: Harcourt, Brace, 1947.
Schelling, Thomas C. *Micromotives and Macrobehavior*. New York and London: W. W. Norton, 1978.
Schnee, Heinrich. Review of *Rahel Varnhagen*, by Hannah Arendt. *Historisches Jahrbuch* 80 (1960): 458–59.
Seligman, Adam B. *The Idea of Civil Society*. New York: Free Press, 1992.
Shklar, Judith N. "Hannah Arendt as Pariah." *Partisan Review* 50 (1983): 65–77.
Shumer, Sara Mayhew. "Power/Alienated Power." Unpublished paper presented at the annual meeting of the American Political Science Association, 1990.
Skilling, H. Gordon, and Paul Wilson, eds. *Civic Freedom in Central Europe: Voices from Czechoslovakia*. New York: St. Martin's, 1991.
Sontag, Susan. "The Imagination of Disaster." In *Against Interpretation*. New York: Farrar, Straus and Giroux, 1986.
Spelman, Elisabeth V. *Inessential Woman: Problems of Exclusion in Feminist Thought*. Boston: Beacon, 1988.
Spiegelberg, Herbert. "On the Right to Say 'We.'" In *Phenomenological Sociology*, ed. George Psathas. New York: Wiley, 1973.
Stern, Daniel. *The Interpersonal World of the Infant: A View from Psychoanalysis and Developmental Psychology*. New York: Basic, 1985.
Sumner, Gregory D. *Dwight Macdonald and the politics Circle: The Challenge*

of *Cosmopolitan Democracy*. Ithaca and London: Cornell University Press, 1996.
Taminiaux, Jacques. *La fille de Thrace et le penseur professionel: Arendt et Heidegger*. Paris: Editions Payot, 1992.
Tester, Keith. *Civil Society*. London: Routledge, 1992.
Tewarson, Heidi Thomann. *Rahel Levin Varnhagen*. Hamburg: Rowohlt, 1988.
Thomas, Paul. *Alien Politics*. New York and London: Routledge, 1994.
Tocqueville, Alexis de. *Democracy in America*. Ed. J. P. Mayer, trans. George Lawrence. Garden City, N.Y.: Doubleday, 1969.
———. *The Old Regime and the French Revolution*. Trans. Stuart Gilbert. Garden City, N.Y.: Doubleday, 1955.
———. *Recollections*. Trans. Alexander Teixeira de Mattos. New York: Meridian, 1959.
Unger, Roberto Mangabeira. *False Necessity: Anti-necessitarian Social Theory in the Service of Radical Democracy*. Cambridge and New York: Cambridge University Press, 1987.
Villa, Dana R. *Arendt and Heidegger: The Fate of the Political* Princeton: Princeton University Press, 1996.
Whitfield, Stephen. *Into the Dark: Hannah Arendt and Totalitarianism*. Philadelphia: Temple University Press, 1980.
Williamson, Oliver. *Markets and Hierarchies: Analysis and Antitrust Implications*. New York: Free Press, 1975.
Winner, Langdon. *Autonomous Technology: Technics-out-of-Control as a Theme in Political Thought*. Cambridge: MIT Press, 1977.
Winnicott, D. W. *The Child, the Family, and the Outside World*. Harmondsworth, U.K.: Penguin, 1964.
———. *The Maturational Process and the Facilitating Environment*. New York: International Universities Press, 1965.
———. *Playing and Reality*. Harmondsworth, U.K.: Penguin, 1974.
Wittgenstein, Ludwig. *Philosophical Investigations*. Trans. G. E. M. Anscombe. 3d ed. New York: Macmillan, 1968.
Wolin, Sheldon S. "Hannah Arendt and the Ordinance of Time." *Social Research* 44 (spring 1977): 91–105.
———. *Politics and Vision*. Boston and Toronto: Little, Brown, 1960.
Yack, Bernard. *The Longing for Total Revolution: Philosophical Sources of Social Discontent from Rousseau to Marx and Nietzsche*. Berkeley and Los Angeles: University of California Press, 1992.
Young-Bruehl, Elisabeth. *Hannah Arendt: For Love of the World*. New Haven and London: Yale University Press, 1982.
———. *Mind and the Body Politic*. New York and London: Routledge, 1989.
Ziff, Paul. *Semantic Analysis*. Ithaca: Cornell University Press, 1960.

Index

abstraction
　as agent, 233–39
　Arendt's attitude toward, 46–48, 50–52, 60, 99, 114, 145, 147, 149, 152–54, 159, 162–65, 208, 217
　the Blob and, 6, 74, 194, 232–39
　concept of, 237–38
　in contemporary thought, 279
　déformation professionelle and, 46–47, 50–51, 147, 232, 233, 248, 272, 276
　"empty" and "full," 75, 88, 237
　gender and, 149, 152–54, 157–65, 232
　in Hegel, 234, 236–38
　hypostasization and, 227
　as impracticality, 27, 64–65, 75, 154, 157–59, 232, 259, 279
　individual uniqueness and, 46–47, 50, 67, 75–76, 124, 147, 157–59, 183–84, 191, 233–36, 249
　in Kierkegaard, 185
　in Marx, 130–31, 135, 139, 141–42, 234, 236–37
　particularity and, 147, 157–59, 241–50, 252, 256, 270, 277–78
　parvenu and, 26–27, 31, 169, 236
　philosophy and, 147, 159, 162–65, 242–43, 248–50
　reality of, 98, 141, 238–39, 319–20n. 25
　stereotyping and, 21, 67, 75–76, 91, 158–59, 183–84, 204, 232–33, 266
　storytelling and, 277–78
　in Tocqueville, 124, 234–38
　as unavoidable, 159, 236, 246
Achilles, 263, 314n. 70
acquisitiveness
　bourgeois, 85–87, 93–94
　Tocqueville on, 118, 120, 122
　in United States, 118, 120, 122
action
　by abstractions, 76, 117, 123–24, 127, 131, 133, 142, 144, 202, 212, 231, 233–39, 251
　activism and, 59, 82–84, 106, 160–61, 173–75, 231, 284
　agency, effective, and, 8, 16–17, 19–20, 48, 98, 192, 242, 252
　behavior and, 2, 14, 178–82, 191–93, 197, 200, 225, 240
　capacity for, 111, 131, 172, 244, 246, 251, 265–66, 282
　causation and, 197–200, 281, 284, 314n. 70
　in conceptual triad, 132, 145–48, 162, 165–66, 169, 175, 177–78, 231
　concerted, 9, 56, 60, 63, 88, 121, 180, 193–96, 198–200, 209, 215, 227, 245, 253–54, 256–57, 259–60, 268, 274, 280–81, 310n. 1, 313n. 54
　conscious pariah and, 68, 71–72, 76, 98–99, 178

action (continued)
  consequences of, controlling, 9, 11–12, 139, 146, 178, 180–81, 197–200, 209, 220, 239, 252, 268, 279–81, 314n. 70
  as creativity, 146–47, 196, 283
  as duty, 77, 248
  economics and, 11–17, 179–80, 239, 258–60, 268, 279, 322–23n. 17
  explanation and, 124, 126–27, 143, 204, 225, 235–36, 239, 249, 280–81
  founding and, 110–11, 146–47, 176, 196, 216, 239
  freedom and, 1–4, 14, 50, 66, 68, 88, 166, 175, 177, 196, 221, 225, 239, 243–44, 249, 256–57
  inaction and, 181, 217
  "Just do it!" path and, 254, 280–84
  labor and, 132, 146, 178–83
  lost meaning of, 110–11, 143, 147, 274, 280
  in Marx, 131, 133, 142, 231, 233
  parvenu and, 27, 30–31, 56, 178
  peer equality and, 146, 199–200, 266, 314n. 66
  politics and, 1–4, 14, 50, 66, 68, 88, 175, 177, 196, 221, 225, 239, 243–44, 249, 256
  preconditions for, 197–200, 229–30, 253–84, 314n. 70
  relationships, web of, and, 146, 178, 180–81, 197, 200, 283
  self-realization and, 109–11, 157–58, 175–76, 264, 314n. 70
  solidarity and, 27, 56, 182, 186, 194
  spontaneity and, 1, 14, 56, 88, 110–11, 124, 146–47, 157, 176, 178–79, 197, 202, 218, 225, 254, 260, 266, 268
  thought and, 63, 73, 114, 149, 181, 191, 212, 253–54, 269–79
  time and, 190, 267–69, 324–25n. 54
  in Tocqueville, 117, 119–27, 147, 196, 234–38, 283
  totalitarianism and, 70, 87–93, 198, 211–12, 215–16
  in United States, 101, 117, 120–24
  for world's sake, 176, 179, 181, 195, 199–200, 263–64
  work and, 132, 146, 178–83, 200
administration. See administrative despotism; bureaucracy, colonial
administrative despotism, 118–22, 229
Adorno, Theodor, 9
adventurers. See secret agents
Africa, 80, 293n. 16
agency. See action
alienation
  in Marx, 138, 140, 188, 301nn. 70, 71, 301nn. 70, 71, 302n. 80
  from self, 133–34, 265
  the social and, 139–43, 163
  from world, 133–34, 140, 265, 303n. 93
ambition
  Arendt's, 48, 145, 149–51, 153–54, 156, 168, 232, 290n. 37
  Eichmann's, 206
  gender and, 147–54, 156–57, 162, 164
  Luxemburg's, 156
  parvenu's, 33, 52, 229
  Varnhagen's, 28–29
ambivalence
  Arendt's
    about ambition, autonomy, gender, 127, 168
    about control of consequences, 197–200
    about evil, 208, 210–12, 216–17
    about Marx, 127–34

Jaspers's, 210–11
meaning of, 252
America. *See* United States
amor mundi
  action and, 176, 198, 265
  Arendt's, 106, 153, 198
  as intended title, 106, 153
  lack of, today, 133
animal laborans. *See* labor
anti-Semitism
  in Arendt's life, 35–37, 44–45, 48–49, 57, 101, 156, 162
  Eichmann and, 206, 212
  explanation of, 69–76, 83, 95
  gender and, 174
  Nazi, 20, 45, 52–53, 56, 62–63, 66–67, 70–72, 74–75, 83, 127, 206, 213
  in *Origins of Totalitarianism*, 69–76, 85
  pariah and, 21, 23–24, 57
  parvenu and, 21, 23–24, 48–49, 56–58, 70–76, 94
  racism and, 50–51, 72, 78–79, 83, 191
  resistance to, 30, 36–37, 47, 55, 59–65, 67, 213–17
  social and political, 47, 53, 56, 62–64, 72–76, 94, 233, 293n. 10
  stereotyping and, 57, 70, 75–76, 91, 232–33, 266, 293n. 9
  in United States, 101, 103
  in Varnhagen's life, 23–25, 28–29, 35, 49, 56
appeasement. *See* collaboration
Arabs, 67, 105–6, 322n. 17
Arbeit. *See* labor; Marx, Karl; work
Arendt, Martha (mother)
  character, 36–38, 149–52
  femininity and, 37–38, 149–50
  in France, 37, 52, 150–51
  Jewishness and, 36
  politics of, 36–39, 65, 101, 129
  relationships
    with Blücher, 47–48, 151
    with daughter, 36–40, 43, 52, 65, 100–101, 149–53
    with Stern, 43
    in United States, 52, 100, 151–52
Arendt, Max (grandfather), 38, 174
Arendt, Paul (father), 37–38, 40, 65, 149, 153
aristocracy, 19, 32, 83, 85, 86, 203
  in Tocqueville, 121–22
  See also class, social
Aristotle, 10, 132, 188, 243, 300n. 59
art of association
  in anti-Nazi resistance, 110–11, 176, 216
  council system and, 257–58, 260
  founding and, 94, 146–47, 196, 218–25, 239, 310n. 85
  in revolution, 218–25
  in Tocqueville, 117, 119, 121–23, 147, 196
  See also action, concerted; freedom, of Brutus
assimilation, Jewish
  in Arendt's life, 35–37, 47–48
  explanation of, applied to anti-Semitism, 69–76, 95
  impossible under Nazis, 74, 185
  parvenu and, 19–24, 28–30, 33, 35, 51, 61, 68, 70, 87
  politics and, 30–31, 33, 62–68, 72
  refugees and, 51, 57–58, 61, 68, 69, 70, 76
  in Varnhagen's life, 19–24, 28–30, 33, 35, 51, 61, 68, 70, 87
Augustine, Saint, 41–44, 265, 306n. 34
authority
  absence of, 115–44, 162–65, 251
  Arendt as, 154, 243, 275
  Arendt's concept of, 310n. 85
  authoritarianism and, 294n. 40
  contemporary, 131, 251, 273, 283
  on etymology, 275–76
  gender and, 145, 148–49, 154, 159–65, 169, 173–74

authority (*continued*)
  German deference to, 55, 101
  Greeks as, 148, 164–65, 276
  Heidegger as, for Arendt, 35–36, 39–41, 45–46, 49–51, 99, 115, 150, 152–53, 161–64
  Marx as, for Arendt, 115–16, 127–34, 144, 161–63
  personal, in leadership, 263
  Tocqueville as, for Arendt, 115–16, 123, 127, 143–44, 161–64
  in United States, 117–18, 218
autonomy
  action and, 59, 70, 182, 199, 244
  Arendt's attitude toward, 162, 168
  in judgment, 4, 26–27, 33, 56, 88, 169, 182, 184–85, 218, 251, 271
  politics and, 59, 70, 175, 182, 194, 209, 244
  psychology of, 171–75, 185, 268

Bamm, Peter, 214–15
banality of evil. *See* evil, banality of
Barnouw, Dagmar, 3
Beaumont, Gustave de, 121
Beerwald, Clara (stepsister), 38
Beerwald, Eva (stepsister), 38, 151, 153
Beerwald, Martin (stepfather), 38
behavior
  action and, 2, 14, 178–82, 191–93, 197, 200, 225, 240
  behaviorism and, 190–91, 274
  conformism and, 13–15, 17–18, 45, 49–50, 52–53, 58–59, 61, 78, 81, 112, 171–86, 191–94, 217, 261–62, 271
  as isolating, 181
  labor and, 178–83
  misbehavior, non-behavior and, 178, 181
  moral standards and, 179
  pariah, parvenu, and, 178–81
  population and, 259
  relationships, web of, and, 180
  as serially enforced, 194–95
  the social and, 14–15, 171, 174, 197
  storytelling and, 311n. 14
  work and, 178–83
Being and Time (Heidegger), 49
Benhabib, Seyla, 18, 160, 162, 163, 273, 311n. 11, 320–21n. 38
Benjamin, Jessica, 247
Benjamin, Walter, 55, 268, 278, 324–25n. 54, 325–26n. 78
Bergson, Henri, 147
Berking, Helmuth, 170
Bernstein, Richard, 22
Between Past and Future, 107–8, 149, 267–68
biology
  economics and, 11–13, 19, 70, 186–87, 189
  family and, 13
  gender and, 155–56, 162
  Jewishness and, 69, 72–76, 94
  in Marx, 133, 136
  in motion pictures, 171
  nature and, 11, 15, 70, 77, 186–87, 190, 195, 221
  naturalization, spurious, and, 69–70, 72–74, 76, 78, 81, 94, 190–91, 195, 216
  pariah and, 24–25
  process and, 11, 13, 15, 70, 187, 189–90
  the social and, 11, 13–15, 17, 19, 177–86, 190–94
  technology and, 254–55, 260
birth, 32, 132, 167, 187, 307–8n. 55. *See also* natality
Blob, the
  Arendt's abandonment of imagery of, 211–12, 216–17, 225, 284
  concept of, 4–5
  explanation of the social as, 4–6, 226–51
  in Hegel, 234, 236
  in Marx, 142, 144, 231, 233–34, 236–37
  as regression fantasy, 230–31, 250

INDEX 343

as science-fiction fantasy, 4–5, 93, 177, 251
the social as, 4–5, 127, 144, 176, 177, 202, 212, 226, 251, 284
in theorizing, 6, 17, 202, 211, 225, 232
in Tocqueville, 120, 123–24, 127, 144, 170, 231–32, 234–38
totalitarianism and, 87–97, 124, 210–12, 228–29, 250
Blücher, August Charles Heinrich (father-in-law), 47–48, 150
Blücher, Heinrich Friedrich Ernst (second husband), 47–48, 52, 86, 100, 102, 129–30, 150–52, 155–56
Blücher, Klara Emilie Wilke (mother-in-law), 47–48, 150
Blumenfeld, Kurt, 44, 46, 155, 174
body
  action and, 239
  in Augustine, 42
  in Christianity, 42
  Greeks and, 165
  labor and, 132, 145, 178
  in Marx, 138
  nature and, 132
  necessity and, 11, 13–14, 70, 132, 220
  politic, 218–20
Boers, 70, 79–82, 85, 92, 94
bourgeoisie,
  as agent, 85–87, 233
  civil society and, 78, 87
  competitive isolation and, 86, 92
  deviants and, 71, 73–74, 83, 85
  hypocrisy of, 80, 82–83, 86–87, 94, 186, 204, 221, 272
  in Marx, 233
  profit motive and, 78, 85–87, 93–94
  revulsion against, 80, 82, 83, 186, 206
  salon society and, 13–14, 27, 52, 59, 71, 73, 75, 85, 186, 204, 288n. 20

totalitarianism and, 79, 85–86, 94
See also class, social
Brecht, Bertold, 113
Browning, Elizabeth Barrett, 40
Bulgaria, resistance in, 216
bureaucracy
  colonial, 70, 79–81, 84–85, 87, 92, 261
  Eichmann and, 207
  as governmental form, 12, 16, 293n. 17, 310n. 1
  in Hegel, 188, 201
  "institutional" path and, 254–60
  as isolating, 236
  market and, 12, 189, 193–94, 254
  as onion, 89–91, 95, 97, 255, 262, 272
  parvenu and, 79, 261
  totalitarianism and, 69, 78–79, 89–91, 94
  in United States, 102, 255, 262, 272
  as unwieldy, 194, 255

"can," as problematic concept, 197, 240–42, 253. See also freedom, of the will; paradox
Canovan, Margaret, 17–18
Capital (Marx), 136, 137, 139
capitalism, 15, 85, 137–38, 187
Castle, The (Kafka), 62
causation
  action and, 1, 20, 76, 124, 197, 214, 235–36, 249, 268
  in history, 130, 214, 217, 276, 294n. 33, 318n. 57, 324–25n. 54
  in Kant, 20, 76, 132
  nature and, 20, 76, 132, 145, 190
  necessity and, 190–92, 195, 245
  in Tocqueville, 235–36
  as unavoidable concept, 246
centralization
  Arendt on, 123, 257, 283
  localism now and, 102, 258–60
  Tocqueville on, 118, 120, 122–23, 257

Chaplin, Charles, 62
Char, René, 109, 111, 283
character
  individual, 24, 192–93, 196, 201
  national, 261
"characterological" path, 253, 260–69, 272, 279–80, 282–83. *See also* identity; individuality, as uniqueness; psychology
childhood
  Arendt's, 36–39, 101, 149–50
  "bad" mother in, 170–75
  character formation in, 253, 268, 273
  gender and, 160–61, 172–74
  "lord of dreams" and, 63, 65–66, 264
  pariah and, 65, 105, 265–66
  parvenu and, 14, 105, 264
  regression to, 170–75
Christianity
  in Arendt's thought, 41–44, 149–50
  birth metaphor in, 307–8n. 55
  equality and, 73, 81
  as established religion, 19, 29, 37, 74–75
  in Kierkegaard, 185
  in Tocqueville, 125
  in United States, 125
  in Varnhagen's life, 19, 28, 30
citizenship
  free, Arendt's theory of, 112–14, 145, 147–48, 162, 165, 175–76, 282
  identity and, 157–59
  judgment and, 274
  peer equality and, 30, 73, 105, 122, 146, 199, 266, 314n. 66
  preconditions for, 239, 251, 256, 262–69, 274, 278, 280
  respect and, 182
  responsibility and, 74, 194–95, 268–69, 279, 282, 284
  revolution and, 218–19, 223–25
  semantic analysis and, 276
  solidarity and, 72, 93, 111, 182, 216, 241–42
  thinking and, 269–81
  time and, 267–69
  in Tocqueville, 117–18, 121
  in United States, 101–2, 117–18, 121
  or world, 157–59, 259
civil rights movement (U.S.), 229, 322n. 8
civil society
  bourgeoisie and, 78, 87
  contemporary views on, 282–83, 315nn. 75, 76
  in Hegel, 12, 62, 188, 201
  in Marx, 12, 62, 188, 201
  the state and, 12, 62, 72, 78, 188, 201, 227
class, social
  of Arendt's second husband, mother, 150
  high society as, 32, 74, 183
  among Jews, 23
  in Marx, 140, 237
  the mass and, 83, 85, 183
  the mob and, 82
  parvenu and, 21–22, 32
  as system, 32, 83, 85, 183
  in United States, 101, 103
  Varnhagen and, 19
clichés
  autonomous thinking and, 271
  as dead words, 274–75
  Eichmann and, 207, 269–70
Cohn, Rafael (maternal uncle), 38
Cold War
  disappearance of, 7
  Human Condition and, 16, 100, 131–32
  international, 99–100, 106, 112
  in motion pictures, 5, 170–71
  in United States, 102–4, 106, 131–32
collaboration
  anxiety and, 59, 113, 209
  conformism and, 194, 261

Jewish, 213–14, 217
  in occupied Europe, 215–17
  parvenu and, 45, 53, 56, 58–59, 66, 80, 83, 94, 194, 208–10, 213–16, 228–29
  as ruthlessness, work mentality, 147
  totalitarianism and, 59, 80, 209, 211–16, 228–29, 262
colonial administrators. *See* bureaucracy, colonial; imperialism, colonial administrators, secret agents in
common sense
  conformism and, 82, 84, 88, 271
  philosophy and, 46, 164, 279
communism
  Arendt's opposition to, 12–13, 16, 131–32, 322n. 17
  totalitarianism and, 69, 98–100, 112, 131–32
Communist Manifesto, The (Marx and Engels), 139
Communist Party, 43, 100, 102
computers, 255, 273
concentration camps, 52, 97, 213
  Arendt's experience of, 55–56, 193, 210, 268
  Eichmann and, 206
  as laboratories, 92–93, 95
  as radical evil, 108
  totalitarianism and, 70, 92–93, 95
Condorcet, Marie Jean Antoine Nicolas Caritat, marquis de, 218
conformism
  Arendt's personal, 151
  behavior and, 13–15, 17–18, 45, 49–50, 52–53, 58–59, 61, 73, 80, 112, 177–86, 191–94, 217, 261–62, 271
  bourgeoisie and, 86–87
  as character structure, 193, 204, 261–62
  as childishness, 264
  conformity and, 182, 184–85
  in Tocqueville, 103–4, 118, 123

totalitarianism and, 45, 53, 56, 58–59, 66, 80, 83, 94, 194, 208–10, 213–16, 228–29
  in United States, 100–104, 106, 118, 123
conscious pariah
  as adulthood, 63, 65, 264
  identity and, 65–67, 110
  Jewishness and, 62–68, 71–72, 76
  as political alternative, 62–68, 71–72, 76, 98–99, 112–14, 123, 178, 192
  rebellion and, 82, 93
consequences of action
  control over, 9, 11–12, 139, 146, 178, 180–81, 197–200, 209, 239, 252, 268, 279–81, 314n. 70
  large-scale, 11–12, 62, 201–2, 209, 238–39, 252, 268, 279–81
  as relationships, web of, 146, 178, 180–81, 197, 200, 283
  as stories, 146, 311n. 14
Constant, Benjamin, 131
constitution
  as activity of constituting, 218, 284
  United States, 103, 219–25
contradiction
  in theorizing, 239–50
  in word meanings, 219
  See also dialectics; dichotomization; paradox; triad; words
control over consequences. *See* consequences of action, control over
conundrums. *See* freedom, of the will; "micro-macro" conundrum; paradox
convergence theories, 100, 170
council system
  Arendt's view of, 105, 257–58, 260
  in France, projected, 111
  in Middle East, projected, 105
courage
  Achilles and, 263

courage (*continued*)
  cynicism and, 274
  endurance and, 166
  Greek view of, 148, 164, 176
  Hercules and, 166
  for political action, 55, 64, 175–76, 263, 268–69, 274, 279, 282
  in resistance, 110, 113–14, 263
  storytelling and, 276
  See also heroism
creativity. *See* spontaneity
Critique of Pure Reason (Kant), 37
culture
  European prejudice about, 293n. 16
  gender and, 159–61, 173
  as human characteristic, 233
  in Marx, 136, 141
  meaning of, 146, 286n. 12
cynicism
  conspiracy theories and, 82–84, 91
  contemporary, 256, 273, 279
  courage and, 274
  in the mass, 84
  in the mob, 82–83
  totalitarianism and, 91

Dante Alighieri, 264
das Man, 49–51, 60–61, 163, 227, 291n. 63
deceit. *See* hypocrisy
déformation professionelle
  of historians, 233, 276
  of philosophers, 46, 48, 50, 163, 232, 243
  of social, behavioral scientists, 233
democracy
  Athenian, 17, 139, 164
  contemporary, 16, 257
  in Marx, 139, 303n. 86
  in Tocqueville, 116–27, 234–36
  totalitarianism and, 100
Democracy in America (Tocqueville), 115–27
  Arendt's reading of, 115–16, 124, 297–98n. 3
  two volumes, relationship of, 117–20, 124, 289n. 9
demonization
  abstraction and, 239
  hypostasization and, 226
  Jaspers on, 129–31, 143, 210–11
  organizing and, 229–30
  as rhetorical device, 228–30
  totalitarianism and, 95–96, 205–12, 228
  See also evil; personification
Denmark, resistance in, 215–16
dialectics, 246–50, 278, 302n. 80
dichotomization
  in *Human Condition*, 143, 148, 165–68, 175–77, 249
  in Marx, 143
  wartime choices and, 63–64, 68, 113, 230
  in word usage, 219
Dietz, Mary, 165–68
Dinesen, Isaak (Karen Christenze Dinesen, Baroness Blixen), 157, 277
Dinnerstein, Dorothy, 173
Disch, Lisa Jane, 278
dissertation, Arendt's. *See Love in Saint Augustine*
diversity. *See* individuality, as uniqueness
dyad. *See* dichotomization; triad

earth
  homo faber as endangering, 167–68
  as mother, 113, 153, 167–68
  nuclear weapons as endangering, 106–7, 112, 229, 251
  ordinary language as located on, 247
  world and, 153, 303n. 93
economics
  action and, 11–17, 179–80, 239, 258–60, 268, 279, 322–23n. 17

bourgeoisie and, 78, 85–87, 93
global, 258–60, 279
market, rise of, and, 11–14, 16–17, 19, 254
in Marx, 133, 136–38, 140–42, 195, 302n. 80
in Middle East, 106
in Myrdal, 188
politics and, 11–12, 140, 179–80, 239, 322–23n. 17
the social and, 11–15, 17–18, 70–87, 177–89, 191–94, 217
in Tocqueville, 118, 120, 122
totalitarianism and, 70, 77–78, 82, 85
in United States, 118, 120, 122, 224
efficiency. *See* technology; utilitarianism; work
Eichmann, Adolf
character and life of, 205–7, 212, 262
holocaust and, 205–7
narration of life by Arendt, 277
as parvenu, 206–7
thoughtlessness of, 269–72
Eichmann in Jerusalem, 204–17
controversy over, 155, 186, 204, 208, 213–14
explanation in, 204, 212–17, 225, 239, 318n. 57
theoretical difficulties in, 202, 204, 212–17, 219, 225, 239, 318n. 57
1844 Manuscripts (Marx), 134, 137
elections
Arendt's views on, 223–24, 257–58
Tocqueville on, 118–20
elite. *See* aristocracy
Engels, Friedrich, 234
equality
economic, 322n. 17
natural, 63, 73
peer, of citizens, 30, 73, 105, 122, 146, 199, 266, 314n. 66

social leveling and, 33, 72, 101, 119
Tocqueville on, 116–17, 119, 122, 236
essentialism, 159, 320–21n. 38
Ettinger, Elzbieta, 38, 39–40, 48, 152
evil
Arendt's view of, 208–13
banality of, 207–9, 211–13, 256
Jaspers on, 129–31, 143, 208, 210–11, 299–300n. 46
Kant on, 95
organization and, 229
radical, 95–96, 208, 210–12, 316n. 18
exceptionalism
American, 124–25
individual
Jews and, 23–24, 26, 72, 83, 85, 150, 155, 213
parvenu and, 23, 56, 92, 123, 150, 155, 213
women and, 150, 155–56
in Tocqueville, 123–25
exchange. *See* market
existentialism, 176, 280
expertise. *See* technology
explanation
action and, 124, 126–27, 143, 204, 212–25, 239, 249
of the Blob, 226–50
historical, 130, 214, 217, 276, 294n. 33, 318n. 57, 324–25n. 54
of holocaust, 69, 76, 96, 318n. 57
"Just do it!" path and, 280–81
in Tocqueville, 235–36

family
and gender, 29, 153–54, 159–61, 165, 172–74, 188
as institution, 105, 160–61, 268
metaphorical
in structure of *Human Condition*, 174–76
in Tocqueville, 120

family (*continued*)
  parvenu motivation and, 29, 59, 179, 195, 209, 264
  the social as facsimile of, 13–15, 174
  as unit, 11, 13, 188
Farmer, James, 229
father figures
  Arendt's
    as authorities, 115–16, 127–34, 144, 152–53, 161–65
    Blumenfeld as, 38, 174
    Danish king as, 216
    grandfather as, 38, 174
    Heidegger as, 40–41, 115–16, 153, 161–64
    Jaspers as, 40, 129–30
    Marx as, 115–16, 127–34, 144, 161–63
    own father's death and, 37–38, 40, 65, 149, 153, 161–62
    Tocqueville as, 115–16, 123, 127, 143–44, 161, 163–64
  in infancy, 172–74
  as protection against "bad" mother, 161–62, 168, 174–76, 231, 279
  in structure of *Human Condition*, 161–62, 175–76
  as symbolizing autonomy, 120, 170, 173–74
  as symbolizing subjection, 153, 173–76
federalism
  Arendt's view of, 257, 259
  in France, projected, 111
  in Middle East, projected, 105, 123
  Tocqueville on, 118, 120, 122–23, 257
  in United States, 118, 123, 257
Feldman, Ron H., 52
Feuerbach, Ludwig, 141–42
fiction
  ideology and, 91, 95, 107, 186, 213, 271–74
  "lord of dreams" and, 63, 65
  storytelling and, 276–78

films. *See* motion pictures
founding, 94, 146–47, 196, 218–25, 239, 310n. 85
France
  anti-Semitism in, 57
  Arendt in, 46–47, 52, 55–57, 107, 116
  Martha Arendt in, 37, 52, 150–51
  occupation of, by Germany, 55, 107–8, 114, 229
  politics in, 57, 107–12, 283
  resistance in, 107–14, 123, 148–49, 176, 181–82, 185, 193, 217, 229, 283
  revolution in, 116, 217, 219–23
  Tocqueville on, 124, 126–27, 283
  Varnhagen in, 28, 109
freedom
  action and, 1–3, 19, 68, 88, 111, 166, 239, 244–45, 257, 266, 274, 280
  Arendt's concept of, 2, 68, 111, 147, 245
  the Blob and, 2, 8–10, 114, 144, 197
  of Brutus, 111
  causation and, 20, 76, 132
  civil society and, 201
  as creativity, 146–47, 196
  in Kant, 20, 76, 132, 320n. 30
  liberty and, 298n. 7
  as lost concept, 1, 109–12, 274–76, 280
  in Marx, 130, 133, 135–36, 138–39, 141–43, 190
  necessity and, 2, 43, 143, 190, 196, 220–22, 224–25, 245, 274, 302n. 83, 317n. 55
  neighborly love and, 28, 175, 274
  paradox of, 6, 136, 142, 190, 196, 217, 225, 239–40, 245, 256
  peer equality and, 146, 199, 266, 314n. 66
  personal and public, 209, 228, 248
  politics and, 1–3, 19, 68, 88, 111, 166, 239, 244–45, 257, 266, 274, 280

preconditions for, 8, 143, 239, 257, 260, 262–63, 268, 281–84, 322–23n. 17
in resistance, 107, 109–11, 176, 230
revolution and, 218–25
teaching of, 124, 144, 231, 239, 274
in Tocqueville, 117–19, 121–25, 196, 244
totalitarianism and, 100
in United States, 100–104, 117–18, 122–23, 163, 257, 310n. 85
of the will, 9, 42–43, 119, 125, 147, 163, 239–50, 320n. 30
world government and, 157–58, 259
Freud, Sigmund, 267, 268, 316n. 18

gender
Arendt's experience of, 37–38, 43–44, 48, 145, 147, 149–59, 161–65
Arendt's views on, 29, 35–36, 47–48, 65, 127, 147, 154–56, 168
homosexuality and, 73, 83, 85
in *Rahel Varnhagen*, 29
in structure of *Human Condition*, 148, 161, 165–71, 174–76, 308–9nn. 62, 65
in Tocqueville, 120, 125–26, 170
and "woman problem," 29, 36, 38, 153–54, 159
generalization. *See* abstraction
genocide. *See* holocaust
German Ideology, The (Marx and Engels), 137, 139
Germany
as agent, 241
Arendt in, 35–37, 39, 45–46, 48, 67, 99, 149, 232
authority in, 55, 101
Jews in, 21, 23, 28, 56–58, 63, 162
language, 78, 207, 227

philosophy in, 163–64, 227, 234
resistance to Nazis in, 214–15
war and, 55, 59, 107–8, 238
Weimar, 100, 102
Gilligan, Carol, 160–61, 164, 173
Goldenberg, Naomi, 4–5
greed. *See* acquisitiveness
Greece, ancient
authority of, 148, 164–65, 276, 310n. 85
German philosophy and, 163–64
on heroism, 148, 164, 176
in *Human Condition*, role of, 17, 36, 148, 162, 164–65, 168, 174–76, 231, 310n. 85
in Marx, 139–40
politics in, 11, 13, 17, 73, 139, 164–65, 219
Grundrisse, The (Marx), 137, 237

Hartsook, Nancy, 165
Havel, Václav, 273
Hegel, Georg Wilhelm Friedrich
on abstraction, 234, 236–38
on civil society, 12, 62, 188, 201
on dialectics, 247, 249, 302n. 80
Jaspers on, 130
Marx and, 139, 141
Heidegger, Elfriede, 40–41, 45, 86, 152
Heidegger, Martin
Arendt's relationship with, 35–36, 39–41, 43–45, 48–51, 149–53, 159, 163–64, 169
as authority for Arendt, 49–51, 99, 115, 152–53, 161–64
Being and Time, 49
das Man in, 49–51, 60–61, 163, 227
as elite, 86
as Nazi, 45, 49, 232
as philosopher, 40–41, 44, 46, 49–51, 60, 99, 147, 159, 163–64, 227, 232, 243, 272, 325–26n. 78
as teacher, 39, 325–26n. 78
on world, 303–4n. 93

Heine, Heinrich, 63
Hercules, 166
heroism
   Achilles and, 263, 314n. 70
   Eichmann and, 206, 207
   everyday, 175–76, 263
   Greek view of, 148, 164, 176
   Hercules and, 166
   in resistance, 110, 113–14, 148, 263
   storytelling and, 276
   totalitarianism and, 88, 206, 214–15
Heydrich, Reinhardt, 211–12, 262
history
   causal explanation in, 130, 214, 217, 276, 294n. 33, 318n. 57, 324–25n. 54
   déformation professionelle of, 233, 276
   desire to enter, 157, 206
   "making" of, 314n. 66
   in Marx, 128, 130, 136–37, 140
   in *On Revolution*, 204
   paradoxes in, 241, 254
   reality and, 98, 177
   as storytelling, 277
   in Tocqueville, 235–36
   twentieth-century, 66, 149, 209
   understanding one's own, 20, 31, 62
   world, in Arendt's life, 45, 129, 150
Hitler, Adolf, 44–46, 94, 96–97, 206, 211–12, 262
Hobbes, Thomas, 8, 237
holocaust
   bureaucracy and, 79–80, 194, 213
   collaboration and, 59, 73, 209, 212–17, 228, 262
   Eichmann and, 205–7
   evil of, 95–96, 208–12, 228
   explanation of, 69, 75–76, 96, 228, 318n. 57
   irrationality of, 69, 75, 87–88, 94, 96
   Jewish leadership in, 213–14
   Origins of Totalitarianism to explain, 69–71, 75, 87–88, 96
   stereotyping and, 75, 232–33
   survivor guilt and, 108, 145, 152, 228
homo faber. *See* work
homosexuality. *See* gender
Honig, Bonnie, 155–57
Horkheimer, Max, 9
housekeeping
   Arendt's view of, 165–67
   Greek view of, 11–12, 15–17, 19
   as labor, 166–67, 171
   as myopic perspective, 236
   Myrdal on, 188
   rise of, as the social, 11–12, 16–17, 168, 186–88, 193
Human Condition, The
   abstractness of, 114, 131, 145, 150, 152, 162–64
   Greeks in, 17, 36, 148, 162, 164–65, 168, 174–76, 231, 310n. 85
   intellectual influences on, 41, 115–34, 143–44, 161, 164, 170, 188, 243, 312n. 34
   project of, 98, 112–14, 145
   social as Blob in, 3–4, 10, 15, 19, 21, 95, 177–202, 226–50
   structure of, 132, 143, 145–46, 148–49, 161–62, 165–71, 174–77, 231
   thinking in, 4, 112, 149, 162, 269, 272
   writing of, 98–114, 151–53
   mentioned, 18, 70, 157, 158, 174, 203, 210, 233, 253, 254, 264, 276
Humboldt, Wilhelm von, 22
Hungary, 1956 uprising in, 100
Husserl, Edmund, 39–40
Huyssen, Andreas, 170
hypocrisy
   bourgeois, 80, 82, 83, 86–87, 94, 186, 204, 221, 272
   fictitious world of ideology and, 91, 95, 186, 207, 213, 271–74

individual, 29–30, 33, 61, 110, 195
  Nazi language rules and, 207
  parvenu, 26, 28–30, 33, 80, 82, 86
  the social and, 29–30, 33, 52, 61, 87, 183, 186, 192
hypostasization
  the Blob and, 3, 217, 226–28, 250
  in German philosophy, 227
  in Heidegger, 49, 164, 226–27
  of "political," none, 226, 318n. 1
  of "social," 3, 164, 168, 180, 201

"ideational" path, 253, 269–83
identity
  Arendt's as problematic, 48, 145, 149–53, 156–58
  citizenship and, 157–59
  gender and, 160–62
  pariah and, 19, 157–59
  recent interest in, 17, 282
  regression and, 170–71
  the social and, 14, 170–71
  solidarity and, 65–67
  as unique, 88, 146–47, 157–59, 183, 197–99, 234–36, 265–66, 282, 306n. 34
ideology
  Arendt's concept of, 87, 94, 247–48, 294–95n. 47
  disorientation and, 84, 91, 271–74
  fictional world in, 91, 95, 186, 207, 213, 271–74
  in French politics, 109
  as irrational policy, 87, 94
  language and, 207, 247, 276
  in United States, 104, 272–73
"Ideology and Terror," 96
imperialism
  bourgeoisie in, 79, 82–83, 85–86
  components of, 69–70, 79
  colonial administrators, secret agents in, 79–85, 261
  development of, 80–85, 94
  economic social and, 70–71, 186, 189, 192
  nature of, 77, 89
  as policy, 192
individuality
  abstraction and, 21, 67, 72, 75–76, 91, 124, 147, 157–59, 183–84, 191, 204, 232–36, 249, 266
  action, concerted, and, 194–96, 198–200, 281, 286n. 15
  as autonomy, 42–43, 103, 124, 144, 157, 171, 174, 182, 185, 194, 199
  "bad" mother and, 171, 174
  concept of, as problematic, 92–93, 144, 239, 244, 261
  in Heidegger, 49–50
  as isolation, 50, 79, 84–86, 89, 117, 119, 121–23, 167, 181, 193–95
  in Kierkegaard, 185
  in Marx, 133, 139, 141, 144, 234, 243
  "micro-macro" conundrum and, 246, 248–49, 320n. 30
  in Myrdal, 188
  neighborly love and, 42–43, 48, 175
  parvenu exceptionalism and, 23, 56, 92, 123, 150, 155, 213
  political theory and, 99, 112, 124, 131, 145, 147, 159, 235–37, 270–71, 277–78
  the social and, 14, 17, 61, 174–75, 181–86, 191–96, 199, 202, 204, 230
  storytelling and, 277
  in Tocqueville, 103, 117, 119, 121–24, 144
  totalitarianism and, 88–93, 193
  as uniqueness, 124, 146–47, 157–59, 183, 191, 197–99, 220, 233–36, 265–66, 282, 306n. 34
  in United States, 103, 117–19, 121–24
initiative. See spontaneity
innovation. See spontaneity

"institutional" path, 253–60, 268–69, 279–80, 282–83
institutional structure. *See* structure, institutional
instrumentalism. *See* utilitarianism
interest
  action and, 179, 239
  bourgeoisie and, 86
  of a collectivity, 13, 88, 133, 188
  displaced by "image," 272
  in the mass, 84
  self-, and self-sacrifice, 65–67, 88, 92, 153, 175–76, 264
  totalitarianism and, 69, 88, 91–92
internment camp. *See* concentration camp
introspection. *See* psychology
Isaac, Jeffrey C., 228, 257, 320–21n. 38
Israel, 67, 104–6, 112, 322n. 17
  Eichmann trial and, 205, 213–14

Japanese internment in United States, 101
Jaspers, Gertrud, 40, 152
Jaspers, Karl
  Arendt's letters to, 101–4, 106, 131, 151, 155, 186, 209, 210
  Arendt's relationship with, 37, 39–40, 45, 129, 152
  on evil, 129–31, 143, 210–11
  as father figure, 40–41, 129–30
  on Marx, 129–31, 143, 211
  on philosophy, 37, 41, 278
  on present moment, 267
  Psychologie der Weltanschauungen, 37
Jefferson, Thomas, 257
"Jew as Pariah: A Hidden Tradition, The," 62–66
Jew as Pariah, The, 52, 62–68, 104, 209
Jews
  biologically defined, 69, 72–76, 94
  as citizens, 104–6, 113, 158–59
  collaboration with Nazis by, 213–14, 217, 229
  as collectivity, 241
  gender of, as symbols, 174
  hatred for, 71–72, 83
  Jewishness and, in Arendt's life, 35–37, 43–45, 47–48, 101, 122, 144, 154–57, 162, 164, 290nn. 37, 44
  Jewishness and, in Heine, 63
  Jewish Question and, 20, 44, 154, 155, 159, 216
  Jewish state and, 67, 104–6, 322n. 17
  as pariahs, 21–37, 43, 50–53, 56–58, 62–64, 66–68, 70–71, 75, 105, 159, 213–14
  as parvenus, 21–32, 35, 50–53, 56, 71–76, 83, 85–87, 94–95, 150, 155, 213
  politics and, 72–73, 75, 105–6, 158–59, 324–25n. 54
  resistance to Nazis by, 213–14, 217
  salon society and, 52, 59, 71, 73, 83, 85
  self-hatred in, 23–24, 36, 57, 94, 209, 214, 217
  stereotyping of, 67, 72, 75–76, 91, 232–33, 266, 293n. 9
  in United States, 101, 103
  Zionism and, 44, 46, 67, 106, 214
  See also anti-Semitism
Jogiches, Leo, 156
Judaism. *See* Jews
judgment
  abstraction and, 159, 266, 270–72
  capacity for, 110, 218, 244, 251, 265–66, 276, 282
  citizenship and, 110, 157, 218, 270–72, 274
  dialectics and, 278
  social behavior and, 27, 33, 56, 76, 79, 84, 169, 178, 182, 184–85, 188, 206, 266, 272, 273

totalitarianism and, 70, 88
"Just do it!" path, 254, 280–84
justice
    abstraction and, 159, 161
    in Arendt personally, 130, 274
    and equity, 73
    international, 258
    as key word of politics, 275
    in Marx, 129–30
    politics and, 227, 275
    reality of, 274

Kafka, Franz, 10, 61, 62, 184–85, 269
Kant, Immanuel
    antinomies in, 320n. 30
    Arendt's attitude toward, 37, 39, 76, 130, 154
    causation in, 20, 76, 132
    evil in, 95
    freedom in, 20, 76, 132
    kingdom of ends in, 167
    nature in, 20, 76, 132
kibbutz, 105
Kierkegaard, Søren
    Arendt's reading of, 37, 49
    as Christian thinker, 44, 185
    philosophic tradition and, 131, 243, 271
    the public and, 185
Kirchheimer, Otto, 181
Kraus, Karl, 46
Krushchev, Nikita, 100

labor
    abstraction and, 236, 248
    behavior and, 178–80, 183, 187
    biology and, 132, 166, 178–79, 187
    Boers and, 81
    in conceptual triad, 132, 145–48, 162, 165–66, 169, 175, 177–78, 231
    definition of, 132, 145, 179
    division of, 11, 187, 237
    as feminine, 166–68, 307n. 54, 309n. 65

    as isolating, 167, 320–21n. 38
    in Marx, 132–34, 136, 138, 143, 234, 237, 302n. 83
    as *mentalité*, 147, 179–80, 192, 266
    in modernity, 178, 262
    movement, 180
    as myopic perspective, 236, 272
    nature and, 81, 132, 145, 166, 178
    necessity and, 132, 145, 178–80, 187
    politics and, 147, 158, 179, 181–82, 192, 266
    process and, 178, 187
    the social and, 15, 168, 177, 187
    work and, 132–34, 178, 266
language. *See* words
Lazare, Bernard, 21, 63–67
Lenin, Vladimir Ilyich, 44, 308n. 56
Levin, Rahel. *See* Varnhagen, Rahel
liberté. *See* freedom
"A Little Fable" (Kafka), 10
localism. *See* centralization
Locke, John, 15, 132
"lord of dreams," 63, 65–66
lost treasure
    pearl diving and, 276, 278
    politics and, 1–3, 110–11, 143, 147, 274, 280
    as public, 109–11, 176
    of *Résistance*, 109–12
    as spirit of revolution, 218–19, 223–25
    thought and, 149, 224–25, 243
    in United States, 223–25
    words and, 276, 278
love. *See amor mundi*; Augustine; neighborly love; Varnhagen, Rahel
Love in Saint Augustine, 41–44, 145, 289–90n. 33, 290nn. 37, 44
Lukács, Georg, 9, 134
Lummis, C. Douglas, 176, 263
Luxemburg, Rosa, 39, 129, 156, 289n. 14, 290n. 37

Machiavelli, Niccolò, 267, 274
Magnes, Judah L., 106, 323n. 29
Man, das. See *das Man*
market, the
  bureaucracy and, 12, 189, 193–94, 254–60, 322n. 17
  as isolating, 86, 137, 141, 188, 193–96, 256
  Marx on, 136–38, 141–42, 195, 302n. 80, 304n. 99
  politics and, 106, 125, 322n. 17
  rise of, 11–17, 19
  the social and, 77–87, 177, 187–88, 193
  as value setting, 187–88, 224, 312n. 34
Marx, Karl
  abstraction in, 130–31, 135, 139, 141, 142, 236–38
  action and, 128, 131, 133, 142, 231, 233
  alienation in, 133–34, 138, 140, 177
  Arendt's view of, 12–13, 16, 44, 115, 127–34, 140–44, 161, 162–64, 243, 249, 272
  the Blob and, 141–42, 231, 233, 236–37
  on bourgeois political economists, 141–42, 188
  Capital, 136–37, 139
  on civil society, 62, 188, 201
  Communist Manifesto, 139
  on democracy, 139, 303n. 86
  on economics, 125, 136–38, 141–42
  1844 Manuscripts, 134, 137
  on Feuerbach, 141–42
  on freedom, 130, 133, 135–36, 138–39, 141–43, 190, 196, 302n. 83
  German Ideology, The, 137, 139
  Grundrisse, The, 137, 237
  Hegel and, 139, 141, 234, 237
  on history, 128, 130, 136–37, 140, 324–25n. 54
  on individuality, 133, 139, 141, 144, 234, 243
  on institutions, 257
  Jaspers and, 129–31, 143, 211
  on labor, 132–34, 136, 138, 143, 234, 237, 302n. 83
  on the market, 136–38, 141–42, 195, 302n. 80, 304n. 99
  on nature, 131–35, 138, 141, 143, 188, 302n. 80, 304n. 99
  on necessity, 133, 142, 190, 196, 302n. 83, 304n. 99
  paradox and, 239, 243, 245, 249
  philosophy and, 130–31, 234, 236, 271
  political theory and, 144, 236, 238, 243, 245, 249
  on power, 136, 138, 141
  on process, 133, 140
  on revolution, 142, 188, 304n. 101
  on society, 137, 141
  Sorcerer's Apprentice story in, 137, 189
  on species-being, 133–35, 138–39
  on the state, 62, 139
  on technology, 137–38
  Tocqueville and, 115, 143–44
  totalitarianism and, 98, 112, 127–31, 145
  on work, 132–34, 136, 138, 143, 234, 237, 302n. 83
  on the world, 133, 135–36, 138, 140, 303n. 93
mass
  the Blob as, 93, 104, 186, 193, 202, 220
  as feminine, 170–71
  movements, 89–90, 262
  murder, 108, 209–10
  in *The Origins of Totalitarianism*, 70, 79, 84–87, 94, 193–94, 262
  poverty, 220, 222
  society, 5, 16, 83, 85, 88, 92, 96, 170–71, 261
  United States as, 103–4, 123, 220

mastery. *See* consequences of action, control over
McCarran-Walters Act, 102
McCarthy, Senator Joseph, 102–4, 106, 123
McLuhan, Marshall, 273
media, 7, 45, 170–71, 252, 254–55, 268, 273
mentalité. See ontology
metaphor
　Arendt's use of, 94, 277, 307–8n. 55
　the Blob as, 3–4, 182–83, 226
　chronological, 142, 243–44
　explication and, 230, 250
　spatial, 190, 243–44
"micro-macro" conundrum, 241–50, 252, 256, 286n. 15, 320n. 30
Middle East. *See* Israel; Palestine
Milgram, Stanley, 262
Mills, C. Wright, 256
mob
　as adolescent rebellion, 181
　disappearance of, 84–85, 94, 262
　imperialism and, 70, 79, 81–87, 94, 294nn. 24, 28
modernity
　equality and, 73
　labor and, 178
　in Marx, 136
　paradox of, 5–9
　revolution and, 109, 111
　as self-centered, 2, 35, 74, 176, 261
　the social and, 10–11, 60, 98, 197, 203, 244
　thinking and, 272
monarchy, 15–16, 216, 221, 244
mother figures
　Arendt's relationship with own, 36–40, 43, 52, 65, 100–101, 149–53
　"bad," 171–76, 230–31
　the Blob as, 171–75, 230–31, 279
　in structure of *The Human Condition*, 161–62, 165–75

in Tocqueville, 120, 170
motion pictures, 4–5, 170–71, 285–86n. 4. *See also* media
mutuality. *See* solidarity
Myrdal, Gunnar, 188

natality, 165–66, 307–8n. 55. *See also* birth
nationalism
　anti-Semitism and, 72
　Arendt's concept of, 81, 294n. 21
　Israel and, 67, 105
　land and, 81
　nation-state and, 258, 310n. 1
　pariahs and, 67, 105
　in United States, 101, 105
nature
　Boers and, 81
　as causal necessity, 76, 186, 190, 221
　as childhood, 65, 78, 80–81
　equality and, 63, 73
　as "green things," 28, 31, 66, 77, 265
　as helpless dependence, 20–21, 24, 32, 64, 264
　in Kant, 76
　in Marx, 131–35, 138, 141, 143, 302n. 80
　native peoples and, 78, 81
　as problematic concept, 77, 141, 239, 312n. 34
　as regression, 65, 78, 80–81, 264
　society and, 76, 168, 312n. 34
　spurious naturalization and, 72–74, 76–79, 94, 190, 192, 195
　as threatened by *homo faber*, 168
　as threat to civilization, 26, 78, 81, 145, 166–67, 170, 190
　in Tocqueville, 126
Naziism
　in Arendt's life, 44–46, 49–50, 67, 107–8, 150
　as causing moral collapse, 214
　citizenship potential in, 113

Naziism (*continued*)
  as diabolical, 95–96, 208, 210–12, 228, 316n. 18
  Eichmann and, 205–7, 212–13, 217
  human nature and, 92–93, 208
  ideology and, 87–88, 91, 95–96, 186, 213, 272–74
  Jews and, 20, 45, 52–53, 56, 62–63, 66–67, 70–72, 74–75, 83, 127, 206, 213
  parvenus and collaboration in, 45, 56, 59, 80, 83, 94, 194, 208–10, 212–16, 228–29
  as stimulus to resistance, 53, 63, 76, 112–13, 145, 149, 175, 214–15, 228–30
  in United States, 103–4
necessity
  Arendt's concept of, 2, 11–12, 14, 244–45
  Augustine on, 43
  false and real, 77–78, 83, 94, 106, 190–92, 195, 220–22, 224–25, 239–40, 274
  freedom and, 2, 43, 143, 190, 193, 196, 220–22, 224–25, 245, 274, 317n. 55
  individual and collective, 187, 194–96
  labor and, 132, 145, 178–80, 187
  in Marx, 133, 142, 190, 196, 302n. 83, 304n. 99
  in motion, 70, 192
  nature and, 76, 186, 190
  as problematic concept, 190, 313n. 44
  the social and, 186–87, 190, 220–25, 317n. 41
neighborly love
  in Arendt's life, 41–44, 48, 150
  in Augustine, 41–44, 265
  identity and, 42–43, 48, 175
  romanticism and, 43–44, 48, 150, 175, 210, 265, 272
  as term in conceptual triad, 41–43, 145

Nietzsche, Friedrich
  amor fati in, 106, 265
  conflict in, 266
  as moralist, 268
  philosophy and, 131, 243, 271
  on resentment, 262
nuclear weapons, 5, 99, 102–3, 106–7, 112, 229, 251

O'Brien, Mary, 165, 168
On Revolution, 204–5, 217–25, 239, 317n. 55, 318n. 57
ontology
  of Arendt's concepts, 179–80, 239, 320–21n. 38
  of behavior, 180
  and "ideational" path, 253
  of the social, 31–33, 50–53, 59–62, 98, 141, 184–85, 192–93, 224–25, 239
opinion, 13, 270–72, 278. *See also* public opinion
"ordinary language" analysis. *See* words, meanings of
Origins of Totalitarianism, The
  abstraction in, 232
  action in, 209, 215
  anti-Semitism in, 69–76, 85
  the Blob in, 87–96, 211, 228
  bourgeoisie in, 71, 73–74, 78–87, 90–94, 186, 204, 272
  Cold War and, 100
  explanation in, 267, 318n. 57
  imperialism in, 69, 77, 79–85, 94, 189
  Marx and, 128, 130, 143
  mass in, 70, 84–87, 193
  mob in, 70, 81–87, 181
  the present in, 267
  radical evil in, 95–96, 208, 210–12
  the social and, 77–81, 83, 89
  the state in, 78, 201
  Tocqueville and, 116
  unfinished tasks of, 98–99, 113–14
  writing of, 68, 127, 151, 261

Palestine, 67, 104–6. *See also* Israel
paradox
  as explanation of the Blob, 239–50, 320n. 30
  of founding, 218–19, 257
  of freedom, 6, 136, 142, 190, 196, 217, 225, 239–40, 245, 256
  in Kafka, 61
  in Marx, 239, 243, 245, 249, 302n. 80
  of modernity, 5–9
  political theory and, 240–50
  in Tocqueville, 236, 239, 243–45, 248
  See also dialectics; freedom, of the will; "micro-macro" conundrum
pariah, the
  Arendt as, 155–56, 164, 174
  citizenship potential in, 113, 157
  concept of, 21, 43, 50–51, 58–62
  as created by society, 21, 32–33, 52, 59–60, 66–67, 193, 197
  every human as, 43, 58–60, 264
  gender and, 19–20, 29, 169
  Jew as, 21, 23, 63–68
  nationalism of, 105–6, 112, 158–59, 229
  options open to, 21–22, 30, 60, 62–64, 71, 74, 98–99, 108, 192, 227
  in *Origins of Totalitarianism*, 79–80, 82, 84
  refugee as, 52–68
  social and political, 47, 52–53, 62–64
  solidarity with, 99, 131, 150, 155–57
  thinking and, 269
  Varnhagen as, 21–33
parvenu, the
  Arendt as, 35, 48–49
  banality of evil and, 208–9, 212
  behavior and, 178–81
  childhood and, 14, 105, 264
  collaboration and, 45, 53, 56, 58, 66–73, 94, 209–13, 228
  concept of, 21–22, 43, 51, 54, 58–62, 92
  Eichmann as, 206–7
  gender and, 169–70, 173
  hypocrisy of, 26, 28–30, 33, 80, 82, 86
  Jew as, 21–37, 43, 50–53, 56–58, 62–64, 66–68, 70–71, 75, 105, 155, 159, 213–14
  nonpariah as, 43, 54, 56–59
  obsessive activity of, 24–25, 74, 82–84, 181, 194
  options alternative to, 21–22, 30, 60, 62–64, 71, 74, 98–99, 108, 192, 227
  price of becoming, 22–27, 34, 84, 109–10, 162, 184–86, 192, 197, 210, 213, 232, 236
  refugee as, 51–56, 59, 61–62, 66, 68, 69, 94, 185–86, 191, 261
  resentment in, 23, 54, 56, 82–84, 94, 169, 255–56, 262, 267–68, 279
  as scoundrel, 24, 56, 94
  self-abnegation in, 24–26, 41, 43, 48, 54–56, 74, 95, 206, 266
  the social and, 33, 47–51, 72–73, 81–82, 85, 96, 98, 106, 112, 177–86, 189, 191–94, 196, 197, 217, 261, 270
  in the United States, 101–2
  Varnhagen as, 21–31, 35, 49, 191
"pearl diving," 274–76, 278, 325–26n. 78
peers. *See* equality
Pericles, 139
personification
  hypostasization and, 226, 228, 230
  in Marx, 141–42, 144, 231, 233–34, 236–37
  of the social, 3, 6, 74, 226, 228, 230
  in Tocqueville, 231–32, 236
  of totalitarianism, 87–97, 124, 210–12, 228–29, 250

philosophy
  Arendt's view of, 37, 39–40, 46–48, 50–52, 60, 76, 99, 114, 150, 159
  conundrums in, 241–50
  déformation professionelle of, 45–46, 48–51, 147, 149, 159, 232, 261, 271, 276
  dialectics and, 240–50, 278, 302n. 80
  German, 163–64, 227
  Greek, 163–64, 227, 243
  Heidegger and, 39–46, 48–52, 60, 99, 147, 150, 152, 159, 163–64, 227, 232, 243, 272, 325–26n. 78
  hypostasization in, 227
  Jaspers and, 41, 278
  Kant and, 154
  Marx and, 130–31, 234, 236, 271
  Plato and, 130, 243
  political theory and, 1, 99, 131, 147, 159, 162–65, 242–43, 248–50
  Socrates and, 247, 268, 278
  Western tradition of, 128, 130–31, 271
  the world and, 106
Piaget, Jean, 160–61, 164, 173
Pierpont, Claudia Roth, 209
pity, 216, 221–23, 266, 270
Plato, 130, 243
plurality. *See* individuality, as uniqueness
Poland, 100, 214
Polanyi, Karl, 312n. 34
Political Element in the Development of Economic Theory, The (Myrdal), 188
political parties
  contemporary, 257
  Communist, 43, 100, 102
  Nazi, 83–84, 90, 206
political theory
  abstraction in, 124, 147, 159, 235–37, 270–71, 277–78
  Arendt's role in, 1–2, 17, 36, 99, 131, 147, 163–64, 225, 239, 242–43, 248–50, 254, 277–78
  as "Big Boys' game," 162–65
  the Blob and, 6, 17, 144, 202, 211, 225, 231–32
  memory and, 225
  nature of, 226–50
  paradox in, 202, 204–5, 225, 240–50
  philosophy and, 1, 99, 131, 147, 162–65, 242–43, 248–50
  as task of *Human Condition*, 112, 131, 145, 147, 162
  Tocqueville on, 124, 235–39, 243–45, 248
poor, the. *See* economics; social question
population, 14, 191, 237–38, 258–60, 279
poverty. *See* economics; social question
power
  "alienated," 176, 194, 282, 292n. 12
  as concerted action, 121–22, 193, 215, 218, 257, 261
  individual, 20, 25, 33, 66, 190, 194, 209, 261
  in Marx, 136, 138, 141, 304nn. 89, 102
  of mothers, 172–74
  as problematic concept, 7, 9, 17, 255–56, 258, 272, 275, 292n. 12, 322nn. 7, 8
  of society, 31–33, 50–53, 59–62, 98, 119–20, 141, 192–93, 195, 225, 239
  in Tocqueville, 118–22
  totalitarianism in, 89, 95
present, the
  Jaspers on, 267
  as locus of action, 267–69
  as locus of thought, 267
  messianic "now" and, 324–25n. 54

paradox of freedom and, 142, 190, 245
pretense. *See* hypocrisy
Princeton University, Arendt lectures at, 103, 130, 155, 243
process
  causal, 76, 268
  ideology and, 87, 294–95n. 47
  labor and, 131, 145, 167, 178
  life, 13, 133
  in Marx, 133, 140
  natural, 15, 70, 76–79, 81, 293n. 14
  politics and, 77–78, 112
  the social and, 86, 187, 189–90
  surrender to, 70, 77, 79–85, 189, 192, 194, 220
  in totalitarianism, 89
projection
  of future republic, 105, 110–11, 251, 284
  psychological, distorting reality, 270
  the "they" of society as, 31–33, 49–53, 59–62, 79, 98, 141, 163, 184–85, 192–93, 227, 250
  of words into new contexts, 201
property. *See* economics
Proust, Marcel, 73–74
Psychologie der Weltanschauungen (Jaspers), 37
psychology
  Arendt's view of, 2, 36, 147, 261
  "characterological" path and, 258, 260–69, 272, 274–80, 282–83
  of Eichmann, 205–7, 269–70
  as explanation of the Blob, 230–32, 250
  mass, 170
  of pariah, 158
  of parvenu, 22–27, 34, 54–56, 74, 82–84, 109–10, 162, 169, 181, 184–86, 192, 194, 197, 210, 213, 232, 236, 255–56, 262, 267–68, 279

  psychoanalytic, 36, 153, 171–73, 231, 240, 276, 316n. 18
  of science fiction, 5, 170–71
  society and, 33, 61, 109, 118, 180, 204
public and private
  blurring of distinction between, 27, 74, 259
  bourgeoisie and, 78, 85–86, 209, 228
  as dyad in *Human Condition*, 148, 166
  economics and, 11, 16, 186–87, 220–21, 223, 256
  in Kierkegaard, 185
  privatizing withdrawal from public, 14, 224
    bourgeoisie and, 78, 85–86
    introspection and, 35, 74
    Jewishness and, 74
    quotidian pettiness and, 109, 114, 122–23
public deliberation, 256–57
public happiness, 317n. 54
public opinion, 59, 103–4, 118–20, 271, 274
public realm, *Résistance* as, 108–11, 283

racism
  anti-Semitism and, 50–51, 72, 78–79, 83, 191
  Arendt's attitude toward, 78–79, 81, 100–101, 293n. 16
  Boers and, 81, 85
  in imperialism, 69, 78–79, 94
  in Israel, 67, 105, 296n. 21
  secret agents and, 82–83
  Tocqueville on, 125–27
  in United States, 100–101, 223
radical evil. *See* evil, radical
Rahel Varnhagen
  Jewishness in, 19–22, 43, 47
  gender in, 29, 35–36, 153
  nature in, 28, 31, 76
  parvenu in, 21–31, 185
  politics in, 30–33, 61–62, 271

Rahel Varnhagen (continued)
  the social adumbrated in, 19–34, 35, 42, 52, 93, 227
  writing of, 35–36, 47–48, 98, 149
realism
  action and, 182, 185–86, 213, 232, 274, 284, 268, 272–74
  Arendt's, 4, 43–44, 47–48, 50, 150, 175, 209–11, 249–50, 251, 265, 271, 274, 279
  art and, 63, 204, 277
  about the Blob, 209, 211, 229, 250, 251–52
  Eichmann and, 207, 212–13, 270
  gender and, 155, 162
  in Marx, 234
  nature and, 26, 31, 66
  neighborly love and, 43, 175, 210, 265, 272
  parvenu's lack of, 186, 265
  refugee's lack of, 54, 62, 186
  resistance and, 109, 112
  about the self, 25–27, 61–62, 67, 157–59, 182
  time and, 267–69
  totalitarianism and, 89–91, 95, 186, 207, 213, 270
  Varnhagen's lack of, 26–29, 33, 68, 186, 232
  about the world, 26–27, 82, 177, 181–82, 232
rebel
  as adolescent, 82, 181, 265
  Arendt as, 131, 154, 157, 265
  artist as, 204
  conscious pariah as, 82, 93
  Marx as, 130
  pariah as, 29–30, 61–62, 64–65
  Varnhagen as, 29–30
  world as source of, 265
rebellion
  and founding, 147
  prerequisites for, 282
  resistance and, 176
  revolution and, 218
  in television plots, 273

refugee
  Arendt as, 46–47, 52, 55, 57, 67, 100–101, 127, 150–51, 228
  the assimilated and, 57
  as parvenu, 51–56, 59, 61–62, 66, 68, 69, 94, 185–86, 191, 261
  realism and, 109, 228
regression
  the Blob and, 170–74, 230–32, 250
  Boers and, 78, 80–81
reification, 10, 134, 233, 304n. 99
Reinhardt, Mark, 125–26, 196, 255, 257, 261
relationships, web of
  action and, 2, 111, 146, 178, 180–81, 197, 200, 268, 293
  behavior and, 178, 180–81
  infancy and, 172
  institutional structure and, 193
  in Marx, 133, 136
representation
  legislative, 82, 84, 223–24, 257
  as presentation of a false self, 25–26, 28–30, 54
  in thinking, 270–71, 278
resentment
  as acquiescence, 53, 56, 255, 260, 273
  in Nietzsche, 262
  parvenu and, 23, 54, 56, 82–84, 94, 169, 255–56, 262, 267–68, 279
  in Tocqueville, 293n. 4
  violence and, 262
resistance, anti-Nazi
  Bulgarian, 216
  Danish, 215–16
  French
    citizenship, theory of, and, 112–14, 145, 229–30
    freedom in, 107, 109–11, 176, 230
    heroism and, 110, 113–14, 148, 263

as public, 108–11, 176, 196, 283
self-discovery in, 110, 182, 185, 193, 263
as self-organization, 108, 110–11, 113, 123, 149, 176
social question and, 217
Jewish, 213–14, 217
utility of, 110, 215
responsibility
action and, 74, 194–95, 198, 231, 238–39, 246, 268–69, 279, 282, 284
in American Revolution, 220
Arendt's experience of, 45, 210–12
as duty, 65–67, 76–77, 109, 283
in *Eichmann in Jerusalem*, 204, 206, 209, 212–14, 217
in imperialism, 79
toward people, 265–67
power and, 322nn. 7, 8
for totalitarianism, 85–87
toward world, 264–65
revolution
American, 217, 222–25
concept of, 217–19, 275, 282
freedom and, 218–25, 282
French, 16, 217, 219–23
industrial, 187
lost treasure of, 109–12, 143, 147, 149, 176, 218–19, 223–25
in Marx, 142, 188, 304n. 101
spirit of, 218–19, 223–25
violence and, 218, 220
Rich, Adrienne, 165
Riesman, David, 106, 261–62, 323n. 29
Riley, Denise, 170
Robespierre, Maximilien Marie Isidore, 220–21
Rogin, Michael, 4, 36, 170–71
romanticism
in Arendt's life, 40–41, 43–44, 47, 49, 150, 152
Heidegger's, 40, 46–47, 50

as self-abnegation, 41, 43–44, 49, 152, 261
as self-centeredness, 47, 150
as withdrawal inward, 19, 25, 27–28, 84, 232, 271–72
Ross, Andrew, 273
Rothschild, Baroness Germaine de, 57
Rothschild, Robert de, 57
Rousseau, Jean-Jacques, 14, 131, 180, 219
Russia. *See* Soviet Union

Sabbatian movement, 324–25n. 54
schlemihl, 24–25, 63, 65
Schmidt, Anton, 214–15, 282
Scholem, Gershom, 39, 324–25n. 54
science
natural, 2, 191, 258–60, 272, 294–95n. 47
social, 191, 261, 276
science fiction
the Blob as, 4, 177, 229, 251, 284
motion pictures, 4–5, 170–71, 285–86n. 4
secret agents, 70, 79–82, 84–85, 87, 92, 261
Selbstdenken, 271–72
semantic analysis. *See* words, meanings of
Seneca, 10
Shakespeare, William, 275, 324–25n. 78
Shils, Edward, 203
slavery
Boers and, 81
citizenship potential in, 64, 158
in Greece, ancient, 17, 148
of Jews, 56
Marx on, 140
Tocqueville on, 119, 126
in United States, 126, 223
socialism, 12, 16, 38, 129. *See also* communism
social question, 217, 220–24, 317n. 41

"Society and Culture," 203–5, 317n. 41
sociology, 240, 320n. 31
  sense of "society" in, 32, 50–51, 60, 68, 201, 239
Socrates, 247, 268, 278, 314n. 57
solidarity
  among citizens, 65, 72, 93, 111, 182, 216, 241–42
  individuality and, 65–67, 141, 182
  "Just do it!" path and, 254
  with pariahs, 30, 37, 48, 65, 150, 155–56, 158
  parvenu and, 27, 56, 58, 79, 81, 82, 261
  pity and, 266, 270
  in Tocqueville, 123
Sontag, Susan, 4
Sorcerer's Apprentice story, 95, 137, 189
Sorel, Georges, 267, 268
sovereignty, 199–200, 266, 314n. 66
Soviet Union
  in Cold War, 99–100, 112, 131–32
  Marxism, role of in, 98, 112, 128–29
  in *Origins of Totalitarianism*, 69, 93, 98, 112, 128
  as totalitarian, 69, 93
Spartacist rebellion, 38–39, 47, 129
species-being, 133–35, 138–39, 233
spontaneity
  action and, 1, 14, 56, 88, 110–11, 124, 146–47, 157, 176, 178–79, 197, 202, 218, 225, 254, 260, 263, 266, 268
  the Blob and, 202
  bureaucracy and, 79
  institutionalizing of, 218–19, 239
  parvenu and, 25, 56, 70
  in Tocqueville, 117, 122–23
  totalitarianism and, 88
  in United States, 117, 122–23
Stalin, Joseph Vissarionovich, 69, 96–97, 99–100
state, the
  as agent, 12, 33, 52, 60, 75, 241
  civil society and, 12, 62, 68, 78, 188, 201, 227
  council-, 257
  in global economy, 258–60
  Hegel on, 12, 62, 139, 188
  Marx on, 12, 139, 188, 201
  politics and, 33, 62, 72, 75
  totalitarian, 89, 95
  welfare, 16, 100, 170, 322–23n. 17
stereotyping
  artist and, 204
  essentialism and, 67, 158–59, 183–84
  of Jews, 67, 72, 75–76, 91, 232–33, 266, 293n. 9
Stern, Clara, 43
Stern, Günther (first husband), 43, 46–48, 129
Stern, William, 43
storytelling, 38, 146, 276–78, 311n. 14
structural conditions, 258–60
structure
  institutional, 192–96, 201, 218, 257, 261, 280
  social, 105–6, 192
Sumner, Gregory D., 111

Taminiaux, Jacques, 163
technology
  contemporary, 2, 170, 249, 254, 257–60, 279
  in Marx, 137–38
  as mode of thought, 13, 178, 249, 257, 268, 272
  the social and, 254, 257–60, 279
  work and, 132, 146–47, 166–68, 178, 264, 266, 268, 272, 281
television, 7, 252, 255, 273
Tempest, The (Shakespeare), 275
theory. *See* abstraction; political theory; philosophy; thinking
thinking
  autonomous, 4, 26–27, 271

citizenship and, 269–81
in *Human Condition*, 4, 112, 149, 269
"ideational" path and, 269–80
"representative," 270–71, 278
thoughtlessness and, 207, 248, 269–72, 274, 276
time. *See* present, the
Tocqueville, Alexis de
abstraction in, 124, 234–38
on action, concerted, 120–21, 124, 125–27, 283
on administrative despotism, 118–22, 229
on aristocracy, 121–22
on art of association, 117, 119, 121–23, 147, 196
as authority for Arendt, 115–16, 123, 127, 143–44, 161, 163–64
the Blob and, 120, 123–24, 127, 144, 170, 231–32, 234–38
on centralization, 118, 120, 122–23, 257
on conformism, 103–4, 118, 123
democracy, concept of, 116–17
Democracy in America, 115–27
Arendt's reading of, 115–16, 124, 297–98n. 3
two volumes, relationship of, 117–20, 124, 298n. 9
on economics, 118, 120, 122
on elections, 118–120
on equality, 116–17, 119, 122, 236
on federalism, 118, 120, 122–23, 257
on French politics, 117, 124, 126–27, 283
on gender, 120, 125–26, 170
on individuality, 103, 117, 119, 121–24, 144
on *liberté*, 117–19, 121–25, 196, 244
Marx and, 115, 143–44
in *Origins of Totalitarianism*, 116

paradox in, 236, 239, 243–45, 248
on penal system, 121
political theory in, 124, 235–39, 243–45, 248
on public opinion, 103, 118–20
racism in, 125–27
on religion, 125–26, 235
on slavery, 119, 126
on United States, 103–4, 116–27, 163, 235–36
totalitarianism
action and, 70, 87–93, 198, 211–12, 215–16
as Blob, 87–97, 124, 210–12, 228–29, 250
concept of
authoritarianism and, 294n. 40
as explanation of the social as Blob, 228–29, 250
origin of, 292–93n. 1
as requiring Nazi-Soviet parallel, 69, 98, 100, 112
complicity in, 45, 53, 56, 58–59, 66, 80, 83, 94, 194, 208–10, 213–16, 228–29, 261–62
contributors to rise of, 69–70, 79–87, 92, 94, 193–94
decline of, 96, 99–100, 103–4, 105
Eichmann and, 205–12, 269–72
as explanation of holocaust, 69, 76, 96
ideology and, 91, 95, 186, 207, 213, 248, 272
individuality and, 88–93, 193
Israel and, 105
Marx and, 98, 112, 127–31, 145
as radical evil, 95–96, 208, 210–12
the social and, 96–100, 104, 107, 114, 117, 124, 144, 175, 228–30, 272
in United States, 103–4
as unprecedented, 69, 87, 130–31, 267
treasure, lost. *See* lost treasure

triad
  in *Human Condition*, structure of, 148–49, 165–68, 175–76
  labor, work, and action as, 132, 145–48, 162, 165–66, 169, 175, 177–78, 231
  neighborly love as element in, 41–43, 145
Trotsky, Leon, 44, 129
truth. *See* hypocrisy; ideology; realism
"tyranny of the majority," 118–20

Unger, Roberto Mangabeira, 192
United States
  as agent, 241
  American exceptionalism and, 124–25
  Arendt's view of, 100–104, 116, 163, 272, 295nn. 7, 9, 310n. 85
  in Cold War, 102–4, 106, 131–32
  conformism in, 100–104, 106, 118, 123
  penal system of, 122
  political freedom in, 100–104, 117–18, 122–23, 163, 257, 310n. 85
  refugees and, 52, 54, 102
  Tocqueville on, 103–4, 116–27, 163, 235–36
  at war, 52, 100, 238
utilitarianism, 87, 146, 167

Varnhagen, August, 28–29
Varnhagen, Rahel
  Arendt and, 20, 43, 48–50, 277, 287n. 2
  change of mind, 20, 28–31, 193, 287n. 2
  character, 24–31, 181, 272, 288n. 23
  life of, 19–20, 22, 28–31
  as pariah, 21–33
  as parvenu, 21–31, 35, 49, 191
  romantic introspection in, 19, 27–28, 271–72
Villa, Dana R., 163

violence
  Boers and, 81
  courage and, 55
  Jaspers on, 130
  in Marx, 130
  mob and, 82–83
  resentment and, 262
  revolution and, 218, 220
  work and, 167–68
virtual reality, 254–55, 272–74. *See also* media; motion pictures; television
vita activa, 132
vocabulary. *See* words

war
  danger of World War III, 106, 145, 229
  World War I, 38, 47, 83
  World War II, 52, 55, 59, 99–102, 107–14, 228
  See also Cold War
"we," *See* "micro-macro" conundrum
"We Refugees," 54
web of relationships. *See* relationships, web of
Weber, Max, 189, 227
"who." *See* individuality, as uniqueness
Williamson, Oliver, 254
Winters, Francis X., 208–9
Wittgenstein, Ludwig, 248, 320–21n. 38
women. *See* gender
words
  abstract, 237
  hypostasization of, 3, 49, 164, 168, 180, 201, 203, 217, 226–28, 250, 318n. 1
  key, of politics, 275
  meanings of, 177, 200–201, 226–27, 244, 246–47. *See also under particular words*
  "ordinary" usage of, 219, 246–47
  "origins" of, etymological, 163, 275–76, 278, 286n. 20. *See also under particular words*

work
  action and, 132, 146, 178–83, 200
  Boers and, 81
  concept of, 132, 145, 180
  in conceptual triad, 132, 145–48, 162, 165–66, 169, 175, 177–78, 231
  control in, 197, 200
  labor and, 132–34, 178, 266
  in Marx, 132–34, 136, 138, 143, 234, 237, 302n. 83
  as masculine, 166–68, 309n. 65
  politics and, 158, 167, 236, 272
  relationships in, 167, 268
  technical efficiency and, 132, 146–47, 166–68, 178, 264, 266, 268, 272, 281
  world and, 132, 197, 200, 248
world, the
  action and
    as concerned with, 113, 176, 179, 181–82, 195, 199–200, 263–64
    as constituting, 283
  alienation from 27, 133–34, 140, 186, 265
  Boers and, 78, 80–81
  Christian and, 42
  citizenship of, 157–59, 259
  earth and, 303n. 93
  economics, global, and, 258–60, 279
  as endangered, 65, 113, 143, 145, 167–68, 174, 197, 264–65
  fathers as symbols of, 173
  government of, 157–58, 259
  Heidegger's concept of, 303–4n. 93
  history of, 45, 129, 150, 157, 206
  love of, 106, 133, 153, 176, 198, 265
  in Marx, 133, 135–36, 138, 140
  reality and, 177, 180–82, 237, 240, 250, 265, 270, 273, 276
  totalitarianism and, 91, 95, 186, 213
  Varnhagen's, 26, 28–29

Yahil, Leni, 216
Young-Bruehl, Elisabeth
  on Arendt
    in France, 56, 57
    and Heidegger, 39–40, 46
    and mother, 149–51
    personal recollections about, 56, 154, 275
    and semantic analysis, 275
    in United States, 100
  Hannah Arendt: For Love of the World assessed, 17–18, 113, 208, 210

Zionism, 44, 46, 67, 106, 214

www.ingramcontent.com/pod-product-compliance
Lightning Source LLC
Chambersburg PA
CBHW032127010526
44111CB00033B/153